For Pam, an old and dear friend. All the best!

Ross

Quantitative Investing for the Global Markets

Strategies, Tactics, and Advanced Analytical Techniques

PETER CARMAN, Editor

Glenlake Publishing Company, Ltd.

Chicago • London • New Delhi

Fitzroy Dearborn Publishers

Chicago and London

ISBN: 1-888998-03-2

Library edition: Fitzroy Dearborn Publishers, Chicago and London
ISBN: 1-884964-71-0

GPCo
1261 West Glenlake
Chicago, Illinois 60660
glenlake@ix.netcom.com

To Peter Bernstein,
my friend and mentor

CONTENTS

PREFACE

Looking back over the last 25 years, it is apparent that quantitative techniques have had a major impact on investment management firms, in terms of both their approach to managing money and the type of products that they provide to their clients. Important as they may have become, practical applications of quantitative approaches emerged slowly. Those applications were delayed and diluted by suspicion, misunderstanding, and by a lack of communication between academics and practitioners at the time when quantitative approaches first started to receive significant attention in the early 1970s. Academics believed so much in the purity and academic rigor of their research that they perceived practitioners to be superficial readers of tea leaves, whose aggregate results showed no value added. Active money managers, however, viewed quants as a hopelessly naive group of ivory-tower theorists who, despite their command of the intricacies of advanced mathematics, totally misunderstood the way that capital markets and money managers really worked.

Despite the initial mismatch, the ultimate collaboration of the two groups over the subsequent 25 years resulted in an extraordinary list of investment management innovations. A partial list includes

- Performance related analytics such as normal portfolio definition, style definitions, and attribution analysis.
- Passive portfolio construction using broad indices and style-specific indices.
- Multivariate screens used by traditional managers to qualify potential investments and used directly by purely quantitative managers to build portfolios.
- Increasingly widespread uses of present-value methodologies for equity valuation.
- Use of optimization for risk control for both pure-quantitative and more-traditional portfolios.

Three broad factors facilitated the evolution of these innovations and the shift to more systematic investment processes. First, trade publications, such as the *Financial Analyst Journal* and the *Journal of Portfolio Management*, exposed quantitative ideas to line investment managers. Second, institutional clients and consultants pressured investors (1) to define investment styles in order to facilitate performance measurement, and (2) to formalize investment processes in order to increase confidence that past results were repeatable. Finally, managers reacting to client demands found it in their interest to implement formal methods to control risk.

The systematization of active-management processes turned out to provide the basis for cooperation. So, ultimately, working together, both academics and practitioners turned their attention to the opportunity provided by quantitative tools and improvements in technology. They began to exploit new ideas for identifying market inefficiencies. Coincidentally, those systematic approaches to the capital markets also improved operating efficiency and, at the same time, added to the marketability of investment products.

Until the beginning of this decade, most quantitative equity research had been focused on the U.S. market for two mutually reinforcing reasons. First, the amount of data available in foreign markets, the quality of that data, and problems associated with accounting and reporting differences among countries made the potential output from that research problematical. Second, the natural customers for that research were U.S. money managers and pension plan sponsors that had little exposure to, and little historic interest in, global equity investing.

As we moved into the 1990s, U.S. pension plan sponsors began to increase their commitment to foreign equities, and U.S. managers quickly followed, bringing with them an already developed infrastructure of investment system and process. As a consequence, despite all the shortcomings associated with information available from less-mature equity markets, quantitative methods have been increasingly applied to the global market for stocks.

The drivers of this change are clearly related to, and analogous to, the adoption of quantitative approaches by U.S. investment managers.

- U.S. firms have recognized that the asset-management business is global and that their familiarity with systematic decision-making represents a competitive advantage.
- Non-U.S. financial institutions were early in viewing investment management as a global process. However, more recently, they recognized that the U.S. firms had both an intellectual and practical advantage in their more-quantitative approach to investing. Many non-U.S. institutions have recognized that some of their revenues and client relationships would be vulnerable to U.S. competitors, if they did not change.

- Graduates of U.S. business schools and CFA-trained foreign nationals have facilitated the internalization of quantitative approaches.
- Non-U.S. countries with private pension plans are witnessing the emergence of a pension-investment-consulting community.
- The privatization of companies and pension plans in the rest of the world suggests that the trend toward global equity investing is likely to continue.
- Databases on which quantitative processes depend for product validation and screening are improving rapidly in order to service the need.

The final but not the least important facilitator of the changes is the organization and publication of research. This research advances the state of the art and provides practical guideposts that help practitioners understand the options available for systematically improving their investment processes. That, of course, is the purpose of this book.

In conclusion, I would like to express my gratitude for the help provided to me by John DeTore and Keith Quinton of Putnam Investments' quantitative department, and for the invaluable assistance provided by Robert Klein and Jess Lederman that made this book possible.

Peter Carman

CONTRIBUTORS

Geert Bekaert

Dr. Bekaert is associate professor of finance at the Graduate School of Business at Stanford University. He is also associated with the National Bureau of Economic Research in Cambridge, Massachusetts. Dr. Bekaert earned his Ph.D. at Northwestern University. His research interests include exchange rates and emerging equity markets. He serves as associate editor for the *Review of Financial Studies* and the *Journal of Empirical Finance.*

Ross Paul Bruner

Mr. Bruner is a managing director at the Istituto Mobiliare Italiano (IMI) Group. Previously, Mr. Bruner was a vice president of global equity strategy at ABN AMRO Hoare Govett and a portfolio strategist at Dean Witter. Mr. Bruner holds a B.A. in history from Rutgers College and an M.S. in investment management from the Lubin School of Business. He is a Greenwich- and Extel-rated strategist and is registered as a supervisory analyst with the New York Stock Exchange.

Peter Carman

Mr. Carman joined Putnam Investments, Inc., in 1993 as senior managing director, chief of equity investments. He is a member of Putnam's operating, management, and executive committees. Mr. Carman has investment responsibility for Putnam's approximately $72 billion in equities under management, including product development, research, equity trading, and portfolio management. Prior to joining Putnam, he was a partner with Sanford C. Bernstein and Co., where he was chief investment officer, chairman of the U.S. Equity Investment Policy Committee, and a member of Bernstein's board of directors. His professional career since 1972 has been exclusively in investment management. Mr. Carman received a bachelor of arts degree from Brown University and a master of business administration degree from Harvard Business School.

Claude B. Erb

Mr. Erb is a managing director in First Chicago NBD Investment Management Company's Global Investment Strategy and Asset Allocation

Group. He is responsible for the day-to-day management of global asset allocation portfolios. Mr. Erb's published research has appeared in journals such as the *Financial Analysts Journal* and the *Journal of Portfolio Management*. He is on the board of directors of the Chicago Quantitative Alliance. Mr. Erb received an A.B. in economics from the University of California at Berkeley and an M.B.A. from the University of California at Los Angeles.

Michael Even

Mr. Even is executive vice president and director of quantitative research with Independence Investment Associates, Inc., where he is responsible for the development and application of quantitative techniques and the management of pension accounts. Mr. Even has B.A. and B.S. degrees from Cornell University and an M.B.A. from Sloan School of Business at Massachusetts Institute of Technology.

Dennis Fogarty

Mr. Fogarty is vice president at Independence International Associates, Inc., where he is responsible for market valuations and optimized stock selection for actively managed portfolios. His work focuses on investment strategy research and development, the interaction of market-valuation levels, stock market performance, active currency hedging, and international stock-selection strategies within markets. Mr. Fogarty has eight years of investment research experience in international equity management. Previously, he spent several years managing design teams during the planning of office projects worldwide, including two years in Athens, Greece. Mr. Fogarty has completed the C.F.A. Levels I and II. He has B.S. and M.S. degrees from the Massachusetts Institute of Technology.

Campbell R. Harvey

Dr. Harvey is J. Paul Sticht Professor of International Business at Duke University's Fuqua School of Business. He is also a research associate with the National Bureau of Economic Research in Cambridge, Massachusetts. Dr. Harvey earned his Ph.D. at the University of Chicago. His research interests include global asset allocation, dynamic trading strategies, and emerging equity markets. He serves as associate editor for the *Journal of Finance*, the *Journal of Financial Economics*, the *Journal of Financial and Quantitative Analysis*, the *Journal of Empirical Finance*, the *Pacific Basin Finance Journal*, the *Journal of Fixed Income*, the *European Journal of Finance*, and the *Journal of Banking and Finance*.

William J. Kennedy, Jr.

Mr. Kennedy is vice president of Independence Investment Associates, Inc. Previously, he was with John Hancock Investment & Pension Group, and Equitable Capital Management. Mr. Kennedy holds a B.S. degree from Susquehanna University.

Rosemary Macedo

Ms. Macedo is senior vice president of quantitative research and international equities at Bailard, Biehl & Kaiser. Previously, after a year-long fellowship from the Thomas J. Watson Foundation, she was with First Quadrant. Ms. Macedo has been involved in equity style management research since 1989. Ms. Macedo received a B.S. degree from the California Institute of Technology.

Michael P. McElroy

Mr. McElroy is senior vice president at Independence Investment Associates, Inc., where he is responsible for the application of quantitative modeling techniques to aid in valuation and portfolio optimization and electronic trading oversight. Mr. McElroy has five years of investment experience in design of financial-software decision-support tools and optimization modeling, and he has three years prior investment experience in commodity fund management. Previously he was with Digital Equipment Corporation and Intermarket Capital Associates, L.P. Mr. McElroy is a member of the Boston Security Analysts Society, Association for Investment Management and Research, the International Society of Financial Analysts, the Society of Industrial and Applied Mathematics, the Institute for Management Science, and the Boston Stock Exchange Electronic Products Advisory Committee. Mr. McElroy is a C.F.A., and he holds B.S., M.S., and M.B.A. degrees from Massachusetts Institute of Technology.

Carole A. Ryavec

Ms. Ryavec is a managing director for Plexus Group. She oversees Alpha Capture Global Monitor® and Alpha Capture Sponsor Review services. Previously, she was involved in foreign equities sales for Salomon Brothers U.S.; served as Japanese equities technology analyst for Merrill Lynch and Salomon Brothers, and as a loan officer with Chemical Bank, Tokyo. Ms. Ryavec holds a doctorate degree and master's degree in Japanese legal history from Columbia University, and she received a bachelor's degree in history from the College of the City of New York.

H. David Shea

Mr. Shea is vice president at Independence International Associates, Inc., where he is responsible for implementing a historical database of security, market, and benchmark data, which he uses to support modeling and back-testing of active international-equity-investment strategies. Mr. Shea provided all development, and he supports the system for generating and distributing the IIA International Style Indices. These indices track value/ growth and small-cap/large-cap segments of 47 international markets and numerous regional combinations of markets. Mr. Shea has eight years of experience in providing technical and quantitative database and software development for investment management firms. Previously, he was with Massachusetts Financial Services, Oracle Corporation, Massachusetts Institute of Technology, and Raytheon Company. Mr. Shea holds a B.S. in computer science from Tufts University.

Laurence B. Siegel

Mr. Siegel is director of quantitative analysis in the investment division of the Ford Foundation in New York, a position he has held since 1994. Prior to that, he was managing director of Ibbotson Associates, a Chicago-based firm that he helped found in 1979. He has also worked at the Marmon Group and the American Enterprise Institute, and he has served on advisory boards at Moody's and the Common Fund. In addition, he has been a trustee of the Oberweis Emerging Growth Fund and the Household Personal Portfolios. Mr. Siegel is an editorial board member of the *Journal of Portfolio Management* and the *Journal of Investing*. Mr. Siegel received a B.A. in urban studies and an M.B.A. in finance from the University of Chicago.

Lawrence Speidell

In overseeing the activities of the entire global/systematic team, Mr. Speidell is responsible for portfolio management and the development, enhancement, and application of the firm's quantitative disciplines. He also guides the firm's international, domestic, and global research efforts. Prior to joining Nicholas-Applegate in 1994, Mr. Speidell spent 10 years with Batterymarch Financial Management where his wide-ranging responsibilities for portfolio management included development of domestic and international portfolio strategies, portfolio optimization, trading techniques, and client relationships. He was also senior vice president and portfolio manager at Putnam Management Company from 1971 to 1983, and served as a member of that firm's investment policy committee. He is a past president of the Boston Securities Analysts Society and a past director of the Investor Responsibility Research Center in Washington, D.C. Mr. Speidell earned his B.E. in mechanical engineering from Yale University and his M.B.A. from Harvard University. He has 25 years of investment experience.

Douglas B. Stone

Mr. Stone has responsibilities for research, asset allocation, and performance analysis. Prior to joining Nicholas-Applegate, he was senior research analyst and vice president with the Frank Russell Company where he managed international equity strategy research. Included among Mr. Stone's responsibilities were the editing and publishing of the *Russell Research Commentaries,* the development of an international equities profile system, and the co-development of the Salomon-Russell Indices. Previously, he was a lecturer at the University of Washington School of Business and an economist with the U.S. Department of Interior. Mr. Stone has published articles in economics and finance journals and is a member of the advisory board of the *Journal of Investing.* He earned his M.B.A. in international finance from the University of Washington and his B.A. in political science from Northeastern University. He has 22 years of investment experience.

David A. Umstead

Dr. Umstead is senior vice president at Independence International Associates, Inc., where he is leads the research efforts and searches for better ways to make disciplined investment decisions. Dr. Umstead has 24 years of quantitative research experience and 18 years of experience in managing international equity portfolios. Previously, he was with State Street Bank and Trust Company, Putnam Management Company, and The Wharton School of Finance at the University of Pennsylvania. Dr. Umstead serves on the investment committee and acts as a client contact. He is a member of Association for Investment Management and Research and the Boston Security Analysts Society. Dr. Umstead is a C.F.A., and he holds a B.S. degree from the University of Vermont, an M.S. degree from Massachusetts Institute of Technology, an M.B.A. from Boston University, and a Ph.D. in finance from the University of North Carolina at Chapel Hill.

Tadas E. Viskanta

Mr. Viskanta is a vice president in the investment strategy and planning group of First Chicago NBD Investment Management Co. He is the co-author of a number of papers on global asset allocation topics in leading practitioner journals. Previously, Mr. Viskanta was a first scholar with the First National Bank of Chicago. He received his M.B.A. with honors in finance from the University of Chicago. He also received a B.A. with highest distinction in economics and political science from Indiana University.

Wayne H. Wagner

Mr. Wagner is president of Plexus Group. He directs strategic product development and provides senior consulting to clients. Previously, Mr. Wagner was a cofounder and chief investment officer of Wilshire Asset Management, where he managed $2.5 billion in pension assets, and he served as vice president of the management science department at Wells Fargo Bank. Mr. Wagner is a well-known writer and speaker on financial topics, and he is the winner of two Graham and Dodd Awards for excellence in financial writing. Mr. Wagner holds a master's degree in statistics from Stanford University and a bachelor's degree in business administration from the University of Wisconsin.

Jarrod W. Wilcox

Dr. Wilcox is director of research at PanAgora Asset management, where he also serves as director of currency investments. PanAgora is a global, structured investment manager serving large institutions. Dr. Wilcox previously served as director of global investments and director of international equities at PanAgora and Batterymarch respectively, as well as chief investment officer at Colonial Management Associates. Earlier he was a management consultant at the Boston Consulting Group and a member of the faculty at M.I.T.'s Sloan School of Management. Dr. Wilcox is the author of investment journal articles on stock valuation, investing in emerging markets, international asset allocation, trading costs, and on selling bottlenecks. He was educated at M.I.T., where he received his bachelor's, master's and Ph.D. degrees in management.

Michael F. Wilcox

Mr. Wilcox is founder and chief executive officer of Alford Associates. In his 20-plus years of investment management experience, he has developed investment research and management solutions for major institutions in Hartford and New York, and, most recently, he was an international equity portfolio manager and the head of global asset allocation at a leading Boston investment house. Mr. Wilcox spent 10 years in the Wall Street environment, the last five of which he was head of quantitative research in the equity research department at Morgan Stanley.

Mr. Wilcox is an active member of several professional groups, and has served as an adviser to the board of directors of INQUIRE Europe. He is an internationally recognized authority on quantitative investment methods, and he speaks frequently at international investment conferences. He is a specialist in the areas of asset allocation and currency management, and has broad experience in the valuation and trading of all types of securities and derivatives. He is also the editor of the *Thrift Savings Investment Quarterly*. Mr. Wilcox received the C.F.A. designation in 1981 and became a registered securities agent in 1982. Mr. Wilcox holds a master's degree in economics from Trinity College in Hartford.

CHAPTER 1

The $40 Trillion Market: Global Stock and Bond Capitalizations and Returns

Laurence B. Siegel
Director, Quantitative Analysis
The Ford Foundation

Introduction

The wealth of the world is a compelling topic for at least three reasons:

- It represents the stock of resources available to the people living in the world.
- It is, in at least some abstract sense, the opportunity set for investors. The return on a market-capitalization-weighted portfolio of the financial wealth of the world, therefore, represents an all-country, all-asset benchmark that may be appropriate as a basis of comparison for the performance of large, diversified pools of assets.
- It is the market portfolio—and, consequently, the mean-variance efficient portfolio of risky assets—in the capital asset pricing model and in Richard Roll's critique of that model.

This chapter focuses on the subset of world wealth that is represented by publicly traded stocks and bonds. We present the market capitalization and historical returns of stocks and bonds in a broad sample of developed and emerging national markets. A base of information that is at the same time global (reaching across space) and historical (across time) provides the investor with a perspective that he or she cannot obtain in any other way, and that is almost invariably useful in the pursuit of that investor's specialty.

Review of Literature

The literature on world market capitalizations and returns is relatively limited. Roll (1977) asserted that the capital asset pricing model (CAPM) is untestable because a test of the CAPM would require the measurement of period-by-period returns on the world portfolio of all risky asset classes. Such a measurement was and is not available, because the largest components of world wealth—human capital and privately held real estate—have no price-discovering markets. In a kind of response to Roll's critique, Ibbotson and Siegel (1983), and Ibbotson, Siegel, and Love (1985), measured the returns on the components of world wealth that have price-discovering markets or, in the case of real estate, periodic appraisal-based valuations. Despite their efforts, these authors admit that the assets excluded are much larger than those included. This chapter, which updates and in some ways expands on those articles, has the same limitations.

Macroeconomists and government organizations have also made contributions to the study of world wealth and return. Robert J. Barro and Raymond W. Goldsmith are among the economists who have contributed to the thinking on world wealth, its size, importance, and interpretation.[1] The Organisation for Economic Cooperation and Development (OECD), the International Financial Corporation (IFC), the Bank of Japan, and the U.S. Department of Commerce are representative of the organizations that have devoted resources to measuring the stocks of wealth, both physical and financial, in single countries and around the world, as well as stock prices, bond prices, and interest rates.

Data bases published by the great private data gathering organizations have had more to say about world wealth and return than academic and professional authors. In particular, all users of world equity market indices are dependent on the return and market capitalization data collected by Capital International and its successor, Morgan Stanley Capital International (MSCI); the Frank Russell Company; and the Financial Times-Actuaries (FTA) World Indices. On the fixed-income side, Salomon Brothers, Merrill Lynch, J. P. Morgan, and Lehman Brothers have made the principal contributions to the stock of useful data.

Inclusions and Exclusions

Stocks and Bonds

The decision to include stocks and bonds is easy. These assets represent the vast majority of the liquid, publicly traded securities available for purchase. Moreover, data on their capitalization and returns are widely circulated.

What parts of the world represent opportunities for would-be stock and bond holders? The spread of capitalism and capital markets has progressed to the point where the frontier is vanishingly small. Batterymarch Financial Management tracks stock market data even for Kyrgyzstan, Botswana, and Mauritius.[2] The great population centers of China and India have long since joined the list of emerging markets. We would thus like to cover every country in the world, but data are limited for some countries. High-quality stock market data are available for some 47 countries; the number is smaller for bond markets.

Our coverage of stocks is guided by the Morgan Stanley Capital International (MSCI) indices, which comprise most but not all of the large and medium-sized companies in each country's economy.[3] As of mid-1996, the United States was the largest country, with $6.8 trillion in stock market capitalization. The smallest was Sri Lanka, with $2 billion. Note that a few countries with regionally important economies, particularly in the former Soviet Union and in Africa, are not included in the MSCI indices; China only began to be included in November 1995.

Our current coverage of bond capitalization is guided by the Merrill Lynch publication, *Size and Structure of the World Bond Market*, which provides data for bonds denominated in the currencies of 35 countries, plus the European currency unit or ECU.[4] The currency with the largest bond capitalization as of late 1994 is the U.S. dollar with $8.6 trillion, and the currency with the smallest is the Uruguayan peso with $300 million. Historical (as opposed to current) market capitalization data are provided by Salomon Brothers, covering a smaller sample of 22 currencies. Bond returns are drawn from the Ibbotson Associates, Salomon Brothers, J. P. Morgan, and Lehman Brothers government bond indices, covering 15 currencies. Capitalization data include various sectors of the debt markets, including central government, other government and agency, corporate, mortgage, and other types of bonds; return data are limited to government issues. This is acceptable because interest rate and currency changes tend to affect all bonds of like duration in similar ways, so that government bond returns are reasonably representative of the broader bond market. Short-term bonds and bills (cash equivalents) are excluded from the capitalization and return measurements. Brady bonds (issued in U.S. dollars by governments of less-developed countries) are also excluded.[5]

Human Capital, Real Estate, and Other Assets

The value of the assets we exclude is many times larger than the value of stocks and bonds. Human capital—the capitalized value of wages, salaries, and other payments expected by workers—is by far the largest repository of wealth in the world. The global stock of human capital is about four times larger than all other wealth combined. However, there are no *capital* markets for this form of wealth—because slavery is illegal, there are no markets in which human capital can be sold; it can only be rented for wages in the labor market.

The market value of the world's real estate is also likely to be larger than the value of its stocks and bonds. However, most real estate is in private or corporate hands and does not trade as a financial asset, so capitalizations and returns are difficult to measure. To give a sense of scale, Ibbotson, Siegel, and Love (1985) estimated that the market value of real estate in the United States alone was $3.2 trillion as of 1984, compared to $4.3 trillion for global stocks and $4.1 trillion for global bonds in the same year. (Their estimate included all forms of U.S. real estate, including private homes, apartments, and farms, as well as commercial property.) Of course, the market value of non-U.S. real estate is much larger than that of U.S. real estate.

Private equity and debt, commodities, currencies, and gold round out the list of major asset classes not covered in this study. The value of private equity and debt is vast—sole proprietorships, partnerships, and untraded corporations probably represent more wealth than the New York Stock Exchange—but the magnitude of this wealth is not known, and estimating it is an interesting challenge to economists. The other assets listed certainly constitute wealth, although some of their value is held by entities already counted (through the stock- and bond-market measures), and we should not double count them. The part that is not double-counted is a conscious omission from this study.

Stock Market Capitalization

Table 1 provides an overview of the countries in the world that have stock markets. As of June 1996 the capitalization of the world's equity markets summed to $17.8 trillion.[6] Along with current (June 1996) market capitalizations of each country's equity market, we provide data on population, gross domestic product (GDP), per capita stock-market capitalization, per capita GDP, and per capita GDP measured at purchasing power parity.[7] Countries are presented in descending order of stock-market capitalization. The inclusion of all countries in one table without regard to location or stage of development provides a bias-free view. The per capita stock market and GDP data, in contrast, show that the first world as traditionally defined, plus some newcomers such as Hong Kong and Singapore, enjoys a large income and wealth advantage over the rest of the world.[8]

TABLE 1. A World Overview: Stock Market Capitalization, Population, and Gross Domestic Product in 47 Countries

Country	Stock Market Capitalization (US$ billions)	Population (millions)	Stock Market Capitalization per Capita (U.S. dollars)	GDP (US$ billions)	GDP per Capita (U.S. dollars)	PPP GDP per Capita (U.S. dollars)
United States	6,809	258	$26,354	6,658	$25,770	$25,770
Japan	3,667	125	29,444	4,765	38,260	21,140
United Kingdom	1,348	59	22,841	1,055	17,876	17,970
Germany	588	81	7,243	2,190	26,975	19,480
France	565	66	8,553	1,572	23,796	19,670
Switzerland	414	7	59,723	271	39,094	25,150
Canada	371	29	12,909	527	18,337	19,960
Netherlands	337	24	13,925	545	22,519	18,750
Hong Kong	311	7	43,822	152	21,418	NA
Australia	262	18	14,815	338	19,113	18,120
South Africa	258	42	6,143	125	3,010	NA
Malaysia	249	19	12,859	73	3,770	8,440
Taiwan	248	21	11,810	243	11,517	NA
Italy	239	57	4,188	1,014	17,768	18,460
Sweden	201	9	22,981	202	23,095	17,130
Brazil	191	159	1,201	536	3,371	5,630
India	188	914	206	279	305	1,290
Spain	162	39	4,137	489	12,489	13,740
Korea	161	45	3,578	367	8,217	10,540
Singapore	143	3	49,986	72	25,168	21,900
Thailand	139	59	2,356	130	2,213	6,870
Mexico	107	92	1,163	369	4,012	7,050
Belgium	105	11	9,649	258	23,710	20,270
Indonesia	81	190	426	168	883	3,690
Philippines	76	66	1,152	63	956	2,800

TABLE 1 *(continued)*

Country	Stock Market Capitalization (US$ billions)	Population (millions)	Stock Market Capitalization per Capita (U.S. dollars)	GDP (US$ billions)	GDP per Capita (U.S. dollars)	PPP GDP per Capita (U.S. dollars)
Chile	74	14	5,286	50	3,581	9,060
Denmark	61	5	11,759	154	29,687	19,880
Norway	48	4	11,127	113	26,194	20,210
Finland	47	5	9,225	106	20,806	16,150
China	47	1191	39	630	529	2,510
Argentina	44	34	1,294	276	8,061	8,920
Austria	38	8	4,752	205	25,635	19,560
New Zealand	33	3	9,517	55	15,862	15,870
Israel	33	5	6,037	78	14,463	15,690
Turkey	30	61	492	149	2,451	4,610
Ireland	29	4	7,910	55	15,001	13,550
Portugal	29	10	2,908	92	9,398	12,400
Czech Republic	20	10	1,951	33	3,210	7,910
Greece	17	10	1,615	80	7,712	11,400
Peru	14	23	609	44	1,893	3,690
Colombia	13	36	361	59	1,623	5,970
Pakistan	10	126	79	56	440	2,210
Poland	7	38	184	95	2,470	5,380
Venezuela	5	21	238	59	2,757	7,890
Hungary	4	10	412	39	3,839	6,310
Jordan	4	4	952	6	1,381	4,290
Sri Lanka	2	18	94	12	641	3,150

Sources: Morgan Stanley Capital International EAFE and World Perspective, July 1996 (developed country capitalizations), data as of June 1996; Morgan Stanley Capital International EMF and Emerging Markets Perspective, July 1996 (emerging country capitalizations, population, GDP, GDP per capita, PPP GDP per capita), data as of June 1996; MSCI Methodology and Index Policy (population, developed country GDP, GDP per capita), data as of 1994; World Development Report 1996, published by the World Bank (developed country PPP GDP per capita), data as of 1994.

Despite this advantage, we find the per capita GDP levels of the middle-income countries remarkable, considering the poverty of most of these countries only one or two generations ago.

Table 2 provides an episodic picture of the tremendous growth of stock market capitalization over time. (We have data for only a sampling of countries and dates: notable omissions for 1969 and 1981 include the United Kingdom, Germany, and Canada.) Japan provides perhaps the most remarkable story of growth in the modern era. At the end of 1969, the total capitalization of the Japanese stock market was $46.4 billion; by 1995 it was $3,667 billion, nearly 80 times as much. The capitalizations of other countries' stock markets follow similar paths, although at less-extreme rates of growth. Much of this growth can be attributed to the capital appreciation of shares that existed at the beginning of the period, including appreciation that merely compensated investors for consumer price inflation. A substantial fraction of this growth, however, is due to new issues.

TABLE 2. Growth of World Stock Market Capitalization, 1969–1996

Country	1969	1981	1991	1996
	Total Capitalization of Stock Markets, in Billions of U.S. Dollars, at Year-End			
United States	598.7	1112.9	3702	6809
Japan	46.4	400.3	2996	3667
United Kingdom	NA	NA	954	1348
Germany	NA	NA	369	588
France	22.7	38.3	347	565
Switzerland	12.4	40.8	199	414
Canada	NA	NA	232	371
Hong Kong	1.5	40.9	119	311
Australia	31.6	59.6	137	262
Italy	13.7	24.1	154	239
Sweden	5.4	17.6	104	201
Spain	12.1	16.7	120	162
Singapore	2.2	34.9	82	143
Mexico	1.8	9.5	NA	107
Denmark	1.0	4.3	45	61

Source: For all non-U.S. markets for 1969 and 1981, Sikorsky, Nilly, "The Origin and Construction of the Capital International Indices," Columbia Journal of World Business, Summer 1982; for 1991 and 1996 for all countries, Morgan Stanley Capital International Perspective. For the United States, 1969 and 1981 data are for the New York Stock Exchange only, and are from the Center for Research in Security Prices at the University of Chicago as reported by Ibbotson and Brinson (1993), pp. 156-157.

Stock Market Returns

Developed Markets

Tables 3 and 4 together present cumulative indices of annual returns in the most prominent national stock markets over the period 1959–1995, expressed in U.S. dollars. We present index levels rather than annual percentage returns so that the reader can better follow the progress (or regress) of a dollar invested over time. Note that Table 3, covering the first 11 years of that period, contains only capital appreciation returns (excluding dividends), while Table 4, covering the remaining 26 years, contains total returns (including dividends).[9] Thus the rates of return in the two tables are not comparable.[10]

The long historical period covered in these tables is instructive because it supplements the recent history with which many investors are familiar. While most U.S. investors avoided international equities during the first half of this period, it is helpful to know what returns would have been available from such a strategy. Moreover, some European investors—notably the Scottish trusts and the Robeco investment fund in the Netherlands—were very large participants in international markets at that time. At the same time, a few pioneering American investors, including John Templeton, John Clay, and Harry Seligman, managed international portfolios throughout all or most of the period studied.

Europe

The European markets boomed very early—the late 1950s and early 1960s—but then made little progress for a decade. By 1974 the British market was more depressed, relative to most measures of fundamental value, than it had been at the bottom of the Great Depression of the 1930s, while other European markets fared somewhat better. A sharp rebound in the late 1970s was followed by another period of stagnation caused by inflation, high interest-rates, and depressed earnings. Finally, in 1985 and 1986, European markets rose spectacularly, with stock prices more than tripling in most countries over a two-year period. Since that time, Europe has had other strong years, notably 1989 and 1993, but nothing like the fireworks of 1985–1986. A review of European stock market results in the middle 1980s is instructive for today's investor questioning whether there are any gains to be had from international diversification. Although the conditions that caused these returns are not apparent in any markets at the time of this writing, they surely will occur again somewhere.

TABLE 3. World Equities 1959–1969: Cumulative Wealth Indices of Capital Appreciation Returns in U.S. Dollars (Year-End 1958 = 100)

Year end	Australia	Canada	France	Germany	Italy	Japan	Nether- lands	Spain	Switzer- land	United Kingdom	United States
1958	27.13	61.25	75.74	35.38	56.24	33.37	57.43	52.29	32.47	47.85	57.32
1959	39.31	64.50	98.94	64.47	95.53	46.50	71.48	29.37	47.78	68.92	61.45
1960	38.60	59.09	103.49	90.18	128.86	62.44	72.45	31.96	68.33	65.77	60.04
1961	43.61	76.10	126.13	89.48	145.73	51.98	79.05	42.69	103.67	70.36	74.50
1962	43.10	66.34	126.90	67.74	126.27	52.70	72.44	49.57	79.53	69.92	65.61
1963	52.70	73.23	106.13	75.72	105.70	54.46	82.63	48.16	77.36	82.04	78.53
1964	54.24	88.91	102.20	76.92	73.96	58.11	87.81	51.55	70.08	79.92	88.58
1965	48.08	90.29	94.99	64.36	92.04	66.57	77.31	57.83	60.20	79.40	97.02
1966	49.11	78.44	82.93	52.67	96.54	69.48	61.78	62.96	50.96	73.12	84.84
1967	69.91	86.45	80.26	76.41	90.37	63.39	82.57	55.34	75.73	81.50	104.46
1968	85.72	100.17	87.32	84.19	90.22	77.77	109.23	70.31	97.29	117.93	115.30
1969	100.00	100.00	100.00	100.00	100.00	100.00	100.00	100.00	100.00	100.00	100.00

Source: Sikorsky, Nilly, "The Origin and Construction of the Capital International Indices," Columbia Journal of World Business, Summer 1982. Returns in local currency, reported by Sikorsky, were converted to U.S. dollars using exchange rates in R. L. Bidwell, Currency Conversion Tables (Rex Collings, London, 1970), for 1958-1960; and Ibbotson Associates' EnCORR/Analyzer for 1961-1969. Exchange rates were unavailable for Australia for 1958-1960 and are assumed to be constant.

TABLE 4. World Equities 1970–1995: Cumulative Wealth Indices of Total Returns in U.S. Dollars (Year-End 1969 = 100)

Year end	Australia	Canada	France	Germany	Hong Kong	Italy	Japan	Mexico	Netherlands	Singapore	Spain	Switzerland	United Kingdom	United States
1969	100.00	100.00	100.00	100.00	100.00	100.00	100.00	100.00	100.00	100.00	100.00	100.00	100.00	100.00
1970	80.59	114.87	95.48	77.03	144.94	82.75	88.66	104.85	94.15	96.46	96.77	86.84	93.96	104.83
1971	79.64	130.93	96.32	95.84	254.74	72.67	136.44	104.31	95.13	158.17	121.56	110.63	139.60	118.98
1972	98.37	174.64	120.78	113.53	670.83	83.39	308.70	120.83	123.46	504.66	171.49	142.13	145.17	138.69
1973	81.71	170.03	129.96	108.43	406.88	92.93	246.87	127.39	117.54	332.84	216.08	137.92	107.35	116.16
1974	55.36	124.08	97.08	127.03	175.18	61.15	208.07	138.53	98.74	180.30	196.77	120.52	52.99	84.01
1975	82.46	143.09	140.48	165.31	372.54	55.86	249.63	152.37	148.75	285.77	196.94	170.40	114.47	114.10
1976	73.95	157.34	112.34	176.31	523.73	41.02	314.18	109.35	174.21	326.30	125.70	188.20	100.12	140.63
1977	82.93	154.09	118.94	222.07	464.83	33.32	364.11	115.42	202.17	344.20	82.68	242.92	158.68	129.35
1978	101.17	185.78	205.96	276.88	550.29	48.78	558.05	227.19	245.16	500.85	89.27	295.83	181.76	137.07
1979	145.30	284.14	266.14	265.34	1007.24	57.34	491.96	374.12	292.36	645.96	93.73	334.68	221.63	156.87
1980	224.98	344.57	261.93	238.53	1745.36	103.45	643.03	364.47	332.81	1044.84	97.80	308.46	313.48	204.00
1981	171.57	310.05	184.97	212.92	1468.80	93.00	742.89	208.22	286.20	1236.89	109.58	277.60	282.14	195.58
1982	133.14	318.11	178.97	236.16	814.69	75.46	738.81	42.00	335.76	1032.48	77.42	287.34	307.24	238.89
1983	208.34	420.55	237.27	292.58	793.36	78.33	920.78	87.35	462.54	1358.05	73.37	342.69	360.89	291.50
1984	182.03	390.61	250.50	277.49	1165.74	85.58	1081.77	95.04	517.28	995.94	103.98	305.83	379.40	308.92
1985	219.41	454.05	456.33	655.91	1767.63	200.68	1552.81	119.96	833.80	774.72	162.78	630.43	582.91	410.10
1986	316.45	502.89	816.48	891.97	2760.69	417.65	3111.01	186.30	1187.34	1124.14	362.97	851.07	739.78	481.97
1987	349.24	577.53	714.09	679.33	2651.63	335.64	4449.45	198.04	1295.92	1151.97	506.98	779.46	999.28	500.82
1988	482.26	680.38	983.25	819.36	3390.95	374.78	6015.88	297.06	1482.39	1531.62	573.43	830.38	1058.82	580.52
1989	534.90	852.30	1346.45	1206.27	3677.60	451.05	6123.20	612.16	2042.45	2183.70	634.36	1054.72	1290.95	762.61
1990	449.39	748.36	1168.31	1100.96	4015.59	368.70	3918.35	1102.42	2004.65	1932.43	554.01	1001.97	1423.98	746.71
1991	609.25	838.36	1386.54	1198.83	6008.63	366.85	4275.18	2602.33	2392.71	2409.92	648.75	1171.25	1652.90	980.62
1992	548.49	741.39	1428.68	1078.02	7940.34	287.23	3360.78	3171.22	2464.78	2562.87	511.83	1378.63	1589.79	1052.81
1993	750.95	879.10	1735.71	1469.52	17218.05	371.77	4225.34	4636.37	3364.42	4305.62	673.09	2020.92	1979.03	1158.83
1994	799.09	857.61	1654.69	1544.85	12235.42	417.13	5147.78	2772.64	3789.48	4574.76	646.38	2106.01	1947.33	1181.99
1995	898.36	1020.70	1894.26	1800.74	14993.06	423.64	5169.43	2073.65	4870.32	4875.91	844.80	3046.09	2361.53	1633.36

Source: Morgan Stanley Capital International data as reported in Ibbotson Associates' EnCORR/Analyzer (used with permission), with the following exceptions: returns for Mexico over 1988-1995 represent the Financial Times-Actuaries index as reported by Ibbotson Associates; returns shown in the column for Singapore over 1970-1992 are the MSCI Singapore/Malaysia index; the Singapore return for 1993 is from the January 1994 MSCI publication; and the return for Australia for 1973 was calculated by the author.

Japan

Japan was the highest returning market over most of the period studied, and by the late 1980s was one of the two preeminent economies in the world. While Japan kept up with Germany and other successful stock markets of the 1960s, it did not really break out of the pack until the next decade. From the 1970 low to the 1972 high, Japanese stocks more than tripled, then fell back only temporarily in the 1973–1974 bear market. They tripled again by 1980. This was only the beginning of the Japanese superboom: by the end of the 1980s, the Japanese stock market would rise again almost tenfold in total return terms, the market capitalization of those stocks would exceed that of U.S. market, and—most incredibly— the market value of Japanese real estate would be measured at *five times* the value of all the real estate in the United States.

Although few investors anticipated a decline in the Japanese economy and stock market, it now looks inevitable in hindsight. Stock prices fell by more than half over 1989–1992, and rebounded relatively slowly after that. Even in total return terms (with dividends included), the 1989 highs have not been approached as of this writing. Because of the vast size of the Japanese market in comparison to other non-U.S. markets, this poor performance in the 1990s has dragged down the EAFE index and other indices of non-U.S. stock market performance, leading some investors to believe that non-U.S. investing has been fruitless since the highs of 1989. In fact, one would have only had to avoid Japan to do very well in non-U.S. markets in the 1990s.

United States

The United States was a below-average performer over the period studied, although its recent stellar performance has masked the longer-term trend. Because of its mature, diversified character, the U.S. economy offered stability to investors, except in the great bear market of 1973–1974 when U.S. stocks fell more than those of most other countries. This stability came at a price: the best years for the U.S. stock market have had returns in the range of 30 to 40 percent, compared with 126 percent for Japan, 136 percent for Germany, and 116 percent for the United Kingdom.[11] (Some smaller markets have had even higher returns, but the proper comparison is with the largest non-U.S. markets.) Because of its size and dominance in the world financial system, action in the U.S. market has influenced returns around the world over the entire period. The most notable example of this effect was the crash of 1987, in which U.S. stock prices fell 21 percent in one calendar month, and which reverberated as far as Australia (-45 percent), Hong Kong (-46 percent), South

Africa (-29 percent), and Norway (-29 percent).[12] No country had a positive return in October 1987; the best-performing large market was Japan, which declined 8 percent.

Other Countries

The rest of the world contains relatively few markets with a long data history. Over 1970–1995, Hong Kong was the best-performing market in the world, with a 21.3 percent compound annual return, but it had a high level of volatility. Singapore's market was another stellar performer, while Australia had disappointing returns. We have included Mexico, a strong but extremely volatile performer, with the developed markets because Capital International (the "CI" in MSCI) included it in its original study; we also include some Mexican data in our section on emerging markets.[13]

Summary Statistics and Correlations

Table 5 contains summary statistics of the returns in Table 3, covering the years 1959–1969. Using annual standard deviation as the measure of volatility, high-returning Switzerland had the most variable returns, while low-returning Canada, France, and the United States were the most stable.[14] This relationship did not hold up everywhere: Japan and Australia had high returns and low volatility, and Italy had a low return and high volatility. We omit the correlations of returns over 1959–1969 because of the antiquity of the data.

   Tables 6 and 7 together present summary statistics and correlations of the returns in Table 4, covering the years 1970–1995. Risk, as measured by standard deviation, was only loosely related to return over this period. Hong Kong had both a high return and high standard-deviation, but Italy (the lowest-returning country) had nearly as high a risk level. The United States had the lowest standard-deviation. The correlations of annual returns, displayed in Table 7, show the linkages among the world's markets.

   We do not present aggregations of country indices—such as the MSCI EAFE (Europe, Australia, and Far East) index—because presenting them would substantially expand the length of this chapter and start arguments over which aggregations are relevant and properly constructed. It should be noted, however, that most investors build portfolios that are much more diversified, and consequently less risky, than the single-country portfolios shown here.

TABLE 5. Summary Statistics of Annual Capital Appreciation
Returns on World Equities in U.S. Dollars, 1959–1969

	Compound Annual Return (%)	Standard Deviation (%)
Australia	12.59	18.16
Canada	4.56	13.68
France	2.56	14.49
Germany	9.91	31.82
Italy	5.37	27.62
Japan	10.49	17.81
Netherlands	5.17	18.19
Spain	6.07	23.40
Switzerland	10.77	29.60
United Kingdom	6.93	19.89
United States	5.19	14.12

Source: Calculated by the author from data in Sikorsky (1982).

TABLE 6. Summary Statistics of Annual Total Returns on World
Equities in U.S. Dollars, 1970–1995

	Compound Annual Return (%)	Standard Deviation (%)
Australia	8.81	26.98
Canada	9.35	17.01
France	11.98	30.23
Germany	11.76	31.07
Hong Kong	21.25	52.73
Italy	5.71	40.88
Japan	16.39	36.07
Mexico	12.37	51.59
Netherlands	16.12	19.25
Singapore	16.12	50.63
Spain	8.55	33.03
Switzerland	14.04	26.04
United Kingdom	12.93	31.56
United States	11.34	16.37

Source: Calculated by the author from data in Morgan Stanley Capital International Perspective.

Changes in Correlation over Time

Many investors recently have expressed the concern that correlations are
rising and that opportunities for international diversification are therefore falling. To investigate this question, we calculated the correlations of

TABLE 7. World Equities: Correlations of Total Annual Returns in U.S. Dollars, 1970–1995

	Australia	Canada	France	Germany	Hong Kong	Italy	Japan	Mexico	Nether- lands	Singa- pore	Spain	Switzer- land	United Kingdom	United States
Australia	1.00													
Canada	0.72	1.00												
France	0.64	0.51	1.00											
Germany	0.30	0.20	0.69	1.00										
Hong Kong	0.55	0.58	0.37	0.18	1.00									
Italy	0.52	0.34	0.74	0.63	0.30	1.00								
Japan	0.44	0.39	0.47	0.32	0.52	0.48	1.00							
Mexico	0.50	0.36	0.51	0.20	0.20	0.23	0.03	1.00						
Netherlands	0.70	0.57	0.79	0.73	0.48	0.61	0.45	0.30	1.00					
Singapore	0.50	0.57	0.27	0.07	0.76	0.16	0.72	0.17	0.35	1.00				
Spain	0.32	0.21	0.55	0.33	0.34	0.67	0.60	0.19	0.39	0.23	1.00			
Switzerland	0.43	0.35	0.71	0.89	0.41	0.58	0.35	0.18	0.81	0.22	0.36	1.00		
United Kingdom	0.60	0.40	0.45	0.38	0.47	0.29	0.26	0.10	0.64	0.27	0.15	0.55	1.00	
United States	0.59	0.62	0.47	0.38	0.50	0.38	0.27	0.17	0.74	0.35	0.18	0.54	0.57	1.00

Source: Calculated by the author from data in Morgan Stanley Capital International Perspective.

the four largest non-U.S. markets with the U.S. markets using *monthly* returns over rolling 60-month periods spanning the last 26 years. These correlations are graphed in Figure 1. There are short-term trends such as the sharp upward spike in correlation that accompanied the international crash of October 1987, and the decline in correlation five years later when the crash was no longer included in the sample. However, over the whole time-span the correlations are trendless. Moreover, the correlation of the world's largest two markets, the United States and Japan, has fallen slightly over the last quarter century.

Emerging Markets

Although we have overlooked some small but important developed countries, we now turn to the emerging markets, which have captured the imagination of investors in recent years. Emerging countries have always been attractive to investors. The United States was an emerging market in the 19th century, attracting the speculative capital of Great Brit-

FIGURE 1.   Changes in Correlation of Major Non-U.S. Stock Markets with U.S. Market (Correlation of Monthly Returns for 60 Months Ending on Date Shown)

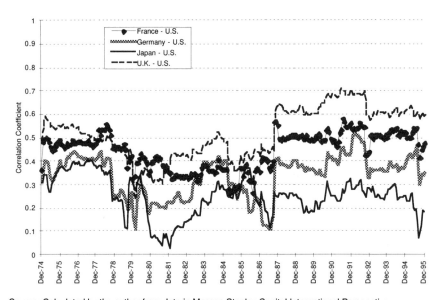

Source: Calculated by the author from data in Morgan Stanley Capital International Perspective.

ain. Having once dominated the economic world, Continental Europe was emerging (or re-emerging) in the period immediately following World War II. In the 1960s and 1970s, Japan was emerging. Today the rest of the world is emerging, and a substantial number of countries—Korea, Taiwan, Malaysia, Israel, South Africa, Mexico, and Chile—are a little more than emerging: they are the developed markets of the very near future.

Table 8 presents annual returns in 25 emerging markets covering the period from 1988 to 1995, or a shorter period where data are unavailable for the whole time-span; Table 9 presents summary statistics of these returns.[15] The returns shown are total returns (including dividends) in U.S. dollars, before adjustment for dividend withholding taxes. Annual returns, rather than cumulative index levels, are presented because the differing starting dates of countries in Table 8 would make index levels difficult to interpret. (Table 9 shows the end-of-period cumulative index level for each country, along with the compound annual return and standard deviation.) For some countries, MSCI calculates both ordinary and "free" indices, where the latter exclude shares that are not purchasable by foreigners; we use the ordinary, not the free, indices.

For countries having eight full years of data (1988–1995), Chile had the highest rate of return, 40.6 percent per year, closely followed by Argentina. Argentina, however, had several times more risk than Chile. Such rates of growth are very unlikely to be sustainable for very long. The lowest returning country was Portugal, which showed a loss over the period (-1.9 percent per year). Looking at year-by-year returns, some of the results are astonishing: the record is held by Poland, with a 754 percent gain in one year (1993). These markets can fall quickly, too. Brazilian stocks fell by more than 60 percent in 1990, and Turkish stocks fell by nearly that much in 1988. The standard deviations in Table 9 show the extent to which these markets have been riskier, on average, than developed markets. As a market becomes more developed, its risk level can be expected to decline, but its potential for extremely high returns will be more limited too.

Bond Market Capitalization

Table 10 shows that the capitalization of the world bond market was $21.1 trillion at the end of 1994, slightly more than that of the world stock market. We should be careful not to interpret this number as wealth in the macroeconomic sense. The world cannot be net long in bonds; if all the borrowers prepaid their bonds today, the wealth of the world would not

TABLE 8. Emerging Market Equities: Total Annual Returns in U.S. Dollars, in Percent, 1988–1995

	Argentina	Brazil	Chile	Colombia	Czech Rep.	Greece	Hungary	India	Indonesia	Israel	Jordan	Korea	Malaysia
1988	102.62	103.36	40.24			-0.88			258.12		-17.65	96.62	27.34
1989	81.19	38.70	64.02			95.96			81.90		-16.25	1.66	57.01
1990	-6.10	-61.59	31.06			90.39			6.39		-10.59	-27.34	-7.03
1991	405.00	172.16	116.10			-20.73			-44.53		19.66	-15.49	5.84
1992	-38.50	6.72	21.89			-30.25			-0.24		40.15	1.56	18.56
1993	58.39	77.74	36.56	31.32		41.00		34.64	105.68	15.60	20.91	31.37	109.53
1994	-23.63	65.73	44.75	21.30		0.54		9.93	-25.92	-32.35	-8.70	23.67	-20.13
1995	12.86	-19.25	-2.66	-25.54	-19.86	10.94	-17.13	-30.94	9.18	23.57	7.47	-3.32	4.68

	Mexico	Pakistan	Peru	Philippines	Poland	Portugal	South Africa	Sri Lanka	Taiwan	Thailand	Turkey	Venezuela
1988	66.07			31.57		-28.48			119.65	47.30	-59.33	
1989	90.25			62.32		42.17			84.88	114.43	547.18	
1990	49.97			-53.96		-30.15			-55.18	-27.32	-5.26	
1991	124.28			78.73		-4.84			12.68	22.74	-18.47	
1992	31.10			37.76		-16.57			-23.66	35.40	-44.64	
1993	47.00	64.09	26.58	131.19	753.97	34.91	72.98	65.69	84.61	103.59	220.47	20.88
1994	-43.39	-7.09	45.42	0.80	-54.71	11.95	31.42	-3.03	20.78	-9.03	-50.49	-14.55
1995	-21.94	-36.46	23.31	-15.07	-2.79	1.01	19.98	-31.25	-29.32	-3.76	-2.82	-22.67

Source: Morgan Stanley Capital International

17

TABLE 9.   Emerging Market Equities: Summary Statistics of
                 Total Annual Returns in U.S. Dollars

Country	Period	Growth of $1.00 Invested at Beginning of Period	Compound Annual Return (%)	Standard Deviation (%)
Argentina	1988-1995	$14.62	39.83	142.94
Brazil	1988-1995	7.48	28.61	73.68
Chile	1988-1995	15.28	40.61	34.85
Colombia	1993-1995	1.19	5.85	30.35
Czech Republic	1995	0.80	-19.86	NA
Greece	1988-1995	3.22	15.72	48.04
Hungary	1995	0.83	-17.13	NA
India	1993-1995	1.02	0.73	33.12
Indonesia	1988-1995	6.38	26.07	98.72
Israel	1993-1995	0.97	-1.13	30.25
Jordan	1988-1995	1.23	2.59	21.05
Korea	1988-1995	1.96	8.76	38.56
Malaysia	1988-1995	4.09	19.24	41.50
Mexico	1988-1995	9.05	31.70	55.11
Pakistan	1993-1995	0.97	-1.05	51.70
Peru	1993-1995	2.27	31.42	11.93
Philippines	1988-1995	4.79	21.64	57.96
Poland	1993-1995	3.76	55.50	452.65
Portugal	1988-1995	0.86	-1.86	27.11
South Africa	1993-1995	2.73	39.72	27.89
Sri Lanka	1993-1995	1.10	3.37	49.86
Taiwan	1988-1995	2.47	11.95	63.23
Thailand	1988-1995	6.80	27.08	51.60
Turkey	1988-1995	1.74	7.13	211.60
Venezuela	1993-1995	0.80	-7.22	23.16

Source: Morgan Stanley Capital International

change. This is in contrast to equities, which are real assets and whose capitalization represents real wealth. An exception is that part of the bond market ($5.4 trillion according to Table 10) that represents corporate leverage. Since corporate bonds are part of the aggregate capitalization of businesses, they represent real corporate assets over and above that which is measured by stock market capitalization. By the same logic, mortgage bonds (to the extent these are measured in the data) pick up some of the value of real estate.

The ranking of the world's countries in terms of bond market capitalization is dramatically different than the ranking in terms of stock mar-

TABLE 10. World Bond Market Capitalizations

	Bond market capitalization (US$ billions)			
Country	Total	Government	Corporate	Foreign, Eurobond, and Other
United States	8,592	5,489	2,247	856
Japan	4,533	2,977	1,221	335
Germany	2,598	1,236	927	435
Italy	981	799	136	46
France	792	513	144	135
United Kingdom	523	331	29	163
Canada	467	335	51	81
Belgium	335	193	115	27
Netherlands	327	253	24	50
Denmark	232	72	see note	160
Switzerland	217	37	88	92
Sweden	203	70	129	4
Spain	175	136	26	13
ECU	172	94	51	27
Australia	124	82	see note	42
Austria	119	52	60	7
Brazil	103	103	0	0
Korea	97	36	61	0
India	84	73	11	0
Argentina	58	46	12	0
Norway	46	26	19	1
Singapore	45	42	3	0
Finland	44	22	20	2
Malaysia	40	33	5	2
Taiwan	38	30	6	2
China	33	33	0	0
Philippines	25	25	0	0
Ireland	23	22	1	0
Chile	15	0	2	13
New Zealand	15	14	0	1
Thailand	14	10	4	0
Mexico	13	1	11	1
Hong Kong	12	0	5	7
Turkey	8	8	0	0
Indonesia	2	1	1	0
Uruguay	0	0	0	0

Notes: Data are year-end 1994, except Australian and Japanese data, which are as of June 30, 1994, and March 31, 1995, respectively. Foreign bonds are bonds issued by nonresidents in the domestic bond market and denominated in the local currency. The "other" category includes miscellaneous institutions for the Canadian market; corporate and foreign issuers for the Danish market; supranational issuers for the ECU (European Currency Unit) market; corporate, foreign, and public issuers for the Australian market; foreign and other miscellaneous issuers for the Finnish market; central bank issues for the Malaysian, Philippine, and Chilean markets; and Hong Kong Monetary Authority bonds for the Hong Kong market.

Source: "Size and Structure of the World Bond Market: 1995," Merrill Lynch & Co., (Global Securities Research & Economics Group, International Fixed Income Research), New York, 1995.

ket capitalization. This is because a substantial fraction of bond capitalization reflects not private wealth but government debt. Thus Italy, with a small stock market, has a vast government bond market amounting to nearly $1 trillion. In Germany, equity financing of corporate balance sheets is traditionally less important than debt financing; this is reflected in the data. In contrast, the data for the United Kingdom reflect an equity culture: most corporate risk is on the equity side of the balance sheet, and even the government bond market is small compared to the size of that country's economy.

In Table 11 we outline the historical growth of the world bond market. Unlike stocks, bonds have no expected capital-appreciation component; any appreciation that does occur is a historical accident. Thus, the tremendous growth in the capitalization of world bonds is almost entirely due to new issues, net of redemptions.

TABLE 11.   Growth of World Bond Market Capitalization, 1970–1994

| Country | Total Capitalization of All Categories of Bonds in Billions of U.S. Dollars, at Year-End | | | |
	1970	1980	1990	1994
United States	485	1377	5667	8023
Japan	47	569	2192	3674
Germany	48	321	1139	1962
Italy	NA	161	718	960
France	20	110	572	893
United Kingdom	62	212	367	502
Canada	30	99	321	401
Belgium	20	106	272	347
Netherlands	4	41	184	281
Denmark	11	75	213	251
Switzerland	8	54	192	232
Sweden	16	74	185	211
Total, 12 largest markets	752	3198	12022	17737

Note: Bonds included in capitalization totals include central and non-central government issues, government agency and government guaranteed bonds, corporate bonds, international bonds (foreign and Eurobonds), and various miscellaneous categories.

Source: Benavides, Rosario, "How Big is the World Bond Market? - 1995 Update," Salomon Brothers Economic and Market Analysis (International Bond Market Analysis), August 1995. Capitalizations in local currency, reported by Benavides, were converted to U.S. dollars using data in Ibbotson Associates' EnCORR/Analyzer.

Bond Market Returns

Methodology

Unlike the global stock market, where the MSCI indices provide a reasonably consistent and satisfactory source of data going back to the 1950s, the collection of bond market returns requires some methodological decisions. So that our data can be interpreted properly, we reveal our decision-making processes here.

It is more difficult to decide how to construct a bond index than to decide how to construct a stock index. There are important theoretical and practical reasons why a stock index should be a market-value-weighted, total-return index of all of the stocks in a market. While the total-return concept carries well to bonds, market-capitalization weighting is less clearly necessary or desirable.

First, as we have already noted, the capitalization of a government bond market is related more to the willingness or need of the government to become indebted than it is to the wealth of the country. Thus a global government bond portfolio constructed using market-capitalization weights would be biased toward the riskier, more heavily indebted countries. Second, the maturity distribution of a government bond market is not clearly the outcome of market forces; the distribution is whatever the government wants it to be. We do not mean to imply that governments are blind to market demand when selecting the maturities they want to sell, but they have total control over the supply of bonds, and distortions are easily produced. Thus some index constructors, including Ibbotson Associates, whose indices we use in the early part of the period studied, prefer constant-maturity series capturing the long-term end of the market—the market segment where a "full unit" of bond risk is priced.

Ibbotson long-term bond data for non-U.S. markets are constructed from yields provided by the International Monetary Fund in its *International Financial Statistics* publication. The IMF states a maturity or maturity range for the long-term-bond yield series for each country. Yields are converted to total returns by calculating the capital gain or loss that arises from the change in yield, assuming that the bond was "bought" at the stated maturity and "sold" one period later at a maturity shorter than the original maturity by the length of the holding period. The income return implied by the initial yield is then added to the capital appreciation return to arrive at a total return. For the United States, Ibbotson constructs a one-bond portfolio with approximately 20 years to maturity and measures the actual (not modeled) total return.

Market capitalization-weighted bond indices, however, have gained currency in the last decade or so, and are actually more relevant to the task we are trying to accomplish: measuring the return on that part of world wealth represented by bonds. Such indices are constructed by bond dealers, such as Salomon Brothers, Lehman Brothers, and J. P. Morgan. These indices reflect the actual total return on a portfolio of all bonds having the relevant maturity characteristics. For each country, we splice the Ibbotson data in the earlier part of the study period with the dealer-supplied data in the later part of the period, and start the dealer returns at the earliest date for which they are available.

We select Salomon as our principal source for the non-U.S. markets, because it provides the longest data history (returns for most of the countries that it covers start in 1979). The Salomon series cover all government bonds with five years or more to maturity. We use J. P. Morgan data for Italy and Sweden starting in 1988. For the United States, we use the Lehman government bond index starting in 1973; this index contains all Treasury and agency bonds with one year or more to maturity. Because it includes one- to five-year bonds, the Lehman index has a noticeably shorter maturity, and is thus less sensitive to changes in interest rates than the indices used for other countries.

We start our data series in 1967 (with an index base-date of year-end 1966) because, remarkably, the Japanese government was not constitutionally permitted to issue bonds until 1966. We wanted a common starting date for all important countries, and clearly 1967 is the first full year with Japanese government bond returns.

Return Data

Table 12 shows the year-by-year results, with summary statistics shown in Table 13. We present cumulative indices because all of the countries have a common start date and because this format makes it easier to follow the progress of a dollar invested over time.

Japan was the highest returning bond market over the period, largely due to the appreciation of the yen. South Africa had the lowest-returning bond market. In general, differences in rates of currency appreciation or depreciation against the dollar explain much of the differences in bond market returns. While returns expressed in local currency as well as in U.S. dollars might be more instructive (showing separately the effect of interest-rate and exchange-rate changes), for brevity and consistency, we show only the returns in U.S. dollars. A more complete discussion of world bond returns, yields, inflation rates, exchange rates, and currency hedging is in Ibbotson and Siegel (1991).

The history of the world bond market over this period consists of a severe bear market at the beginning, a recovery after the interest rate

TABLE 12. World Bonds 1967–1995: Cumulative Wealth Indices of Total Returns in U.S. Dollars (Year-End 1966 = 100)

	Australia	Belgium	Canada	France	Ger-many	Ireland	Italy	Japan	Nether-lands	New Zealand	South Africa	Sweden	Switzer-land	United Kingdom	United States
1966	1.00	1.00	1.00	1.00	1.00	1.00	1.00	1.00	1.00	1.00	1.00	1.00	1.00	1.00	1.00
1967	1.06	1.09	1.00	1.05	1.13	0.93	1.06	1.06	1.08	0.84	1.07	1.02	1.05	0.88	0.91
1968	1.14	1.15	1.02	1.07	1.25	0.95	1.14	1.15	1.13	0.88	1.13	1.15	1.12	0.86	0.91
1969	1.08	1.15	1.03	0.89	1.32	0.93	1.13	1.23	1.10	0.94	1.22	1.11	1.08	0.85	0.86
1970	1.03	1.24	1.29	0.98	1.39	1.02	1.05	1.31	1.22	0.99	1.19	1.19	1.11	0.89	0.96
1971	1.25	1.54	1.44	1.13	1.72	1.23	1.33	1.60	1.47	1.12	1.15	1.38	1.36	1.20	1.09
1972	1.49	1.67	1.49	1.25	1.81	1.16	1.53	1.86	1.60	1.18	1.25	1.49	1.45	1.04	1.15
1973	1.43	1.84	1.54	1.34	2.19	1.06	1.58	1.90	1.76	1.43	1.59	1.65	1.65	0.91	1.19
1974	1.26	2.11	1.57	1.41	2.69	0.96	1.09	1.86	2.17	1.40	1.53	1.87	2.12	0.78	1.27
1975	1.26	2.16	1.60	1.71	2.96	1.07	1.21	2.06	2.27	1.13	1.29	1.75	2.40	0.89	1.37
1976	1.16	2.47	1.88	1.62	3.79	0.98	0.91	2.37	2.75	0.97	1.34	1.96	3.03	0.83	1.54
1977	1.46	3.11	1.85	1.87	5.08	1.71	1.03	3.55	3.27	1.05	1.52	1.87	4.07	1.41	1.59
1978	1.71	3.79	1.76	2.50	5.92	1.89	1.29	4.69	3.98	1.21	1.79	2.20	5.52	1.46	1.62
1979	1.61	3.70	1.76	2.50	6.35	1.99	1.43	3.68	4.23	1.05	2.11	2.32	5.54	1.64	1.70
1980	1.58	3.37	1.78	2.31	5.72	2.10	1.26	4.54	4.00	1.16	2.22	2.30	5.00	2.11	1.79
1981	1.47	2.94	1.74	1.93	5.22	1.82	0.95	4.79	3.67	1.16	1.80	2.03	4.89	1.71	1.96
1982	1.69	2.90	2.37	1.98	5.95	2.27	1.06	4.94	4.26	1.15	2.04	1.74	4.95	2.16	2.50
1983	1.70	2.92	2.59	1.91	5.49	2.14	1.22	5.54	3.88	1.31	1.78	1.89	4.67	2.18	2.69
1984	1.78	2.94	2.81	1.96	5.44	2.08	1.48	5.72	3.79	0.75	1.11	1.84	4.03	1.89	3.08
1985	1.56	4.58	3.31	2.94	7.71	3.47	2.04	7.81	5.34	0.93	0.93	2.45	5.31	2.66	3.70
1986	1.83	6.98	3.88	3.94	10.68	4.06	3.84	11.21	7.27	1.19	1.46	3.41	7.21	3.05	4.27
1987	2.37	9.63	4.21	5.02	13.89	6.27	4.39	15.82	9.71	1.82	1.18	4.19	9.63	4.51	4.37
1988	3.09	8.59	5.05	5.20	12.97	7.02	4.34	16.44	9.07	2.12	1.04	4.48	8.39	4.68	4.67
1989	3.27	8.83	5.97	5.63	13.72	7.48	5.01	13.99	9.42	2.46	1.38	4.51	7.77	4.49	5.34

TABLE 12 *(continued)*

	Australia	Belgium	Canada	France	Germany	Ireland	Italy	Japan	Netherlands	New Zealand	South Africa	Sweden	Switzerland	United Kingdom	United States
1990	3.81	10.97	6.33	6.79	15.45	9.09	6.45	14.69	10.78	2.76	1.68	5.71	9.44	5.80	5.80
1991	4.82	12.60	7.86	7.92	17.35	10.45	7.43	18.22	11.96	3.52	2.04	6.98	9.60	6.63	6.69
1992	4.87	14.09	7.88	8.25	18.46	10.13	6.36	20.39	13.13	3.90	1.68	6.13	9.94	6.40	7.18
1993	5.89	15.22	9.04	9.79	20.11	11.65	7.23	26.64	14.49	5.12	2.58	6.28	11.37	7.87	7.94
1994	6.04	16.34	7.95	9.76	21.45	11.74	7.39	28.69	15.22	5.06	2.40	6.72	12.54	7.57	7.67
1995	7.09	21.44	10.10	12.73	27.48	14.37	8.92	31.97	19.74	6.13	3.50	8.97	16.34	8.86	9.08

Source: Used with permission from Ibbotson Associates for all non-U.S. markets over 1966–1978; Salomon Brothers for all non-U.S. markets over 1979–1995, except Italy and Sweden (1988–1995) from J. P. Morgan. U.S. data are from Ibbotson Associates (1966–1972) and Lehman Brothers (1973–1995).

TABLE 13. Summary Statistics of Total Annual Returns on World Bonds, 1967–1995

	Australia	Belgium	Canada	France	Germany	Ireland	Italy	Japan
Compound Annual Return	6.99%	11.15%	8.30%	9.17%	12.10%	9.62%	7.84%	12.69%
Standard Deviation	13.08%	16.74%	11.20%	15.29%	13.80%	21.67%	22.32%	16.37%

	Netherlands	New Zealand	South Africa	Sweden	Switzerland	United Kingdom	United States
Compound Annual Return	10.83%	6.45%	4.42%	7.86%	10.11%	7.81%	7.90%
Standard Deviation	13.14%	18.26%	22.50%	13.84%	15.82%	21.27%	7.84%

Source: Calculated by the author from data in Table 12.

spike of 1974, a second bear market ending in 1981, and a tremendous recovery or boom starting in 1982. The levels of interest rates reached in the 1974 and 1981 episodes are unprecedented in modern developed economies: long-term U.S. Treasury yields exceeded 15 percent in the second episode. German and Japanese bonds provided the best protection against these storms, not only because their currencies were strong, but because yields in those countries never reached the extreme levels attained in the United States, the United Kingdom, and other markets.

While the bull markets of the 1980s and 1990s suggest a return to more normal behavior in bond yields and returns, it should be noted that the 7 percent yield that has become typical in the United States in recent years was never reached in that country between 1817 and 1973; it was not even reached during the Civil War. High bond yields, of course, are caused by inflation expectations; and low or negative bond returns are caused by a shift in bond yields from low levels to high. Thus, inflation is at the root of the trouble that was experienced by bond investors around the world in the first half of the period shown in Table 12. Without resorting to a lecture on good management of the global monetary system, sound government finance, or right living, we note that at least in the United States, it was possible to suffer booms and depressions of the most extreme kind, fight wars, and wage peace for 15 decades without experiencing the kind of sustained inflation that makes high bond yields possible and necessary. One would think the world had learned from Weimar Germany that inflation is destructive, but it did not. Only today, after a spasm of inflation that was far more widespread and far longer in duration (though less extreme in its pace) than the German hyperinflation of 1923, is moderation in inflation and bond yields becoming the rule in practically every country.

Unfortunately we do not have enough data on emerging bond market returns to make a useful table. Paul Kaplan's (1996) description of the Brady bond market sheds some light on the fixed-income investment opportunities in these countries.

Implications for the Future

Expected Returns on Financial Assets

The data presented here give a backward-looking picture of the world's stock and bond markets. Based on this information, we can hazard some guesses about the future.

World stock and bond markets can be expected to continue to grow, although not at the explosive pace of the past few decades. Some of the past growth has been due to rises in nominal asset prices that merely compensate for inflation; such rises are likely to be at lower rates in the future. But we should be concerned not with nominal quantities but with real ones.

In the end, the capitalization of corporate financial assets (stocks and corporate bonds) must reflect the capitalization, or value, of the real economic assets against which the stocks and bonds are a claim. They cannot in the aggregate grow at rates faster than the rate of real economic growth, or more specifically the rate of real growth of the global corporate sector. This rate has averaged 3 percent per year in the United States in this century, somewhat faster in rapidly growing countries such as Japan, and somewhat slower in stagnating countries. We know of no reason why this stable and basically healthy rate should change much. Thus, a first-order approximation of the capital-gain return on corporate financial assets is 3 percent in real terms. In addition, investors expect to receive the dividend yield, which is now at a historically low level of 2.1 percent for the MSCI World Index.

We recognize that there is some (not much) leverage in the corporate balance sheet; because bonds have no expected capital gain, the expected capital gain on stocks is a little higher. (The boost from leverage is dampened by the extraordinarily high real rates that firms have to pay to bondholders at this time.) In addition, new issues and buybacks add some complexity to the equation that we will not address here. Setting aside these considerations for the sake of conservatism, we can project the total return on stocks as the sum of the 3 percent real economic growth rate, the 2.1 percent dividend yield, and an assumed 3 percent inflation rate. Dropping the decimal to avoid false precision, we arrive at a forecast of 8 percent.[16]

What could cause our forecast to be substantially wrong? Three considerations come to mind. First, unforeseen technological advances or difficulties could change the long-term rate of real global economic growth. This century has seen the emergence of a great many valuable general-purpose technologies: the automobile, airplane, computer, telephone, electrical power, the assembly line, the democratization of education (even if the per-unit quality is suffering), and the mechanization of agriculture have all exerted upward pressure on the growth rate. Environmental and population pressure, war, and tyranny have detracted. On net, we believe the 20th century growth rate is on the high side as a long-run forecast.

The valuation of stocks, relative to measures of fundamental value, could change, rendering our forecast wrong. (With regard to fundamental value, we have focused here on assets, but earnings or cash flows could be equally relevant.) Given today's level of valuation, the change is more likely to be down than up, but stocks have occasionally sold at valuations higher than those of today and could do so again.

Finally, a subtle technical point could cause us to be wrong. Our forecast relies on a comparison of dividends paid on stocks to a conceptual "dividend" on the capital stock of the real economy, where the conceptual dividend consists of current consumption. (That which is not consumed is available for use in a later period—it remains part of the capital stock.) There is some evidence that the real-economy dividend is substantially higher, expressed as a percentage yield, than the 2.1 percent stock-market dividend. The reader will be relieved to hear that, if this is true, it would cause us to raise our forecast for the stock market.

International Diversification

At the time of this writing, many investors in the United States are looking back at the recent past and questioning the wisdom and practicality of international diversification. Two issues appear to concern investors: (1) correlations appear to be rising, so that diversification does not "work" as well as it once did; and (2) the United States looks more promising, over the long run, than many other developed markets.

As we have shown in Figure 1, correlations of monthly returns are not rising, at least in any pronounced way. But a persistent element of investment folklore says that, at least in the short run, world markets are moving together much more than they used to. Folklore that cannot be empirically confirmed should not be ignored. Perhaps another researcher can find rising correlations in daily or weekly returns, or in returns collected only on days when the U.S. stock market is down.[17] If it turns out that correlations are perceived to be high because the correlation *conditional on a falling U.S. market* is high, investors should still diversify internationally: sometimes the U.S. market will rise a little and foreign markets will rise much more.

Moreover, there is a powerful reason why correlations should not be rising. Although increased international linkages might lead to rising correlations, another factor should lead to *falling* correlations. If each country is an autarchy, with no trade, then the business mix of every country will be more or less the same, reflecting the necessities of living: one-seventh in agriculture, one-seventh in mining, and so forth. The correlations of country stock markets in such a world would naturally be high. Now, when countries trade, they specialize. The Americans invent computers; the Japanese manufacture cars; the Swiss run banks; the British produce public television shows. Correlations fall.[18]

The second argument is that the developed world, other than the United States, is in a funk and that only the United States has the capital resources, labor market flexibility, and entrepreneurial drive to sustain strong economic growth. This is an exact repeat of the argument, commonly made in the 1980s, that only Japan had the right mix of ingredients for growth. It was wrong then, and it is wrong now. International competition and mean reversion are very powerful effects. We do not know what country or countries will next challenge the United States, just as we did not know in 1989 who would benefit from the decline of Japan. We only know that the challenge will take place, and that the only prudent investment position to take in the context of such knowledge is a global one.

Endnotes

1.   See, for example, Barro (1974) and Goldsmith (1984).

2.   We thank Steve McCarthy of Batterymarch for this nugget.

3.   To measure market capitalization, we use the MSCI measure of the total capitalization of all the stocks in a country, not the total capitalization of the stocks in their return indices (a smaller number). Total country market capitalization includes all companies which MSCI determines to be domiciled in a particular country, and each company is counted at its full capitalization; crossholdings, government holdings, and other noninvestable shares are not taken out of the measure. The MSCI return indices use substantially fewer stocks, typically comprising 60 percent of total country market capitalization, but each company that is included in the return indices is counted at its full capitalization.

4.   In the bond market, the currency of denomination—not the home country of the issuer—is the variable according to which issues are classified.

5.   For information on Brady bond returns, see Kaplan (1996).

6.   This number is not float-adjusted. A substantial fraction of this total represents closely held shares, government-owned shares, and cross-holdings (i.e., shares owned by corporations that are themselves counted in the total).

7.   We use purchasing power parity (PPP) exchange rates to convert foreign *per capita* GDP data to U.S. dollars so that the reader can make intercountry standard-of-living comparisons. PPP exchange rates are the number of units of a foreign country's currency that would buy, in that country's domestic market, the same quantity of goods and services as one dollar buys in the United States. Such hypothetical rates are often quite different from actual market rates; they lower the estimate of the standard of living in expensive countries (compared to the United States) and raise it in inexpensive ones. Thus the *per capita* GDP in Mexico is $4,012 at market exchange rates, but almost twice as much—$7,040—at PPP exchange rates, because a dollar goes farther in Mexico than it does in the United States.

8.   By the traditional first world we mean the United States, Canada, Western Europe, Japan, Australia, and New Zealand. Of course, Japan is itself a relative newcomer; despite some prewar prosperity it had the lowest per capita GDP in the world in 1946 ($29 per year, not PPP-adjusted, in then-current U.S. dollars).

9.   Ibbotson and Brinson (1987), page 107, constructed total returns for the MSCI national indices over 1960–1969 by adding an estimate of dividends to the capital appreciation returns presented here. They present only compound rates of return over two five-year periods (1960–1964 and 1965–1969), not year-by-year returns.

10.   We do not advise chain-linking indices that are constructed using different rules (capital appreciation and local currency in the 1958–1969 period, and total return and U.S. dollars in the 1969–1995 period). However, our two sets of indices are presented using a common base date (December 31, 1969, equals 100), and the reader can accordingly chain-link them at his or her own risk.

11.   For consistency with other countries, we use the MSCI United States index, rather than the more familiar S&P 500 or Wilshire 5000, to represent the U.S. stock market. This index has some oddities: Ford, the second largest U.S. company as ranked by sales, is excluded so as not to overrepresent the automotive industry.

12.   Returns are in U.S. dollars. See Roll (1988).

13.   We also repeat some Malaysian data in the sense that the MSCI Singapore/ Malaysia index is used to proxy the Singapore return over 1970–1992 in our section on developed markets, while Malaysia taken alone is treated as one of the emerging markets in that section.

14.   Because these returns reflect capital appreciation, not total return, the averages in Table 5 (geometric mean and arithmetic mean) are not comparable to the total return averages in other tables. However, because dividends are not highly variable, the standard deviations in Table 5 are roughly equal to those that would have been computed using total returns, and can therefore be compared to standard deviations of total returns shown in other tables.

15.   Our coverage is guided by that of MSCI. Thus, no data are available for China, which was added to the MSCI database in November 1995. Many of the countries shown in Table 8 have longer data-histories, collected by the International Financial Corporation, an affiliate of the World Bank; for summary data through 1990, see Ibbotson and Brinson (1993), page 142. The Financial Times-Actuaries (FTA) indices cover South Africa starting in 1981; Capital International created an index of South African gold mining stocks starting much earlier than that.

16.   This is a forecast of the compound annual rate, or geometric mean; the arithmetic mean (the return that is expected in each year) is higher. For U.S. stocks over 1926–1995, the arithmetic mean return exceeded the geometric mean return by 2 percent per year. The reader may react to this forecast by saying that an 8 percent nominal return on stocks is too low, considering that long U.S. Treasury bonds currently yield 7 percent. We would respond that stocks are, at this time in history, not dramatically riskier than bonds and thus may not command much of a risk premium over bonds. Moreover, our forecast may well be too low; it implic-

itly assumes that plowback (the portion of earnings not paid out as dividends) must remain as high as it is now in order to support a real economic growth rate of 3 percent. This has not been historically true. The average dividend yield over the last 70 years was 4.6 percent, and real economic growth close to 3 percent was supported under those conditions. If dividend yields somehow rose to their historical average level without a large initial drop in stock prices, our forecast method would yield a result of 10.6 percent for the nominal total return on stocks, exactly equal to the historical (1926–1995) return. Finally, a compound annual return of 5 percent in excess of the inflation rate is nothing to sneeze at, it makes stocks well worth owning, and it is not available from any other asset.

17.   A superb article that we received after writing this chapter (Solnik, et al. [1996]) finds that cross-country correlations of equity markets are higher in down markets than in up markets. This phenomenon presents some additional downside risk to investors who diversify internationally. It does not, however, reduce the power of international diversification to provide high returns. Investors should presume that their own country will not always have the highest-returning market, or the market with the highest risk-return tradeoff, and should consequently diversify.

18.   The author is grateful to the late Fischer Black for his assistance in elucidating this argument.

References

Barro, Robert J. "Are Government Bonds Net Wealth?" *Journal of Political Economy,* vol. 82, no. 6 (November/December 1974), pp. 1095-1117.

Benavides, Rosario. "How Big Is the World Bond Market?—1995 Update." New York: Salomon Brothers, August 1995.

Goldsmith, Raymond W. "National Balance Sheets as Tools of International Economic Comparisons," in *Comparative Development Perspectives: Essays in Honor of Lloyd G. Reynolds,* edited by Gustav Ranis, et al., Westview Press, Boulder, Colorado in cooperation with the Economic Growth Center, Yale University, 1984.

Ibbotson Associates. *EnCORR/Analyzer,* software and data service, Chicago, IL: Ibbotson Associates, Inc., July 1996 and other releases.

Ibbotson, Roger G., and Gary P. Brinson. *Investment Markets: Gaining the Performance Advantage.* New York: McGraw-Hill, 1987.

Ibbotson, Roger G., and Gary P. Brinson. *Global Investing.* New York: McGraw Hill, 1993.

Ibbotson, Roger G., and Laurence B. Siegel. "The World Market Wealth Portfolio." *Journal of Portfolio Management,* vol. 9, no. 2 (Winter 1983).

Ibbotson, Roger G., and Laurence B. Siegel. "The World Bond Market: Market Values, Yields, and Returns." *Journal of Fixed Income,* vol. 1, no. 1 (June 1991).

Ibbotson, Roger G.; Laurence B. Siegel; and Kathryn S. Love. "World Wealth: Market Values and Returns." *Journal of Portfolio Management,* vol. 12, no. 1 (Fall 1985).

Kaplan, Paul D. *Stocks, Brady Bonds, and Currencies: Investment Opportunities in Latin America,* Chicago, IL: Chicago Mercantile Exchange, 1996.

Merrill Lynch. *Size and Structure of the World Bond Market: 1995.* New York: Merrill Lynch & Co., 1995.

Morgan Stanley Capital International. *EAFE and World Perspective.* New York: Morgan Stanley & Co., July 1996 and other issues.

Morgan Stanley Capital International. *EMF and Emerging Markets Perspective,* July 1996 and other issues.

Morgan Stanley Capital International. *Methodology & Index Policy.* New York: Morgan Stanley & Co., 1996.

Roll, Richard. "A Critique of the Asset Pricing Theory's Tests." *Journal of Financial Economics,* vol. 4, no. 2 (March 1977).

Roll, Richard. "The International Crash of October 1987." *Financial Analysts Journal,* vol. 44, no.5 (September/October 1988).

Sikorsky, Nilly. "The Origin and Construction of the Capital International Indices." *Columbia Journal of World Business,* vol. 17, no. 2, November 1982.

Solnik, Bruno, Cyril Boucrelle, and Yann Le Fur, "International Market Correlation and Volatility," *Financial Analysts Journal*, vol. 52, no. 5 (September/October 1996).

World Bank. *From Plan to Market: World Development Report 1996.* New York: Oxford University Press, Inc., 1996.

CHAPTER 2

Why Invest Globally?

Jarrod W. Wilcox
Director of Research
PanAgora Asset Management

Introduction

Investing in foreign markets means venturing into the unknown. You meet unfamiliar political and economic environments. Financial reporting is strange and less reliable. Transaction costs are higher. You face unstable currencies. The homebound will criticize you. As a global investor facing uncertainty, it will be helpful to keep in mind why you are here.

We will describe useful basic ideas in three steps. First, we will show why investing globally is likely to raise returns. Second, we will show why it can be expected to lower investor risk. Third, we will describe agent risk in the international investing context and the innovation diffusion process that is gradually overcoming it.

We will use for illustration MSCI equity index returns (for the United States and for Europe, Australia, and the Far East, or EAFE) for developed country markets over the last 20 years.[1] Similar concepts also apply to bonds and real estate, but these are not covered here. The analysis in this chapter is brief and used only to highlight our argument.

We will also refer to typical findings from the academic and professional investment literature, primarily to provide the reader with a springboard for further reading. A good journal review of many of the issues covered here may be found in Odier and Solnik (1993). More recently, a critique of international diversification benefits by Sinquefield (1996) deserves a considered response. There has also been a coincident and ironic drop in correlations between U.S. returns and foreign returns in the mid-1990s as Japan's business cycle got out of phase with that in the United States. Finally, the practical problem of agent risk, not investor risk, is increasingly recognized as the key determinant of the speed of investment globalization.

Investing for Greater Return

International investing is likely to be helpful both to passive investors and to skillful active investors. First, though, let us consider the bedrock, the return benefit to the passive investor willing to diversify outside the United States.

Passive Return Enhancement for Risk-Bearing

Investors require higher expected returns for taking higher expected risks. If you as an investor are better able than average to bear risks, you can earn higher returns without undue discomfort.

In the United States, both risk and return grow as we move from the safest short-term Treasury bills through risky small stocks.[2] The return difference is stable only over time horizons of 20 years or more. But it is quite strong. Large stocks have enjoyed about a 5 percent long-term return advantage versus bonds, and 6 percent versus Treasury bills. Small stocks have gained another 2 to 3 percent.

Modern portfolio theory (MPT) obscures the long-term link between volatility and average return. MPT assumes fully integrated and efficient markets with identically informed investors. It concludes that nondiversifiable risk will be rewarded on average, while diversifiable risk will not.[3] Careful study shows this to be contrary to fact. However, when we restrict the range of volatility by looking only within stocks, additional attributes of small size and low price-to-book ratio appear stronger determinants of relative return.[4] Part of this is a by-product of the higher volatility of small stocks. However, they also have less liquidity, less available data, and less cachet among the public than do the stocks of larger companies. Stocks with low price-to-book are generally those of companies that have been less profitable, as measured by return on equity.[5] They are thus likely to be underpriced by investors who wrongly identify good stocks with good companies.

Risk, whether measured by volatility, low liquidity, or low social acceptance, implies higher long-term returns because it creates a reluctance to own, which must be compensated. Risk is the most useful place to start in comparing expected rates of return. Higher risk means higher expected return.

How do foreign stocks rate versus U.S. stocks in risk? Investors from key wealthy countries such as the United States and Japan still hold considerably less than market capitalization weights in foreign markets. For example, InterSec Research Corporation estimates that 9 percent of U.S. pension assets were invested abroad at the end of 1995. However, at least 60 percent of the developed world equity market lies outside the United States. If we included emerging markets, the figure would be considerably higher. Unconstrained foreign investing is still seen as unconventional.

The intrepid investor in foreign securities must face not only a residue of social skepticism but also an unaccustomed environment. In many countries, liquidity and availability of company data are less than in the United States. Trading costs in countries like Spain are higher than in the United States. Audited quarterly reports are generally unavailable over most of the rest of the world. Even audited annual reports may be particularly uninformative in countries like Germany where profit may be tucked away in reserves for a rainy day. For such qualitative reasons, U.S. investors in foreign securities face higher risks.

They also face higher risks measured as volatility, or standard deviation of return. Many foreign markets are much more volatile than in the United States. See Table 1 for a comparison of equity return volatility measures across the developed countries. Return volatility is given for both returns in dollars and in local currencies.[6] The United States is almost at the bottom of the list. Such mature economies as the United Kingdom, Germany, and France are substantially riskier. Japan is far riskier. Consider countries like Hong Kong, Malaysia, Finland, Norway, and Italy. Their annualized standard deviation of equity market return has been about twice that of the United States. Clearly many foreign markets are riskier than those in the United States, and these markets offer increased return opportunities.

Table 1 does not show rankings for systematic risk, or beta, versus a world return index. To do so would give more precision and credibility to the MPT estimates of appropriate risk premium than is warranted by the evidence. The argument here is that higher return is available, and that it is valuable precisely because it is associated with risk that can be diversified away. This places us in direct opposition to MPT as a descriptive theory. Nondiversifiable risk should get a higher reward. But in an imperfect world, even diversifiable risk may be rewarded to a surprising degree.

Of course, the expectation for higher return may be met by very large returns for only a few of the available assets. If the 18 countries in EAFE from mid-1976 through mid-1986 are ranked for risk, Hong Kong,

TABLE 1. Countries Ranked by Volatility Risk

	Dollar Return	Local Return	Currency Return
HONG KONG	34.93	33.09	5.76
MALAYSIA	34.04	35.56	9.42
FINLAND	32.76	34.73	12.67
NORWAY	30.61	29.26	10.68
ITALY	30.45	29.27	11.61
SPAIN	27.58	26.17	12.30
SINGAPORE	26.55	26.51	4.63
AUSTRIA	25.91	24.74	12.91
JAPAN	24.68	20.09	13.37
FRANCE	24.60	22.05	12.41
SWEDEN	23.92	26.66	11.83
AUSTRALIA	23.77	20.49	9.31
BELGIUM	21.31	19.31	13.60
GERMANY	20.48	18.37	12.90
SWITZERLAND	20.08	17.68	15.06
UK	19.96	17.32	11.24
DENMARK	18.20	19.37	12.38
CANADA	18.01	15.72	4.79
NETHERLANDS	16.21	15.31	13.08
NEW ZEALAND	14.96	14.88	5.97
USA	14.08	14.08	0.00
IRELAND	11.17	10.90	10.05

Source: Morgan Stanley Capital International (MSCI).

Italy, and Norway top the list with more than 30 percent annualized risk. In the 10 years since 1986, Hong Kong returned in local currency a fantastic annualized 25 percent, while Italy returned only 3 percent per year, and Norway 10 percent. For the U.S. investor, these countries returned 23 percent, 2 percent, and 10 percent respectively.[7]

The Currency Return Controversy

Some disparage investing outside the United States because about 2 percent of EAFE's return over the last 20 years has come through declines in the value of the U.S. dollar.[8] The implication is that currency return is clearly separable from stock returns and that currency return differentials are somehow less predictable than stock return differentials. The opposite is true in both cases.

First, consider the assumption of separability. For Canada and the EAFE countries for the 80 quarters ending June 1996, there was a negative correlation between local stock returns and currency returns for the U.S. investor of –0.15. For example, in the first quarter of 1996, Australia, New Zealand, and Italy had the worst local returns of the developed countries. But they also had the best currency gains versus the dollar.

The reliability of this negative relationship gets much greater as one examines longer-periods. Consider 10-year returns rather than quarterly returns. The 10-year MSCI index returns of local stocks and their currency returns for the U.S. investor for the decade ending in mid-1986 have a –0.49 correlation. The 10-year returns ending in mid-1996 show a correlation between local stock returns and their currencies of –0.28. Persistent differences in the rate of inflation and in changes in the terms of trade are probable influences here. Since these differences are only a small part of short-term fluctuations in currency values, typical studies relating returns measured in monthly or quarterly intervals do not reveal this powerful negative relationship. Nevertheless, we cannot fully separate currency from local return, because they are partial substitutes. A long-term decline in the value of the dollar is very likely part of the reason for the long-term bull market in stocks we have seen in the United States in recent years, measured in dollars of declining value.

Second, consider currency trend predictability. Are differences in currency returns less likely to persist over long periods than those of stocks or bonds? There is no justification for this inference. Various studies have shown currencies to be *more* likely to follow long-term trends than are either stocks or bonds.[9] The strong currencies of much of the rest of the world, as exemplified not only by Japan and Germany but also by some emerging markets such as Singapore, are a reflection of a long-term erosion in the dollar. While there have been intervals of recovery, the example of Great Britain in the first half of the twentieth century reminds us that such trends can continue for decades.

On both counts, it is a poor argument to say that we should discount the future excess returns of international securities because in the past a significant portion has been based on currency.

Enhancing Compound Return through Diversification

Passive investors can expect higher return not only from bearing the risks implicit in global investing but also from diversification effects versus U.S. returns. This is because higher return, not just lower risk, results from diversification among two equally risky securities as long as they are less than perfectly correlated.[10] Markowitz pointed out this source of additional return in the 1950s.[11] Because this phenomenon is widely unknown or ignored, it is worth a few minutes of reflection.

Contrary to intuition, the return of an average, that is, a portfolio, will be slightly greater than the portfolio-weighted average return of its constituents. Booth and Fama (1992) give an example of a U.S. portfolio of 50 percent bonds and 50 percent stocks gaining an annual 0.28 percent over a 50-year period. The incremental gain from diversification is positively related to the variances of the component asset returns and negatively related to the correlation among them.[12]

Suppose that in the first year of a single-security investment, we get a 100 percent return. The second year, we get a loss of 50 percent. The arithmetic average is 25 percent, while the compounded return is only 0 percent. This example does get across the idea that variance somehow lowers compound return.

It can be shown that a good approximation of the expected compound return is expected average return converted into log form less half its expected variance. (The log return is simply the natural log of the sum of one plus the arithmetic return expressed in decimal form.)

Consider the impact of this relationship when we combine securities in a portfolio. Suppose there are two securities, each with the same mean and variance of return. However, the fluctuations in return of the two are not perfectly correlated. Consequently, the variance of returns of a portfolio composed of the two securities will be reduced. The expected arithmetic return is unaffected. Therefore the expected compound return of the portfolio will be greater than the expected compound return of either security in isolation. Although rebalancing the securities to constant 50-percent proportions will keep the diversification effect at its maximum, it is not necessary to rebalance in order to achieve some expected return benefit.

Finally, consider an EAFE + Canada portfolio combined with a U.S. portfolio of equal size. Their average correlation of returns is about 0.6 and the typical annual risk for them each is about 15 percent. (The actual figures over 20 years based on quarterly data are 0.56, 17 percent, and 14 percent.) Let us compare this portfolio with a pure U.S. holding. The return gain will be approximately half the reducton in portfolio variance. In this case, that works out at 0.22 percent annually. If this is allocated to the diversifying foreign asset, the incremental return benefit is twice that, or 0.44 percent. This increment results solely from the diversifying impact, without taking into account any increased expected return from foreign stocks in isolation. While this benefit may seem small, recall that it is quite reliable, since it results merely from better financial engineering rather than from expected return enhancement for particular assets.

So far we have shown that there are attractive return benefits to global investing for even the passive investor. The active investor with the ability to exploit market inefficiencies has even bigger fish to fry.

Active Return Benefit from a Bigger Universe

The simplest active return benefit arises from the mere increase in the number of investable securities. A typical large U.S. investor may select from among 300 to 1500 securities, depending on investigational resources, liquidity requirements, and type of expertise. The investor employing extensive qualitative fundamental analysis will be at the low end. The quantitative investor using simple computer screens is at the high end. In either case, the expansion into international and emerging markets more than doubles the number of opportunities. How much is it worth, for example, to be able to search not just in the United States but also in Italy and Poland for undervalued growth companies?

We can get an insight into this by an example. Suppose that the investor needs a portfolio of 50 stocks, all with market capitalization of at least 300 million dollars, in order to provide sufficient diversification and liquidity. The investor can identify stocks that can earn an extra 4 percent annually after trading costs, but only under special circumstances. Suppose he or she can identify these excellent opportunities only if they are at least two standard deviations better from the average composite of identifying characteristics. For example, the composite might be a score based on a combination of value and earnings momentum measures combined with subjective assessments of barriers to competitors and management's ability to articulate a growth strategy. If the characteristics are normally distributed, 2.3 percent of available companies will meet this screen. Suppose there are 1000 companies available in the United States. On average, 23 U.S. companies will meet the screen. If the investor limits the portfolio to U.S. companies, then slightly less than half of the portfolio will be excellent opportunities, and the rest will be undistinguished. Portfolio return will be better than average by a little less than 2 percent. However, if the investor can double his or her universe by searching globally, the pool will be 2000 stocks. Nearly the whole portfolio will be excellent opportunities earning an additional 4 percent, approximately doubling the value added of the pure U.S. portfolio.

Although the example is simple, it does capture the basic elements to be considered, with one exception. We have not subtracted the costs of additional searching. These will vary depending on how extensible the investor's techniques and on the size of the portfolio over which these costs may be amortized.

Active Benefits from Less Efficient Markets

Active management implies that markets do not process all available information immediately or correctly. The types of processing delays and mistakes each market makes are a function of the types of investors and traders populating that market. Market inefficiencies also depend on the information infrastructure that has grown up to support the efforts of their participants.

Although there is a flow of investors among them, markets are not identical. As you move from the least-liquid emerging markets up through relatively efficient markets such as that of the United States, you see increasing depth and variety of investors. You also see better information resources and a more sophisticated regulatory environment.

In their early stages, stock markets are dominated by insiders, and trading is light. A typical example today might be the Egyptian stock market. As more informational sources open up and more nonprofessional investors enter the market, professional investment analysts begin making better financial estimates. Less-informed investors attempt to take advantage of this second-hand information. The Warsaw Stock Exchange comes to mind here.

As still more investors enter the market, the usefulness of access to particular fundamental research declines. Technical methods for capturing trends become more useful, creating momentum investors. In this environment, "retail" investors tend to buy in waves, sensing that underneath price momentum there must be some real opportunities. Prices may far overshoot fair values, creating exploitive opportunities for a new class of investor, the value-oriented investor. The latter bases investments on a comparison between prices and some yardstick of fair value, but does not require extensive fundamental knowledge if there are many more momentum than value investors. In recent times, the Japanese stock market may fairly be placed here. A different, slower, evolution has governed the larger European markets such as are found in France and Germany. Such markets have considerable volume and are old enough to have a full range of investor types, but the information and trading substructure still is lacking transparency, except, perhaps, in the United Kingdom. Finally, the market evolves to become so deep and efficient that index investors may flourish, catching a free ride on the valuation and low trading-costs caused by active investors. This is a reasonable description of the U.S. market.

Within this spectrum, there are ample opportunities for quantitatively based active global investors. Fifteen years ago one heard Japanese brokers saying that it would be hard for outsiders to do well in that market, because it worked so differently. For example, there were stocks whose prices were set precisely for extended periods by major banks. Where prices did float freely, they were highly influenced by concerted retail-brokerage selling campaigns. Anecdotally, the Japanese market turned out to be the easiest major market for quantitative global investors to make money in, because the Tokyo market suffered from a shortage of value-oriented investors. Their criteria were particularly amenable to quantitative methods that provided a discipline within which one could more safely buy when all around were selling, and vice versa. Today, foreigners still play this role in Tokyo.

Quantitative active investing methods have not been limited to value investing, however. Momentum investors can exploit new infrastructure such as electronically available IBES earnings estimates. These massive, constantly updated compilations of broker and bank earnings estimates can serve as an invaluable support for fast-moving quantitative investors wanting to focus on earnings estimate revisions and earnings surprise opportunities. These occur when the market does not efficiently digest new information. Global quantitative investors who are experienced in quickly using the earnings estimates provided by I/B/E/S Inc. in the United States may even have a jump on local investors.

Detailed examples of foreign market opportunities at the stock selection level may be found in the investment literature.[13] Typical market inefficiencies described are international corollaries of the Fama and French finding for the United States that small stocks and stocks with low price/book ratios provide superior average returns.[14] Other anomalies characteristically found in the United States are also found internationally, sometimes with greater strength.

Evidence of both the low price/book and the small capitalization effect exists at the country level as well. It is harder to show statistical significance at the country level than at the stock selection level, however, because there are so many fewer observations.

We explore this briefly using our MSCI country database of index returns and characteristics. Table 2 shows the result of regressing country returns against price/book and market capitalization over the last 20 years. Both price/book and total market capitalization of the country index were put in log form. Each quarter the cross-sectional means of these variables were subtracted from the raw measure to put the independent variables into excess form. The same was done for the subsequent quarter's dollar-based index returns expressed in percentage terms.

On average and other things equal, a country that was one standard-deviation lower in log price/book provided a return 0.24 percent per quarter higher than average. A country one standard-deviation

TABLE 2. Low Price/Book and Small Size as Predictors of MSCI
          Index Return

. fit xrtn xpbln xmkt

Source	SS	df	MS
Model	334.141	2	67.071
Residual	131426.953	1497	87.794
Total	131761.094	1499	87.899

Number of obs	= 1500
F(2, 1497)	= 1.90
Prob > F	= 0.150
R-squared	= 0.0025
Adj R-squared	= 0.0012
Root MSE	= 9.370

xrtn	Coef.	Std. Err.	t	P>|t|	[95% Conf. Interval]	
xpbln	-.682	.725	-0.94	0.35	-2.104	.740
xmkt	-.214	.169	-1.27	0.20	-.545	.117
_cons	-.000	.242	0.00	1.00	-.475	.475

Note: Standard deviations: xrtn 9.375%, xpbln 0.357, xmkt 1.533.

smaller in terms of log market capitalization provided a return 0.33 percent higher than average. The effects are in the predicted direction and are of an economically significant size. However, they are so variable that they are not statistically significant. It should be noted that in the last 10 years the impact of price/book has been of somewhat greater significance than shown here for the 20-year sample. It is also possible to improve on both our indicators with variants that take into account measurement issues and potential variability of impact through time.

Global Investing for Less Investor Risk

We could simply say that global investing decreases portfolio risk through better diversification of sources of return and stop there. However, effective use of this insight benefits from more detailed knowledge.

The Concept of the Efficient Frontier

We will use the idea of an efficient frontier to discuss risk reduction without sacrificing expected return. We could also use it to discuss return enhancement for a given level of risk. Investors hold stocks and bonds as part of collections called portfolios. For any given level of expected portfolio risk, one should prefer the portfolio with the highest expected return. We measure risk as the statistical variance of future returns up to some investment time-horizon. Return is the expected growth rate of portfolio value.

One can derive the expected risk and return for any portfolio using three types of inputs. They are the expected mean return for each asset, the expected standard deviation of return for each asset, and the expected correlation between the returns of every pair of assets. Iterative mathematical procedures can then be used to identify which of the possible portfolios for each successively higher level of risk has the highest expected return. The set of all these "best" portfolios over different risk levels is known as the *efficient frontier.*

We will show how introducing the potential for international diversification expands the efficient frontier. It thus allows both improved expected return and reduced risk from a starting point consisting only of U.S. securities. In so doing, we use the Markowitz mean-variance framework.[15]

For example, consider the average risk of quarterly U.S. and Japanese stock returns. Over the last 20 years, the standard deviation for arithmetic quarterly returns for the United States has been 7.04 percent. (Note that for a series of nearly independent returns, quarterly standard deviations are approximately half of annual standard deviations.) However, the more volatile Japanese market, including currency and local returns together, has a quarterly risk of 12.34 percent. What would be the risk of a portfolio rebalanced quarterly to maintain proportions of 75 percent in the United States and 25 percent in Japan? If you guessed the weighted average risk at $(.75)(7.04) + (.25)(12.34) = 8.36\%$, you would be mistaken. The actual quarterly risk is a little less than for the United States by itself, a reduction from 7.04 percent to 7.00 percent. The relatively high individual-risk of holding Japanese securities surprisingly resulted in a slight lowering of portfolio risk. The reason was that the Japanese returns to the U.S. investor had a relatively low correlation with the U.S. returns, only 0.35.

We can tell whether small amounts of a foreign country's equity will reduce the risk of a U.S. equity portfolio by calculating that market's *beta* to the United States. This is the product of correlation with the United States times the ratio of the foreign risk in isolation to the U.S. risk in isolation. If it is less than one, the country has some diversification value. Table 3 is based on quarterly risks and correlations. It shows us that each of the developed countries, considered in small proportions, would have had the effect of lowering total portfolio risk for a U.S. investor. This was true even though some are much riskier individually than the United States. The most useful are small countries like Finland and New

TABLE 3. Ability to Diversify U.S. Equity

	Correlation	Std. Dev.	Beta to US
FINLAND	-0.01	16.38	-0.02
NEW ZEALAND	0.24	7.48	0.25
IRELAND	0.37	5.58	0.29
DENMARK	0.35	9.10	0.45
AUSTRIA	0.25	12.96	0.46
GERMANY	0.39	10.24	0.57
JAPAN	0.35	12.34	0.61
MALAYSIA	0.28	17.02	0.68
NETHERLANDS	0.60	8.11	0.69
BELGIUM	0.48	10.66	0.73
NORWAY	0.34	15.30	0.74
ITALY	0.35	15.23	0.76
SWITZERLAND	0.54	10.04	0.77
UK	0.55	9.98	0.78
SPAIN	0.40	13.79	0.78
FRANCE	0.45	12.30	0.79
AUSTRALIA	0.51	11.89	0.86
SWEDEN	0.54	11.96	0.92
CANADA	0.73	9.01	0.93
SINGAPORE	0.50	13.27	0.94
HONG KONG	0.39	17.47	0.97
USA	1.00	7.04	1.00

Source: Morgan Stanley Capital International (MSCI).

Zealand, but even big markets like Japan and Germany have been excellent potential diversifiers.

Of course, as more international assets are added to the mix, the relevant beta should be measured with respect to a mixed portfolio that has become less like the United States. Thus the final calculation of an optimum portfolio is complicated and requires a computer program to solve. Nevertheless, foreign holdings have clear ability to reduce the risk of a U.S. portfolio.

You may recall that even if their individual expected returns were merely equal to those of the United States, the total portfolio would have not only lower risk but also have slightly increased expected return. This is because modestly higher compounded return comes through the impact of reduced risk discussed earlier.

Japan is very important because it comprises about 40 percent of the non-U.S. developed market.

Figure 1 shows a very simple efficient frontier constructed around only three asset classes—cash, U.S. equities, and Japanese equities—without currency hedging. For mean returns, we assume cash at 5 percent, U.S. stocks at 11 percent, and Japanese stocks at 12 percent. This recognizes that the higher volatility in Japanese returns may be associated with higher expected returns. For risks, we will use actual historical risks, annualized from our quarterly data: cash 0 percent, U.S. stocks 14.08 percent, and Japanese stocks plus currency exposure at 24.68 percent. The U.S. versus Japanese stock correlation is 0.35, and we will assume correlations between cash and stock returns at zero.

In Figure 1, the efficient frontier is approximately 0.4 percent to the left of the "U.S. Alone" point that lies below and to the right of the efficient frontier. At that expected return, Japanese equities are about 20 percent of the total portfolio. Alternatively, the efficient frontier at the point of equivalent risk to a pure U.S. equity portfolio has more return.[16] By adding additional diverse international assets, it is possible to move the efficient frontier farther up and to the left, toward more return for less risk.

FIGURE 1. Simple Efficient Frontier

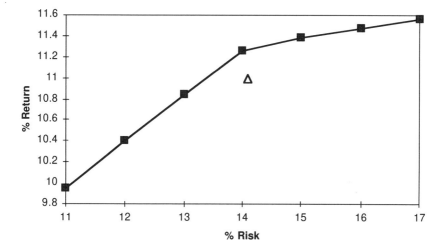

Whither Correlations?

Critics of international investing often remind us of a future with less diversification potential. Will correlations of U.S. returns with international returns stay low enough to provide significant diversification benefits? After all, we see around us ample daily evidence of increased world integration in culture, economic activity, and investor diversification.[17] These should, over time, cause correlations between returns in different countries to increase. How fast is this happening?

Figure 2 shows rolling five-year correlations based on quarterly data of EAFE + Canada returns to U.S. investors with U.S. stock returns. There is no identifiable long-term increasing trend. Quite the opposite, in the last few years the five-year rolling correlation fell from about 0.7 to about 0.2. This fall has been a consequence of two factors. First, there has recently been relatively little volatility in U.S. returns. Second, Japan's business cycle has gotten very much out of phase with that in the United States. Business recovery from the last recession in the United States began in 1991. In Japan, undergoing the aftermath of a gigantic real estate bubble, recovery only got strongly underway in 1996.

The Spike Scenario

Will international diversification be there when you really need it?

FIGURE 2.   EAFE + Canada 5-Year Rolling Correlation with U.S.

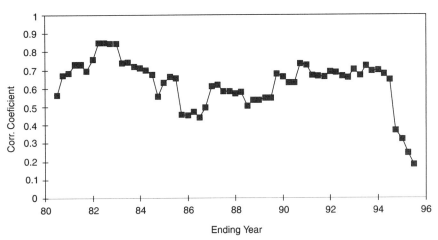

Source: MSCI.

Another source of potential doubt in global diversification's ability to reduce risk was raised by studies of daily volatility around the world-wide stock market crash in October 1987. It is true that on a daily basis correlations rose during this period. However, there is no real cause for doubt, for three reasons.

First, the coincidence in volatility was short-lived. Over periods long-enough for making policy decisions concerning the degree of global diversification, what counts are average correlations and risks. These are better estimated by long-term rolling averages than by events on a weekly, or even daily, timescale.

Second, dollar returns were less affected than local returns by the market break, because currency tended to offset some of the stock market action. In the fourth quarter of 1987, the U.S. market lost 23 percent. In yen terms, the Tokyo market was down a comparable 19 percent. But an offsetting fall in the dollar caused a net fall of only 2 percent to the U.S. investor in Japanese stocks.

Third, this concern fails to recognize that diversification benefit is not only a function of correlation but also of the volatility of U.S. returns. During October 1987, correlations were higher, reducing percentage volatility reduction from diversification. However, since volatility sharply increased, the impact was much more favorable than is apparent from looking at correlations alone. As a rough estimate, the benefit is proportional to the reduction in correlation from unity times the U.S. risk. For example, if current correlation increased from 0.6 to 0.8, cutting the correlation benefit in half, but U.S. volatility more than doubled, then the diversification benefit might have risen, not fallen. Without a more detailed study, one cannot determine the net benefit. However, anecdotally, U.S. investors were quite glad of the diversification provided by EAFE at the time. While the United States fell 23 percent, EAFE lost only 11 percent.

For all these reasons, it is very clear that the benefits of international diversification are far from declining. And even if some day the correlations between U.S. returns and developed country returns begin to increase beyond the average of the last 20 years, it is likely that there will be ready replacements maturing from today's emerging markets.

Extra Dimensions Provided by Emerging Markets

Although great practical opportunities are available through diversification into emerging markets, no new principles are involved beyond those described in earlier sections. Therefore, we need not go into detail here.

Everything we have said about the developed markets as represented by the MSCI indices applies with greater force when emerging markets are included. Higher returns may be expected passively, because these markets are individually much more volatile and less accepted by investors in the major investing countries. Higher returns are also possible through the diversification effect because, in general, correlations with the United States are somewhat lower than for developed markets. (Although the correlation of International Finance Corporation's market capitalization-weighted composite emerging-market index returns with U.S. returns is not much different from that of EAFE; the correlations of individual component countries, especially the smaller ones, are much lower.) Higher returns from emerging markets may also be available for active investors who are good enough to earn excess returns in the U.S. market. These opportunities are not restricted to investors relying on qualitative fundamental analysis. There are now good databases of prices and returns and at least minimal databases of earnings, dividends, and book value for many hundreds of emerging market stocks.

Finally, the lower correlations with U.S. returns of most emerging market countries as compared to developed markets give rich opportunities to reduce risk. The opportunity here is not so much in the larger countries included in emerging market indices, for example Mexico, Malaysia, and South Africa. It is more in assembling low-risk portfolios of smaller, individually still more volatile markets. It is not difficult to put together a portfolio of emerging market stocks that is both lower in its own risk than the EAFE bundle and lower in correlation with the U.S. market. This provides a double risk reduction benefit for U.S. investors.

Extra Dimension Provided by Currency Hedging

In the example efficient frontier shown in Figure 1, we considered only unhedged Japanese equities. We can change the nature of the efficient frontier available to us by introducing a new asset, currency-hedged Japanese equities. These can be purchased either by buying stocks and hedging them in the currency market or by buying Japanese stock futures on margin.

The addition of a fourth, hedged, asset into our simple asset allocation question cannot reduce our efficient frontier, and may increase it. We very conservatively estimate expected return will be that of Japanese equities less a frictional hedging cost of 0.4 percent. Hedged returns are approximated as local returns less local short-term interest plus domestic short-term interest. However, the short-term interest components contribute little to the risk picture. Let us estimate hedged risk with the correlations and standard deviations that we have observed for local Japanese returns over the last 20 years. The annual risk is 19.98 percent, the correlation with the United States is 0.41 and with Japanese unhedged equities is 0.84. The new efficient frontier using this asset is shown to the left of the old one in Figure 3.

The addition of currency hedging opportunities helps increase available return by about 0.1 percent in the 13 percent risk area, where risk and return trade-offs are typical of institutional clients. At that point, the efficient frontier contains 3 percent cash, 70 percent U.S. stocks, 2 percent Japanese stocks, and 25 percent hedged Japanese stocks. (At higher levels of risk, the sacrifice of 0.4 percent in return versus unhedged Japanese stocks causes reduced levels of hedging.) With hedging, the total allocation to Japanese stocks, hedged and unhedged, increases from the 10–15 percent range to the 25–30 percent range at normal institutional risk-tolerance levels. This example shows that the potential for currency hedging greatly adds to the optimal foreign allocation.

Agent Risk

We alluded earlier to the risk of investing in foreign securities as having qualitative components, including the risk of social disapproval. This broader concept is especially important when we consider the problems of risk for investment agents as opposed to investment principals. There are usually several layers of agents hired to protect the interests of the

FIGURE 3.   Efficient Frontier with Hedging

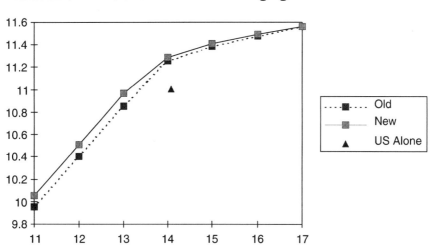

final investor. For a pension plan, for example, the pension fund committee or board are agents of the corporation (for defined benefit plans) or even of the employee (defined contribution plans). In turn, an internal staff is hired as their agent. The staff may, again in turn, hire outside investment managers and consultants. These people all influence the amount and type of global diversification. As they consider risk, it is transformed from the risk of investor loss to the risk of being sued, the risk of losing one's job, or the risk of losing a profitable business arrangement and incurring a loss of business reputation. These kinds of risks may be as much a function of being unconventional as of investor loss. As someone once said, it is often better to fail conventionally than to succeed unconventionally.

Agent risk is therefore more a matter of tracking error versus an accepted benchmark than it is a matter of total volatility. And it is probably more of a matter of lack of attention to the proprieties than to tracking error. What has this got to do with global investing? For U.S. investors, a great deal.

The same optimal portfolio studies that currently say to put 30–40 percent of your equity portfolio outside the United States were available 15 years ago. Then, most U.S. pension funds had no significant international holdings. However, the proportion, as reported by InterSec Research Corporation, has risen from insignificant levels in 1980 to 4 percent at the end of 1990 and to 9 percent at the end of 1995. This trend has continued through good times and bad for international returns. It is safe to say it will continue for some time to come. What has been happening during this period?

Since the investment benefit was at least as great in 1980, in some sense the costs of foreign investing must have been falling. While it is true that trading costs have come down and liquidity has risen in certain countries such as Spain and Italy, that cannot be the primary answer. The cost of trading Japanese securities in size was comparable to U.S. costs even 15 years ago. What seems to have changed is agent risk. It has fallen as a result of accumulated experience with gradually increasing numbers of U.S. participants. As more people invest abroad, they provide models for those investors uninitiated.

If this diagnosis is true, then the expansion of global investing is probably forecastable in the same way that the conversion of sailing ships to steam was possible. The process of conversion is proportional both to the population of those already converted and to the population yet to be converted. This is similar to epidemic dynamics in which the number of new cases is a multiplicative function of both how many people are already infected and how many people are yet to be infected. Conversions first grow exponentially and then began to slacken as the market becomes saturated, following an S-shaped logistic curve. Optimal portfolio models currently suggest a 30–40 percent foreign holding for U.S. investors. This implies we are still short of the midpoint of the "epidemic," with the greatest absolute growth, remarkably, still to come.

Compounding the revolution we face, a new factor, emerging markets, has entered the scene. Today investment in emerging markets appears regarded as about as risky as developed international markets were perceived to be a dozen years ago. Current investment is near the 1 percent level of institutional portfolios. Optimal portfolio analysis suggests that this figure will go much higher. A figure of 15 percent of total assets is certainly plausible, especially since it may not be realized until today's emerging markets are considerably bigger. This substitution is still in its very early stages, and we can expect to see rapid growth for many years. Consider, for example, the enormous potential not only of today's accepted emerging markets like Mexico but of the newer markets in Eastern Europe, China, and even Russia.

The challenge for international investors, then, is to ride this substitution wave as rapidly and as comfortably as possible. This means reducing agent risk. The centrality of agent risk in governing growth of international investing offers a particularly sharp dilemma for the quantitative international investor. Quantification and uncertainty do not naturally fit together in the minds of many. How can the quantitative investor produce attractive investment results, both increased return and decreased risk, in a way that results in lower agent risk?

Tracking error, which gives rise to agent risk, can be reduced by educating investors toward better benchmarks. These include global indices, indices that include emerging markets, and mandates for the freer, more flexible use of currency hedging. But this effort is only a first step.

It is also helpful to meet the unconventionality-driven objections engendered by foreign investments. For example, if the problem is anxiety about foreign accounting differences, master the details and discuss where they are relevant and how to handle this problem. If the fear is of currency fluctuations, show how the risk of currency can be controlled effectively and what the benefit of exposure to foreign currency can be versus long-term U.S. risks of inflation. If the objection simply reflects lack of personal familiarity, provide opportunities for orientation. This dimension of investment management is easy for a quantitative investor to ignore, since it may have little demonstrable relationship to investment returns. From practical experience, one does so at his or her own peril.

If you succeed in reducing the agent risk, you will help accelerate the trend toward global investing. However, if not, just wait. Open borders, low transaction costs, better information, and the gradually increasing sophistication of investors have made further diffusion of this innovation inevitable.

Summary

First, we showed why investing abroad is likely to raise *passive* returns. Passive returns are likely to be higher based on the higher return required to finance investments with greater immaturity and volatility. Passive returns will also tend to be higher based on the diversification effect. Far from increasing, correlations between U.S. and foreign equity returns have fallen in recent years. The U.S. dollar's decline has aided past foreign returns to the U.S. investor. Some have raised fears that this help will no longer continue. However, a full understanding of long-term currency and stock market behavior suggest future international combined currency and stock returns for foreign countries are just as likely as before to exceed those of the United States.

Second, a successful *active* investor has increased opportunity from investing globally simply based on increased numbers of securities meeting investment criteria. Beyond this, reason suggests that foreign markets less liquid and mature than that of the United States will embody greater market inefficiencies that the active investor may exploit. Japan, where straightforward value-oriented quantitative investing has typically been profitable, is an excellent case in point.

Third, we showed how global investing can be expected to lower investor risk by improving the efficient frontier of available portfolios. Greater diversity leads to reduced portfolio return volatility. This effect will likely last a long time because, as noted above, average correlations among returns in different countries are increasing, if at all, only very slowly. In fact, the recent trend has been down, not up.

Finally, we described agent risk as partly the risk that returns will differ from those of a conventional portfolio benchmark and partly the result of unconventionality in practices. Both these obstacles are shrinking as more critics become fellow global investors. The result is a true diffusion process for innovation that is almost certain to continue. Global investing will replace parochial home-country investing much as steamships replaced sailing vessels. It was a process that took decades, but the outcome was never in doubt.

Endnotes

1. The MSCI indexes are published by Morgan Stanley and include the Europe, Far East, and Australia (EAFE) index as well as separate return indices for each component country as well as the United States and Canada. The indices used provide total return net of unrecoverable dividend withholding tax. The data referred to in the text are quarterly ending June, 1996. The rolling correlations for periods ending earlier than 1987 were produced by reconstructing an index of EAFE+Canada based on published individual country returns and market capitalization weights.

2. See Ibbotson and Sinquefield (1976), for the early study, followed by regular publications by Ibbotson Associates, (1991).

3. After Sharpe (1964) and others proposed the capital asset pricing model, academics for a few years debated whether specific risk is rewarded. Specific risk is the part of risk not captured by the systematic risk indicated by the regression coefficient of excess returns of an asset to the excess market return, or beta. Although the evidence of several careful investigators suggested that variance had a stronger claim to empirical validity than did beta, this thought was allowed to go fallow. See studies by Black (1993), by Black and Litterman (1992), by French, Schwert and Stambaugh (1987), by Friend, Westerfield, and Granito (1978), by Mayshar (1983) and by Lakonishok and Shapiro (1986).

4. The most famous of the studies showing a widespread relationship between return and market capitalization and price/book ratio antecedants is that of Fama and French (1992).

5. See Wilcox (1984).

6. Although local returns are not equivalent to currency hedged returns, their risks are quite similar. Currency-hedged returns may be approximated as foreign local returns plus domestic short-term interest, less foreign short-term interest.

7. There is a technical argument for expecting a very small pure currency risk premium, though it cannot be large since both sides of any exchange rate would have to benefit. See Black and Litterman (1992). The terms *Siegel's paradox,* and the possibly more accurate *Jensen's inequality* may ring a bell for some readers. This issue may be a red herring for long-term policy purposes. Regardless of the answer for currency in isolation, if currency and security returns are negatively correlated, the total risk premium for the bundle should be considered regardless of whether it comes from currency or the security.

8. Sinquefield (1996) cites the 1970–1994 compound return of the United States (10.97 percent) versus EAFE (13.21 percent) of which (2.37 percent) is based on currency, as evidence for skepticism on international returns. Here we argue the opposite. He also regards correlations as likely to increase; the opposite occurred while his article was being published. Sinquefield performed a very valuable service, however, by indicating the greater potential rewards from international diversification of small stocks than for diversification of large stocks.

9. See Holton (1992), who points out that the risk characteristics of returns of major asset classes such as stocks, bonds, and currencies change in unexpected ways as we measure them at different frequencies. For example, stock returns have a slight tendency to exhibit trends when measured at frequencies of a year. However, if stocks do unusually well over a longer, five-year period, they have a modest tendency to do worse than average over the next five years. This kind of reversion to the mean is a basis for contrarian equity-investing strategies. Currencies are very different, showing a pronounced tendency to trend when measured at low frequncies. Consequently, there is at least some reason to suspect that long-term declines in the dollar will continue.

10. Booth and Fama (1992) provide a nice primer on the mathematics of portfolio return.

11. See Markowitz (1959).

12. Ibid.

13. See, for example, Chan, Hamao, and Lakonishok (1993). Although there is much to be learned from such studies of "anomalies" over particular periods, two limits are always present. First, the period over which data are collected may not be representatitive, especially of the future. Second, it is usually possible to "data mine," creating indices that will "explain" the sample data, but generalize poorly. These authors try hard to avoid these problems, but to some extent they seep into every quantitative study. The only cure is to keep testing on fresh data.

14. See Fama and French (1992).

15. The mean-variance framework has defects, but is quite practical for long-term asset allocation decisions. One defect often cited is that risk is practically defined as the risk of loss. However, a measure of dispersion such as the return variance, or the related standard deviation, will also be a good measure of the potential for losses if the probability distribution for returns is reasonably symmetric. Another possibility, "fat-tailed" return distributions so extreme that the variance is undefined, is not characteristic of domestic and foreign stocks and bonds in aggregate form. Recent studies indicate the tails are fatter than log-normal, but not so fat as to have an infinite variance. Third, as long-term policy makers, we need not concern ourselves with possible complications from between-period linkages such as trading costs and so are not injured by using a one-period model. Finally, because we are dealing with relatively few asset classes, we need not be overly concerned about the inflation of apparent benefit that results from deterministic optimizing using inputs that are themselves subject to estimation error. That is, we need not be afraid the optimizer will "dive" on coincidentally low correlations, artificially moving the apparent efficient frontier upward and to the left. See Jorion (1985).

16. Following convention, the efficient frontier shows only the weighted average of the individual asset returns, omitting the extra boost from the impact of diversification on compounded return of the total portfolio.

17. The 1996 Sinquefield article assumed without question that correlations are increasing, while in fact they were sharply decreasing.

Bibliography

Black, Fischer. "Beta and Return," *Journal of Portfolio Management*, 20(1), Fall 1993, pp. 8–18.

Black, Fischer. and Robert Litterman. "Global Portfolio Optimization," *Financial Analysts Journal*, September/October 1992, pp. 28–43.

Booth, David G., and Eugene F. Fama. "Diversification Returns and Asset Contributions," *Financial Analysts Journal*, May/June 1992, pp. 26–32.

Chan, Louis K. C.; Yasushi Hamao; and Josef Lakonishok. "Can Fundamentals Predict Japanese Stock Returns?" *Financial Analysts Journal*, July/August 1993, pp. 63–9.

Fama, Eugene F., and Kenneth R. French. "The Cross Section of Expected Stock Returns," *Journal of Finance*, June 1992, pp. 427–65.

French, K. R.; G. W. Schwert; and R. F. Stambaugh. "Expected Stock Returns and Volatility," *Journal of Financial Economics* 19, 1987, pp. 3–30.

Friend, Irwin; Randolph Westerfield; and Michael Granito. "New Evidence on the Capital Asset Pricing Model," with "Comments" by William Sharpe, *Journal of Finance* 33(3), June 1978, pp. 903–20.

Holton, Glyn A. "Time: The Second Dimension of Risk," *Financial Analysts Journal*, November/December 1992, pp. 38–45.

Ibbotson, Roger. *Stocks, Bonds, Bills and Inflation, 1991 Yearbook*, Chicago: Ibbotson Associates, 1991.

Ibbotson, Roger, and Rex Sinquefield, "Stocks, Bonds, Bills, and Inflation: Year by Year Historical Returns (1926–1974)," *Journal of Business* 49(1), 1976, pp. 11–47.

Jorion, Philippe. "International Diversification with Estimation Risk," *Journal of Business* 58(3), 1985, pp. 259–78.

Lakonishok, Josef, and Alan C. Shapiro. "Systematic Risk, Total Risk and Size as Determinants of Stock Market Returns," *Journal of Banking and Finance* 10, 1986, pp. 115–32.

Markowitz, Harry M. *Portfolio Selection*, New Haven, Conn.: Yale University Press, 1959.

Mayshar, Joram. "On Divergence of Opinion and Imperfections in Capital Markets," *American Economic Review* 73, March 1983, pp. 114–28.

Odier, Patrick, and Bruno Solnik. "Lessons for International Asset Allocation," *Financial Analysts Journal*, March/April 1993, pp. 63–77.

Sharpe, William S. "Capital Asset Prices: A Theory of Market Equilibrium Under Conditions of Risk," *Journal of Finance* 19, September 1964, pp. 425–42.

Sinquefield, Rex A. "Where Are the Gains from International Diversification?" *Financial Analysts Journal*, January/February 1996, pp. 8–14.

Wilcox, Jarrod. "The P/B–ROE Valuation Model," *Financial Analysts Journal*, January/February 1984, pp. 3–11.

Quantitative Investing

Jarrod W. Wilcox
Director of Research
PanAgora Asset Management

Introduction

Do you notice whether an idea is on the way in or on the way out? There are deep analogies between the world of fashion in art, music, and clothing, and the world of investing. It is better to shop in boutiques than in warehouses, and it is better still to have the sensitivity to changing trends that allow you to join in successful fashions while they are fresh. Best of all is to be able to put together your own innovative personal taste and have it be imitated. The same is true in investing.

Do you look at facts unemotionally and revise your opinions based on careful experimentation? The world of investing is like the world of science, only at fast speed and with somewhat less sense of community. Scientists have learned to overcome the inertia of personal prejudice and cultural tradition through an organized process for creating new knowledge rapidly. The best scientists cooperate with one another while striving to stay ahead of contenders for leadership in the process we call the scientific method. The same is true in investing, although we do not usually think of it that way.

Are you relentless in constantly improving your decision making in order to be more prompt and accurate? In today's relatively efficient markets, the world of engineering has much to offer. The task of the engineer is to design what is competitively viable and then to continuously upgrade that design. It is necessary to focus on the essentials because rivals keep improving and because new techniques lead to new opportunities. The same is definitely true in investing.

The investing environment is an arena with thousands of intelligent competitors. It is constantly changing as market participants learn new techniques and as market infrastructure improves. It rewards those who combine the qualities of fashion leader, scientist, and engineer.

This chapter's purpose is to introduce and to provide perspective on several quantitative investment ideas adapted from science and engineering. It may seem a radical thought to even mention fashion in a serious discussion. We offer no special expertise in how to sense the social dynamics in thought patterns that result in fashion, the interplay of those seeking to differentiate versus those seeking to imitate. But to ignore fashion is to ignore the cause of the ineffectiveness of many investors who seek to use quantitative techniques.

The science of economics, and its offshoot, finance, though they purport to deal with investments, give little attention to differences in ideas among investors, much less to the dynamics of these differences. However, even a glance at market participants detects ripples of newly perceived facts. It may take only a few minutes for the market to absorb a new fact along dimensions familiar to it. Examples include a large buy or sell order, a change in interest rates, or in an earnings estimate. Still, this process is not instantaneous, and the time lag offers opportunities to the market participants who do the work of collecting and interpreting new information. It takes longer to absorb the impact of less familiar events or more broad-ranging events, such as a change in trade policy. Watch over a few months and you will see that among brokerage research reports there are waves of realization that this or that causal influence is now a key factor in judging the market. Even in a circumscribed market such as Germany, one can see the irregular rotation of ideas. For a while, attention focuses on the Bundesbank's policy on interest rates, then on business activity, then on political factors in Europe, and finally on the value of the U.S. dollar. Companies are judged on dividends, then on earnings, and finally on cash flow. Active investment managers provide value-added by anticipating these changes.

Extend your study over several years, and you will discover noticeable changes resulting from the slower diffusion of new techniques for analyzing causal relationships. Market participants sometimes focus on accounting reports, then on technical charts, technology stories, government reports, only to eventually refocus on accounting.

The tools of quantitative active investors are subject to the iron laws of fashion as well. A successful fashion is one that establishes a difference. It also contains the seeds of its destruction as more and more people imitate it and destroy its differentiating value. The quantitative investor does not have a vantage point outside this process but must operate within it.

One example is the impact of mean-variance optimization on greater institutional diversification not only into smaller developed countries, such as Austria, but also into a wide variety of emerging markets. Another example is the recent respectability of low price/book value investing. A third example is the increased reliance on quick reactions to changes in consensus earnings estimates made available through the IBES database. It seems clear that quantitative investment tools are not only the means for assessing fashion trends and for determining pockets of opportunity created by the long out-of-fashion—they are fashions themselves, fashions that will gradually tend to become obsolete as they are imitated.

Our plan is to first examine basic conceptual building blocks useful for quantitative investing, and then to discuss some examples that will show the real-world application of these ideas. In the first part, we begin with the relevance of quantitative techniques for *passive* investing. We will then review the main arguments for *active* quantitative investing. Next, we note the limitations of quantitative investing, particularly in a global context. It is important to realize where quantitative techniques are not well-suited so that we can focus on the areas where they can have a more substantial benefit. In the second part, we will give three examples of how quantitative techniques are being used. They are (1) computer screening and scoring, (2) econometric estimation of returns, and (3) the use of Markowitz mean-variance analysis for portfolio construction. This list is not exhaustive. We do not explore option models. There are even newer techniques such as neural nets and genetic algorithms. But our examples are those most frequently encountered in practice. When we close, you will be in a good position to appraise and assimilate more extensive and detailed information on quantitative investing.

Concepts

Better Passive Investing

At the most basic level, a good investor need not beat the market. It is a worthwhile task simply to do a good job in matching a portfolio of securities to a set of investment needs. This could be to finance an individual's retirement, for example, or to grow an endowment at a rate faster than inflation without having substantial year-to-year setbacks. A portfolio invested 60 percent in the S&P 500 Index and 40 percent in U.S. Treasury bonds has historically been a good combination of moderate risk and long-term return, and performs well against active managers taking comparable risks.

However, a quantitative analysis of more efficient diversification can lead to better passive returns. This involves better diversification at the asset-class level by using international stocks and bonds, including emerging markets, and reweighting country exposures in order to get greater use of low-correlation countries. It involves selective use of index futures to avoid more expensive currency hedging for a portion of the international equity portfolio. And it involves diverting much of the U.S. and international stock exposure to higher-return, more-diversifiable small stocks. Better diversification, primarily in equities, reduces volatility of the equity portion so that the portfolio, as a whole, can carry more equity and consequently earn a higher rate of return without additional risk. The benefit of this improved asset diversification may be a 1 percent increment in annual return at the same level of risk.[1]

This kind of analysis is generally carried out through a Markowitz mean-variance optimization.[2] Given the asset weights in a portfolio, the expected average returns and risks for each asset, and the correlations expected in returns between all pairs of assets, one can estimate the return and risk of the portfolio composed of these weights. Mathematical techniques can then be used to discover the set of weights which provide the least risk for a given expected return. The set of all such portfolios is the efficient frontier, and the portfolio on the efficient frontier that balances risk and return consistent with the investor's preferences is selected as optimal.

A benefit of 1 percent annually, through better diversification, may seem modest, but is not. The return above inflation of a 60 to 40 mix has averaged over the long term only about 4 percent. (Returns in the mid-1990s have been far above average and should not be extrapolated.) Raising 4 percent to 5 percent constitutes a notable improvement in the growth of real wealth. For example, a dollar invested at 4 percent will after 20 years be worth $2.19. At 5 percent it will be worth $2.65. The 20-year-profit comparison is between $1.19 and $1.65, an increase of 39 percent.

Quantitative analysis is extremely powerful if it can persuade us to put aside tradition and diversify globally in an optimal way, even though we may consider this to be "only" a passive application.

Quantitative Can Be Active

Reporters and the investing public often think there is a contradiction between active and quantitative investing. The active investor attempts to deliver better results through trading or holding a portfolio that differs widely from a benchmark portfolio. Quantitative investing may be defined most simply as measured, disciplined investing. There is no necessary contradiction between these two approaches. Quite the opposite, there are excellent reasons why the combination of the two will often be highly synergistic.

Human Nature and the Need for Investment Engineering

As Walt Kelly, the cartoonist, had Pogo say, "We have met the enemy and he is us." Human decision-making has evolved physically and culturally to meet a variety of environmental and social situations far-removed from investing in stocks, bonds, and currencies. Here are just a few examples.[3]

In our noninvesting lives, when we are elated we press ahead, when we are afraid we retreat. When we do well, we generalize, thinking that we are certainly intelligent enough to win at this game, and buy more. When we do poorly, we lose self-confidence, and sell out. These emotions are disastrous when investing in liquid securities because the crowd behavior that such emotions create sets up speculative cycles that lead to a pattern of buy high, sell low. A better-engineered investment process will remove the extremes of emotion.

We normally do not have to generalize from situations in which there is a great deal of essentially random noise and only an occasional small valid signal. Yet the competitive impact of thousands of intelligent investors has created, not a perfectly efficient market, but an uncomfortably efficient market, leaving just this situation. To do well, one often has to refine the ore tailings; the easy-to-get nuggets have already been taken away.

In normal life, there is great value to consensus among organization-members; agreement is essential to arrive at decisions that will be carried out. In the securities markets, trading by committee decision is likely to implement a fashion that is on the way out. A better-engineered process preserves independent sources of information, taking into account the likelihood that viewpoints that are widely shared are probably already incorporated in market prices.

Outside of the investment arena, we would think that desirable company attributes, such as high profits and superior management, would lead to better results. In highly efficient stock markets, it is surprise that leads to higher returns, and this often appears to be just as likely, or even more so, among companies with low profits and mediocre management. We must make sure that our investment process is based on a reality test: is the type of information we are using really correlated with higher future profits from holding securities?

In general, it is helpful that human nature tends to sustain past commitments. But in the securities markets, this tendency can result in greater difficulty in selling than in buying. Difficulty in deciding to sell can cause portfolios to become choked with stale ideas. A better-engineered process will eliminate selling bottlenecks. One way to do so is by using the same quantitative score or expected-return scale for both buying and selling.

For all these reasons—emotions, inattention to occasional details, urge for agreement with fellows, confusion between the company and the stock, and inability to shed past commitments—many otherwise admirable active investors are ineffective in the market arena. Will we be slaves to fashion, or will we be its masters? Quantitative models can give us the structure within which to carry out sound investment and trading strategies.

When a decision rule has been fully articulated to the point that it can be carried out by computer, we are less emotional and can focus on creative devising of new and better decision-making rules. But we do so on our best days, at a time-scale that allows thorough evaluation and recognition of our behavioral biases.

The benefit of quantitative decision-making in avoiding psychological biases may be particularly applicable in international markets because of their greater unfamiliarity and complexity. The words *currency* and, in the case of emerging markets, *political risk,* seem to conjure up primitive dangers that heighten the susceptibility to emotional and group pressures on investment decisions.

Because there are so many human biases in typical investment organization decision-making, there is ample opportunity for engineering far-reaching improvement. The rapidly expanding field of behavioral finance is a source of new insight both into market imperfections and into tendencies that we should guard against in our investment choices.[4]

The Advantage of the Scientific Method

Scientists can also lend us useful ideas and superior methods for adapting to evolving market conditions which require new knowledge. As an example of the former, consider the idea of the efficient market. It may not be exactly true, but it is not a bad first approximation. Economists and mathematicians note that if markets do instantly absorb all available information, the change in that information will inevitably be a surprise and will therefore appear random. That insight helps us as investors to focus on specific exceptions where the market appears to be inefficient, rather than to dilute our efforts by trying to predict all price changes.

Through the efforts of those seeking to disprove the efficient market hypothesis, there has gradually grown up a list of *anomalies* or predictable return patterns. This list is a valuable compendium of potentially profitable investment tactics.[5] The discovery and dissemination of this knowledge took place under the umbrella of the scientific method. Investors should take advantage of the publicly revealed anomalies so long as they remain profitable. That is, use them until their fashion has been adopted by the mass of investors.

Investment organizations competing in global markets face markets at different states of maturity. Many of these immature markets appear to be significantly less-efficiently priced than the U.S. market. It seems likely that the market inefficiencies characteristic at various periods in U.S. history, many of which have been quantified, will offer profitable opportunities within these foreign markets for a considerable period. One of the best examples in recent years has been the Japanese stock market, which appears to still be driven largely by growth stories of the sort that confuse the company with the stock. U.S. quantitative value-oriented investors appear to do well there.[6]

We need not stop with anomalies which are well-established in the public investment literature. We can use the tools of science to generate proprietary knowledge that has not yet found its way into the public domain. We now have enormous statistical databases and the latest econometric modeling techniques to discover predictive relationships. We can use computer simulations to better understand the behavior of our decision rules, both with real and realistic data. There are also other tools now coming out of engineering and computer science, such as neural nets and genetic algorithms.[7]

Possibly more important than specific techniques are the adoption by some investment organizations of more scientific attitudes, which has accelerated the rapid discovery and adoption of new ideas. It should be emphasized that active investment can never be a science. Full community sharing, testing, and replication of newly discovered active investment truths will lead to the falsification of those truths as competitors imitate the techniques of the innovators. However, there is great advantage in what one might call private science, which involves many of the same mechanisms. For example, the value placed by scientists on clearly articulating evidence and theory allows very effective collaboration among colleagues in the same firm. It allows one person to trust more readily the findings of another, because knowledge is replicable.

Clear articulation of an idea also allows it to be more effectively challenged, whether simply by new data, or by colleagues and by junior portfolio managers and analysts. When we put on the mantle of science, even if only partially (as we must do for private knowledge to remain proprietary), we improve our ability to seek disconfirming evidence. Scientific ethics also reduce the chance that supporting data will be distorted or that decisions will be made solely by the more powerful person in the investment organization.

The point is to provide for more rapid creation of investment knowledge in a constantly changing competitive environment. As the Red Queen told Alice in Lewis Caroll's fable, "We have to run as fast as we can just to stay in the same place. To get anywhere we have to run twice as fast as that."

Impact of Growing Computational Resources

One of the key stimuli for the greater use of quantitative methods, whether for investment engineering or proprietary investment science, has been the incredible expansion of computational resources at low cost. Thirty years ago it was possible with some labor to screen from about a thousand U.S. stocks based on a few simple ratios published by the *Value Line Survey*. Now large computer-readable databases make the same screens the work of a few seconds, and make much more elaborate screens carried out over a much larger global universe the work of a few minutes.

We have more data available, including essentially all balance-sheet and income-statement items. We have frequently updated analysts' earnings-estimates. We have detailed minute-by-minute data on interest rates and currency exchange rates. We can study massive databases of returns that allow us to better see what securities are moving together subject to what influences. We can also carry out elaborate statistical analyses and simulations that thirty years ago would have been prohibitively expensive and time-consuming. We can therefore make more sophisticated investment models involving more factors, more customization, and more ability to vary their structure over time.

We can also make higher-quality inferences because they are supported by many more observations at a higher level of detail. We need not form investment policy based solely on the few investment events, such as the crash of October 1987, that are so striking that they fix themselves in our memory. Instead, for example, we may look for consistencies in the differing impact of revisions in analysts' earnings estimates over the business cycles of each country.

Finally, computerized decision rules have made it possible to make much faster decisions, and to make them at a more detailed level, than would be practical without them. It is possible using computer assistance both to trade faster and to have portfolios diversified over more issues without loss of expected return.

These labor-saving advantages are particularly relevant in global investing. As of June 1996, the U.S. market accounted for only 41 percent of the Morgan Stanley Capital International (MSCI) World Equity Index. The rest of the world is substantially bigger than the United States, both in economic size and its universe of securities. There are thousands of foreign companies covered by electronic databases. Combined with the need to use customized approaches in many markets, this large securities universe offers a great practical advantage to the investor who takes advantage of the computer. Full advantage can mean more than simply storing and retrieving data, although that alone is significant. It can also mean freeing the time of expensive analysts and portfolio managers for the most critical qualitative information-gathering and for the creative effort needed to further improve the decision-making process.

Limits to the Quantitative Approach

We have discussed the aid to investors offered by quantitative approaches, whether in engineering better choices given current knowledge or in using proprietary science to discover new knowledge. We have cheered the advent of the computer. You will need, however, to recognize the limits of this approach if you are to be most skilled in its use. We have already noted that, because of fashion, the underlying structure of market behavior is subject to continual change. Even if it were a stable process, however, returns would be difficult to predict.

Economic behavior is exceedingly complex and nonlinear. The failure of even expert economists to correctly forecast economic turning points is a subject of continuing humor and derision. Overlay this with a securities market where investors seek to guess when and in what direction other investors are likely to change their minds. Now you have encrypted whatever is predictable in the economy with another layer of highly unstable code. Magnify the problem by setting up a series of parallel markets in different countries, competing for the global investor, only partly coupled through business activity, with additional fluctuations in linking currency exchange-rates. Put on the added blinders confining us to the simple models we can reasonably construct with limited relevant history. What we have is a recipe for poor prediction, punctuated by only occasional and modest success.

Those who use quantitative models given limited relevant history must make many qualitative judgments: what factors to include, what observations to pool, and what history will be most representative of the immediate future. These judgments are often wrong, particularly when they overlook their topic: fashions in information-processing subject to sudden change. For example, in the period leading up to 1992, quantitative investors found differences in interest rate an excellent guide to currency-adjusted profits on short-term bonds. During the next few years, this signal proved largely perverse, as the special conditions created by recognition of potential currency merger among European countries were reevaluated. Quantitative investors do not necessarily make such mistakes more often than their purely subjective brethren. However, when mistakes in qualitative judgments by quantitative modelers occur, they are often slow to be rectified while data is accumulated that provides statistically significant evidence of the need for change. This does provide opportunities for agile and fashion-sensitive rivals who do not feel the need to base their conclusions on statistical tests.

There are many useful areas for investment judgment where quantitative models never become practicable. In 1996, what did investors say would be the impact on Hong Kong stock values when that British colony reverts to mainland China in 1997? There are simply not enough cases of very similar type to do a least-squares regression of returns versus possible governing factors. One may do better by forming a subjective judgment, reasoning from cases that are similar enough to offer analogy, but that are not similar enough to use for statistical analysis.

Another limitation on quantitative models is the absence of measurements of the crucial variables for prediction. Consider the case of management turnarounds. Even though there are many possible observed cases of new management of troubled companies around the world, the key factors determining whether new management will succeed may simply not be measured. Skilled fundamental analysts may be able to form subjective impressions of management's ability and of the company's competitive opportunities that are far superior to quantification based on financial statements.

Even when quantities are measured, they may be measured in a way that requires considerable local knowledge to interpret, and so may be unavailable to the less-informed global investor. Examples include the use of accounting reserves in many European countries, the incompatibility of accounting measurements under different rates of inflation, and differences in whether research and development expenses are capitalized. Examples also include interpretive context; for example, in emerging markets the potential availability of additional resources through government or family connections can be an offset to a leveraged balance sheet.

Note, however, that the issue is not whether quantitative models have good data with which to work. The issue is whether they will bring an advantage over the mental models used in setting prices in a particular market. Some of the arguments that one hears—for example that certain accounting ratios are meaningless in such and such country—miss this point. Poor data that measures the right thing may still be superior to a qualitative subtlety that judges the wrong thing. This is often brought out in discussions regarding the superiority of local investment expertise over centralized global decision-making. If local investors are unduly swayed by a speculative fever, even very crude measurements of price/ book ratios may encourage the correct decision to lessen investment weight in that country.

Finally, we return to where we started. The investor relying more on subjective analysis and intuition will continue to play an important role in helping the market digest information that is relatively unique and unmeasured. However, he or she will not have the discipline of a quantitative approach to help withstand the tides of emotion. Inappropriate cognitive biases will interfere with fact collection. He or she will not have the apparatus of science and the important values of scientists to help promote the creation of new insights. Many of the important competitive edges offered by computers will be forgone. These disadvantages seem to point toward the need for effective synthesis of quantitative and qualitative approaches, even for those who prefer to be less quantitative.

Practical Examples

Computer Screening and Scoring

There are thousands of investment securities available and generally suitable for a diversified global portfolio. How can an investor select a subset that will probably have better than average returns? The answer depends on the conceptual equipment the investor brings to the task. If you think like everyone else, then your only hope for results better than chance is in speed of access to information and speed in acting on it.

However, suppose you have a specialized skill that can be applied to the analysis of particular securities. In this case, the computer can be of great aid in reducing the time and expense of applying that skill. It can simply store and retrieve available data, even in text form. But you can also use the computer to focus your attention on the relatively small number of cases that are most likely to favor the application of your specialized skill. This is computer screening.

For a value-oriented investor, this might consist in screening for companies with low price/book ratios or high dividend-yields. The growth-oriented investor may ask for a list of small companies with high and consistent rates of sales growth. The momentum investor might ask for charts showing security price-behavior, which he or she can scan in a few minutes for companies that look interesting. The investor may then conduct a highly qualitative subjective exploration, but one that is more effective because more in-depth information can afford to be collected. Then he or she could review industry conditions, read brokerage reports assessing the country and company of interest to determine the information already in the market, and perhaps even conduct company visits. These activities are simply too expensive if they have to be applied to every stock, but they may generate above-average profits if concentrated on the most likely candidates. The advantage of initial computer screening may be very significant in international investing, where the cost of investigating many securities in Japan or France or Italy will be high for a U.S. investor.

Where there are anomalies in market pricing that you believe will persist on a broad scale, computer screening may be carried forward to purchase and sale criteria. For example, you could simply build a portfolio of a random sample of stocks from the lowest decile, ranked by price/book ratios, perhaps constrained to those large enough to have low trading costs. The hope is that that other investors will continue to underestimate the ability of such stocks of companies in trouble to exhibit more upside than downside surprises as profitability regresses toward the mean. This has been a very useful strategy over the last several decades, as documented by a number of published studies.[8] Although turnover would be low, this is still active management, because the investor is betting against a broader benchmark and selling off stocks that become too expensive.

Another fairly widespread idea is a growth-at-a-price model. This selects stocks based on a combination of growth measures such as high profitability and consistent growth in sales, with a measure of pricing such as a price-earnings ratio. A score may be constructed, such as growth rate divided by price-earnings ratio, and stocks bought based on their rank when sorted by the score.

Momentum investors may base their purchase and sale decisions on specific cutoffs for earnings-estimate revisions, insider trading, and recent return patterns.

The following recipe for a computerized strategy is loosely paraphrased from an actual process constructed in the early 1990s by the author as one of several diversified strategies used in managing an international portfolio. It selects successful growth companies on a global scale based on value and timeliness. The hypothesis was that at times the market will favor the most successful companies; for example, during periods of increasing uncertainty. At those times it may be helpful to be able to swiftly allocate more of the portfolio to a process that is already investing within this group selectively.

1. Categorize common stocks by country, geographical or trading region, and industry sector. Make sure the stock is covered by the MSCI database. Ascertain that preliminary classification data are available. These include five years of return on equity, current market capitalization, debt/assets, five years of total return, latest book/price, cash earnings/price, and proprietary momentum scores based on both price and earnings estimate revisions. Get current holdings.

2. Rank stocks by their latest return on equity (ROE), five-year earlier ROE within global major industry, and debt/assets by global major industry. Provide default values for financial sector debt/assets. Construct initial competitive success scores by aggregating these ranks, and re-rank them. Then rank within each country to discover companies most likely to survive globalization. Exclude stocks smaller than 300 million dollars in market capitalization. Re-rank and select a quota from each country, based on country market capitalization, filling quota in order of this rank. The total quota is 200 companies. This procedure is intended to produce a list of the world's most competitively successful companies. In the early 1990s this included Coca Cola, Siemens, and Nintendo. Note both the strength and the weakness of the quantitative screening process. At a group level, the collection of 200 stocks looked very much as the investment intuition underlying it would have hoped. However, at the individual stock level, qualitative judgments could have improved the list. For example, even then it was apparent that Nintendo's long-term success was threatened by the more aggressive Sega.

3. Separately rank for reversal of five-year return, both overall and within country, high book/price within country, high cash earnings/price ranked by major industrial sector within region, and proprietary momentum scores worldwide. These criteria were partly based on work published by Lakonishok, partly on experience as a value-oriented investor, and partly from private science showing the effectiveness at that time of various earnings-estimate-revision factors. Construct separate composite rankings for both momentum and value. Weight these scores to a final attractiveness score based on past usefulness of each of these broad categories.

4. Combine a weighted average of world competitiveness rank and attractiveness score. Further down-rank scores of these stocks in

the bottom three deciles of momentum, giving negative momentum an effective nonlinear veto over value.

5. Use percentile-rank cutoff limits based on the combined attractiveness score from step 4 to establish *buy, hold* and *sell* categories. Mark for sale any stocks currently held in strategy categorized as *sell*. Additionally mark for sale sufficient *hold's* to bring each country's holdings to within a percentage threshold over its market capitalization weight. Allocate the difference between the strategy's budget (as a percentage of total portfolio) and the remaining strategy holdings to the *buy* list.

6. On a daily basis, send stocks marked as purchase and sale candidates to the trading process, subject to overall firmwide constraints on ownership, minimum and maximum holding-percentages for particular clients, the ratio of the day's total orders to average daily trading volume in each stock, cash availability and other risk-control considerations.

This screening and scoring process used the computer effectively to focus attention and also made some use of then-current investment knowledge to select stocks within a relatively short list of successful companies. It was engineered to exclude emotion and selling bottlenecks. Because it was not based on econometric modeling, there was no discipline to try to make sure the weights of different criteria were optimal. However, it included features, such as a cutoff for poor momentum, that reflected judgment as to the increasing institutional popularity of earnings-estimate revision that would have been difficult to support based on past data. Possibly the biggest negatives were on the qualitative rather than on the quantitative sides. The process contributed nothing to timing its own application to periods when successful companies would be most fashionable, and it did not make use of obvious exceptions that could have been noted judgmentally on a stock-by-stock basis.

An investment organization may assemble a number of different types of such strategies, which must be combined within the portfolio. The weights given to value-oriented versus growth strategies, or to strategies intended to exploit the changing preferences of different classes of investors, may be varied over time based on judgment or based on a higher-level model. Of course, any such approach may be combined with a variety of rules constraining weights by industry and country in order to ensure reasonable diversification of risk.

Problems Engendered by Quantitative Screening and Scoring

The validity of computer screening followed by qualitative investigation depends on the validity and skillfulness of the investor's quantitative description of the universe. Typically, investors greatly overestimate the precision and power of their decision-making. This technique could be more valuable if the investor monitors the success rate of the judgmental as well as the quantitative parts of the process. Thus, detailed performance attribution reporting is both highly desirable and is made more revealing by the structure provided by a repetitive quantitative policy.

When carried forward to the actual purchase and sale decisions, computerized decision-making injects new problems.

First, there will likely be surprising difficulty in choosing the best way to combine different criteria. For example, what do you or your investment organization do with stocks that are a *buy* based on *momentum* and a *sell* based on *value?* The culture and beliefs of those used to the frequent rewards of high-turnover momentum trading offer a sharp contrast to the more contrarian and patient value-oriented investors. Of course this issue of what to do with conflicting criteria is also present with subjective judgments. However, articulating them in a quantitative model focuses the attention of portfolio managers on differences in one another's assumptions. This awareness, which the management texts often say is a good thing, may or may not be dysfunctional. It enhances the potential for organizational infighting at the same time as it enhances the potential for organizational learning.

A second problem typically occurs when, after painful effort, a stable resolution of conflicting public criteria is reached. Publicly communicated criteria produce powerful pressures for organizational consensus. Unfortunately, the securities markets do not reward consensus thinking with above-average returns. Innovative investment ideas that could be hidden among variant separate portfolio managers may be squeezed out of the process once publicity exposes them to the rest of the investment community. If not carefully managed, quantitative computer scoring may lose track of a basic goal—to be able to benefit from changing fashion. These benefits can be found either on fashion's leading edge or on the currently unfashionable, but not in the middle of the pack.

Third, public quantitative models tend to be sticky. If you have spent energy in defending a particular decision, it may be hard to give it up when it should be abandoned or set aside for a while. Both proponents and customers look for the Holy Grail of a consistent model that will work forever. But even successful approaches typically depend on a linear extrapolation of what has worked in a past period of similar economic circumstance and market infrastructure. The inexorable march of the fashion of ideas ensures that a successful process will be imitated, thus changing the market infrastructure. New skills need to be continually under development. Though an explicit screening and scoring model facilitates learning, the higher expectations of clients and colleagues for consistency in applying a quantitative model may perversely decrease the ability to adapt to changed circumstances.

Fourth, once computerized methods are embraced, the qualitative judgments that are still called for may suffer. Needs for so-called manual overrides based on additional subjective considerations may be organizationally difficult to accomplish or may be delayed past usefulness. Manual overrides may be of worse quality than in a good qualitative decision-making framework because infrequency has allowed regular procedures for qualitative decision-making to lapse.

In applying quantitative screens and decision-making, it will be advantageous to control these problems by focus on the most repetitive or long-lasting of market inefficiencies. It will be helpful to retain regular procedures for the qualitative decisions that will need to operate outside of the quantitative domain. For long-term success, it is important to encourage as much diversity and experimentation as the need for organizational efficiency will permit.

For example, some organizations find it desirable to have some customization of decision models for different categories of countries, such as the United States, other developed countries, and the emerging markets. The intended benefit is to get specialized knowledge. The by-product is to encourage more experimentation with new ideas. The U.S. stock-selection process may develop more refined momentum estimates, the international process may develop better appreciation of alternate value measures, and emerging markets may encourage a keener interest in keeping down trading costs. But these ideas, once developed, may cross-fertilize into the other areas.

Econometric Return Models

One way to minimize arguments about conflicting criteria is to embrace a common yardstick that will be the measure of all subsidiary criteria. Setting aside the issue of risk, we can go a long way toward effective integration by basing our purchases and sales on an agreed procedure for estimating expected return. Arguments about which period of history to use in order to base statistical inference, for example, seem less heated than whether one should focus on value or growth. The large body of techniques known as econometrics or statistical estimation gives us a convenient means to carry out this approach.

Many investment organizations spend considerable time and energy modeling past returns based on earlier quantified signals, typically through least-square's regression or some variant. The takeoff point may be a published study of some market anomaly. However, the possibilities for variations on these themes are vast.

To give a simple, concrete example using well-known principles and public data, let us do a multiple regression that forecasts country-index quarterly returns. The resulting return-forecasting equation might be implemented using country index funds or futures, or its results could be combined with other individual stock-return forecasts. The purpose is to show many of the issues facing econometric return modeling; we will be taking some shortcuts that would require further refinement in practice.

One of the most popular, though still controversial, findings in the public investment literature is that low price/book and small market capitalization are indicators of greater reward for investors.[9] The theory is that these indicate either risk factors or persistent confusion of the stock with the company. Assuming that this finding is still controversial or little-known enough to still be valid going forward, could the same thing apply to countries? We will examine 20 years of quarterly data ending June 1996, on MSCI stock return indices for the EAFE (Europe, Australia, Far East) countries, plus the United States, and Canada.

Assume that we will always remain fully invested in equities. Our job, then, is to forecast differences in return from average equity returns based on prior differences from average in price/book and market capitalization. In each case, we will recast the variables in log form to make their distributions more symmetric. To reduce noise from currency fluctuations, we will forecast local returns. Of course, local returns are only an approximation of the attainable currency-hedged returns, but they may be instructive nevertheless. Finally, we will examine the first 10 years and the second 10 years separately. This is both to simulate what a quantitative investor might have achieved beginning in mid-1986 based on ideas that were then current among value-oriented investors, and to check the consistency of the relationships that we find.

Table 1 shows correlations and a regression equation based on the 10 years ending in mid-1986. Excess local returns show correlations of −.08 and −.05 for excess log price/book and excess log market-capitalization, respectively. In combination, the statistical significance of the regression equation is 0.11, which, while not good, is promising.

In the mid-1980s in the investment community as well as published in research, both price-earnings ratios and dividend yields were strong

TABLE 1. Country Local Return Explained by P/B and Size

```
. corr xfrtnloc xlpb xlmktcap if date<=86.5 & date>76.5
(obs=720)

         | xfrtnloc    xlpb xlmktcap
---------+-----------------------------
xfrtnloc|   1.0000
    xlpb|  -0.0788   1.0000
xlmktcap|  -0.0529   0.3330   1.0000


. regress xfrtnloc xlpb xlmktcap if date<=86.5 & date>76.5

    Source |       SS       df       MS              Number of obs =     720
-----------+------------------------------           F(  2,   717) =    2.53
     Model | 479.845544      2 239.922772           Prob > F      =  0.0804
  Residual | 68019.8384    717 94.8672781           R-squared     =  0.0070
-----------+------------------------------           Adj R-squared =  0.0042
     Total | 68499.6839    719 95.2707704           Root MSE      =    9.74

------------------------------------------------------------------------------
  xfrtnloc |      Coef.   Std. Err.        t    P>|t|     [95% Conf. Interval]
-----------+------------------------------------------------------------------
      xlpb | -1.596166   .9162854    -1.742    0.082    -3.395089    .2027574
  xlmktcap |   -.18633   .2447887    -0.761    0.447    -.6669182    .2942582
     _cons |  1.88e-08   .3629878     0.000    1.000    -.7126459    .7126459
------------------------------------------------------------------------------
```

Source: MSCI

contenders with price/book as indicators of value. Perhaps we can improve our results further by adding these signals.

Price-earnings ratios can be high for two very different reasons: great prosperity and negligible earnings. Also, unlike book-value expectations, earnings expectations often differ wildly from current earnings, especially when the latter are negative. Both of these complications are lessened by using average return-on-equity over a three-year period, combined with current price/book, to calculate normalized-earnings-to-price ratios. Because normalized earnings still can be negative or near zero at a country level, we do not try to produce a more symmetrical distribution by putting the ratio in log form.

Table 2 shows the result of adding excess normalized-earnings-to-price to our model. Now the total regression is statistically significant at the 3 percent level, meaning that there is less than a 3 percent chance that we would see this much relationship as a coincidence. The t-statistic for each explanatory variable is greater than one, though barely so for price-to-book (P/B) and market cap. At least these variables are not subtracting from the accuracy of the forecast, and they are in the direction predicted by investment lore. The single-factor correlations with return have values in the predicted direction of –.08, –.05 and .09 for P/B, market cap and

TABLE 2. Adding Normalized-Earnings-to-Price to Explain Excess Returns

```
. corr xfrtnloc xlpb xlmktcap xyield xnep if date<=86.5 & date>76.5
(obs=702)

         | xfrtnloc    xlpb xlmktcap   xyield     xnep
---------+-------------------------------------------------
xfrtnloc|   1.0000
    xlpb|  -0.0808   1.0000
xlmktcap|  -0.0595   0.3353   1.0000
  xyield|   0.0469  -0.6944  -0.1527   1.0000
    xnep|   0.0832  -0.2214   0.0361   0.2220   1.0000


. regress xfrtnloc xlpb xlmktcap xnep if date<=86.5 & date>76.5

   Source |       SS       df       MS              Number of obs =     702
---------+------------------------------           F( 3,   698) =    3.03
   Model |  870.969296     3   290.323099           Prob > F      =  0.0289
Residual |  66932.022    698   95.891149           R-squared     =  0.0128
---------+------------------------------           Adj R-squared =  0.0086
   Total |  67802.9913   701   96.72324            Root MSE      =  9.7924


------------------------------------------------------------------------------
xfrtnloc |      Coef.   Std. Err.       t    P>|t|     [95% Conf. Interval]
---------+--------------------------------------------------------------------
    xlpb |  -1.14223   .9599421    -1.190   0.234    -3.02695    .7424898
xlmktcap |  -.2857673  .2510759    -1.138   0.255    -.7787219   .2071872
    xnep |   14.8015   7.766727     1.906   0.057    -.4474517   30.05044
   _cons |   2.33e-08  .3695904     0.000   1.000    -.7256421   .7256422
------------------------------------------------------------------------------
```

Source: MSCI

normalized-earnings-to-price, respectively. (Newcomers to quantitative investing find such correlations shockingly low, having been taught somewhere that such small correlations are usually neither statistically nor economically significant. In the securities markets, where assets can be assembled into portfolios, and where the effect can be repeated over multiple periods, these modest correlations can still be profitable.)

Table 2 also shows the correlation of dividend yields with subsequent returns, a still potentially useful 0.05. However, it also shows that there is a very strong correlation between dividend yield and log price/book, -0.69. In the presence of this multicollinearity, including dividend yield in the model would worsen overall statistical significance.

Suppose that we freeze the model relationship between price/book, market capitalization and normalized-earnings-to-price, on the one hand, and subsequent excess local returns, on the other, as of the data collected through June 30, 1986. What would be the usefulness of forecasts generated by this relationship and by the evolving independent variables over the next 10 years?

Table 3 shows the correlation of the forecast to actual excess returns, and shows the single variable regression of returns to forecast. The forecast has a correlation with actual of 0.10, a regression coefficient of 0.83, and an excellent statistical significance. The combined model relationship has been even stronger in the more recent decade than it was in the first 10 years. (The reason is that the strength of the price/book effect became greater, though it was of marginal value in the earlier period.)

Finally, if we were to assume that both sets of data have equal validity for forecasting, our best model would be based on the pooled data, and this is shown in Table 4. Our normalized price/earnings indicator worked better in the first 10 years, and price/book in the second 10 years. The recurring fashion cycles that may exist in the market give us little reason to abandon the earnings-based indicator.

Critique of Econometric Example

In this example, we were good engineers. We did well in eliminating the impact of emotion. We avoided confusing economic success of a country with success in its investments. We also made use of unobtrusive but relevant details possibly below the threshold of memory and perception.

TABLE 3. Success of True Forecast in Second 10 Years

```
. corr xfrtnloc pxrtnloc xlpb xlmktcap xyield xnep if date>86.5
(obs=773)

         | xfrtnloc pxrtnloc    xlpb xlmktcap   xyield     xnep
---------+------------------------------------------------------------
xfrtnloc|   1.0000
pxrtnloc|   0.0981   1.0000
    xlpb|  -0.1240  -0.6606   1.0000
xlmktcap|  -0.0648  -0.5979   0.4278   1.0000
  xyield|   0.0923   0.4552  -0.4627  -0.0154   1.0000
    xnep|   0.0305   0.6732  -0.0779   0.0523   0.4779   1.0000


. regress xfrtnloc pxrtnloc if date>86.5

  Source |       SS       df       MS              Number of obs =     773
---------+------------------------------           F(  1,   771) =    7.49
   Model |  455.209609     1  455.209609           Prob > F      =  0.0064
Residual |  46884.7329   771  60.8102892           R-squared     =  0.0096
---------+------------------------------           Adj R-squared =  0.0083
   Total |  47339.9426   772  61.3211691           Root MSE      =  7.7981


------------------------------------------------------------------------------
xfrtnloc |      Coef.   Std. Err.       t     P>|t|     [95% Conf. Interval]
---------+--------------------------------------------------------------------
pxrtnloc |   .8300118   .3033661      2.736   0.006     .2344903    1.425533
   _cons |   .0509142   .2805081      0.182   0.856    -.4997361     .6015644
------------------------------------------------------------------------------
```

Source: MSCI

TABLE 4. Explanation of Country Index Returns over 20 Years

```
. regress xfrtnloc xlpb xlmktcap xnep if date>76.5

    Source |       SS          df        MS                    Number of obs =    1475
-----------+------------------------------------              F(  3,   1471) =    6.20
     Model | 1438.76596          3   479.588653               Prob > F       =  0.0003
  Residual | 113704.747       1471   77.2975844               R-squared      =  0.0125
-----------+------------------------------------              Adj R-squared  =  0.0105
     Total | 115143.513       1474   78.1163586               Root MSE       =  8.7919


------------------------------------------------------------------------------------
  xfrtnloc |      Coef.   Std. Err.          t     P>|t|       [95% Conf. Interval]
-----------+------------------------------------------------------------------------
      xlpb | -1.856415    .6982293     -2.659     0.008      -3.226047    -.4867841
  xlmktcap | -.2089812    .1632745     -1.280     0.201      -.5292569     .1112946
      xnep |  9.407287    5.036984      1.868     0.062      -.4731494     19.28772
     _cons |  .0263709    .2289436      0.115     0.908      -.4227198     .4754615
------------------------------------------------------------------------------------
```

Source: MSCI

Application of econometric methods to investment problems often is based on periods that were too short to show a reasonable range of different behaviors. In this case we went back 20 years, which is good. Another typical problem is data-mining, or overfitting the model to the sample by experimenting with too many trial independent variables. Here, by pooling countries and time periods, we had a total of almost 1500 observations and tried only a few model ingredients. In this we were assisted by confining our hypothesized predictive variables to those suggested by basic investment principles, rather than trying for statistical correlations with probably irrelevant variables.

The typical problem in regression studies of multicollinearity of independent variables was minimized. We dropped dividend yield because its information content in the first 10 years was fully captured by book/price.

Some things that we did were problematic. Would we really use price/book and market capitalization, when each showed a t-statistic only slightly above 1.0 during the first decade? The author would use them so long as they were key variables in investment theory and did not subtract from statistical significance. However, many good econometricians would tend to ignore so slight a statistical relationship.

The choice to forecast local returns rather than total return (including currency) was good. It filtered out an overlay of noise. However, we did not investigate the independence of currency returns and local stock returns. Also we did not go to the trouble of constructing currency-hedged returns, which incorporate short-term interest rate differentials. So our study would need considerable follow-up to be practically useful.

Our choice to pool data across all time periods and countries could also be questioned, though our approach has merit. Our model-estimates could be made slightly more accurate by recognizing differences in error variance (heteroscedasticity). It conceivably could be improved more notably by testing the hypothesis that the responses of each country to changes in the independent variables were equal. Because we want the benefit of pooling data, we begin with the hypothesis that responses of different countries are the same, but we did not test this here. (Because it seems obvious that each country is different, one is frequently surprised when the number of countries failing the test of uniformity does not exceed that expected by chance. This is another manifestation of the problem of limited data.)

We were perhaps too casual in using a countrywide measurement of market capitalization to measure a company-level idea. For example, we might have tried to measure the average size of the companies within each market.

Finally, there is the issue of fat-tailed return distributions. We know that, in general, security returns are leptokurtic, with many more outlier observations than can be accounted for by either a normal or log-normal distribution. Measuring kurtosis here at above six, we could use methods more robust to outliers than ordinary least-squares regression. Doing so here would have revealed that the power of small market-capitalization to forecast higher returns was confined to the outliers. We might, or might not, choose to disregard the small-cap effect.

These fairly technical issues, however, pale in comparison to more fundamental questions.

On a very broad level, our quantitative model is incomplete. It assumes static relationships when they are likely to be dynamic, and it assumes that the optimal forecast return can be determined in isolation from the way it will be implemented.

We have stated that fashion makes the process unstable, yet we have used a model that assumes both local and long-term stability. This issue may be viewed in part as one of choosing weights for the different observations on which our model is based. Should we put more weight on the most recent observations? Perhaps we should put least weight on the observations likely to be attended to by other investors. We could use both more-recent data and more very-old data than our competitors in order to encourage a contrarian view. Whatever the answer, we made no attempt to discover it.

We could also have extended our model to try to determine whether the response to price/book, market cap, and normalized-earnings-to-price is time-dependent. Figure 1 shows the example for price/book. It provides a plot through time of the single-period cross-sectional regression coefficients between quarterly returns and the prior log price/book for each country, in the context of a multiple regression including excess normalized-earnings-to-price. (Market capitalization was a bit too highly correlated with price/book to give us a clear picture here.) The vertical axis gives the t-statistic for each quarter's local regression coefficient that links excess-return to excess price/book. The solid line is a smoothed curve drawn through the points. When it is below zero the effect is in the predicted direction. Note that this form of value investing would have worked very well in 1992–1993 and earlier in 1983–84. It would have worked poorly recently (1994–1995) and also would have been disappointing from 1987 through 1991. Do time variations in the smoothed curve differ significantly from those expected by chance? Could we predict them? These are the kinds of questions that today are in the realm of private science, but that may enter the public domain soon.

Our regression model is also too pristine in its indirect assumption that minimizing squared forecast-error is the best way to get a forecast to be used in day-to-day portfolio revision.

For example, in the actual investment process, we may not be able to take short positions. In the present context, this means that we cannot fully take advantage of a negative forecast for small countries such as Austria, Finland, and New Zealand. Our model will give too much weight to relationships that worked well for small countries, and not enough to what works well for the United States and Japan. This is true

FIGURE 1. Effectiveness of P/B over Time

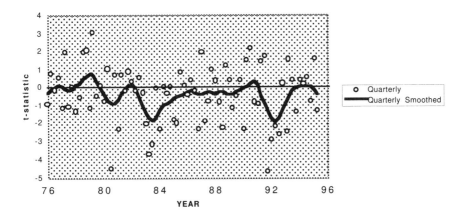

because we can implement more substantial underweights from benchmark or average in the latter countries.

In the actual process, there is a wedge between return forecasts and asset positions which is created by the need to take trading costs into account. Although it did not happen here, regression models may be based on forecast variables that imply very high turnover. For example, earnings-estimate revision is such a variable. Then, when the forecast must be implemented, a good trading process will ignore much of that signal because it is too expensive to trade. If the forecast model allows too much weight to independent variables with such low persistence, the result may be to drive out of the model other variables that contended for the same multicollinear slot. These abandoned variables might be more persistent and therefore more implementable.

Finally, the simple regression forecast takes no account of the ability of an investor or of an investment manager to sustain the process over time. This topic might be rephrased as *risk control,* but it has a place in forecasting return as well in providing for coordination between the forecast and portfolio construction. Other things equal, we would prefer to forecast the excess returns of stocks that are lower in risk. This idea applies either to total volatility risk, or, for an agent, to residual risk against a benchmark. We will come back to the opposite side of this coin in the next section.

The dry spells in the return to low price/book shown in Figure 1 can be uncomfortable. The same argument that was made for trading costs applies here. We should not wait until implementation to control risk if a candidate predictor with poor risk characteristics may drive a more attractive one out of its multicollinear slot in the regression equation. We may want to give somewhat more emphasis to predictive variables that produce steadier excess returns, even if the long-term compounding rate is not as great. For example, this principle might lead us toward the use of composites such as a value index rather than the more parsimonious use of variables that a static econometric analysis would recommend.

A few quantitative investors have developed two-layer models in which forecast coefficients for each independent variable are themselves subject to a dynamic process. However, these have usually been a simple exponentially weighted moving-average of what has worked in the most recent past, rather than a model reflecting, for example, the state of the economy or of the market. Even fewer investors have modified-regression procedures to take into account the adaptive control structure in which return-forecasts must be embedded, complete with holdings constraints, trading costs, and risk control. No doubt the future will see progress in both of these areas. Meanwhile, though, econometric modeling is already a powerful way to collect good investment ideas.

Mean-Variance Analysis for Portfolio Construction

We earlier defined the idea of an efficient frontier of portfolios. Each portfolio on the efficient frontier has the best expected return for a given level of expected standard deviation of returns. For our purposes, it does not matter how the efficient frontier is actually discovered. We are primarily interested in what our investment process will be like if we embrace this concept as a practical means of managing portfolios on a day-to-day basis.

In the original form of analysis, the inputs are expected returns and standard deviations for each of n assets, together with an n by n array of expected correlation coefficients. These may be used to figure the expected return and risk of the portfolio determined by a vector of asset weights summing to one. Where short-selling is forbidden, there are also constraints against negative weights.

Table 5 shows the excess-returns forecast made in June 1996 for 22 countries from the example of the preceding section, as well as the standard deviations of local return for the 20-year period. Note that expected quarterly returns have been multiplied by four, and expected quarterly risks by two, to annualize them. Table 5 also shows, for reference only, recent market-capitalization weights. Since one of our forecast ingredients was small market capitalization, we should not be surprised that the larger countries show negative expected-excess-returns. However, high price/book is also working against countries such as the United States, Japan, and the United Kingdom at mid-1996. Table 6 shows correlation coefficients derived from quarterly returns over this period. Note how many inputs are required, and that some of the in-sample correlations are quite low—for example, 0.05 between Austria and Japan.

Table 7 shows predicted risk and return for five portfolios. At the left is a "naïve" market-capitalization-weighted portfolio. To its immediate right we can compare a proposed improvement: the portfolio on the efficient frontier with the same risk. The rows below risk and return show weights by country. The best return portfolio with the same risk as a capitalization-weighted portfolio, assuming our inputs, need contain only six countries: about 85 percent is in New Zealand, Denmark, and Belgium, with smaller amounts in Austria, Norway, and Canada. According to our example model, it has an annual expected return of 2.5 percent above the

TABLE 5. Model Return Forecast, June 1996

Country	Forecast Excess Annual Return %	Annual % Risk	Observations	% MSCI World Index
AL	0.91	20.49	80	1.55
AT	1.92	24.75	80	0.24
BE	2.27	19.31	80	0.64
CA	-0.55	15.72	80	2.22
DK	1.15	19.37	80	0.44
FI	2.05	32.54	34	0.28
FR	-1.15	22.05	80	3.68
GE	-3.47	18.37	80	3.83
HK	0.73	33.09	80	1.86
IR	3.27	23.04	34	0.17
IT	0.61	29.27	80	1.55
JA	-5.92	20.09	80	22.30
MA	-3.65	26.70	34	1.38
NE	0.35	15.31	80	2.36
NZ	3.39	18.84	34	0.21
NO	4.10	29.26	80	0.27
SI	1.38	26.51	80	0.81
SP	2.78	26.17	80	1.07
SWE	-0.01	26.66	80	1.21
SWI	-1.66	17.68	80	3.29
UK	-2.65	17.32	80	9.08
US	-5.82	14.09	80	41.56

equal-weighted average of our country list. In contrast, the "naïve" cap-weighted portfolio has an annualized return of 4.1 percent *below* the equal-weighted average.

The additional columns in Table 7 show portfolios on suboptimal efficient frontiers that were derived after constraining the solution. In the middle column, no country can be more than 20 percent of the portfolio. In the next, no country can have more than 5 percent of the portfolio more than its capitalization weight. In the right-most column, no country can be more than 5 percent above or below its capitalization weight, restraining the United States, Japan, and the United Kingdom to have substantial representation. These three portfolios might be considered more practical, because they are less concentrated and would behave more like an index benchmark that is capitalization-weighted. Note again that because our return model assumes return differentials working against the United States, Japan, and the United Kingdom, these larger-capitalization countries have very little role in the optimal portfolios except where constrained to do so. Another way of saying this is that the inclusion of large

TABLE 6. Correlation Coefficients

	AL	AT	BE	CA	DK	FI	FR
AL	1.00						
AT	0.24	1.00					
BE	0.41	0.22	1.00				
CA	0.65	0.18	0.38	1.00			
DK	0.30	0.28	0.31	0.33	1.00		
FI	0.42	0.28	0.42	0.40	0.46	1.00	
FR	0.36	0.33	0.58	0.33	0.25	0.42	1.00
GE	0.42	0.63	0.55	0.33	0.52	0.44	0.53
HK	0.52	0.33	0.29	0.34	0.16	0.26	0.26
IR	0.58	0.47	0.70	0.61	0.51	0.61	0.70
IT	0.31	0.27	0.41	0.29	0.37	0.69	0.53
JA	0.27	0.05	0.43	0.34	0.19	0.23	0.31
MA	0.50	0.44	0.40	0.57	0.37	0.40	0.56
NE	0.54	0.33	0.71	0.58	0.52	0.56	0.52
NZ	0.81	0.19	0.27	0.47	0.12	0.33	0.31
NO	0.48	0.35	0.46	0.46	0.36	0.59	0.39
SI	0.55	0.17	0.32	0.50	0.36	0.47	0.21
SP	0.42	0.21	0.50	0.28	0.25	0.64	0.39
SWE	0.34	0.27	0.53	0.38	0.54	0.75	0.41
SWI	0.45	0.52	0.59	0.46	0.42	0.51	0.51
UK	0.46	0.15	0.56	0.50	0.28	0.45	0.42
US	0.61	0.29	0.50	0.74	0.35	0.29	0.50

	GE	HK	IR	IT	JA	MA	NE
GE	1.00						
HK	0.42	1.00					
IR	0.60	0.49	1.00				
IT	0.46	0.21	0.54	1.00			
JA	0.24	0.23	0.47	0.39	1.00		
MA	0.53	0.67	0.50	0.26	0.14	1.00	
NE	0.63	0.53	0.80	0.40	0.39	0.62	1.00
NZ	0.25	0.44	0.38	0.49	0.13	0.41	0.47
NO	0.38	0.39	0.59	0.21	0.17	0.30	0.54
SI	0.33	0.57	0.60	0.20	0.31	0.90	0.56
SP	0.41	0.35	0.76	0.53	0.49	0.47	0.48
SWE	0.52	0.25	0.65	0.53	0.44	0.44	0.62
SWI	0.75	0.45	0.61	0.33	0.33	0.59	0.67
UK	0.43	0.38	0.61	0.38	0.43	0.54	0.69
US	0.45	0.41	0.55	0.37	0.41	0.41	0.68

	NZ	NO	SI	SP	SWE	SWI	UK
NZ	1.00						
NO	0.15	1.00					
SI	0.44	0.30	1.00				
SP	0.48	0.24	0.33	1.00			
SWE	0.48	0.36	0.42	0.58	1.00		
SWI	0.50	0.39	0.37	0.43	0.58	1.00	
UK	0.41	0.30	0.46	0.43	0.47	0.56	1.00
US	0.44	0.35	0.50	0.44	0.50	0.62	0.61

TABLE 7. Optimal and Constrained Portfolios (percent)

	Market Cap. Index	Optimal at Index Risk	Constrained Absolute<=20%	Constrained Relative <+5%	Constrained -5%<=Rel<=5%
Expected Excess Return	-4.13	2.46	2.03	-0.58	-2.18
Expected Risk	13.12	13.12	13.12	13.12	13.12
Weights					
AL	1.55			6.55	0.25
AT	0.24	10.41	14.94	5.24	5.24
BE	0.64	21.61	20.00	5.64	5.64
CA	2.22	1.59	12.26	7.22	
DK	0.44	22.49	20.00	5.44	5.44
FI	0.28				1.30
FR	3.68			5.71	
GE	3.83			1.28	
HK	1.86				
IR	0.17				5.17
IT	1.55				
JA	22.30			8.43	17.30
MA	1.38				
NE	2.36			7.36	
NZ	0.21	39.89	20.00	5.21	5.21
NO	0.27	4.00	6.79	5.27	5.27
SI	0.81			2.54	2.46
SP	1.07		6.01	5.43	6.07
SWE	1.21				
SWI	3.29			8.06	
UK	9.08			14.08	4.08
US	41.56			6.53	36.56

countries is not important from a risk control perspective, where risk is measured as total volatility.

What is good and what is bad about the preceding analysis? One good is that it highlights areas for improvement over a market-capitalization-weighted index fund, given our active assumptions about future return and our passive assumptions about future risk. If we believe that we can add 6.6 percent in return by concentrating in a few small countries that have good expected returns and good diversification potential, we should probably act on it. If we do not do so, then either we have not captured all of the problem or we do not really believe our inputs.

Many quantitative investors who use mean-variance optimization restrict its answers with additional constraints, as we have done in the three rightmost columns in Table 7.

Constraints to Cope with Uncertainty

One of the key reasons why most people add constraints is that they cannot assume the validity of the estimates that they have entered into the decision-making framework. The resulting efficient frontier is particularly sensitive to differences in estimated mean returns.

We know that our return estimates are just that: estimates from a model, whether quantitative or qualitative, with very low statistical precision. Our estimates contain inevitable error. As we put more assets into a problem, the resulting erroneous apparent benefit from focusing on the most attractive estimates is magnified. In addition, the connection between our estimate error and the variance we are putting into the mean-variance framework is typically broken, and for good reason. Observed average returns are much less predictive than observed variance in returns. Consequently, we will probably use past time-series data to estimate variances, but we will not use them for estimating means. For both of these reasons, the true uncertainty in our estimates of the mean return for attractive assets and unattractive assets will not be well-represented in the problem.[10]

Consequently, we may get a better allocation by putting additional constraints on the problem. If we measure risk as volatility of return, the constraints ought to keep us from overconcentration in a few high-volatility assets. The third column in Table 7 moves the solution in this direction.

A more sophisticated approach to achieving this kind of augmented optimum without the use of constraints is to adjust the input parameters. For example, we can reduce expected return differentials substantially so that the resulting optimal portfolio is closer to the minimum variance solution.[11]

Although in small problems the estimates of the mean are most likely to cause problems, in very large problems the estimated correlations are also a source of difficulty. Suppose, for the sake of argument, that all pairs of assets have the same true correlation, but that during our measurement period random noise causes us to measure differences in the correlations. As the number of assets goes up, the number of correlation coefficients goes up in proportion to the *square* of the number of assets. With five assets we have 10 different correlation coefficients to measure. With 20 assets, we have 185. With 1000 assets, as in a stock selection problem, we have 499,500 different correlation coefficients. (We may run out of computer processing power for such a large problem, but that is not what concerns us here.) The large number of possibilities for sampling correlation coefficients assures that a few of them are measured as strongly negative, simply from sampling error. This tends to cause the solution to be pulled toward pairs of such apparently superdiversifying assets. In the limiting case, the whole portfolio might be put into two assets whose returns appeared to be perfectly negatively correlated.

Consequently, mean-variance-based optimizers for practical investment decision-making at the security level should be based on a more compact representation of the risks in the portfolio. There are at least two available approaches. The first adjusts correlations part way toward the mean-correlation among all pairs of assets, or toward group-means given a supposed true risk structure. The second approach uses factor analysis to reduce the number of parameters. For example, each security return might be regarded as composed of a number of common risk factors, say 20 to 100, plus an independent risk specific to that particular security. The common risk-factors may relate to industries, to countries, and to a handful of stock characteristics, or they may be purely statistical. In either case, the size of the problem will go up with the square of the smaller number of factors, not the square of the larger number of securities. This will greatly reduce the sampling-error problem for correlation coefficients. The validity of this approach depends on the accuracy with which risk can be decomposed into common factors, plus a specific risk-factor unique to each asset.

Errors in estimates of variance are typically of lesser import than those for means and correlations. This is because variances are likely to be more accurately estimated, and because their number does not go up as the square of problem size. However, estimates of variances can typically be improved by reducing their dispersion across assets of the same general type.

Constraints to Cope with Other Risks

The second reason people add constraints to the mean-variance solution is to bring into play additional criteria that were not captured in the problem definition. The most common is to bring in a second type of risk consideration. If our original mean-variance analysis is in terms of risk as total volatility, then a second risk dimension, that of residual risk around a benchmark, may be introduced. The resulting solutions will be closer to benchmark weights, as we see in the fourth column of Table 7. Here the maximum resulting weights are constrained not to exceed capitalization weights by more than 5 percent of the portfolio from capitalization weights. There is less improvement over a capitalization-weighted index in terms of estimated return at the same level of risk. However, there is somewhat more practicality in terms of satisfying convention. Finally, the rightmost column shows the result if weights are also constrained on the downside to no less than 5 percent of the portfolio under capitalization weights. This solution requires that we retain significant positions in the United States and Japan, for which our example active model estimated strongly inferior returns. However, we can still modestly improve return while lowering expected volatility.

In the case of the need to include both total volatility and residual benchmark risks, there is a more sophisticated alternative than constraints. Simply use as your risk input the standard deviations and correlations of residual returns around a hypothetical benchmark composed of a weighted average of cash and the true benchmark.[12]

Multiple-Period Optimization

So far we have discussed the mean-variance framework only in terms of a snapshot. This is all we need for long-term asset allocation. When we seek to use it for day-to-day portfolio revisions, new problems appear. First, our friends and colleagues perceive instability of solutions. Second, we lack a theoretically grounded way to take into account transaction costs.

Newcomers to the usage of mean-variance analysis are invariably shocked by what is perceived as the instability of the solution. In any case with more than a few assets, quite small changes in inputs result in very different looking portfolios in terms of the weights given to their component parts. However, the portfolios will be very similar in terms of their expected risk and return.

This is a problem on two levels. The two solutions look very different, even though the optimizer sees them as very close substitutes. This discomfort may relate to very real practical problems in explaining what is going on to clients and colleagues. Second, unless we have injected some stickiness into the optimizer to account for trading costs, the resulting rapid changes in portfolio composition will prove to be expensive and very far from optimal.

A simple first response to both problems is to include as added inputs the existing portfolio and trading costs, proportional to the absolute value of the change in weights between the existing and the optimal portfolio. This is done as an offset to expected-return differentials. While this affords a practical first-order control over trading costs and instability in weights, it is only coincidentally optimal. The reason is that the mean-variance framework is a one-period model. Trading costs arise in the context of transitions between temporary solutions over multiple periods. If we knew ahead of time how long we were planning to hold a particular security, then we could amortize the transaction cost of buying and selling it over that many periods. But we will not know how long we will hold the security until we have solved the problem!

This chicken-and-egg circularity might be used to get a better answer by simulating an extended sequence of optimizations. We could then observe average holding periods. Then we could reset trading-cost amortization fractions per period to be consistent, and repeat the analysis. While this process may converge, with the assumed holding period equaling the average actual holding period, there is no guarantee of a unique solution. Even if there were, the result would still only be approximate because different securities bought for different reasons are likely to have very different holding periods.[13]

In any case, it would be difficult to locate any investment organization going to this much trouble. In practice, those who use optimizers do so in the full knowledge that they produce inaccurate results. They hope, however, that even an approximate answer will produce a better trade-off between risk and return than is produced by seat-of-the-pants methods. For ambitious investors or for investment managers working within tight constraints on risk around a benchmark, the framework offers the potential for better risk-return tradeoffs. However, this potential can only be realized through the exercise of considerable judgment, because the deterministic, single-period assumptions of the model are only a rough fit to the problem.

Summary

We began by comparing investing to fashion design, science, and engineering. Quantitative engineering techniques are obviously relevant to the design of the most efficient passive portfolios. Careful diversification with regular rebalancing offers a significant improvement over traditional allocations in average return at a given level of risk. We suggest the benefit is at least 1 percent annually.

However, if we wish to be more successful than average, we must remember the need for difference and innovation in order to stay ahead of an evolving consensus. Herein lies the analogy between fashion design and the design of active investments.

The main short-term goal of active quantitative investing is to overcome the limits of our instinctive mode of thinking when faced with a problem that is very different from those that shaped our biological and cultural evolution. We want to control emotions. We wish to give adequate attention to small details that are far removed in time and circumstance. We also desire to depart from the consensus of our fellows, who often confuse a company with its securities. Finally, we need to shed commitments as easily as we make new ones. For most of us, this does not come naturally; we have to engineer it.

The main long-term goal of quantitative investment is to accelerate our ability to create new investment knowledge. We do this first by staying in contact with the developing public research on market anomalies. Second, we cultivate our ability to do private research. The conventions of science help us here.

On a global level, an active quantitative approach is rendered even more advantageous by the extremely large number of securities to be considered. Computerized databases and screening, together with computerized analytical methods, offer the investor an efficient way of using costly portfolio-manager and security-analyst time to add value.

There will always be room in the market for investors to seek an edge through nonquantitative means, relying on superior agility in dealing with nonstandard events. In practice, however, this does not imply that fundamentalist local investors have any overall advantage over quantitative global investors. Anecdotally, the case of Japan suggests that global investors employing a value-based discipline have outperformed local investors who rely on traditional growth stories replete with great detail.

In the context of these conceptual underpinnings, we reviewed three common quantitative techniques used in investing: 1) computer screening and scoring, 2) econometric estimation of forecast return, and 3) mean-variance optimal-portfolio construction.

Computer screening can focus expensive judgmental skills on fewer cases, but those having greater payoff. Carrying forward this process to final purchase and sale decisions provides for performance analysis and avoids some, but not all, cognitive limits. For example, we reduce the role of emotion and augment attention to details. Because of its flexibility to use a mixture of science and judgment, this approach is likely to be highly useful to the quantitative investor.

Econometric methods use statistical techniques to test hypotheses and make more efficient use of information to derive the rules used by computer-scoring techniques. However, it should be remembered that these methods are likely to be inferior for problems where there is not enough repetitive data with which to build and apply models. Many economic events are sufficiently unique or sufficiently poorly measured that good qualitative analogy and fact-gathering are likely to represent tough competition for by-the-book quantitative analysis.

Mean-variance optimization is a powerful technique for balancing risk and return considerations and for constructing safer portfolios that are composed of high-return but individually risky ingredients. It is fundamentally a single-period model, and additionally takes inadequate account of the uncertainty surrounding the estimates on which it operates. However, a variety of adjustments can make mean-variance optimization, in the hands of an experienced and wary quantitative investor, a very useful bridge between investment research and final portfolio.

Endnotes

1.   As a first step, suppose that the Morgan Stanley EAFE index of developed country equity markets earns 1 percent more than the S&P 500, and the index's currency-hedged return will be about 0.3 percent less because of frictional hedging costs. Suppose we increase equity from 60 percent to 65 percent of the portfolio and split it equally between the United States and the EAFE, about two-thirds hedged. With typical risk estimates for the component assets, it appears we can achieve a portfolio with the same moderate short-term risk but about 0.45 percent higher annual return than the classic 60/40 mix.

The addition of a 10 percent position in emerging markets, if biased toward an equal-weighting that gives prominence to smaller, less-correlated countries, may be very conservatively estimated as offering a 2 percent higher return than the S&P 500. The risk of an equal-weighted (by country) emerging market index is surprisingly low. It is lower than that of the EAFE when low correlations with the United States are taken into account. The impact on the portfolio is a further return addition of more than 0.4 percent.

There are at least three more sources of return-enhancing diversifications: (1) altering EAFE weights by country toward the low-correlation developed countries, (2) adding value in the United States by substituting diversified U.S. small stocks for a portion of the U.S. stock position, and (3) substituting currency-hedged foreign bonds for part of the U.S. bond position. In each case, the ultimate source of benefit is the lower correlations that permit the overall portfolio to weight higher-return assets more heavily while maintaining overall risk.

Our conservative estimate of a 1 percent benefit does not include other potential passive benefits. These include optimal diversification against additional sources of income such as corporate profits or fund contributions, or of optimal protection against negative factors such as variable liabilities and cash withdrawals.

2.   The ubiquitous references to mean-variance optimization in the professional and academic literature might be more meaningful if you can first find a copy of the original exposition in Markowitz (1959). The notion that the world market capitalization-weighted index lies on a single passive efficient frontier is a later idea that is not well supported by empirical data. [See, though, Chan and Lakonishok (1993).] It perhaps was too good to be true that the best portfolio also happens by definition to be the most conventional. In real life, lack of integration of the global markets means that there are advantages in trying to devise a better diversified portfolio than the market-capitalization-weighted global index.

3. See Shefrin and Statman (1995) as an example of the recent literature in behavioral finance that helps explain the existence of market inefficiencies. See Wilcox (1994a) for a discussion of selling bottlenecks.

4. The hard-science academics of the Chicago school (not to neglect Yale) lent considerable support to the soft-science field of behavioral finance with landmark studies indicating low price/book and small market-capitalization as the primary correlates of higher returns over long periods. These variables captured the contrarian ideas used by value-oriented investors for years. See Fama and French (1992 and 1996). But there were many antecedents. See, for example, Lakonishok and Shapiro (1986). A more recent article weaving together many correlates of realized return is that by Haugen (1996).

5. Many of the effects cited by Fama and French, by Lakonishok and by Haugen in various writings have been documented within a number of countries.

6. For example, see Chan, et al. (1993a).

7. An early application of neural nets to exchange rate forecasting may be found in Weigand, et al. (1992). The best introduction to genetic algorithms may be Goldberg (1989). They were invented, however, by John Holland. The extension of this chapter to cover these emergent applications to investing would have been fascinating to the author but had to be omitted for reasons of space and time. These "quantitative fashions," along with the use of fractals and fuzzy logic, are expanding at a relatively rapid rate, although they are not entirely approved by the investing establishment. For example, there is now a magazine titled *The Magazine of Artificial Intelligence in Finance,* published by Miller Freeman in San Francisco, which was up to Volume 2, Number 3, in the fall of 1995.

8. See Chan, et al. (1993b).

9. See Fama and French (1992 and 1996).

10. See Chopra and Ziemba (1993).

11. See Jorion (1985).

12. For discussions of the difference between tracking-error risk and total risk in optimization, see Roll (1992) and Clarke, et al. (1994). See also Wilcox (1994b) for a brief discussion of the method of combining two kinds of risk in a single optimization.

13. The problem of properly dealing with trading costs may be dealt with partially using heuristics, as in Grinold and Stuckelman (1993). A more complete treatment is given in Wilcox (1993), but at the cost of restricting the problem to a single security.

Bibliography

Chan, Louis K. C.; Yasushi Hamao; and Josef Lakonishok. "Can Fundamentals Predict Japanese Stock Returns?" *Financial Analysts Journal,* July/August 1993a, pp. 63-69.

Chan, Louis K. C., and Josef Lakonishok. "Are the Reports of Beta's Death Premature?" *Journal of Portfolio Management* 19 (Summer 1993b), pp. 51-62.

Chopra, Vijay K., and William T. Ziemba. "The Effect of Errors in Means, Variances and Covariances on Optimal Portfolio Choice." *Journal of Portfolio Management* 19, Winter 1993, pp. 6-12.

Clarke, Roger C.; Scott Krase; and Meir Statman. "Tracking Errors, Regret, and Tactical Asset Allocation." *Journal of Portfolio Management* 20, Spring 1994, pp. 16-24.

Fama, Eugene F., and Kenneth R. French. "Multifactor Explanations of Asset Pricing Anomalies." *Journal of Finance* 51, March 1996, pp. 55-84.

———. "The Cross Section of Expected Stock Returns." *Journal of Finance*, June 1992, pp. 427-465.

Goldberg, David E. *Genetic Algorithms in Search, Optimization and Machine Learning*, Reading, MA: Addison-Wesley, 1989.

Grinold, Richard C., and Mark Stuckelman. "The Value-Added/Turnover Frontier." *Journal of Portfolio Management* 19, Summer 1993, pp. 8-17.

Haugen, Robert A. "The Effects of Intrigue, Liquidity, Imprecision, and Bias on the Cross Section of Expected Stock Returns." *Journal of Portfolio Management* 22 (Summer 1996) pp. 8-18.

Jorion, Philippe. "International Diversification with Estimation Risk." *Journal of Business* 58(3), 1985, pp. 259-278.

Lakonishok, Josef, and Alan C. Shapiro. "Systematic Risk, Total Risk and Size as Determinants of Stock Market Returns." *Journal of Banking and Finance* 10, 1986, pp. 115-132.

Markowitz, Harry M. *Portfolio Selection*. New Haven, Connecticut: Yale University Press, 1959.

Roll, Richard. "A Mean/Variance Analysis of Tracking Error." *Journal of Portfolio Management* 20, Summer 1992, pp. 13-22.

Shefrin, Hersh, and Meir Statman. "Making Sense of Beta, Size and Book to Market." *Journal of Portfolio Management* 21, No. 2, Winter 1995, pp. 26-34.

Weigand, Andreas S.; Bernardo A. Huberman; and David E. Rumelhart. "Predicting Sunspots and Exchange Rates with Connectionist Networks," in *Nonlinear Modeling and Forecasting*, Martin Casdagli and Stephen Eubank, eds., XII Proceedings of the Santa Fe Institute, Redwood City, California: Addison Wesley, 1992, pp. 395-432.

Wilcox, Jarrod. "Selling Bottlenecks: Causes and Treatments." *Financial Analysts Journal*, March/April 1994a, pp. 49-54.

———. "EAFE is for Wimps." *Journal of Portfolio Management* 20, Spring 1994b, pp. 68-75.

———. "The Effect of Transactions Costs and Delay on Performance Drag." *Financial Analysts Journal*, March/April 1993, pp. 45-54, 77.

CHAPTER 4

The Critical Role of Fundamental Research

Michael Even
Executive Vice President
Independence Investment Associates, Inc.

William J. Kennedy, Jr.
Vice President
Independence Investment Associates, Inc.

One of the defining features of money managers today is the decision to either be a practitioner of traditional fundamental research or of quantitative investment techniques. The quantitative manager believes in a structured investment-decision-process using mathematical tools. The manager further believes that the proper application of these tools dominates most investors' abilities to analyze and prioritize multiple factors which affect security valuation. The traditional investor, relying on fundamental research, scoffs at the idea that an investor can capture investment insights with a computer chip. The world changes quickly, and so must the investor. The traditional investor would substitute nothing for the judgment of the experienced investment professional.

The truth lies somewhere in between. Indeed, by integrating the two disciplines of quantitative valuation and fundamental research, the investment process can capture the best parts of human judgment and mathematical valuation.

This chapter explores the benefits of using fundamental research in a quantitative investment process. First, we explore the importance of fundamental data in a disciplined investment process. Then, we consider the advantages of a proprietary fundamental data source, and we share a statistical study of potential value-added and conceptual explanations of the study's success. Finally, we apply these findings to the international investment arena.

The Advantages of Fundamental Research

Every active investment manager sets out to predict the future—to emphasize positions in securities which will do well, and to minimize exposures to securities which will underperform. In order to predict the future, most managers, disciplined or traditional, rely on forward look-ing—expectational—data as opposed to purely historical data. There are many sources of fundamental/expectational data. What data are best and why? What kind of fundamental inputs make quantitative methods shine? Specifically, is an internal fundamental-research team worth the expense or should one rely on consensus-supplied data? Strong argu-ments can be made for how proprietary fundamental-research can enhance the quantitative investment process.

A Changing World

The world changes, and therefore so do investors' views of relative attrac-tiveness. Analysts can interpret major economic, social, and political events and the impact of these events on investment opportunities much more quickly than can quantitative techniques alone. By the time the quantitative manager experiences enough observable data points to con-firm or reject (in a statistically-significant manner) a major shift in invest-ment opportunities, the large excess-returns will have been captured. Fundamental-research analysts have the best opportunity to recognize the changing world of the companies that they research.

Fundamental Changes in Companies

A particularly cumbersome data issue for purely quantitative managers is the handling of changing corporate structures. For example, on Novem-ber, 1994, Sears announced the spin-off of its insurance subsidiary All-state, to be effective June 30, 1995. The next day, how did quantitative investors adjust the model inputs to accommodate this change in corpo-rate structure? For quantitative managers using consensus data, the spin-off posed a problem. Some of the analysts immediately recognized the Allstate spin-off and adjusted the Sears numbers accordingly. Some ana-lysts did not change the numbers for a month, some for six months. This lack of uniformity in data inputs would make this consensus number for Sears difficult to use in an unbiased fashion. The fundamental analyst provides guidance on how valuation-model inputs can be adjusted to most accurately reflect the security's true economic value and earnings potential.

Fundamental Oversight

Every quantitative manager, whether relying on historical data or expectational data, risks losing sight of the fundamentals of investing—of what really drives stock prices and what really influences corporate successes and failures. The focus on statistical methods may lead to models, investment processes, and philosophies which are so far withdrawn from the fundamental basics that their long-term logic and performance are truly suspect. An in-house fundamental staff can keep the whole organization focused on the true drivers of the market.

Good Fundamental Data

Defining the Concept

The philosophical battle between those who would use consensus data and those who support proprietary fundamental-analysis has remained just that—philosophical. Unlike many other investment topics, which are tested and argued about, proprietary research remains just argued about and rarely tested. The reason behind this is that most investors with fundamental-research experience are traditional investors—in their world it is hard to define where research ends and portfolio management begins, where the analyst's value-added ends and the portfolio manager's judgment begins. It is hard to statistically test analysts whose recommendations are not well-defined, in contrast to the alpha predictions of quantitative analysts. Because few concrete data are available, commitment to proprietary research on the U.S. market is difficult for a quantitative equity manager, much less for the complex and expensive task of research on a worldwide basis.

Defining a Good Analyst—The Quantitative Investment Environment

Although fundamental research is usually associated with traditional investors, measuring its added value is more straightforward in a quantitative shop. Consider an investment process which uses fundamental research to provide the necessary inputs for disciplined quantitative valuation and portfolio construction. In other words, the fundamentally based quantitative shop of our example uses fundamental numbers (these could be recommendations, earnings expectations, risk assessments, future price expectations, etc.) to run a disciplined process. These fundamental inputs are used to drive a valuation system (which may be composed of factors such as dividend-discount models and earnings-momentum models) which produces an expected alpha for each stock in the universe. These alphas are then combined in a structured fashion to create portfolios. This disciplined process requires explicit alphas, thus the analyst's alpha is well-defined. A good analyst produces fundamental inputs which make the expected-return series more accurate than a naive input.[1]

Since the inputs fed into the quantitative process are controlled, and the process produces rankings whose effectiveness can be measured, a test can be created to compare the effectiveness of the process by using different inputs. The purpose of the test is to assess the value added by fundamental data. At the lowest level, the effectiveness of the valuation process can be tested using consensus inputs only. This is done by comparing the power of our disciplined approach when the valuation process is fed consensus data versus the effectiveness of the valuation process when naive—historical—data are driving it. A second test can discern the value added of proprietary research by comparing results when using proprietary data with those which use consensus inputs. Finally, specific analyst's inputs can be measured and compared for performance evaluation purposes. For the purposes of this chapter, only the second test is considered—comparing proprietary research to consensus.

A Test of Proprietary Research versus Consensus Data

Since 1983, Independence Investment Associates has been managing portfolios with the combination of proprietary fundamental research and disciplined application described above. The fundamental-research staff provides all the inputs that the various models demand: predicted earnings, predicted earnings-growth, dividend-payout projections, and any other fundamental information that our quantitative models may need. This information is used to construct various models which, in turn, are combined to predict a single expected return for each stock. The quantitative models include numerous value and momentum measures so that the final combined model is not biased in either direction. Since this test commenced real-time in 1985, consensus data have been tracked to generate a second list of expected returns to compare to the ranked list generated by the proprietary fundamental data. These lists of expected returns are identical in construction from a quantitative point of view—they differ only in the inputs on which they rely.

Since 1985, we have compiled:

- *Monthly ranking of stocks using proprietary research.* This list starts with approximately 300 names in 1985 and increases at a steady pace to approximately 500 names at the end of 1995.

- *Monthly ranking of stocks using consensus data.* We generate rankings for any stock which overlaps with the proprietary list, and which has three or more consensus estimates of the data that we need.

Using the BARRA @ PERFAN system we construct "perfect" portfolios out of each of the two models. We then track the performance and risk characteristics of the perfect portfolios over time. We use these results to judge how much value was added by proprietary- versus consensus-driven research.

At each month-end, we feed each of the two models' rankings into PERFAN in order to create a portfolio for each model. This portfolio has the minimum expected risk, a beta close to zero, and a one standard-deviation exposure to the model-ranking on which the portfolio is based. In order to accomplish this, the portfolio has long positions in positively ranked stocks and short positions in negatively ranked ones. We perform return-attribution on each portfolio over the subsequent month and end up with a total active return (which is the difference between the long and short portfolios). We also break up the total active return into components, including systematic (market timing), style and industry timing, and specific stock selection. PERFAN links these monthly results and comes up with a final estimate of model effectiveness through time.

The test is not perfect. To make the results of the two models completely comparable, we used only an overlapping universe. In other words, we excluded stocks which had consensus data but no proprietary data. In so doing, we reduced our universe from an average of approximately 1300 names per month to an average of about 400. This is the right decision in our quest to determine which data source is superior. However, an investment organization which is making a choice between consensus and proprietary data must take into account the reality that proprietary research will limit the universe and, in so doing, could reduce potential returns. We believe that this limitation is insignificant for strategies benchmarked to large-cap indices, since our proprietary universe is diversified and representative of such benchmarks. The second limitation is that our models were tuned to work with our investment process—a process which has depended on proprietary research. It is possible that if we had set out to create a quantitative system which works best with consensus data, we could have improved the consensus results somewhat. For example, our dividend-discount model works less effectively with consensus data. Fine-tuning with consensus data would have probably reduced our emphasis on dividend discount and, perhaps, increased our emphasis on earnings momentum. Once again, although we believe that this is a limitation of the test, we also believe that our models are representative of a broad range of value and momentum models that are available, and that fine-tuning them to consensus data would have made little difference to our conclusions.

Analyzing the Results

Table 1 shows our test yields since 1985.

Two immediate conclusions can be drawn from the results in Table 1:

- The quantitative discipline works—it adds value with either set of fundamental inputs.
- Proprietary research adds significantly to the potential value-added of the disciplined approach.

The strategy's potential value-added is 3.8 percent per annum using consensus inputs. The very same strategy has the potential to add 9 percent per annum when proprietary research is substituted for the consensus (note that both results ignore turnover constraints, transaction costs, shorting restrictions, and fees). The proprietary inputs also create a more consistent strategy (reducing the negative instances from 36 percent to 31 percent), one which is more focused on stock selection and less apt to create industry and style bets.

To emphasize these results, it is important to review how they were generated. All the model data tested were real-time data—none of the

TABLE 1.   Test Results (April 1, 1985 through
           December 31, 1995)

	Consensus-Based	Proprietary-Based Research
Annualized alpha (t-statistics in parenthesis)	3.8% (2.0)	9.1% (5.6)
Sources:		
Stock selection	84%	86%
Industry	−39%	−2%
Style	54%	16%
Beta/market	1%	0%
Tracking error	5.2%	4.7%
Percentage of negative months	36%	31%
Percentage of months proprietary exceeds consensus	65%	

data were backtested. The proprietary-research-based model was used to manage actual equity portfolios. The consensus-based model was being generated simultaneously (though not for portfolio management purposes). Finally, our results make sense. If you cut the 9 percent added-value, which was generated in the test, in half (since most of our strategies use only long portfolios and the 9 percent was generated with a long/short strategy), then cut it in half again (as a basic rule of thumb to account for the trading-cost friction and the realities of day-to-day portfolio management), you end up with a 2.25 percent expected alpha—only slightly above our long-term expectations for our diversified portfolios. The same exercise yields an expected alpha of just under 1 percent for the consensus-based model, which seems very much in line with the long-term expectations of the consensus-based disciplined managers we hear about.

Why Proprietary Fundamental Research Inputs Add Value

Deciding that proprietary research adds value is certainly important—deciding *why* it adds value is equally important. As investment philosophies and processes from the familiar domestic environment are adapted to foreign markets, the hows and whys of proprietary fundamental research must be understood to use it effectively. Ask any director of research about how proprietary research adds value, and the response is often the same: "Our analysts are the most experienced, thorough, professional analysts in the world—they are way ahead of everyone on accuracy and forecasting." But not everyone can have the best analysts—competitors are willing to pay top dollar to attract their own version of the best analysts—so why does proprietary research add value?

We think a very different set of skills is creating this value-added—at least within quantitative investment processes. The best way to explain these key skills is to examine them in terms of the "garbage in, garbage out" adage. Quantitative tools have no judgment—feed them incorrect data and they will produce incorrect results. A proprietary fundamental research feed does not completely eliminate faulty data, but it greatly reduces it. A proprietary research staff eliminates bad data by being:

- Focused—each input is produced by an analyst who understands how the input will be used and why; therefore, analysts are focused on the key elements.
- Timely—not only is each piece of information submitted as soon as it is available, but the information's horizon and span can be made to match those of the rest of the universe.

- Uniform—each input is defined to be comparable across companies. This requires a consistent economic outlook, clear definitions of each required datum, and a consistent interpretation of accounting and reporting subtleties.

It is worthwhile to review why each of these three aspects is so important.

Focus

Consensus analysts are far from focused. Their objectives in providing reports and data vary significantly, and are often at odds with the needs of the quantitative shop. For example, many sell-side analysts produce expectational data as a sideline—their real job is to produce reports, produce opinions, sell themselves to the buy side, and generate investment-banking opportunities. With all these pressures, the Wall Street analyst may spend as much time working on relationships and reports as they will spend on working on company-earnings models and growth expectations A proprietary research effort should be incented and focused on producing inputs for a quantitative process without distractions. A well-managed proprietary research staff focuses directly on the necessary inputs to the quantitative process; the analysts know the relative importance of each input and refine their work to cater to the specifics of the process.

Timeliness

How quickly is new fundamental information incorporated into the quantitative process? With an internal research staff focused on internal needs and valuation, the process can easily incorporate the most recent data. Internal analysts using modern technology can update inputs immediately, whether in their offices or on the road. These updates can be embedded in any investment decisions immediately. Just as important, issues affecting impending portfolio decisions can be reviewed in a timely fashion. A quantitative decision to buy IBM can be reviewed with the IBM analyst to be sure that the inputs used to come to that buy decision reflect the most current beliefs and information. Such a review process would be impossible with sell-side data. In addition, when news affects multiple companies, internal analysts can be not only timely but also coordinated to assure that all of the affected companies are updated simultaneously and that their numbers remain comparable. With consensus data, the quantitative valuation process is at the mercy of the third-party data-provider's efficiency in updating its information.

Uniformity

In many ways, uniformity is the key issue in assuring the quality of data inputs. Only through uniform definitions of information needed and uniform application of methodology across industries can the quantitative process produce a realistic relative ranking of stock to stock. Imagine ranking IBM versus GM using a dividend-discount model (DDM). Most DDMs rely at least on earnings numbers (predicted and historical), earnings growth numbers, and dividend payouts (historical and expected). What if your GM numbers are based on different economic scenarios and different definitions of growth, earnings, and dividend payouts than your IBM assumptions? In such a situation your DDM rankings for IBM and GM may have little to do with each company's prospects and more to do with each analyst's assumptions. Therefore, it is necessary for data to be uniform in order to make stock-to-stock comparisons meaningful.

Consensus data fail the uniformity test. Consider Wall Street's long-term growth numbers. We can observe consensus analysts who contribute data to IBES; the following summarizes the observations:

- Time horizons of long-term growth ranged between 2 and 10 years; it was loosely defined by many analysts.
- The base earnings used for estimating the long-term growth—in other words, the number that is compounded by the growth to yield the earnings at the end of the time horizon—were similarly nonuniform. Some analysts used earnings normalized over the last cycle; others simply used last year's reported numbers; still others used last year's reported numbers adjusted for nonrecurring numbers; and, of course, to add complexity, some used this year's estimated numbers.
- In computing the long-term growth, analysts used an array of economic scenarios. The economic scenarios included a recession, a boom, and completely flat economic growth—some with and some without inflation.
- There was little uniformity in analyst's attitudes regarding their long-term growth projections. Some treated long-term growth as a very important number. Other thought of it as a fallout of a general earnings model. Still others simply generated (i.e., invented) a growth rate to support an opinion on the stock.

Suffice it to say that this kind of nonuniformity is only intensified when companies from fundamentally different industries are compared. It would be next to impossible to rely on growth numbers that were generated with so little uniformity if one wanted to quantitatively compare different companies in different industries and derive an unbiased ranking of securities based on expected alpha.

We believe that the value-added of proprietary research is *not* gained through an improvement in the inherent predictive ability of the data. In other words, we believe that, in the highly-paid investment industry, few incapable analysts are hired, and that the ability to accurately predict the future is fraught with equal difficulties for all of these intelligent analysts. The true advantage of in-house analysts is their ability to focus on the needs of the process and to format the data through uniform, timely, and focused work.

The Next Step—Fundamental Inputs in Foreign Markets

Over the past few years we began to adopt our process (fundamental analysis and disciplined portfolio construction) to foreign markets. Along with adopting the domestic quantitative process, discussed above, to the international markets, we strove to adopt the concepts of focus, timeliness, and uniformity to improving our fundamental inputs in these new arenas. In projecting beyond the United States, we had to resolve one key fundamental-research question: is it necessary to exactly replicate our U.S. proprietary-research function? In other words, did we have to build a huge team of in-house research analysts to fly all over the world, visit company managements, and research product-markets in order to develop data inputs for the quantitative valuation models?

On the surface, the answer would seem to be a resounding yes. One would think that an investor could clearly benefit more from internal research in international markets. After all, information (particularly good clean information) is harder to come by in that market—and is, therefore, worth more. A fundamental-research staff may be able to provide numbers that are simply unavailable from external (consensus) sources, or they may be able to provide numbers of a higher quality than is available in some international markets. Most international markets are not nearly as dominated by institutional investors as the U.S. market, and one consequence of this is less focus on high-quality fundamental research by the sell side. This means that some numbers which we regularly receive in the United States may not be available—consensus long-term earnings growth projections, for example. Fewer high-quality sell-side research teams are available, and this leads to limited depth of consensus numbers. Large-cap domestic consensus projections, for example, are often based on the inputs of more than 20 analysts, while in smaller, less developed markets, the consensus projections are often composed of only one or two inputs. The argument for in-depth proprietary research in foreign markets is, therefore, based on the concept that truly refined and timely fundamental data are unavailable from any other source.

Our experience argues that the common sense answer above is wrong. As we said above, we believe that the key to maximizing the value of fundamental inputs to a quantitative process lies with three concepts: focus, timeliness, and uniformity. We have shown that improving on consensus numbers in these three categories dramatically increases the value-added of a disciplined process. In the United States, consensus data are somewhat focused, somewhat timely, and somewhat uniform. Because of this, it takes in-depth research to improve on the consensus—to focus it further and to make it more timely and fully uniform. As we argue in more detail below, international consensus data are behind U.S. standards in these aspects. Therefore, the proprietary research required to achieve the extra value-added can be structured quite differently.

The argument for a very different internal research effort on the international arena is further buttressed by the fact that the necessary structure of an international research area—analysts working in different regions, with different economic scenarios and with infrequent opportunities to work together—works to undermine focus, timeliness, and uniformity. Finally, we believe that the structure of fundamental research feeding into a disciplined process requires inputs which are ahead of the pack, but not too far ahead. In this respect, too, a U.S.-like structure would produce more problems than solutions. We will, therefore, argue for a very different focus and structure internationally.

Focus

The focus of international sell-side analysts is even less well-honed than that of their domestic brethren. First, the less-developed international investment community demands less focus on numerical estimates and is generally happy with written reports focusing on opinions and qualitative judgments. Second, international standards for release of information by corporations are less stringent by U.S. standards. This makes it difficult to produce accurate numbers. Third, because there is generally less competition among analysts on the sell side in these markets (there are simply fewer analysts), there is less pressure to meet the needs of specific clients—clients who may need good numerical estimates. Using the IBES consensus databases, the average number of estimates for the largest 10 U.S. companies is 30 per company, whereas the same count for Japan yields 15 per company. Finally, because services like IBES are relatively new to these markets, there may be less experience in providing information to consensus services.

Timeliness

Timeliness suffers from the same effects that influence focus. Germany, for example, allows companies to wait up to 9 months before reporting formal, audited numbers (compared with 3 months in the United Kingdom). Imagine the problems that a sell-side analyst would have in introducing timely numbers when they may have to wait many months to see a breakdown of what already occurred. Finally, the likelihood of updating across companies in unison and keeping data current (or the likelihood of analysts trying to beat these reporting delays and problems) is greatly diminished. In addition, the rules taken for granted in the United States regarding insider information and fairness in dealing with clients are less developed in some markets. In these markets, the favored customers will get the most recent updates well ahead of everyone else, and consensus services will probably receive new information last. By the same token, one or two insider analysts may received timely information from some companies while all other analysts languish. This puts the certainty of general timeliness of data in doubt.

Uniformity

Earlier, we discussed the importance of uniformity for fundamental inputs to a disciplined process, and we talked about some of the uniformity problems which plague the consensus data in the United States. All those problems pale when compared to uniformity problems in the international arena. Not only do differences exist between industries, but, internationally, huge differences exist between countries and regions.

To begin with, accounting standards differ dramatically from country to country. Fully diluted earnings in France are lower than in the United Kingdom as UK GAAP does not yet require goodwill to be amortized; it is difficult to compare such distinctly different concepts. Getting past accounting standards, one soon comes head to head with reporting conventions or requirements. In many countries, companies are required to report the bare minimum of information; how does one compare estimates from a country with thorough reporting with those from a country with limited data? Surely some higher level of confidence must be attached to numbers from a more open country.

The regional structure of research departments in many of the big sell-side providers (for example, European analysts operating out of London and East Asian analysts out of Tokyo) may lead to independent (and nonuniform) styles within each organization. Take economic scenarios, for example. Uniformity would require all predicted fundamental numbers to be based on the same economic scenario—but what economic scenario do we use internationally? Should we look for a consistent global economic theme? The odds of finding such a scenario among sell-side shops are certainly small. Should we look for consistent country themes? That would be easier but ineffective in today's global economy. After all, what good are single-country economic scenarios when a French consumer goods producer may be as dependent on the economy in Britain as it is dependent on the economy of France for its success. Uniformity in defining specific numbers and concepts is also practically impossible between global offices and global concepts and ideas which differ from region to region and country to country.

In short, the consensus data which one receives from any of the data providers is likely to be the furthest thing from uniform. The fact that, in most cases, that same data will be based on fewer independent analysts than in the United States makes the possibility that particular idiosyncrasies will average out in the sample less likely. Uniformity, more than any of the other issues, makes the use of consensus data in disciplined environments difficult and uncertain.

With all these consensus problems, why not create a fundamental-research area which functions much as in the United States? We believe that route is less than optimal for the following reasons:

- Uniformity would be very difficult to achieve even with an internal staff. To do truly in-depth analysis would require local presence in many of the markets. But local presence, by definition, takes away from uniformity—how do you hire a staff to specialize in a region, its concepts, accounting, finance, and economy, and then tell that staff to yield to central control and direction? On the other hand, how do you use a centrally based and centrally trained staff to explore the unique issues of each economy? We think the problem is very tough to solve.

- The goal of an internal fundamental staff is to improve on consensus data, not to supplant it. Internal research which is sufficiently different from the locally available data will be useless in the valuation step. Imagine an internal analyst who predicts international companies' five-year earnings growth rates with uncanny accuracy—but only for markets where no one else produces or pays attention to such numbers. The analyst's skill is likely to be wasted, because local valuation ignores it.

■ The goal of developing an internal staff which could compete with the locals is tough. Internationally, being plugged in is even more important than in the United States. In addition, fair play is less common. The probability of creating an internal research staff which could survive and thrive in such an environment is small.

As international markets open up, rules governing them become more uniform, methods of investing draw closer together, and information flows more easily, these three points could well lose their applicability. Until then we recommend the following.

Custom Consensus

Custom consensus is a blend which aims to produce the best of both worlds: local in-depth knowledge combined with focus, timeliness and uniformity. It is based on a simple combination: consensus data modified with proprietary knowledge and skill. We can think of many ways to implement this concept, but they all include three basic steps:

1. Collect the highest-quality consensus data possible.
2. Select a subuniverse of superior consensus providers which will provide your default inputs, assuming you have no further knowledge.
3. Use proprietary research to improve the quality of the inputs further with focus, timeliness, and uniformity—tune your proprietary research efforts to apply their knowledge where they can add the most value.

Though only the third step may sound complex, there are issues which need to be resolved with each of them.

Step 1: Data Collection

On the surface, data collection may be as easy as signing up for electronic delivery by IBES—but even in this first step the custom part of custom consensus can begin. First, through mechanical or manual means, the data can be checked for reasonableness and likely errors. Data-entry errors, missed splits, and very old data mixed with new can all be partially avoided in a process which collects data logically. Second, clearly inferior data can be modified mechanically. For example, consistent long-term earnings growth data is lacking in international consensus data, so we developed an alternative process which formulates a growth rate from

Dupont formula.[2] Finally, the process itself can be designed to assure that the most recent data are supplied each time the valuation process is recomputed. In step 1, without significant human intervention or qualitative judgment, consensus data can be improved significantly.

Step 2: Global Data Screen

Once the best off-the-shelf data are gathered, the first qualitative improvements can be implemented. Step two involves picking a subset of global consensus providers who are a step above the rest in focus, timeliness, and uniformity. We combined a top-down and bottom-up approach to select these super-providers. The top-down screen looked for consensus providers who had broad coverage of the EAFE (Europe, Australia, Far East) universe. The logic behind this was simple:

- Shops with broad coverage are likely to take the research function seriously.
- Broad coverage generally implies some effort at uniformity across countries and industries.
- Most large providers have a strong domestic presence and, therefore, have existing relationships with us, allowing a closer understanding of their analysts by ours and more service of our analyst should further data be needed.

The bottom-up screen was developed by asking internal industry and regional analysts to pick the most influential providers in their area of expertise. In this case the goal was to select firms with local and industry knowledge, as opposed to global presence. We combined the two lists into a final universe of about 20 select providers. Assuming no further inputs from our analysts, we would use this select list (with our cleaning modifications of step 1) to create our custom consensus.

Step 3: Company-by-Company Insights

Overseeing this custom process is our internal research department. Their international focus is significantly different than their domestic focus: domestically they are charged with producing detailed earnings models and expectations for each of their companies, while internationally they are required to be familiar with regional, industry, or company events. This familiarity is translated into improvements on the custom consensus of steps one and two. The assumption is that our analysts cannot compete with locals and still maintain their focus, timeliness, and uniformity. Their knowledge will, therefore, be used to derive a modicum of focus, timeliness, and uniformity from the local experts. Let us demonstrate how this process may work.

Our analysts would familiarize themselves with the issues of their international coverage—industries and companies. Analysts which already cover the same industries domestically are knowledgeable about the key international issues and the main international competitors. A few regional analysts may help industry analysts deal with the complexities of local issues, local accounting, and local customs. The goal of the industry/regional-analyst combination will be to understand the basics of each of their companies and to know the consensus analysts which cover them. On an ongoing basis our analysts would review each of the contributors to their consensus numbers and would look for opportunities to improve on the conglomerate number. The following situations could create opportunities.

Data-Definition Driven. Our analyst can check the inputs of each of the consensus analysts to verify that they are using consistent definitions, and inconsistent inputs can be excluded. For example, all of our input fields are defined in local currencies, so each analyst can automatically exclude or convert inputs in other currencies. As a second example, if our definition of earnings excludes one-time charges and revenues, each of our analysts would check each consensus input for their industries to assure that the definition is adhered to by all consensus participants.

Event Driven. Our analyst realizes that industry group XX in country YY will be effected by very large new tax. She quickly examines the custom consensus numbers and finds that only two out of the five selected analysts have already reflected this event in their numbers. She may choose to delete the lagging three from our custom consensus or, alternatively, she may call each of the laggards, find out if they have revised numbers which have simply not made it through the system yet, and reflect those new numbers in our custom consensus numbers.

Judgment Driven. Our analyst may find that for various reasons one or two consensus providers that have been globally selected for his industry provide subpar numbers, and he may choose to eliminate them from our custom consensus. Alternatively, our analyst may find that one or two consensus entries are dramatic outliers and are simply beyond the range of realistic expectations. Those can also be eliminated from the consensus.

No Availability. After applying all of our screens and data tests we may find that not enough consensus providers remain to create reliable inputs. In such a case, our analyst may be able to provide predicted numbers for the company in question much as she does in the United States—

with a primary research effort and pro-forma earnings statements and balance sheets.

Conclusion

Conceptually, our analysts would work to create a more focused, timely, and uniform data input set. The global selection of consensus analysts is already tuned to emphasize the consensus providers most focused on providing reasonable numbers. Our analysts pick and choose from this global set to select those providers which best address each company. Timeliness is emphasized by excluding numbers which clearly do not reflect recent events. In some situations, our analysts may update expectations from consensus analysts which have recomputed their numbers following a dramatic event but have not yet entered them into the consensus system. In the most extreme situations, our analyst may create their own numbers if consensus is deemed not sufficiently current. Finally, uniformity is approached from two ends—by choosing global firms with some emphasis on uniformity across countries and industries, and by asking our analysts to eliminate data which clearly does not conform with the definitions and methods which we establish for each field.

Beyond ongoing maintenance of the database, our analysts are contacted before major purchases and sales. Their opinion about the accuracy and currency of the consensus numbers for the company in question serve as a final screen before action. An analyst may ask for more time to research a specific situation more closely in order to assure us that our inputs are correct. Alternatively, an analyst may feel secure that the most recent information is imbedded in our consensus numbers and that we are free to act.

It is imperative to acknowledge that these functions are *not* data-cleansing functions, but are professional tasks which require a very high level of understanding of fundamental research, the economies and industries in question, and the quantitative tools for which the data are needed. An analyst must quickly and effectively absorb the issues in a new industry or country and make useful judgments regarding the consensus players in that area. An analyst must efficiently judge the work of others and look for flaws in analysis, definition, or economic assumptions. We believe that this teaming of consensus providers and internal fundamental research is the best way to feed a disciplined process in the EAFE markets. In 10 years we will be able to back this statement with quantitative proof, as we have done domestically. Until then, we depend on our philosophical beliefs and logical extrapolations from the domestic experience.

Endnotes

1.   Note that there are many other effective ways to use fundamental inputs in a disciplined process. For example, analysts may select a subuniverse of "good" securities and a disciplined process may than be used to further screen them and to create a portfolio. Alternatively, a disciplined process may establish a list of possible buys and sells, and a fundamental override may be applied before the final decision. All of these are valid and potentially effective ways to combine fundamental and disciplined methods. We will limit our discussions to the methodology discussed earlier, because it is by far the easiest to test. It is our belief that our test results are representative of the value of proprietary fundamental research in many disciplined applications—we believe our conclusions apply to alternative methodologies.

2.   A "DuPont formula" analysis considers factors such as operating margin, asset turnover and leverage ratios to evaluate how effectively a company is utilizing its resources. A sample formula is:

$$\text{Return on Equity} = \frac{\text{EBIT}}{\text{SALES}} \times \frac{\text{SALES}}{\text{ASSETS}} \times \frac{\text{ASSETS}}{\text{EQUITY}}$$

The formula can be reengineered to produce a sustainable earnings growth rate formula.

CHAPTER 5

Global Sector Allocation

Ross Paul Bruner
Managing Director
Istituto Mobiliare Italiano

Overview

The Sector Dimension

Our global equity strategy is developed from a series quantitative management tools organized around three dimensions: sector, country, and style. For each dimension, we evaluate trailing and forecast valuation premiums, earnings per share (EPS) momentum, estimate error, and quality, as well as performance or valuation anomaly. For the purposes of this chapter, we focus on the importance of the sector dimension in developing a view on global equity strategy.

In terms of relative importance, our work suggests that the sector dimension is as significant as the country dimension in explaining historical equity returns. We developed a 10-year monthly correlation study of sector and market returns in local currency and found that, on average, European and American sectors were more highly correlated with each other (62 percent) than with the country average correlation (49 percent). (See Tables 1 and 2.) In fact, European and American sectors are almost as highly correlated with each other as with the country average correlation relative to our global benchmark (64 percent). Japanese sectors are another story. They are more highly correlated with European sectors than with American sectors (32 percent versus 25 percent), but the absolute level is consistent with Japan's relatively low correlation (38 percent) to other world equity markets.

Global sector correlation also emphasizes the importance of the sector dimension. In fact, the global average sector correlation (63 percent) is only modestly less significant than the country average correlation (64 percent). Interestingly, global sector correlation has declined since 1990 (62 percent) when compared with the preceding five years (68 percent); this same trend has also been at work with respect to country correlation (66 percent versus 62 percent).

Integrate Sector and Country Strategy

As a result of our work on global sector correlation, we decided that a sensible view on global equity strategy should include an evaluation of the sector as well as the country dimension. In terms of our process, we use our sector and country allocation models as tools rather than a "black box." The exercise of judgment is critical to producing sustained relative performance, given problems with premium stability (which will be discussed in greater detail in the next section). For now, just as stocks can be re-rated to reflect enhanced or diminished growth prospects, so can sectors and markets. Sector and market strategy are about equally important in our process: Sometimes sectors drive our selection process, and other times we focus more on the country dimension.

The global model portfolio in Table 3 represents the end result of our three-dimensional selection process. It is a 67-stock equal-weighted portfolio (1/67=1.5%) whose sector and country attributes reflect our recommendations on sector and market strategy. In other words, the aggregate number of names for a particular sector or market times 1.5 equals our recommended exposure to the group. It also implies that we will only overweight a sector or a market to the extent that there are enough shares to own. In terms of stock selection, we evaluate individual shares according to the same methodology as sectors and markets (see Chapter 11).

Methodology

P/E to Inverse Bond Yield

We evaluate stocks relative to bonds by dividing the price-to-earnings ratio by the inverse 10-year government bond yield, which for us represents a kind of equity risk premium. This method of transformation captures the rate at which equity investors capitalize the EPS relative to the pace of economic activity. When the economy is overheating and interest rates are high (e.g., $1/10\% = 10x$), equity price-to-earnings must be reduced to reflect the fact that interest rates offer an attractive alternative

TABLE 1. Correlation by Market (local currency)

	Avg	UK	Germany	France	Nether- lands	Switzer- land	Belgium	Italy	Sweden	Spain	Japan	USA
USA vs	49%	70%	44%	51%	61%	51%	53%	27%	43%	55%	36%	100%
Japan vs	38%	41%	31%	39%	35%	41%	43%	31%	35%	47%	100%	36%
Europe vs	68%	89%	72%	76%	74%	68%	80%	49%	56%	70%	45%	70%
Global vs	64%	71%	54%	63%	63%	63%	65%	44%	54%	66%	79%	78%

TABLE 2. Correlation by Sector (local currency)

			Consumer									
	Avg	Basic	Durable	Merch	Non-dur	Service	Energy	Finan	Health	Indus	Tech	Utility
Europe vs USA	62%	63%	57%	53%	69%	70%	74%	54%	69%	70%	59%	43%
Europe vs Japan	32%	36%	39%	30%	40%	28%	31%	28%	31%	41%	39%	11%
USA vs Japan	25%	27%	30%	25%	28%	23%	22%	28%	27%	23%	19%	19%
Europe vs Global	70%	48%	65%	70%	84%	80%	86%	59%	77%	74%	72%	51%
USA vs Global	75%	55%	61%	83%	87%	85%	92%	57%	89%	62%	80%	73%
Japan vs Global	66%	40%	90%	65%	60%	58%	44%	89%	59%	85%	68%	67%
Global vs Sector	63%	69%	71%	59%	69%	79%	63%	48%	58%	57%	75%	51%

Source: Compustat, WorldScope & IMI estimates.

TABLE 3. Global Model Portfolio (local currency)

31-Jul-96 BENCHMARK	Share Price	1-Week % Chg	1-Month % Chg	Q-T-D % Chg	Y-T-D % Chg	P/E FY +1	P/CF FY +1	P/B FY +1	Yield FY +1	ROE FY +1	EPS Y-Y
GLOBAL 3,500-STOCK INDEX		1.3	-5.2	-5.1	3.0	22.1	12.5	3.1	2.8	18.0	17.6
CYCLICAL INDEX (47% vs. 37%)		2.1	-6.1	-5.7	4.7	22.4	12.0	2.9	2.5	16.8	21.1
BASIC MATERIAL (12% vs. 8%)		1.9	-5.2	-4.7	3.4	20.6	10.3	2.6	2.8	17.7	18.0
AIR LIQUIDE(L')	880.0	1.6	-3.0	-4.6	8.5	18.2	9.7	2.4	3.5	13.2	10.0
BAYER AG	49.5	0.7	-7.4	11.2	30.8	11.8	6.6	2.0	3.0	15.1	10.5
BOC GROUP	9.1	-0.4	-1.4	-0.8	1.0	14.2	7.7	2.6	3.0	17.0	11.1
JAMES RIVER CORP	25.3	1.5	-4.7	-3.8	4.7	14.5	3.4	1.0	2.4	6.4	64.2
NISSAN CHEM INDS	702.0	-2.0	-10.7	-3.4	2.5	37.7	26.3	2.9	1.7	7.6	14.1
NKK CORP	305.0	4.5	-7.6	0.0	9.7	27.5	5.3	2.6	0.0	9.2	27.6
PRAXAIR	38.4	5.1	-7.8	12.9	14.1	15.2	8.5	3.8	2.1	24.7	22.9
AVERAGE		1.6	-6.1	1.6	10.2	19.9	9.7	2.4	2.2	13.3	22.9
CONSUMER DURABLE (12% vs. 6%)		2.1	-6.7	-6.8	8.3	22.6	9.9	2.1	2.6	13.0	22.9
BAYER MOTOREN WERK	825.0	-1.4	-6.4	-2.5	12.2	14.8	4.1	1.9	4.0	12.5	18.8
BOSS (HUGO) AG	1,750.0	0.6	1.2	37.3	46.9	15.3	13.0	4.0	4.9	25.8	10.9
CANON INC	2,020.0	0.0	-11.0	0.0	8.0	20.7	8.6	1.9	1.9	9.2	12.3
GENERAL MOTORS CORP	48.8	4.6	-10.3	-7.4	-7.8	6.8	2.1	1.3	6.4	18.6	17.1
HONDA MOTOR CO	2,580.0	3.6	-9.2	10.3	21.1	16.6	9.1	2.1	2.2	12.8	15.2
MINOLTA CAMERA CO	645.0	-1.2	-11.6	5.7	7.0	27.0	7.6	2.8	1.8	10.3	23.8
NIKE -CL B	102.9	4.0	-1.3	47.5	47.8	17.6	16.0	4.7	1.4	26.9	20.8
PIRELLI SPA	2,470.0	2.5	-2.8	14.1	20.5	10.6	4.2	1.1	4.7	10.3	17.1
SONY CORP	6,750.0	0.7	-6.6	3.1	9.0	21.4	7.5	2.4	0.7	10.7	20.5
AVERAGE		1.5	-6.5	12.0	18.3	16.7	8.0	2.5	3.1	15.2	17.4
CONSUMER MERCHANDISE (9% vs. 5%)		1.2	-5.7	-5.6	9.7	20.9	14.4	3.4	2.3	16.2	16.8
BENETTON GROUP SPA	17,855.0	-3.6	-8.7	-4.4	-5.5	12.0	8.6	1.9	2.2	14.4	9.2

TABLE 3 (continued)

31-Jul-96	Share Price	1-Week % Chg	1-Month % Chg	Q-T-D % Chg	Y-T-D % Chg	P/E FY +1	P/CF FY +1	P/B FY +1	Yield FY +1	ROE FY +1	EPS Y-Y
BENCHMARK											
CIRCUIT CITY STORES INC	31.5	-6.0	-13.7	22.3	14.0	13.9	10.2	2.4	0.8	17.5	17.6
COMPTOIRS MODERNES	2,314.0	6.1	-0.3	31.9	45.5	22.4	10.8	3.6	2.0	16.2	12.9
GAP INC	29.8	0.8	-7.4	26.3	41.7	17.0	12.2	4.1	2.1	24.0	16.7
FAMILYMART CO	4,930.0	-1.2	0.8	6.3	16.4	33.5	26.8	4.3	0.9	12.9	7.6
TOYS R US INC	26.4	1.4	-8.3	19.9	21.3	12.9	9.6	1.8	0.0	14.1	14.5
AVERAGE		-0.4	-6.2	17.0	22.2	18.6	13.0	3.0	1.3	16.5	13.1
CONSUMER NON-DURABLE (6% vs.8%)		1.6	-3.5	-3.2	7.7	20.1	14.3	4.9	3.1	26.7	12.9
COCA-COLA CO	46.9	2.2	-5.1	24.4	26.3	28.6	25.7	13.0	2.3	45.4	18.0
COLGATE-PALMOLIVE	78.5	-4.6	-7.2	6.1	11.7	16.3	11.4	6.4	2.2	35.2	14.5
GILLETTE CO	63.8	0.8	3.0	18.9	22.3	25.4	20.8	8.2	2.3	32.1	16.2
KIKKOMAN CORP	811.0	-0.5	-9.4	-4.6	6.7	29.8	21.0	1.7	1.6	5.6	-1.1
AVERAGE		-0.5	-4.7	11.2	16.8	25.0	19.7	7.3	2.1	29.6	11.9
CONSUMER SERVICE (6% vs.5%)		1.7	-6.9	-6.9	3.9	22.3	14.2	3.9	2.1	16.2	14.3
CANAL PLUS	1,195.0	3.0	-5.5	15.7	30.2	29.6	9.8	3.4	1.7	10.9	25.5
POLYGRAM NV	93.0	5.9	-7.5	-2.8	9.2	17.7	15.3	4.8	2.3	27.2	13.7
TOKYO BROADCASTING	1,750.0	0.0	-8.9	-0.6	2.9	50.1	28.5	1.6	1.3	3.2	12.2
WENDY'S INTERNATIONAL	17.0	-2.2	-10.5	-17.6	-20.0	11.7	8.1	2.2	1.4	17.0	17.9
AVERAGE		1.7	-8.1	-1.3	5.6	27.3	15.4	3.0	1.7	14.6	17.3
ENERGY (3% vs.5%)		-0.8	-4.6	-4.4	6.4	16.9	8.2	2.4	3.4	15.5	9.8
COSMO OIL	673.0	1.5	-1.9	23.0	19.3	31.0	8.5	2.2	2.4	7.1	39.1
SCHLUMBERGER LTD	80.0	-2.4	-5.6	14.1	15.5	20.6	11.0	3.8	1.8	16.8	18.2
AVERAGE		-0.5	-3.7	18.6	17.4	25.8	9.8	3.0	2.1	12.0	28.7
FINANCIAL (12% vs.21%)		1.0	-4.6	-4.2	-0.4	27.2	14.9	2.2	2.9	12.8	22.0
ALLSTATE CORP	44.8	4.7	-3.8	2.9	8.8	9.9	7.4	1.6	5.0	16.3	16.2

TABLE 3 (continued)

31-Jul-96 BENCHMARK	Share Price	1-Week % Chg	1-Month % Chg	Q-T-D % Chg	Y-T-D % Chg	P/E FY+1	P/CF FY+1	P/B FY+1	Yield FY+1	ROE FY+1	EPS Y-Y
BANKERS TRUST	71.9	1.8	-3.5	10.8	8.1	9.8	7.9	1.1	5.6	11.2	12.7
BANK OF YOKOHAMA	924.0	0.3	-6.5	12.8	9.3	43.4	27.3	2.4	0.5	5.5	82.1
CITICORP	81.9	1.6	-1.5	10.8	21.7	9.8	8.4	2.0	1.5	19.7	12.6
DEAN WITTER DISCOVER	50.9	3.3	-11.7	-6.0	8.2	7.9	7.5	1.4	2.6	17.4	17.0
NATIONSBANK	86.0	3.5	2.1	23.1	23.5	9.6	8.7	1.8	2.4	17.0	11.7
PROVIDENT FINL	4.5	9.5	-3.4	12.1	8.8	14.3	13.2	5.2	3.1	30.7	10.0
SUNTRUST BANKS INC	36.8	2.1	-2.0	6.3	7.3	12.3	10.2	1.7	4.5	13.8	9.9
AVERAGE		3.3	-3.8	9.1	12.0	14.6	11.3	2.2	3.2	16.5	21.5
HEALTH CARE (7%)											
ASTRA AB	271.0	0.4	-5.3	-5.0	2.4	18.7	14.4	5.0	2.1	34.5	15.7
JOHNSON & JOHNSON	47.8	5.0	-5.4	-2.7	3.0	14.8	12.6	4.2	2.4	28.3	15.1
PHARMACIA & UPJOHN	41.1	0.5	-3.8	-0.5	11.7	19.4	15.4	5.1	3.2	26.2	14.4
SMITHKLINE BEECHAM	6.8	2.8	-7.3	-1.2	6.1	16.1	11.8	2.9	1.8	18.0	23.2
		-1.2	-1.7	-6.4	-3.9	16.0	12.9	12.6	2.1	75.9	12.8
TAISO PHARM CO	2,300.0	0.0	-1.7	10.0	12.7	24.7	18.7	2.4	1.9	9.5	6.6
AVERAGE		1.4	-4.0	-0.2	5.9	18.2	14.2	5.4	2.3	31.6	14.4
INDUSTRIAL (9% vs. 12%)											
HITACHI CONST MACH	1,340.0	0.6	-6.0	-5.8	3.5	25.5	14.2	2.6	2.5	13.9	19.2
ILLINOIS TOOLWORKS	64.4	2.3	-2.2	8.1	7.2	44.2	22.7	2.3	0.4	na	35.3
KOMATSU	979.0	3.2	-4.6	4.9	9.1	14.9	11.6	3.0	2.5	20.5	12.2
MITSUBISHI HVY IND	905.0	2.4	-6.8	8.5	15.2	38.2	15.1	1.7	0.8	na	19.6
SYSCO CORP	29.0	2.4	-5.0	6.6	10.0	22.2	15.2	2.3	2.4	10.2	12.1
		1.3	-15.3	-9.4	-10.8	16.5	11.9	3.0	3.0	18.2	na
TELEDYNE INC	36.0	2.9	-1.7	44.0	40.5	12.4	8.6	4.4	1.1	30.1	9.8
AVERAGE		2.4	-5.9	10.5	11.9	24.7	14.2	2.8	1.7	19.7	17.8
TECHNOLOGY (15% vs. 12%)											
BRITISH AEROSPACE	9.3	3.7	-6.5	-5.6	4.8	20.5	11.9	3.8	2.1	20.8	23.8
		0.4	-4.8	4.1	16.6	11.6	7.9	4.5	4.2	39.0	24.6

TABLE 3 (continued)

31-Jul-96	Share Price	1-Week % Chg	1-Month % Chg	Q-T-D % Chg	Y-T-D % Chg	P/E FY+1	P/CF FY+1	P/B FY+1	Yield FY+1	ROE FY+1	EPS Y-Y
BENCHMARK											
COMPAQ COMPUTER	54.6	13.2	9.2	15.9	13.8	10.8	9.3	2.3	0.0	21.7	20.5
ERICSSON(LM)TEL	132.5	8.2	-10.2	-5.0	1.9	16.0	11.0	3.7	1.3	20.9	20.3
FUJI PHOTO FILM CO	3,190.0	3.2	-9.1	5.6	7.0	20.2	9.4	1.2	1.3	6.2	6.4
KYOCERA CORP	7,310.0	1.2	-4.7	-3.7	-4.7	19.3	13.8	1.9	2.0	10.1	6.7
MICROSOFT CORP	117.9	2.7	-3.6	27.4	34.3	29.0	26.1	7.8	0.0	27.0	na
MOTOROLA INC	54.0	2.9	-16.3	0.0	-5.3	17.3	8.5	2.5	1.7	14.4	29.3
REUTERS HOLDINGS	6.7	-4.1	-14.2	8.7	14.2	20.0	13.7	8.5	3.1	42.5	14.2
SUN MICROSYSTEMS	54.6	9.0	-9.9	18.8	19.7	16.6	11.9	3.6	0.0	21.9	na
TDK CORP	6,190.0	5.3	-4.6	16.1	17.5	22.7	10.5	2.1	0.8	8.7	-8.3
AVERAGE		4.2	-6.8	8.8	11.5	18.3	12.2	3.8	1.4	21.2	14.2
UTILITY (9% vs. 11%)		0.4	-5.8	-6.0	-4.0	17.1	7.4	2.9	4.0	16.0	8.5
AT&T CORP	52.3	2.7	-15.7	-21.9	-19.3	12.6	7.8	4.4	2.5	na	12.7
CABLE & WIRELESS	4.1	1.8	-3.8	-8.4	-11.5	12.7	7.0	2.8	2.5	19.4	12.8
KOKUSAI DEN (KDD)	11,000.0	-3.5	-0.9	33.5	22.2	42.0	11.3	2.0	1.0	4.7	3.5
KPN	58.3	0.3	-9.6	-8.9	0.0	10.0	4.5	1.8	4.5	16.7	9.4
MCI COMMUNICATIONS	24.6	5.9	-2.5	-14.0	-5.7	12.4	6.2	1.5	0.6	12.2	14.5
VEBA AG	75.0	-0.1	-7.5	13.2	23.1	14.1	5.2	2.1	2.3	13.7	10.4
AVERAGE		1.2	-6.7	-1.1	1.5	17.3	7.0	2.4	2.2	13.3	10.5
MODEL PORTFOLIO (100%)*		1.8	-5.8	7.7	12.2	19.5	11.8	3.3	2.2	18.4	16.9
RELATIVE TO THE MARKET		0.5	-0.6	-0.6	3.7	88.4	94.6	105.4	78.3	102.3	95.6

*Equal-weighted (1/67 = 1.5%) relative to our benchmarks.

TABLE 3 *(continued)*

Country Rotation Strategy

	Y-T-D % Chg	P/E FY +1	P/CF FY +1	P/B FY +1	Yield FY +1	Index %	Portfolio %
Belgium	6.7	12.3	7.2	1.7	4.8	1.0	0.0
France	9.4	16.4	8.4	2.0	3.8	3.0	4.5
Germany	6.8	20.3	8.9	2.8	2.8	4.0	5.5
Italy	2.0	16.3	8.1	1.6	4.2	2.0	2.5
Japan	0.2	44.6	20.1	2.6	1.2	29.0	28.5
Netherlands	11.6	14.3	9.1	2.9	4.7	2.0	3.0
Spain	8.5	12.1	7.4	1.9	4.7	1.0	0.0
Sweden	8.4	12.6	9.0	2.6	4.1	1.0	3.0
Switzerland	5.2	14.9	10.4	2.6	3.1	3.0	0.0
United Kingdom	1.2	13.2	9.5	3.1	4.3	10.0	9.5
United States	3.3	15.1	10.1	3.8	3.0	44.0	43.5

Source: Compustat, WorldScope, I/B/E/S & IMI estimates.

118

to shares. Conversely, when the economy is slowing and rates are lower (e.g., 1/5% = 20x), equity P/E multiples can expand because the valuation backdrop has improved.

Mean Reversion

The concept of mean reversion is important in terms of our view of economic systems, as well as sector and market valuation cycles. In its simplest form, mean reversion is the tendency of systems to move toward a long-term average. With regard to economic systems, when an economy grows beyond its sustainable long-term growth rate, interest rates act to slow the economy and move it back toward the average. Conversely, when an economy is slowing, interest rates act to advance growth toward the long-term average. Sector and market valuation cycles operate in largely the same way. Political, social, and valuation-related events can change the consensus growth-rate forecast for a sector or market. These events create changes in relative valuation, which, like the velocity of economic activity, become exaggerated and ultimately move back toward a historical average. The appropriate average valuation, then, is a function of the forecast growth rate which is naturally a moving target.

Premium Stability

The stability of any equity risk premium is an issue no matter how risk is defined. Our equity risk premiums change over time as sectors or markets develop and mature, causing changes in a consensus growth-rate forecast. Higher growth sectors, markets, and shares command higher premiums to bonds, EPS, and forecast EPS growth rates. Truly superior long-term growth does not continue forever, largely because at some point the sector or stock would become the whole economy or the market. There are structural limits to growth.

Valuation by Scenario

We value sectors, markets, and shares by evaluating trailing and forecast P/E ratios relative to an inverse bond yield against an average rating to produce a fair value return (price) target. As a result, there only two inputs to our model: EPS and rating. If both inputs are correct, the price target will approximate actual performance. To the extent that the EPS or rating is incorrect, the price target will vary from actual performance. Valuation by scenario provides insight as to how the price target changes with varying EPS and rating inputs. The essence of valuation by scenario is to measure risk against return.

When we find sectors, markets and stocks, which are undervalued on trailing and forecast profits, we know that our risk is almost entirely based on the rating which we assign to the EPS. The rating (equity risk premium) is by far the most significant input, particularly since it can and does change over time, as sectors, markets, and shares are re-rated to reflect changes in the consensus growth-rate forecast. In general, we use the longest-term average rating that we can. When a sector, market, or share is being re-rated, a long-term growth rate overstates upside potential, and a shorter-term average or comparable valuation (e.g., P/E / growth rate) should be used. Developing an appropriate rating is the most important single decision and inevitably involves the exercise of judgment.

Once we decide on the appropriate rating, the next step is to evaluate the sensitivity of the price target in relation to various levels of EPS. We begin with the average EPS estimate one-year out (FY +1), followed by the bearish forecast (lowest estimate per company), the bullish forecast (highest estimate per company), and finally the trailing level. Each EPS scenario reveals something as to the nature of risk and return. The scenario which we ultimately accept is largely a function of our view of the profit cycle. If we believe that profits have peaked, we are more likely to use the bearish or trailing inputs than the average or even a bullish estimate. Conversely, if we think profits have troughed, then consensus or bullish EPS may be the correct inputs. Our EPS-estimate error models, which we will discuss shortly, provide valuable insight into the timing of peak and trough profits. See Table 4.

EPS Momentum and Estimate Error

We measure EPS momentum from I/B/E/S consensus 1997 EPS estimates relative to the 1996 estimate indexed to a base of 100, using a percent change formula calculated from absolute difference structure $((1+(X1-X0)/abs(X0))*100)$. This method of transformation allows the model to discriminate between a widening and narrowing net operating loss. The company data are market-capitalization weighted in dollars, using the previous year-end closing price and aggregated into sector, industry, and country benchmarks. An evaluation of the extent to which the consensus 1997 growth rate (+17 percent) is achievable, is the first step to finding the correct EPS input to our model. See Table 5.

TABLE 4. Global Sector Allocation

SECTOR STRATEGY—CONSENSUS EPS

31-Jul-96	P/E LTM	10-Year %	P/E FY +1	10-Year FY +1	Bond P/D	Disc /Prem	10-Year Mean	FVRT %
EURO 1,000-STOCK INDEX	21.0	7.1	14.8	7.9	12.7	1.17	1.56	33.5
USA 1,000-STOCK INDEX	19.9	6.8	15.1	7.6	13.2	1.14	1.25	9.1
JAPAN 1,000-STOCK INDEX *	48.8	3.3	44.6	4.1	24.7	1.80	2.05	13.5
GLOBAL 3,500 INDEX	27.2	5.9	22.1	6.5	15.3	1.44	1.72	19.6
BASIC MATERIAL	23.4	5.9	20.6	6.5	15.3	1.35	1.78	32.6
CONSUMER DURABLE	33.3	5.9	22.6	6.5	15.3	1.48	2.00	35.2
CONSUMER MERCHANDISE	25.4	5.9	20.9	6.5	15.3	1.37	1.67	22.2
CONSUMER NON-DURABLE	26.0	5.9	20.1	6.5	15.3	1.31	1.45	10.5
CONSUMER SERVICE	28.0	5.9	22.3	6.5	15.3	1.46	1.74	19.5
ENERGY	24.1	5.9	16.9	6.5	15.3	1.10	1.38	25.0
FINANCIAL	22.9	5.9	27.2	6.5	15.3	1.78	1.93	8.5
HEALTH CARE	24.8	5.9	18.7	6.5	15.3	1.23	1.52	23.7
INDUSTRIAL	29.9	5.9	25.5	6.5	15.3	1.66	1.95	16.9
TECHNOLOGY	26.6	5.9	20.5	6.5	15.3	1.34	1.70	26.9
UTILITY	19.7	5.9	17.1	6.5	15.3	1.12	1.21	8.1

SECTOR STRATEGY—BEARISH EPS

31-Jul-96	P/E LTM	10-Year %	P/E FY +1	10-Year FY +1	Bond P/D	Disc /Prem	10-Year Mean	FVRT %
EURO 1,000-STOCK INDEX	21.0	7.1	19.0	7.9	12.7	1.50	1.56	4.2
USA 1,000-STOCK INDEX	19.9	6.8	18.0	7.6	13.2	1.36	1.25	-8.4
JAPAN 1,000-STOCK INDEX *	48.8	3.3	54.8	4.1	24.7	2.22	2.05	-7.8
GLOBAL 3,500-STOCK INDEX*	27.2	5.8	26.4	6.5	15.3	1.72	1.72	0.0
BASIC MATERIAL	23.4	5.9	28.5	6.5	15.3	1.86	1.78	-4.3
CONSUMER DURABLE	33.3	5.9	28.4	6.5	15.3	1.86	2.00	7.7
CONSUMER MERCHANDISE	25.4	5.9	24.4	6.5	15.3	1.60	1.67	4.6
CONSUMER NON-DURABLE	26.0	5.9	22.7	6.5	15.3	1.48	1.45	-2.3
CONSUMER SERVICE	28.0	5.9	24.6	6.5	15.3	1.61	1.74	8.5
ENERGY	24.1	5.9	23.0	6.5	15.3	1.51	1.38	-8.4
FINANCIAL	22.9	5.9	30.2	6.5	15.3	1.97	1.93	-2.0
HEALTH CARE	24.8	5.9	22.2	6.5	15.3	1.45	1.52	4.6
INDUSTRIAL	29.9	5.9	30.2	6.5	15.3	1.98	1.95	-1.5
TECHNOLOGY	26.6	5.9	26.1	6.5	15.3	1.71	1.70	-0.4
UTILITY	19.7	5.9	21.1	6.5	15.3	1.38	1.21	-12.6

(*) Four-year average valuation.
Source: Compustat, WorldScope, I/B/E/S & IMI estimates.

TABLE 4 (continued)

SECTOR STRATEGY—BULLISH EPS

31-Jul-96	P/E LTM	10-Year %	P/E FY +1	10-Year FY +1	Bond P/D	Disc /Prem	10-Year Mean	FVRT %
EURO 1,000-STOCK INDEX	21.0	7.1	13.5	7.9	12.7	1.06	1.56	46.5
USA 1,000-STOCK INDEX	19.9	6.8	14.8	7.6	13.2	1.12	1.25	11.7
JAPAN 1,000-STOCK INDEX *	48.8	3.3	37.9	4.1	24.7	1.53	2.05	33.6
GLOBAL 3,500-STOCK INDEX*	27.2	5.8	19.8	6.5	15.3	1.30	1.72	32.9
BASIC MATERIAL	23.4	5.9	17.4	6.5	15.3	1.14	1.78	57.1
CONSUMER DURABLE	33.3	5.9	20.0	6.5	15.3	1.31	2.00	52.9
CONSUMER MERCHANDISE	25.4	5.9	20.8	6.5	15.3	1.36	1.67	22.6
CONSUMER NON-DURABLE	26.0	5.9	19.5	6.5	15.3	1.28	1.45	13.7
CONSUMER SERVICE	28.0	5.9	21.6	6.5	15.3	1.41	1.74	23.5
ENERGY	24.1	5.9	14.6	6.5	15.3	0.96	1.38	44.3
FINANCIAL	22.9	5.9	22.0	6.5	15.3	1.44	1.93	34.3
HEALTH CARE	24.8	5.9	17.8	6.5	15.3	1.16	1.52	30.5
INDUSTRIAL	29.9	5.9	24.0	6.5	15.3	1.57	1.95	24.1
TECHNOLOGY	26.6	5.9	19.1	6.5	15.3	1.25	1.70	36.1
UTILITY	19.7	5.9	16.1	6.5	15.3	1.05	1.21	14.7

SECTOR STRATEGY—TRAILING EPS

31-Jul-96	P/E LTM	10-Year %	P/E FY +1	10-Year FY +1	Bond P/D	Disc /Prem	10-Year Mean	FVRT %
EURO 1,000-STOCK INDEX	21.0	7.1	21.0	7.9	12.7	1.66	1.56	-6.1
USA 1,000-STOCK INDEX	19.9	6.8	19.9	7.6	13.2	1.50	1.25	-16.9
JAPAN 1,000-STOCK INDEX *	48.8	3.3	48.8	4.1	24.7	1.98	2.05	3.6
GLOBAL 3,500-STOCK INDEX*	27.2	5.8	27.2	6.5	15.3	1.78	1.72	-3.2
BASIC MATERIAL	23.4	5.9	23.4	6.5	15.3	1.53	1.78	16.8
CONSUMER DURABLE	33.3	5.9	33.3	6.5	15.3	2.18	2.00	-8.0
CONSUMER MERCHANDISE	25.4	5.9	25.4	6.5	15.3	1.66	1.67	0.5
CONSUMER NON-DURABLE	26.0	5.9	26.0	6.5	15.3	1.70	1.45	-14.7
CONSUMER SERVICE	28.0	5.9	28.0	6.5	15.3	1.83	1.74	-4.6
ENERGY	24.1	5.9	24.1	6.5	15.3	1.58	1.38	-12.4
FINANCIAL	22.9	5.9	22.9	6.5	15.3	1.49	1.93	29.3
HEALTH CARE	24.8	5.9	24.8	6.5	15.3	1.62	1.52	-6.5
INDUSTRIAL	29.9	5.9	29.9	6.5	15.3	1.95	1.95	-0.4
TECHNOLOGY	26.6	5.9	26.6	6.5	15.3	1.74	1.70	-2.2
UTILITY	19.7	5.9	19.7	6.5	15.3	1.29	1.21	-6.2

(*) Four-year average valuation.
Source: Compustat, WorldScope, I/B/E/S & IMI estimates.

We use a similar approach to develop our EPS-estimate error models so that 1997 estimates can be put in the context of the profit cycle and adjusted accordingly. For each year, we express the average estimate in January as a percentage of the final reported number indexed to a base of 100. Analyst estimate-error bottoms at peak EPS levels and is maximized at the trough. By following EPS estimate error, we can better judge relative position in the profit cycle, which, in turn, affects our thinking on the cyclicals (basic material, consumer durable, industrial, and technology) as well as our view on which EPS input is most appropriate to use. See Table 6.

Construction

Segment Revenue Assignment

We assign companies to sectors and industries based on a segment revenue majority and, occasionally, price correlation. For most shares, segment revenue majority provides the best and simplest way to classify stocks, even in the case of conglomerates for which there is no clear majority and for which there is considerable diversity between segments of a company's business portfolio. Occasionally, when there are two large and economically diverse business segments, it makes sense to assign the stock based on how it actually trades.

Homogeneous Sectors

The creation of homogeneous sectors develops from the consistent application of assignment by segment revenue majority. Sectors need to be consistent across markets in order for results to have the maximum predicative value. Consistent sectors also have better correlation with economic cycles and less correlation with each other.

Country Effects

Country effects result from a natural overweight or underweight in a particular sector. For example, the French market has a natural bias toward consumer nondurable and against industrial, technology, and utility as is detailed in Table 7. Germany has a bias toward basic material, consumer durable, and financial, and against consumer nondurable, consumer service, energy, and health care. Italy has a natural overweight in consumer durable, energy, financial, and utility, but is underweight consumer nondurable, consumer service, health care, and technology. Japan is overweight consumer durable, financial, and industrial, and underweight

TABLE 5. Global EPS Estimate Momentum (local currency)

31-Jul-96	% of Total	EPS Y-Y	EPS -1M	EPS -3M	EPS -6M	EPS -9M	EPS -12M
GLOBAL 3,500-STOCK INDEX	100.0	117.2	117.7	118.9	121.0	125.8	127.5
CYCLICAL INDEX	36.4	119.1	119.4	127.5	132.8	143.7	149.8
INDUSTRIAL	11.3	116.2	116.3	120.7	124.0	130.6	139.2
INDUSTRIAL MACHINERY	2.4	115.6	115.7	122.7	117.2	125.3	141.3
COMMERCIAL SERVICE	0.8	115.7	115.5	116.6	118.8	120.8	125.5
CONGLOMERATE	3.0	113.5	113.6	114.1	116.6	119.7	121.3
CONSTRUCTION	2.9	119.0	119.2	122.8	132.8	145.6	155.0
FABRICATED METAL	0.4	124.9	126.1	135.1	148.7	161.0	185.1
MARINE TRANSPORTATION	0.4	127.4	127.2	121.3	131.5	136.6	140.9
SURFACE TRANSPORTATION	1.4	112.4	112.5	125.4	128.6	128.7	137.5
TECHNOLOGY	11.3	121.2	121.6	132.0	134.9	140.6	137.7
AEROSPACE	0.9	130.1	129.9	130.1	128.4	122.6	121.3
ELECTRICAL	2.8	116.1	116.1	118.2	120.0	122.8	122.8
ELECTRONIC	6.1	120.4	121.1	139.0	142.2	152.4	146.7
TELECOMMUNICATION	1.5	128.7	129.1	130.4	136.7	136.2	139.2
BASIC MATERIAL	7.6	117.7	118.4	131.7	143.2	166.9	180.0
ALUMINUM	0.4	134.7	137.9	157.2	164.3	172.7	165.7
CHEMICAL	2.6	113.3	113.7	145.4	141.0	139.9	146.3
CONTAINERS & PACKAGING	0.4	114.8	115.5	123.0	129.2	155.4	170.0
NON-FERROUS METAL	0.9	125.5	127.4	138.5	146.4	167.7	170.4
PAPER	1.2	117.4	117.4	112.0	165.7	256.6	284.2
SPECIALTY CHEMICAL	1.0	113.4	113.5	114.5	116.4	120.0	122.6
STEEL & IRON ORE	1.3	121.1	121.8	126.0	144.1	177.3	211.0
ENERGY	5.6	109.8	109.9	109.5	107.6	112.5	116.0
INTEGRATED OIL	4.1	106.2	106.6	105.5	105.1	109.1	108.6
OIL & GAS PRODUCTION	0.5	122.3	121.6	121.0	115.0	130.6	142.5
OIL REFINING & MARKETING	0.9	117.7	117.2	119.9	114.1	116.7	132.4
FINANCIAL	21.7	121.7	122.9	111.4	111.3	112.3	112.7
BANK	13.2	127.7	129.6	112.7	112.4	113.8	115.0
FINANCE	1.2	116.3	116.2	118.2	117.8	117.1	118.3

TABLE 5 (continued)

31-Jul-96	% of Total	EPS Y-Y	EPS -1M	EPS -3M	EPS -6M	EPS -9M	EPS -12M
INSURANCE	4.5	109.9	110.0	112.0	110.9	107.8	106.0
INVESTMENT FIRM	1.4	124.8	125.4	99.1	96.2	106.9	105.3
REAL ESTATE	1.3	104.3	104.6	102.7	111.8	113.7	116.0
UTILITY	11.5	108.5	108.6	110.7	109.6	109.7	110.3
ELECTRIC & WATER	5.0	106.2	106.1	107.6	107.9	108.3	108.5
NATURAL GAS	0.9	108.3	108.4	110.5	112.8	114.5	113.0
TELEPHONE	5.6	110.6	110.9	113.4	110.6	110.3	111.5
CONSUMER DURABLE	6.2	122.1	122.1	126.8	132.4	144.8	154.1
AUTOMOBILE	2.6	128.7	128.8	133.0	142.7	164.4	185.5
AUTO SUPPLY	1.1	113.8	113.7	118.3	121.4	129.0	137.0
CONSUMER ELECTRONIC	1.7	119.2	119.2	125.8	129.2	128.7	134.2
TEXTILE & APPAREL	0.8	118.0	118.0	119.9	120.1	136.1	116.2
CONSUMER NON-DURABLE	7.9	112.9	112.9	114.4	116.2	117.0	117.5
ALCOHOL & TOBACCO	2.5	110.1	110.0	110.4	113.2	113.4	113.2
FOOD & BEVERAGE	3.8	115.0	115.0	115.9	116.9	119.1	119.7
PACKAGED GOODS	1.7	112.4	112.5	116.9	119.2	117.4	118.9
CONSUMER SERVICE	5.1	121.8	122.8	126.7	138.0	148.8	143.0
AIR TRANSPORTATION	0.7	110.6	110.5	119.8	121.0	121.7	136.6
BROADCASTING	1.3	141.8	145.8	149.3	184.2	218.9	185.6
HOTEL & RESTAURANT	0.9	118.4	117.3	124.1	131.8	131.3	129.4
PRINTING & PUBLISHING	1.5	114.2	114.5	116.1	117.8	121.3	123.0
RECREATION	0.7	116.0	116.1	116.8	117.9	123.0	127.5
CONSUMER MERCHANDISE	4.8	116.9	116.9	118.3	121.9	130.3	133.5
CHAIN STORE	3.5	117.9	118.0	120.0	123.9	134.2	138.0
FOOD CHAIN	1.2	113.8	113.8	113.2	116.2	118.7	120.4
HEALTH CARE	7.2	115.6	115.8	118.0	117.7	117.2	116.7
MEDICAL DEVICE & SERVICE	1.1	119.7	121.1	128.9	128.7	129.2	126.3
PHARMACEUTICAL	6.0	114.8	114.8	116.0	115.6	114.9	114.8

Note: Index value of 100 indicates consensus '97E = '96E.

Source: Compustat, WorldScope, I/B/E/S & IMI estimates.

125

TABLE 6. EPS Estimate Error

GLOBAL SECTOR & INDUSTRY MODEL

9-Aug-96 BENCHMARK	Jan 1987	Jan 1988	Jan 1989	Jan 1990	Jan 1991	Jan 1992	Jan 1993	Jan 1994	Jan 1995	Jan 1996E
GLOBAL 3,500-STOCK INDEX	119	102	116	133	142	147	141	116	120	109
CYCLICAL INDEX	114	91	108	136	158	163	159	113	116	117
BASIC MATERIAL	97	79	107	142	176	180	171	108	100	130
ALUMINIUM	111	51	85	165	212	210	203	76	78	125
CHEMICAL	98	84	106	141	142	194	192	97	91	111
CONTAINERS & PACKAGING	106	98	103	122	129	130	139	119	144	134
NON-FERROUS METAL	98	87	111	129	187	154	169	109	108	119
PAPER	87	88	116	164	209	220	151	112	84	171
SPECIALTY CHEMICAL	91	88	118	124	148	142	147	108	97	107
STEEL & IRON ORE	88	57	107	146	205	214	194	131	101	142
CONSUMER DURABLE	105	95	117	148	149	181	172	108	129	107
AUTOMOBILE	106	102	121	202	183	192	175	83	135	105
AUTO SUPPLY	93	89	154	141	166	135	142	114	121	106
CONSUMER ELECTRONIC	132	98	96	125	128	247	207	105	130	101
TEXTILE & APPAREL	89	90	97	125	120	148	164	132	130	116
CONSUMER MERCHANDISE	108	110	107	110	119	127	138	122	118	110
CHAIN STORE	111	114	115	118	119	138	117	126	129	115
FOOD CHAIN	105	106	99	102	119	116	159	118	106	105
CONSUMER NON-DURABLE	111	98	100	114	116	114	151	106	118	106
ALCOHOL & TOBACCO	104	102	98	134	119	120	138	99	103	104
FOOD & BEVERAGE	97	95	106	108	107	117	119	118	127	107
PACKAGED GOODS	133	96	95	101	121	106	195	100	125	108
CONSUMER SERVICE	112	99	120	132	153	130	130	117	125	115
AIR TRANSPORTATION	109	91	111	175	197	159	157	128	127	102
BROADCASTING	96	102	139	127	159	136	119	115	154	146
HOTEL & RESTAURANT	96	110	108	110	138	122	113	104	113	111
PRINTING & PUBLISHING	112	98	120	124	122	116	113	106	117	110
RECREATION	147	96	120	125	149	117	149	131	113	106
ENERGY	113	120	130	115	169	189	149	119	131	110
INTEGRATED OIL	120	90	135	101	181	164	121	104	118	100
OIL & GAS PRODUCTION	95	152	140	132	220	201	193	143	124	113

126

TABLE 6 (continued)

9-Aug-96 BENCHMARK	Jan 1987	Jan 1988	Jan 1989	Jan 1990	Jan 1991	Jan 1992	Jan 1993	Jan 1994	Jan 1995	Jan 1996E
OIL REFINING & MARKETING	125	117	115	111	107	201	134	109	149	118
FINANCIAL	138	114	117	160	167	159	113	151	125	106
BANK	194	104	139	169	143	157	155	144	155	106
FINANCE	140	118	114	157	125	144	106	109	109	102
INSURANCE	160	137	144	150	172	138	116	125	123	100
INVESTMENT FIRM	101	110	93	216	281	232	70	271	103	112
REAL ESTATE	96	100	95	107	114	126	118	106	137	107
HEALTH CARE	118	134	112	106	109	130	125	111	114	103
MEDICAL DEVICE & SERVICE	133	163	107	106	109	151	122	115	123	103
PHARMACEUTICAL	103	106	116	107	109	108	128	107	105	102
INDUSTRIAL	135	96	100	126	155	154	155	125	121	114
INDUSTRIAL MACHINERY	142	91	119	132	155	189	170	106	99	101
COMMERCIAL SERVICE	127	112	106	116	122	133	140	111	108	103
CONGLOMERATE	116	95	95	122	159	145	147	118	119	110
CONSTRUCTION	116	91	94	122	153	173	138	123	133	129
FABRICATED METAL	141	99	123	139	200	145	171	115	118	125
MARINE TRANSPORTATION	186	93	63	125	129	137	126	147	123	121
SURFACE TRANSPORTATION	114	93	101	123	165	155	195	155	146	112
TECHNOLOGY	116	100	115	131	140	134	133	108	122	111
AEROSPACE	141	99	122	114	154	128	126	118	161	96
ELECTRICAL	119	93	98	138	133	139	139	110	108	110
ELECTRONIC	90	83	121	144	160	171	126	84	102	107
TELECOMMUNICATION	116	125	119	127	112	99	143	121	119	131
UTILITY	125	119	114	121	109	123	139	118	100	105
ELECTRIC & WATER	126	114	130	126	106	114	123	102	106	105
NATURAL GAS	153	122	125	141	124	161	163	159	104	107
TELEPHONE	96	120	85	96	97	94	132	92	89	103

Note: Value of 100 means reported EPS = estimated EPS 12-months forward.

Source: Compustat, WorldScope, I/B/E/S & IMI estimates.

127

TABLE 7. Sector Weights

1. BY MARKET

31-Dec-95 Benchmark	France %	German %	Italy %	Japan %	Dutch %	Spain %	Sweden %	Swiss %	UK %	USA %
GLOBAL 3,500-STOCK INDEX	100.0	100.0	100.0	100.0	100.0	100.0	100.0	100.0	100.0	100.0
CYCLICAL INDEX	31.0	49.6	20.5	48.2	14.5	10.5	63.0	18.6	22.6	35.6
BASIC MATERIAL	7.0	16.2	2.8	7.5	5.5	1.6	14.8	9.3	4.7	6.5
CONSUMER DURABLE	6.6	11.7	9.9	13.0	4.8	0.2	8.8	1.3	1.3	3.6
CONSUMER MERCHANDISE	9.1	2.5	2.0	4.5	3.0	4.9	1.7	0.3	9.3	4.7
CONSUMER NON-DURABLE	16.8	0.0	1.2	3.7	18.7	1.8	0.0	16.3	10.8	10.2
CONSUMER SERVICE	4.1	1.7	1.4	2.7	11.0	0.0	0.9	0.7	6.7	5.8
ENERGY	10.2	0.0	14.4	1.3	25.8	9.7	0.0	0.0	9.3	8.0
FINANCIAL	19.2	32.9	37.8	28.2	21.2	34.0	10.3	31.0	17.1	14.0
HEALTH CARE	4.5	0.7	0.7	2.9	0.0	0.0	19.4	33.1	12.4	10.0
INDUSTRIAL	9.5	9.6	5.6	18.5	3.2	8.5	19.8	4.3	12.1	6.7
TECHNOLOGY	7.8	12.0	2.2	9.2	1.0	0.1	19.5	3.7	4.5	18.8
UTILITY	5.1	12.6	22.0	8.5	5.8	39.2	4.7	0.0	11.8	11.7

2. ACROSS ALL MARKETS

31-Dec-95 Benchmark	France %	German %	Italy %	Japan %	Dutch %	Spain %	Sweden %	Swiss %	UK %	USA %
GLOBAL 3,500-STOCK INDEX	3.4	4.3	1.7	28.4	2.4	1.1	1.2	2.9	9.7	45.0
CYCLICAL INDEX	3.0	5.8	1.1	38.7	1.2	0.3	2.1	1.9	6.0	40.0
BASIC MATERIAL	3.0	9.2	0.7	31.1	1.9	0.2	2.6	3.9	7.1	40.2
CONSUMER DURABLE	3.2	6.8	2.5	55.9	1.8	0.1	1.6	0.6	2.4	25.1
CONSUMER MERCHANDISE	5.5	2.2	0.7	25.7	1.4	1.0	0.4	0.3	18.6	44.2
CONSUMER NON-DURABLE	6.4	0.7	0.3	12.9	5.6	0.2	0.0	6.1	12.5	55.3
CONSUMER SERVICE	4.0	1.2	0.5	15.9	5.6	0.0	0.2	0.4	16.1	56.0
ENERGY	5.7	0.0	4.4	6.6	11.4	1.9	0.6	0.0	15.4	54.6
FINANCIAL	3.7	6.5	3.0	38.5	2.2	1.7	0.6	3.9	8.8	31.2
HEALTH CARE	1.7	1.5	0.2	10.6	0.0	0.0	2.7	11.6	10.9	60.8
INDUSTRIAL	3.5	3.9	0.8	47.5	0.7	0.9	2.2	2.0	10.9	27.6
TECHNOLOGY	2.1	3.4	0.3	20.4	0.2	0.0	1.9	0.9	3.7	67.2
UTILITY	1.4	5.9	3.4	22.4	1.3	3.8	0.5	0.2	10.7	50.4

Note: Section 1 adds to 100% from top to bottom and Section 2 adds to 100% from left to right.
Source: Compustat, WorldScope & IMI estimates.

consumer nondurable, consumer service, energy, and health care. The Netherlands has a natural bias toward consumer nondurable, consumer service, and energy, and away from health care, industrial, technology, and utility. Spain has a bias toward energy, financial, and utility, and away from basic material, consumer durable, consumer nondurable, consumer service, health care, and technology. Sweden is overweight basic material, consumer durable, health care, industrial, and technology, and underweight the balance of the consumer sectors, as well as energy, financial, and utility. Switzerland is overweight consumer nondurable, financial, and health care, and underweight the balance of our sectors. The United Kingdom, and the United States are the most evenly balanced markets. The United Kingdom has a natural bias toward consumer merchandise, and consumer nondurable, and away from consumer durable, and technology. The United States has a natural bias toward health care, and technology, and away from industrial, and financial. In short, sector strategy is, to some extent, inseparable from country strategy.

Results

Global Sector Allocation

Normal exposure to global shares. Our fair value return target (+20 percent) is based on consensus 1997 EPS estimates, a 75-basis-point increase in bond yields and a four-year average valuation. We think a shorter-term premium is warranted, given a re-rating of Japan and Germany. Regionally, we recommend normal exposure to the Euro-Pacific (56 percent) and to the United States (44 percent), with a modest preference for Europe (48 percent versus 46 percent) as opposed to the Pacific (52 percent versus 54 percent). See Figure 1.

Overweight exposure in basic material (12 percent versus 8 percent). With a fair value return target which is greater than the market overall (+33 percent), we prefer the chemical and paper shares to the steel and iron ore and nonferrous metal companies. See Figure 2.

Overweight exposure in consumer durable (12 percent versus 6 percent). Our notion of fair value includes a 35 percent return target for the sector. Unlike industrial, we think selected shares in this group can deliver secular EPS growth over the next several years. See Figure 3.

Overweight exposure in consumer merchandise (9 percent versus 5 percent). Re-rated down from peak valuations in 1990, this sector has significant upside potential. It is created from the chain stores and the food chains, and blends our favorite consumer cyclical and growth themes. We prefer the chain stores to the food chains. Our fair value return target is 22 percent. See Figure 4.

Underweight exposure in consumer nondurable (6 percent versus 8 percent). The sector is approaching fair value (+11 percent); we think investors will not accept a higher-than-average rating for the shares. Overweight food and beverage instead of alcohol and tobacco stocks. See Figure 5.

Overweight exposure in consumer service (6 percent versus 5 percent). This sector also blends consumer cyclical and growth themes; we find the bullish scenario (+24 percent) most credible. Overweight the broadcasting, hotel and restaurant and recreation shares relative to the printing and publishing stocks. See Figure 6.

Underweight exposure in energy (3 percent versus 5 percent). Despite a fair value return target (+25 percent) greater than the market overall, we think the sector deserves a modest underweight, as a hedge against an increase in interest rates and/or inflation. See Figure 7.

Underweight exposure in financial (12 percent versus 21 percent). The group outperformed during the fourth-quarter 1995; we changed our opinion from overweight to underweight in order to facilitate a rotation back into the cyclicals. We think the sector is being re-rated in Japan, which accounts for 39 percent of all financial shares. Our fair value return target is 9 percent. See Figure 8.

Normal exposure in health care (7 percent). Relative valuations versus value shares are approaching neutral for "growth" based on consensus 1997 estimates, and we recommend reducing exposure back to a market weight; our fair value return target is 24 percent. See Figure 9.

Underweight exposure in industrial (9 percent versus 12 percent). The sector has a fair value return target which is greater than the market overall (+17 percent); we reduced our underweight on the basis of our view of the timing of peak EPS. See Figure 10.

Overweight exposure in technology (15 percent versus 12 percent). Our notion of fair value includes a 27 percent return target for these shares. We think technology offers secular EPS growth not widely available in the cyclicals. Overweight the electrical and electronic companies relative to the aerospace and telecom equipment shares. See Figure 11.

Underweight exposure in utility (9 percent versus 11 percent). With a fair value return target of 8 percent, we think the shares deserve an underweight position. Overweight the telephone shares relative to the electric and water and natural gas companies. See Figure 12.

FIGURE 1. Global

Jul-96	1987	1988	1989	1990	1991	1992	1993	1994	1995	FY +1
Y-T-D % Chg	1.1	28.1	25.3	-14.1	21.8	3.9	28.6	-0.8	21.9	3.0
P/E Multiple	28.1	29.3	31.9	25.1	30.2	28.3	28.9	25.0	25.2	22.1
P/CF Multiple	21.0	22.4	23.6	18.0	20.1	18.0	18.7	17.9	21.1	12.5
P/B Multiple	3.5	3.7	3.8	2.7	3.1	2.9	3.1	2.9	3.2	3.1
Dividend Yield	2.1	2.0	1.9	2.5	2.3	2.3	2.1	2.1	2.0	2.8
Fair Value Return Target									→	19.6

EQUITY RISK PREMIUM

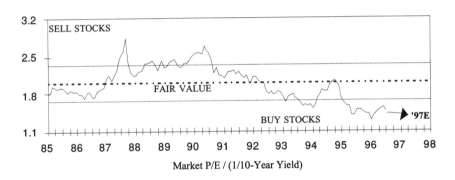

Market P/E / (1/10-Year Yield)

3,500-STOCK INDEX

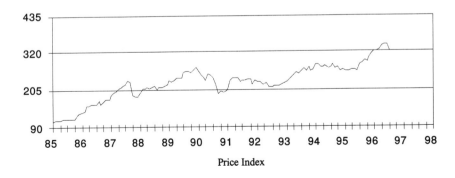

Price Index

Source: Compustat, WorldScope, I/B/E/S and IMI estimates.

FIGURE 2.   Basic Material

Jul-96	1987	1988	1989	1990	1991	1992	1993	1994	1995	FY +1
Y-T-D % Chg	23.3	52.5	18.3	-21.1	15.9	-1.9	27.7	5.5	9.7	3.4
P/E Multiple	26.3	29.6	30.9	20.9	26.8	30.3	32.9	26.6	21.8	20.6
P/CF Multiple	15.9	18.1	20.3	13.1	15.5	13.8	14.5	13.5	18.5	10.3
P/R Multiple	2.8	4.0	3.4	2.1	2.2	2.2	2.5	2.4	2.7	2.6
Dividend Yield	2.1	2.0	2.1	3.1	2.6	2.5	1.9	1.9	2.2	2.8
Fair Value Return Target									→	**32.6**

EQUITY RISK PREMIUM

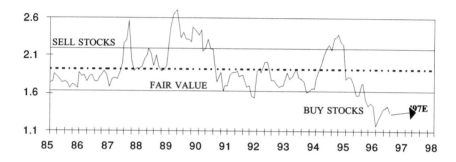

SECTOR BENCHMARK

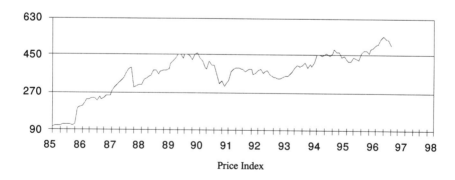

Price Index

Source: Compustat, WorldScope, I/B/E/S and IMI estimates.

FIGURE 3. Consumer Durable

Jul-96	1987	1988	1989	1990	1991	1992	1993	1994	1995	FY +1
Y-T-D % Chg	4.3	32.1	24.7	-26.8	11.2	3.4	27.6	4.2	8.3	8.3
P/E Multiple	21.9	25.5	30.3	23.3	28.3	31.6	38.1	34.9	30.2	22.6
P/CF Multiple	13.0	15.8	18.6	12.8	13.1	11.5	14.7	15.7	25.8	9.9
P/B Multiple	2.0	2.4	2.8	2.1	2.0	1.9	2.1	2.0	2.0	2.1
Dividend Yield	2.1	1.7	1.6	2.3	1.8	1.6	1.2	1.3	1.4	2.6
Fair Value Return Target									→	**35.2**

EQUITY RISK PREMIUM

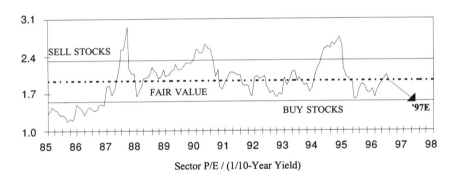

Sector P/E / (1/10-Year Yield)

SECTOR BENCHMARK

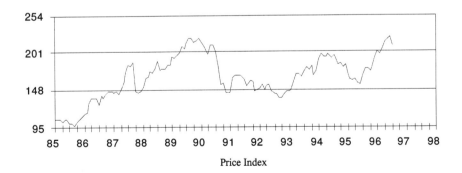

Price Index

Source: Compustat, WorldScope, I/B/E/S and IMI estimates.

FIGURE 4.   Consumer Merchandise

Jul-96	1987	1988	1989	1990	1991	1992	1993	1994	1995	FY +1
Y-T-D % Chg	0.4	25.9	33.6	-5.3	41.6	14.6	22.6	-2.1	12.8	9.7
P/E Multiple	23.2	26.2	32.2	23.2	29.9	28.0	28.6	25.1	24.8	20.9
P/CF Multiple	16.4	21.0	24.5	17.1	21.9	20.1	19.7	17.0	21.0	14.4
P/B Multiple	3.4	3.6	4.4	3.3	4.5	4.2	3.8	3.3	3.4	3.4
Dividend Yield	2.0	1.8	1.5	2.0	1.5	1.5	1.5	1.7	1.4	2.3
Fair Value Return Target									⟶	**22.2**

EQUITY RISK PREMIUM

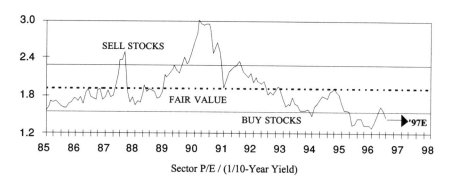

Sector P/E / (1/10-Year Yield)

SECTOR BENCHMARK

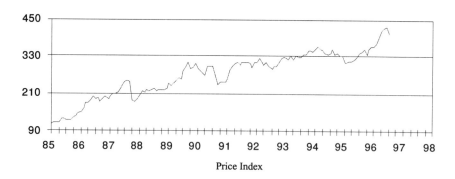

Price Index

Source: Compustat, WorldScope, I/B/E/S and IMI estimates.

FIGURE 5.   Consumer Non-Durable

Jul-96	1987	1988	1989	1990	1991	1992	1993	1994	1995	FY +1
Y-T-D % Chg	7.0	17.5	37.9	4.1	33.9	7.0	9.6	-0.3	24.9	7.7
P/E Multiple	26.8	26.5	24.7	19.3	24.5	22.4	26.1	21.3	23.7	20.1
P/CF Multiple	17.5	18.8	19.6	14.4	16.6	14.9	16.1	14.9	19.0	14.3
P/B Multiple	3.1	3.1	3.9	3.4	4.4	4.6	4.4	3.9	4.0	4.9
Dividend Yield	2.1	2.2	2.0	2.3	2.0	2.1	2.2	2.4	2.2	3.1
Fair Value Return Target									$\longrightarrow$	**10.5**

EQUITY RISK PREMIUM

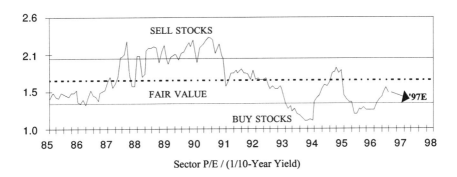

Sector P/E / (1/10-Year Yield)

SECTOR BENCHMARK

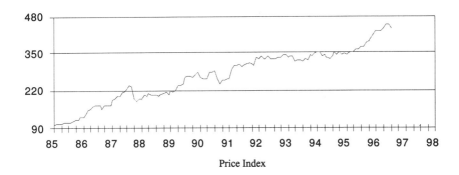

Price Index

Source: Compustat, WorldScope, I/B/E/S and IMI estimates.

FIGURE 6.   Consumer Service

Jul-96	1987	1988	1989	1990	1991	1992	1993	1994	1995	FY +1
Y-T-D % Chg	8.1	22.0	26.8	-18.8	23.3	12.3	38.3	-4.9	22.8	3.9
P/E Multiple	22.2	23.1	22.5	20.2	25.4	26.2	28.9	25.2	26.8	22.3
P/CF Multiple	17.5	17.9	17.3	14.4	18.3	14.5	21.2	16.9	19.9	14.2
P/B Multiple	4.3	4.5	3.9	3.4	3.6	3.7	4.5	4.0	4.1	3.9
Dividend Yield	1.6	1.5	1.3	1.9	1.6	1.6	1.3	1.4	1.3	2.1
Fair Value Return Target									→	19.5

EQUITY RISK PREMIUM

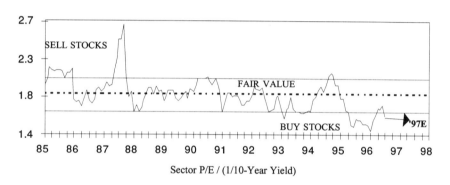

Sector P/E / (1/10-Year Yield)

SECTOR BENCHMARK

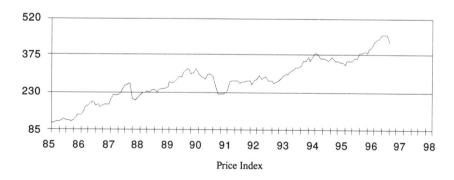

Price Index

Source: Compustat, WorldScope, I/B/E/S and IMI estimates.

FIGURE 7. Energy

Jul-96	1987	1988	1989	1990	1991	1992	1993	1994	1995	FY +1
Y-T-D % Chg	-4.0	19.8	28.1	-1.1	10.6	-4.0	24.7	-2.3	20.2	6.4
P/E Multiple	17.1	16.4	26.1	15.0	22.3	20.7	24.4	20.0	21.5	16.9
P/CF Multiple	7.8	9.0	11.2	7.8	8.9	8.9	10.1	8.5	12.6	8.2
P/B Multiple	1.6	1.9	2.4	1.9	1.9	1.8	2.1	2.0	2.3	2.4
Dividend Yield	4.7	4.4	3.6	4.3	4.1	4.3	3.6	3.6	3.3	3.4
Fair Value Return Target									⟶	25.0

EQUITY RISK PREMIUM

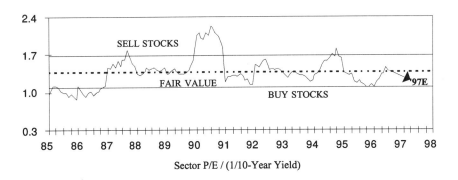

Sector P/E / (1/10-Year Yield)

SECTOR BENCHMARK

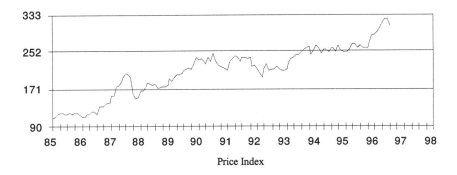

Price Index

Source: Compustat, WorldScope, I/B/E/S and IMI estimates.

FIGURE 8.   Financial

Jul-96	1987	1988	1989	1990	1991	1992	1993	1994	1995	FY +1
Y-T-D % Chg	-4.6	27.8	17.8	-24.3	20.7	4.0	39.0	-6.0	25.1	-0.4
P/E Multiple	37.6	41.0	42.7	38.3	41.9	35.9	30.7	24.7	24.8	27.2
P/CF Multiple	35.9	38.6	38.7	34.0	34.9	32.2	29.4	29.2	24.1	14.9
P/B Multiple	4.2	4.4	4.1	2.4	2.7	2.3	2.5	2.4	2.5	2.2
Dividend Yield	1.5	1.4	1.4	2.2	2.0	2.1	1.7	2.1	1.9	2.9
Fair Value Return Target									→	8.5

EQUITY RISK PREMIUM

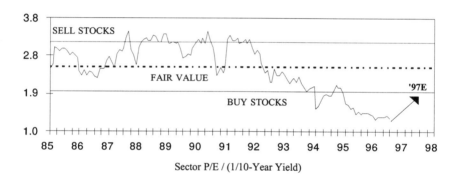

Sector P/E / (1/10-Year Yield)

SECTOR BENCHMARK

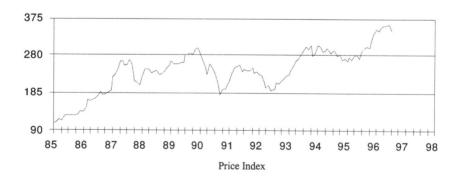

Price Index

Source: Compustat, WorldScope, I/B/E/S and IMI estimates.

FIGURE 9.   Health Care

Jul-96	1987	1988	1989	1990	1991	1992	1993	1994	1995	FY +1
Y-T-D % Chg	-1.3	7.8	29.8	7.7	60.3	2.5	9.3	3.3	45.8	2.4
P/E Multiple	33.3	29.0	29.7	23.4	31.1	25.0	23.7	20.8	24.1	18.7
P/CF Multiple	25.9	23.5	23.1	17.8	23.3	18.7	17.3	16.1	20.7	14.4
P/B Multiple	4.6	4.4	5.0	4.7	6.7	5.6	4.4	4.0	5.5	5.0
Dividend Yield	1.6	1.8	1.6	1.9	1.5	1.8	2.0	2.0	1.6	2.1
Fair Value Return Target									→	23.7

EQUITY RISK PREMIUM

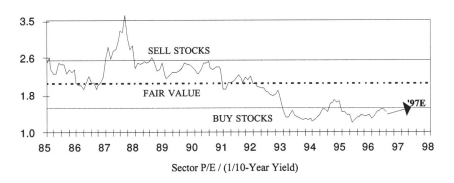

Sector P/E / (1/10-Year Yield)

SECTOR BENCHMARK

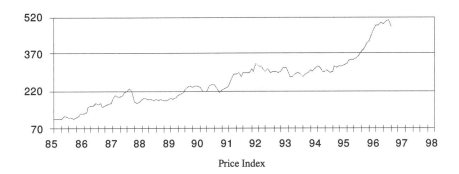

Price Index

Source: Compustat, WorldScope, I/B/E/S and IMI estimates.

FIGURE 10. Industrial

Jul-96	1987	1988	1989	1990	1991	1992	1993	1994	1995	FY +1
Y-T-D % Chg	6.9	43.0	38.3	-24.1	10.6	-4.9	31.9	-2.1	11.4	3.5
P/E Multiple	35.1	37.7	39.6	28.9	33.4	30.8	32.4	32.6	30.3	25.5
P/CF Multiple	26.0	28.9	30.9	20.8	23.0	19.6	20.0	19.6	27.0	14.2
P/B Multiple	3.1	3.9	4.7	2.7	2.8	2.5	2.7	2.5	2.7	2.6
Dividend Yield	1.7	1.5	1.3	2.1	1.9	2.0	1.6	1.8	1.8	2.5
Fair Value Return Target										**16.9**

EQUITY RISK PREMIUM

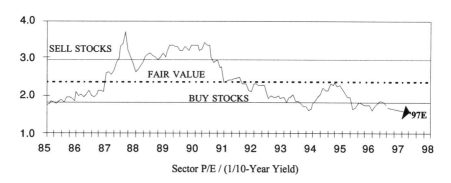

Sector P/E / (1/10-Year Yield)

SECTOR BENCHMARK

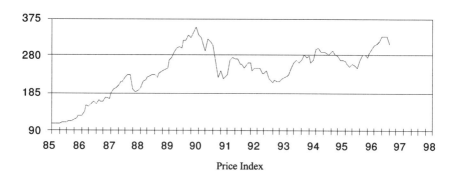

Price Index

Source: Compustat, WorldScope, I/B/E/S and IMI estimates.

FIGURE 11. Technology

Jul-96	1987	1988	1989	1990	1991	1992	1993	1994	1995	FY +1
Y-T-D % Chg	2.7	13.9	21.6	-9.2	19.6	8.0	33.0	10.7	34.0	4.8
P/E Multiple	26.6	23.0	26.1	19.6	28.3	25.8	27.5	25.3	26.4	20.5
P/CF Multiple	13.2	11.9	14.6	10.7	12.9	12.5	15.3	14.0	20.4	11.9
P/B Multiple	2.6	2.5	2.8	2.2	2.8	2.8	3.2	3.2	4.0	3.8
Dividend Yield	2.0	1.9	1.8	2.3	2.1	2.0	3.2	1.4	1.2	2.1
Fair Value Return Target									→	**26.9**

EQUITY RISK PREMIUM

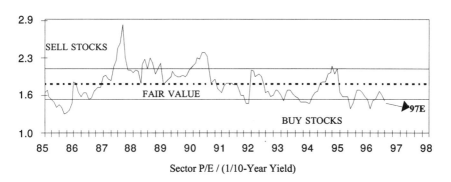

Sector P/E / (1/10-Year Yield)

SECTOR BENCHMARK

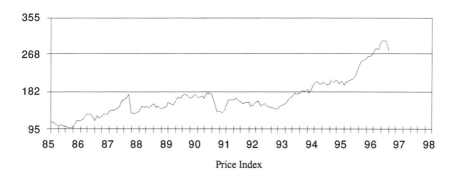

Price Index

Source: Compustat, WorldScope, I/B/E/S and IMI estimates.

FIGURE 12. Utility

Jul-96	1987	1988	1989	1990	1991	1992	1993	1994	1995	FY +1
Y-T-D % Chg	-17.3	36.3	17.4	-11.9	11.0	6.9	28.0	-9.2	17.5	-4.0
P/E Multiple	15.8	18.8	23.9	18.9	19.0	21.7	22.8	17.9	21.7	17.1
P/CF Multiple	13.0	13.5	13.3	8.6	8.9	8.4	11.1	11.8	15.6	7.4
P/B Multiple	4.7	4.1	3.5	2.3	2.3	2.3	2.9	2.7	3.2	2.9
Dividend Yield	3.2	3.1	3.0	4.0	3.8	3.9	3.2	3.6	3.3	4.0
Fair Value Return Target									⟶	8.1

EQUITY RISK PREMIUM

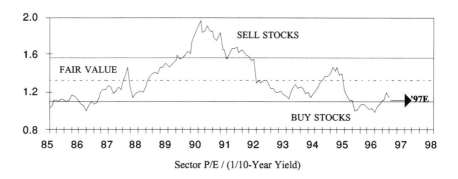

Sector P/E / (1/10-Year Yield)

SECTOR BENCHMARK

Price Index

Source: Compustat, WorldScope, I/B/E/S and IMI estimates.

Conclusion

The long-term performance and valuation illustrated in Figures 1 through 12 show the importance of the sector dimension. Notice the inverse correlation between the equity risk premium and sector performance. The dotted line is a 10-year average valuation plus and minus one standard-deviation to show broadly when stocks are expensive or undervalued relative to EPS and interest rates.

Sectors and markets where valuation premiums are being unwound from exaggerated levels require special care in order to develop an appropriate rating. It is our experience that even three to five years of valuation experience is enough to let various EPS scenarios provide insight into the nature of risk and return. In cases where there is simply not enough valuation experience for a credible historical average, we recommend a P/E to growth-rate comparable valuation to generate EPS scenarios from.

Style-Based Country-Selection Strategies

Rosemary Macedo
Senior Vice President
Quantitative Research and International Equities
Bailard, Biehl & Kaiser

This chapter refines previous research on investment style as it applies to country selection. It aims to distinguish among the many potential explanations for the observed variation in the cross section of national equity-market returns in relation to style factors. Only by understanding the causes of the observed historical relationships can we have confidence in applying these strategies going forward.

Just as in stock selection, country selection reflects distinct investment styles. For example, many stock pickers focus on undervalued stocks or on stocks characterized by high earnings momentum and high price momentum; similarly, many international equity managers focus on undervalued markets or on markets characterized by high earnings momentum and high price momentum. Keppler [1990a, 1990b], Keppler and Traub [1993], and Macedo [1995a, 1995b] have documented the potential benefits of style tilts which are applied to country selection.

New results presented in this chapter show that the excess returns to a value-based country-selection strategy cannot be accounted for solely as compensation for higher fundamental risk; that the excess returns to a relative strength-based (price momentum-based) strategy likewise cannot be accounted for as compensation for buying markets as they become riskier; and that market price momentum is not just a proxy for market earnings momentum.

In stock selection and in country selection, no investment style works all the time. Sometimes undervalued markets become even cheaper before returning to fair value, and no market remains the strongest performer forever. Conventional multifactor tilt approaches seek to smooth this variability in performance rather than to exploit it; style rotation seeks to actively exploit it.

Macedo [1995a, 1995b] hypothesized that global market volatility is a proxy for investor risk-aversion and, thus, should indicate the relative attractiveness of value- and momentum-based country-selection strategies. The linkage between volatility and the subsequent performance of these country-selection styles proved to be quite powerful. The linkage between volatility and risk aversion, however, was not independently tested.

New results employing fundamental risk ratings support the hypothesis that volatility is a reliable proxy for investor risk-aversion.

Direct comparison of a country style rotation strategy with a conventional multifactor tilt strategy reveals a nearly 5 percent per annum informational advantage, with greater consistency in added value and without additional turnover.

Overview

The chapter begins with a discussion of the rationale behind value and momentum strategies, and the evidence to date from stock selection and country-selection research. Political Risk Sciences' *International Country Risk Guide* (ICRG) risk ratings are then described, followed by a section that details the sources and availability of additional data used for this chapter.

Next, style tilts are evaluated. Quartile portfolios based on valuation ratios demonstrate that value effectively discriminates between attractive and unattractive markets. The exposure of these portfolios to fundamental risk, as measured by the ICRG ratings, proves insufficient to explain these excess returns.

Price momentum-based quartile portfolios also effectively discriminate between attractive and unattractive markets. The results are highly statistically significant, even after transaction costs. By comparison, results for earnings momentum are substantially weaker and shorter lived. Earnings momentum does not account for the success of the price momentum strategy. Nor do differences in fundamental risk or in changes in fundamental risk account for the results.

The remainder of the chapter relates to style timing.

The hypothesis that volatility is a proxy for investor risk-aversion is considered first. The flight-to-quality phenomenon suggests volatility as a proxy for risk aversion. Quartile portfolios based on fundamental risk, using the ICRG risk ratings, corroborate this intuition. The premium for investing in riskier markets doubles after periods when volatility has been high, when risk tolerance is presumed to be low.

Volatility is likewise shown to be a powerful ex ante indicator of the subsequent performance of value- and momentum-based country-selection strategies. Value strategies are rewarded when risk aversion is high, momentum when risk aversion is low.

A strategy that changes style between value and momentum, based on volatility, outperforms a more conventional strategy that tilts toward both factors every month. It is noteworthy that it does so with the same turnover as a conventional multifactor tilt strategy.

Indicators

This section discusses the rationale behind value and momentum strategies, presents the evidence to date from stock selection and country-selection research, and describes Political Risk Sciences' *International Country Risk Guide* (ICRG) risk ratings.

Valuation Ratios

The idea behind value-style investing is to buy assets that are cheap relative to some underlying value, such as book value, earnings, or dividends. When discount rates and expected returns are high, it follows from the dividend discount model that dividend yield likewise will be high.[1] The dividend discount model can be recast in terms of price-to-book value (P/BV) and price-to-earnings ratios (P/E). Each ratio captures different aspects of market expectations. Price-to-book value ratios reflect market participants' expectations regarding the level of future profitability. Price-to-earnings ratios reflect expectations regarding changes in profitability.[2]

There is an extensive body of research concerning value-based stock selection strategies. Tilts toward value characteristics have been documented to add value for stock selection in nine markets: Australia, Canada, France, Germany, Japan, Sweden, Switzerland, the United Kingdom, and the United States.[3]

For stock selection, the evidence to date does not support the idea that these ratios are simply proxies for fundamental risk that must be compensated for with higher returns.[4] Instead, the anomalous returns seem to stem from investors' tendencies to have excessively high expectations for "glamour" stocks—those of successful or well-run companies ("winners")—and excessively low expectations for those with recently poor results ("losers"). Aversion to regret reinforces this preference for glamour stocks. The prices of losers consequently end up more depressed than their extra risk justifies.

Shefrin and Statman's behavioral capital asset pricing theory [1994] provides the theoretical foundation for differentials in the returns to various investment styles—in other words, risk premia for investment styles. They support this theory with direct evidence that investment style is linked to investors' perceptions of quality and risk [1995].

With the value effect so widely publicized, how can it possibly continue? The inclination to believe that a good stock is the stock of a good company arises from representativeness, a cognitive error. Cognitive errors by definition are resistant to learning. Hence, despite widespread awareness of the value anomaly, one can expect value investing to continue to work due to this persistent personal and institutional preference for stocks of perceived winners.

Less research has been published regarding the application of value-tilts style to country selection. Keppler [1990a, 1990b] has documented the benefits of value tilts applied to country selection using dividend yield and cash flow-to-price. Keppler and Traub [1993] have documented the benefits of tilting toward smaller markets. Macedo [1995a, 1995b] has compared a variety of value-based strategies.

When applying style factors to country selection, two questions must be addressed. Is it valid to compare these ratios across countries? If so, are excess returns simply compensation for higher fundamental risk, or is there systematic mispricing of risk?

Conventional wisdom objects to comparing valuation ratios across countries because accounting methods are so varied. What matters, however, is that the methods are the relevant local standard. Anecdotal evidence, when individual companies have restated their accounts, shows that in the absence of actual restatements from one country's accounting standards to another's, the markets do not appear to make adjustments for differences in accounting standards. In practice, the differences do not appear to matter.

To sidestep issues of comparability, some practitioners normalize valuation ratios relative to their own history. This is akin to a comparison shopper buying apples for $3 per bag at ABC Market because they had increased only 5 percent from last week's price, rather than buying the apples for $2.50 per bag at XYZ Market which charged 20 percent less the previous week. Furthermore, the markets tend to get "cheap" together and tend to get "expensive" together, relative to their histories. Heckman and Sze [1995] demonstrate that normalizing equity market valuation ratios relative to the ratios' histories lessens their usefulness.

Another objection to direct comparison of valuation ratios across markets argues that the differences in valuation ratios among countries are justifiable on the basis of differing growth opportunities, differing risk, and other factors. The same argument obviously holds true for individual stocks. Yet there is abundant evidence that for individual stocks, systematic mispricing occurs, and there is a wide body of theory as to why.

The evidence from country selection does not support the hypothesis that these ratios are merely proxies for risk. Beta, volatility, and fundamental risk fail to account for the strength of the relationship between value and the cross section of returns.

Momentum

Relative strength, or price momentum, is just the percentage change in the local market index. It is usually measured over one year. An investor who focuses on relative strength, simply overweights those assets whose prices have risen the most, and underweights those whose prices have fallen the most. The idea is to buy assets with improving prospects, which are assumed to have been fairly, but not fully, reflected in price movements.

Macedo [1995a, 1995b] showed that price momentum-based country-selection strategies produce excess returns.

How can such strategies possibly work if markets are efficient? The evidence from the U.S. stock market reveals that it takes time for all relevant information to be fully reflected in stock prices. Chan, Jegadeesh, and Lakonishok [1996] show that momentum strategies work because the markets tend to underreact to news. High-momentum stocks continued to outperform low-momentum stocks *three years* after portfolio formation. The persistence of momentum effects and analyst inertia in revising forecasts support the underreaction hypothesis for why momentum strategies work, and belie the herding and trend-chasing hypothesis.

Chan, Jegadeesh, and Lakonishok further demonstrate that price momentum in stocks is not just a proxy for earnings momentum, which exhibits smaller and shorter-lived effects. Earnings is a short-horizon measure of profitability, whereas prior returns reflect a broader set of market expectations.

Similar results for country selection are presented below. Earnings momentum does not account for the observed success of price-momentum strategies for country selection. The success of momentum strategies does not appear to be a statistical fluke, nor does it appear to be due to higher risk. Rather, the evidence supports the hypothesis that there is systematic underreaction to information.

ICRG Fundamental Risk Ratings

Political Risk Services' *International Country Risk Guide* (ICRG) provides four risk ratings monthly for over 100 countries, beginning in 1984.[5] These risk ratings are forward-looking, and are based on analysis of a mix of quantitative and qualitative information that is pertinent to financial, political, and economic risk. Their composite risk rating is calculated from the three individual ratings.

Erb, Harvey and Viskanta [1996] have demonstrated that changes in the ICRG risk ratings contain information about future return and risk of developed and emerging equity markets.[6] They also have shown that these fundamental risk measures explain a significant proportion of the cross-sectional variation in market valuation ratios.

Data

This study comprised 18 markets up to 1990: Australia, Austria, Belgium, Canada, Denmark, France, Germany, Hong Kong, Italy, Japan, Malaysia/ Singapore, the Netherlands, Norway, Spain, Sweden, Switzerland, the United Kingdom, and the United States. From January 1990, there are 19 markets including Finland.

Morgan Stanley Capital International (MSCI) provided the following month-end valuation ratios for the 20 years from December 1974 through June 1996: price-to-book value, price-to-earnings, price-to-cash flow, and dividend yield. Returns with net dividends were calculated, through July 1996, using MSCI national indices both in U.S. dollars and in local currencies. "Free" indices, which exclude stocks restricted from foreign ownership, were used where and when available.

Relative strength is calculated as the local, no dividend, price return over the preceding 12 months. Past earnings-momentum was imputed from the 12-month percentage change in price-to-earnings and the 12-month percentage change in price.

Hedged returns are calculated assuming that the forward rate is the current exchange rate less the difference between short-term yields of the foreign markets and the United States.[7] Three-month Treasury-bill yields came primarily from Datastream and DRI International. Data from local banks' research departments helped to fill in older history in the smaller markets. Due to limitations in the available histories of cash yields across these markets, the studies in this chapter commence at the end of 1976, rather than at the end of 1974 when the valuation and U.S.-dollar-return data are already fully available.

Political Risk Services publishes country-risk ratings monthly which include political-, economic-, and financial-risk ratings as well as a composite risk rating. These ratings, where a higher score indicates lower risk, were converted to risk indices, where a higher number indicates higher risk, as follows:

$$RI = (100 - ICRG)/ICRG.$$

Ratings are used according to the month in which they were reported. The history begins with ratings, based on January 1984 data, that would have been available at the end of February 1984.

Portfolio Construction Tests

For each indicator, four quartile portfolios were created based on the value of the indicator as of the end of the previous period. Portfolio Q1 contains the four most attractive countries; Q2, the five next-most attractive countries; Q3, the five to six next-least attractive countries; and Q4, the four least attractive countries. All markets are equal weighted within a given portfolio. Figure 1 illustrates this methodology using book value-to-price.

Each indicator's ability to discriminate between attractive and unattractive markets is gauged by the significance of the average difference in returns between portfolios Q1 and Q4. This spread represents the return to a hypothetical long-short investment strategy that is long the markets in Q1 and short those in Q4. Alternatively, it can be viewed as the return advantage of a tilt strategy that overweights the markets in Q1 and underweights the markets in Q4. Since we build these portfolios based solely on information from the previous period, the returns on these quartile portfolios can be viewed as out-of-sample performance of a long-short strategy based on the indicator.

To explore the persistence of returns, tests include portfolios rebalanced monthly, quarterly, semiannually, and annually. Transaction costs of 2 percent round-trip are subtracted from performance.[8] Regardless of rebalancing frequency, all returns are reported annualized in order to facilitate comparison.

Table 1 summarizes the results of the portfolio construction tests based on book value-to-price, earnings-to-price, dividend yield, relative strength (price momentum), and past earnings momentum.

FIGURE 1. Quartile Portfolio-Construction Methodology

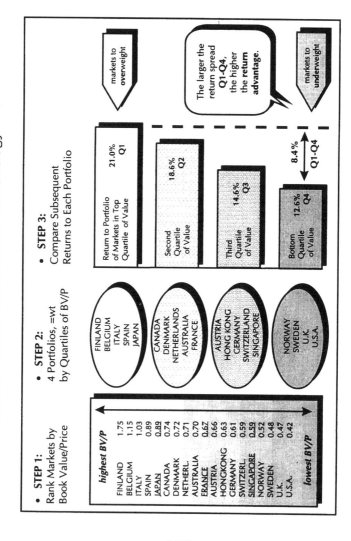

TABLE 1. Quartile Portfolio Spreads, Various Value, and Momentum Indicators

Quartile Portfolios, Average Annual Return Spread, Q1–Q4, Percentage (t-Statistic)   January 1977–July 1996

Indicator	Monthly Rebalancing		Quarterly Rebalancing		Semiannual Rebalancing		Annual Rebalancing	
	US$	Hedged	US$	Hedged	US$	Hedged	US$	Hedged
Book Value/Price	2.98 (0.87)	3.94 (1.21)	3.30 (0.96)	4.86 (1.49)	3.15 (0.86)	5.11 (1.46)	6.55 (1.48)	8.54 (1.99)
Dividend Yield	1.97 (0.61)	3.77 (1.27)	1.21 (0.34)	3.05 (0.97)	1.84 (0.48)	3.50 (1.04)	3.92 (0.83)	5.70 (1.36)
Earnings/Price	2.76 (0.81)	3.12 (0.97)	2.21 (0.63)	2.65 (0.77)	2.05 (0.57)	2.63 (0.74)	1.25 (0.30)	2.97 (0.67)
Relative Strength (Price Momentum)	14.68 (3.76)	11.56 (3.06)	13.39 (3.42)	10.35 (2.83)	11.27 (2.80)	8.57 (2.28)	8.47 (1.90)	4.79 (1.09)
Earnings Momentum	4.36 (1.31)	0.40 (0.13)	2.87 (0.74)	-1.09 (-0.30)	2.00 (0.44)	-1.72 (-0.44)	0.71 (0.12)	-2.99 (-0.61)

Note: Net 2% round-trip transaction costs.

Source: Bailard, Biehl & Kaiser

Value Tilts

Book value-to-price with annual rebalancing discriminated between attractive and unattractive markets the best, with significant spreads between the top and bottom quartiles (Q1–Q4). The spread between markets with high book value-to-price and low book value-to-price was 4 percent to 8.5 percent per annum after transaction costs, and spreads increased as the investment horizon lengthened (hedged returns). In U.S.-dollar terms, however, the results were not quite so good, ranging from 3 percent to 6.5 percent per annum.

Dividend yield and earnings-to-price were not as effective. Dividend yield followed the same pattern that book value-to-price followed with regard to (1) the persistence of returns (returns became stronger as the investment horizon lengthened), and (2) the impact of currency (returns were weaker in U.S. dollars). Spreads to the dividend-yield strategy ranged from 1.2 percent to 5.7 percent per annum. Spreads to the earnings-to-price strategy ranged from 1.3 percent to 3 percent per annum.

Do value tilts work for country selection simply because these markets are riskier? To test whether the excess returns might be fully explained by the higher fundamental risk of the cheap markets, we will predict the returns that would be consistent with the average differences in fundamental risk between the value-based Q1 and Q4 portfolios. To do so, we must first establish the reward-for-fundamental risk.

Table 2 summarizes the results when the ICRG indices are used to form quartile portfolios.[9] Three out of the four indices produced significant spreads; only the economic risk index did not. The composite risk index—by reason of its comprehensiveness and the magnitude, consistency with respect to currency effects, and persistence of spreads for quartile portfolios based on it—was used to make the risk-based forecasts of the return spreads for value quartile portfolios.

Figure 2 plots the actual returns spreads for value-based quartile portfolios (over the same period for which the risk indices were available) against the predicted returns spreads calculated as the relative risk of the value-based quartile portfolios multiplied by the reward-for-risk of the composite risk index-based Q1 and Q4 portfolios. The higher fundamental risk of the value portfolio accounts for less than half of the observed spreads.

The evidence suggests that there is more behind the success of the value tilt strategy than the simple explanation that value markets are riskier than expensive markets. Do global investors make representativeness errors, by assuming that a good equity market is the market of a success-

TABLE 2. Quartile Portfolio Spreads, Various Fundamental-Risk Indicators

Quartile Portfolios, Average Annual Return Spread, Q1–Q4, Percentage (t-Statistic)   *January 1977–July 1996*

Fundamental-Risk Index (ICRG)	Monthly Rebalancing		Quarterly Rebalancing		Semiannual Rebalancing		Annual Rebalancing	
	US$	Hedged	US$	Hedged	US$	Hedged	US$	Hedged
Composite Risk	8.04 (2.21)	9.00 (2.86)	9.14 (2.77)	9.70 (3.22)	9.30 (2.57)	9.88 (2.82)	10.45 (2.57)	10.76 (2.49)
Financial Risk	5.73 (1.67)	6.45 (2.15)	7.16 (2.09)	7.60 (2.49)	7.58 (2.17)	7.58 (2.34)	9.94 (2.58)	9.45 (2.56)
Economic Risk	-1.46 (-0.57)	-1.58 (-0.63)	-0.13 (-0.05)	-0.65 (-0.27)	0.43 (0.15)	0.19 (0.08)	0.76 (0.33)	0.88 (0.36)
Political Risk	6.54 (2.16)	8.46 (3.06)	8.13 (2.68)	9.53 (3.35)	8.41 (2.12)	9.79 (2.64)	9.40 (1.91)	10.25 (2.18)

Note: Net 2% round-trip transaction costs.

Source: Bailard, Biehl & Kaiser

FIGURE 2.   Realized Quartile Portfolio Spreads, Q1–Q4,
            Percentage, for Value Indicators versus Spreads
            Predicted by Differences in Fundamental Risk
            March 1984–July 1996

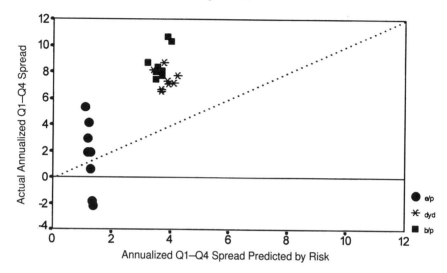

Eight points are plotted for each valuation ratio, corresponding to 1-, 3-, 6-, and 12-month
hedged returns, and 1-, 3-, 6-, and 12-month US$ returns. Fundamental risk does not fully
explain the outperformance of value markets.

Source: Bailard, Biehl & Kaiser

ful or well-run country? This conjecture is intuitively appealing but difficult to prove. Certainly the other two cognitive errors, aversion to regret
and excessive expectations at the extremes, should apply equally to country selection and stock selection.

Momentum Tilts

Relative strength, or price momentum, is a trading-intensive strategy,
with correspondingly high transaction costs. Table 1 shows that among
the five strategies tested, relative strength produced the greatest number
of significant return spreads, even after transaction costs were deducted.
Results ranged from 4.8 percent per annum (with annual rebalancing
and hedged returns) to 14.7 percent (with monthly rebalancing and U.S.-

dollar returns). Relative strength worked better over short horizons, one to three months, though the spreads were still significant six months after portfolio construction, and did not reverse within the first year. Relative-strength tilts performed better in U.S.-dollar terms than when hedged.[10]

Comparison of the strong and persistent results for price momentum with the weak and short-lived results for past earnings momentum (refer to Table 1) leaves little doubt that price momentum must be much more than a proxy for past earnings momentum.

Is a relative-strength strategy equivalent to merely buying markets as they become riskier? The difference in fundamental risk between the momentum quartile portfolios is negligible. Figure 3 shows that it does not account for the spreads. Nor did spreads between the relative-strength quartile portfolios result from differences with respect to changes in risk ratings.

FIGURE 3.   Realized Quartile Portfolio Spreads, Q1–Q4,
             Percentage, for Relative Strength versus Spreads
             Predicted by Differences in Fundamental Risk
             March 1984–July 1996

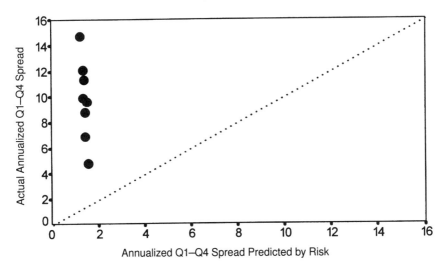

Eight points are plotted, corresponding to 1-, 3-, 6-, and 12-month hedged returns, and 1-, 3-, 6-, and 12-month US$ returns. Fundamental risk does not fully explain the outperformance of markets with high relative strength.

Source: Bailard, Biehl & Kaiser

Value and Momentum Summary

Tilts toward either style worked for investment horizons up to a year. Value tilts performed equally well over shorter and longer horizons, but were less effective when measured in U.S.-dollar terms. The performance of relative-strength tilts decreased as the investment horizon lengthened. Relative-strength tilts looked better in U.S.-dollar returns than hedged.

Relative value and relative strength are *competing* indicators: the markets with the highest relative-value ranks tend to have the lowest relative-strength ranks. A market is highly unlikely to have high scores in both. It is reasonable, therefore, to expect that when value does not work, relative strength does. (By "value works," we mean that the value markets outperform the expensive markets, so that the spread, Q1–Q4, is positive.) Figure 4 confirms the high degree of negative correlation in the performance of the two strategies.

There were periods during which both value and relative strength worked (or did not work), but these tended to be weaker periods for both. While it was often the case that both styles worked, more than half the

FIGURE 4.   Value (Book Value/Price) and Relative Strength
            Quarterly Quartile Portfolio Spreads, Q1–Q4,
            Percentage
            January 1977–July 1996

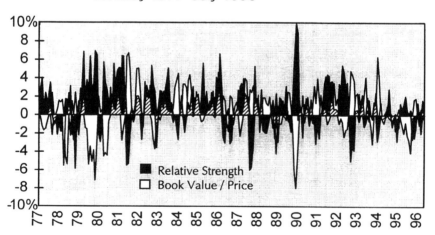

This chart illustrates the negative correlation in the performance of Relative Strength and Value.

Source: Bailard, Biehl & Kaiser

time only one style did. When one of the styles was out of favor, the other style was in favor about 70 percent of the time.

How could *both* value and relative strength work? The answer is that the market rewards these characteristics at different times for different reasons.

Style Timing

How is an investor to know which country-selection style to use when? Shefrin and Statman [1995] provide direct evidence that investment style is linked to investors' perceptions of quality and risk. Their behavioral capital asset pricing theory [1994] provides the theoretical foundation for differentials in the returns to various investment styles—in other words, risk premia for investment styles. And market equilibrium and mean-variance portfolio theory prescribe that a decrease in risk tolerance results in an increase in risk premium. If investors' risk tolerances decrease, the premium to those styles perceived to be riskier must increase.

Neither the risk premium nor societal risk aversion can be measured directly, but we can approximate. As proxies for risk aversion, Sharpe [1989] has used measures of investor wealth, noting several studies that demonstrate the link between (1) whether investors feel rich or poor and (2) their level of aggressiveness in their investment portfolios. The flight-to-quality phenomenon suggests an alternative proxy for risk aversion, one that is more closely coupled with investment style.

The urge to "play it safe" is strongest when investors are most nervous or uncertain. Since market volatility reflects—and perhaps even amplifies—investor uncertainty, a flight to quality is often observed during periods of high volatility. During such times, investor risk-aversion increases, investors bid up "quality," and they oversell assets which they perceive to be riskier. The consequence is a higher premium for bearing risk.

A global market-volatility measure was calculated for each month as the standard deviation of monthly returns to each market over the most recent six months. This measure captures both the volatility of returns over time and, to a lesser extent, the dispersion of returns among countries. Whenever volatility is higher than its prior average, investors are presumed to be risk averse, and the "risk-aversion proxy" variable is defined to be "high." Whenever volatility is lower, investors are presumed to be risk tolerant, and the "risk aversion proxy" variable was defined to be "low" (refer to Figure 5). Note that it is the absolute level of volatility that is important here—whether volatility is particularly high or low relative to prior values—not the differences in volatility among coun-

FIGURE 5. Global Market Volatility

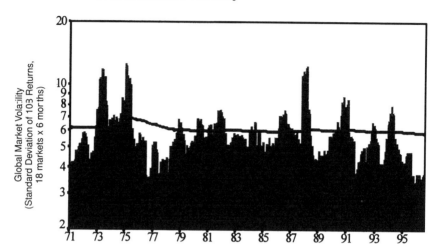

When volatility has been above average, risk *aversion* is presumed to be high; the risk premium for value markets is therefore expected to be high. When volatility has been below average, risk *tolerance* is presumed to be high; the risk premium for value markets is therefore expected to be low.

Source: Bailard, Biehl & Kaiser

tries. No look-ahead bias is introduced, since each month's volatility level is compared to an average of prior months only.

The ICRG composite risk index provides a simple means to verify our intuition that volatility is a reliable proxy for investor risk aversion. Table 3 reveals a dramatic difference when volatility has been above average and when it has been below, in the return spread between quartile portfolios based on fundamental risk, using ICRG's composite risk index. The risk premium doubles immediately following a period when global market volatility has been high. These results strongly support the intuition that volatility is a proxy for risk aversion.

Figure 6 illustrates the dramatic differences in the performance of book value-to-price tilts and relative-strength tilts after periods of high and low volatility, our proxy for risk aversion.[11]

As expected, the contrarian style, book value-to-price, worked substantially better—much larger Q1–Q4 spreads—when volatility had been high and when investors are presumed to have been risk averse. The comfortable style, relative strength, worked better when the risk-aversion proxy was low.

TABLE 3. Global Market Volatility as a Risk-Aversion Proxy

ICRG Composite Risk Index, Annualized Quartile Portfolio Spreads, Q1–Q4
March 1984–July 1996

		Global Market Volatility	
	Holding Period	Below Average	Above Average
Hedged Returns	1 month	0.61%	1.26%
	3 months	1.94%	3.80%
	6 months	1.43%	2.23%
	12 months	10.40%	11.99%
US$ Returns	1 month	0.48%	1.31%
	3 months	1.50%	4.31%
	6 months	1.08%	2.69%
	12 months	9.21%	13.43%

Source: Bailard, Biehl & Kaiser

For book value-to-price, the spread between Q1 and Q4 was not significantly different from zero when the risk-aversion proxy was low. When the risk-aversion proxy [RAP] was high, however, the premium was highly significant, even for long holding periods. More rigorously, there was a statistically significant difference in the premium when RAP was high *versus* when it was not. Figure 7 shows that *when* value is used makes a bigger difference than *which measure* of value is used.

The premium for relative strength also responded as expected. Looking at 12-month relative strength, the risk premium was negative after periods of high volatility and highly positive after periods of low volatility. The difference in the premium when RAP was high *versus* when it was not was highly significant.

These results are consistent with intuition and with theory. If returns to style factors represent risk premia, then when investors' risk tolerance is low, risk premia should be high. These results provide compelling evidence that the hypothesized relation between volatility and the performance of country-selection styles exists.

Multifactor Strategies

The problem that no single indicator works all the time typically is dealt with by using several diverse indicators simultaneously. By design, these models do not adapt to changing market conditions. Some refer to this inflexibility as a "feature," more disciplined than, and superior to, *qualita-*

FIGURE 6.   Quartile Portfolio Spreads, Q1–Q4, Percentage,
             Relative Strength and Book Value/Price versus
             Global Market Volatility
             January 1977–July 1996

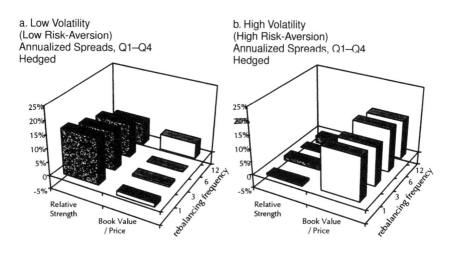

a. Low Volatility
(Low Risk-Aversion)
Annualized Spreads, Q1–Q4
Hedged

b. High Volatility
(High Risk-Aversion)
Annualized Spreads, Q1–Q4
Hedged

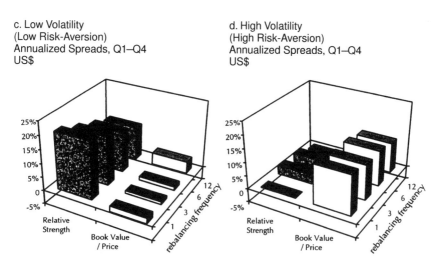

c. Low Volatility
(Low Risk-Aversion)
Annualized Spreads, Q1–Q4
US$

d. High Volatility
(High Risk-Aversion)
Annualized Spreads, Q1–Q4
US$

Source: Bailard, Biehl & Kaiser

FIGURE 7. Value Timing Compared with Value Tilts Quartile Portfolio Spreads, Q1–Q4, Percentage, January 1977–July 1996

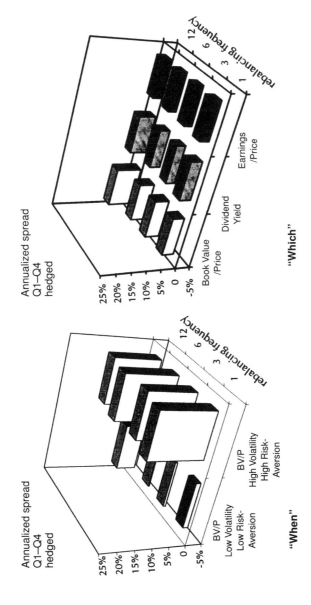

When to emphasize value markets is more important than which valuation ratio to emphasize.

Source: Bailard, Biehl & Kaiser

163

tive managers who automatically focus on different indicators under different market conditions. But discipline and adaptability are not mutually exclusive.

Good quantitative strategies are characterized not just by high R^2s but also by whether the indicators and relationships make sense. If we have an idea why an indicator should work, we should also have insight as to when it should work. A quantitative strategy that incorporates such insights can be both disciplined and adaptive. Furthermore, such an approach does *not* necessitate increased turnover.

The results above suggest a simple model for style rotation: use relative value when volatility is above average, relative strength when below. As before, four portfolios were created monthly from January 1977 through June 1996, using data available at the end of the previous month. Portfolio Q1 contained the markets with the best forecast each period, and Q4 contained the markets with the worst forecast.

To see how such a strategy compared with the more conventional multifactor approach, quartile portfolios were constructed based on the sum of each country's ranked book value-to-price and ranked relative strength. It is noteworthy that these portfolios had interquartile turnover just as high as the style-rotation strategy, about 15 percent per month.

The style-rotation strategy outperformed the conventional strategy by almost 5 percent per annum, with far more consistent performance, as can be seen in Table 4.

TABLE 4. Comparison: Multifactor Tilts Conventional Strategy versus Multifactor Timing Style-Rotation Strategy

January 1977–July 1996

	Conventional Value and Momentum		Style Rotation Value or Momentum	
	US$	Hedged	US$	Hedged
Annualized Return	13.5%	11.8%	18.4%	16.0%
Annualized Risk	14.0%	13.3%	16.6%	15.4%
t-Statistic	4.24	3.92	4.90	4.57
Monthly consistency	63%	60%	66%	66%
Annual Consistency	75%	83%	87%	91%

Note: Net 2% round-trip transaction costs.

Source: Bailard, Biehl & Kaiser

Conclusion

New results presented in this chapter showed that the excess returns to a value-based country-selection strategy cannot be accounted for solely as compensation for higher fundamental risk; that the excess returns to a relative strength-based (price momentum-based) strategy cannot be accounted for as compensation for buying markets as they become riskier; and that market price momentum is more than a proxy for market earnings momentum. Fundamental risk ratings provided indirect evidence which supports the hypothesis that volatility is a proxy for investor risk aversion.

These results enrich our understanding of how investment style applies to country selection. With this understanding, we can exploit patterns in when each style is likely to be most effective.

By knowing when to use them, value and relative strength can be more effective components in any country-selection discipline. Furthermore, the relations described here are consistent with investment theory, they can exist even if everyone knows about them, and they can be expected to work out-of-sample.

Endnotes

1.   Eugene F. Fama and Kenneth R. French, "Business Conditions and Expected Returns on Stocks and Bonds," *Journal of Financial Economics* 25, 1989. pp. 23–49.

2.   Patricia M. Fairfield, "P/E, P/B and the Present Value of Future Dividends," *Financial Analyst Journal*, July–August 1994.

3.   Refer to Carlo Capaul, Ian Rowley, and WIlliam F. Sharpe, "International Value and Growth Stock Returns," *Financial Analysts Journal*, January–February 1993 and to John Meier, "Do Styles Make Sense Globally? Growth vs. Value." BARRA International Research Conference in Berkeley, California, May 1992.

4.   Josef Lakonishok, Andrei Schleifer, and Robert Vishny, "Contrarian Investment, Extrapolation, and Stock Returns." Working Paper, University of Illinois, 1992.

5.   More information can be found at Political Risk Services' website: http://www.polrisk.com/.

6.   Claude B. Erb, Campbell R. Harvey, and Tadas E. Viskanta, "Political Risk, Economic Risk, and Financial Risk." published at http://www.duke.edu/~charvey/Country_risk/pol/pol.htm.

7.   Arbitrage on short-term interest rates guarantees that this estimate for the forward rate should be very accurate.

8.   Commissions, trading taxes, custody, and the bid/offer spread make international equities more expensive to trade than domestic equities. This 2 percent esti-

mate for round-trip total cost was for EAFE + 1/2 Japan, from Grantham [1990]. Derivatives might be used as a cheaper alternative. Currently, derivatives are available for 15 out of the 19 markets studied. Of these, eight out of the nine larger markets had a higher average daily volume in futures and options than in the underlying stocks, and five of the six smaller markets exceeded 50 percent of the stock volume in futures and options volume. Averages for 1993. Source: Goldman Sachs.

9.   Note that these portfolios represent high risk and low risk, not increasing risk and decreasing risk as in Erb, Harvey, and Viskanta [1996].

10.   The results when relative strength is measured over periods other than 12 months, ranging from one month to two years, can be found in "Country-Selection Style" [Macedo 1995b]. The superiority of 12-month relative strength for country selection, versus longer and shorter measurement-intervals, is consistent with Engerman's findings for stock selection in the United States, the United Kingdom, and Japan [Engerman, 1993].

11.   Tables with detailed results for all the indicators during periods of low and high presumed risk-aversion are presented in Macedo [1995b].

References

Arnott, Robert D.; John L. Dorian; and Rosemary Macedo. "Style Management: The Missing Element in Equity Portfolios." *Journal of Investing,* Summer 1992.

Arnott, Robert D.; Charles M. Kelso, Jr.; Stephan Kiscadden; and Rosemary Macedo. "Forecasting Factor Returns: An Intriguing Possibility." *Journal of Portfolio Management*, Fall 1989.

Arnott, Robert D., and Roy D. Henriksson, "A Disciplined Approach to Global Asset Allocation." *Financial Analysts Journal*, January/February 1989.

Capaul, Carlo; Ian Rowley; and WIlliam F. Sharpe. "International Value and Growth Stock Returns." *Financial Analysts Journal*, January–February 1993.

Chan, Louis K. C.; Narasimhan Jegadeesh; and Josef Lakonishok. "Momentum Strategies," Working Paper, February 1996, forthcoming *Journal of Finance.*

Clarke, Roger, and Meir Statman. "Growth, Value, Good, and Bad." *Financial Analysts Journal*, November–December 1994.

Engerman, Mark. "Reversal and Momentum Strategies." BARRA Equity Research Conference, Pebble Beach, June 1993.

Erb, Claude B.; Campbell R. Harvey; and Tadas E. Viskanta. "Political Risk, Economic Risk, and Financial Risk." published at http://www.duke.edu/~charvey/Country_risk/pol/pol.htm (presented at the Chicago Quantitative Alliance Conference, September 1996).

Fairfield, Patricia M. "P/E, P/B and the Present Value of Future Dividends." *Financial Analysts Journal*, July–August 1994.

Fama, Eugene F., and Kenneth R. French. "Business Conditions and Expected Returns on Stocks and Bonds." *Journal of Financial Economics* 25, 1989, pp. 23–49.

Grantham, R. Jeremy. "Dirty Secrets of International Investing," in *Investing Worldwide,* Association for Investment Management and Research, 1990.

Heckman, Leila, and Holly Sze. "Absolute versus Relative Valuation Measures for Cross-Market Comparisons." Smith Barney Research Note, November 20, 1995.

Keppler, Michael. "Further Evidence on the Predictability of International Equity Returns." *Journal of Portfolio Management,* Fall 1990a.

Keppler, Michael. "The Importance of Dividend Yields in Country Selection." *Journal of Portfolio Management,* Winter 1990b.

Keppler, Michael, and Heydon Traub. "The Small Country Effect," in *Small Cap Stocks,* Robert A. Klein and Jess Lederman, eds. Chicago, IL: Probus Publishing, 1993.

Lakonishok, Josef; Andrei Schleifer; and Robert Vishny. "Contrarian Investment, Extrapolation, and Stock Returns." Working Paper, University of Illinois, 1992.

Macedo, Rosemary. "Value, Relative Strength and Volatility in Global Equity Country Selection." *Financial Analysts Journal,* March/April 1995a.

Macedo, Rosemary. "Country-Selection Style," in *Equity Style Management,* Robert A. Klein and Jess Lederman, eds. Chicago, IL: Irwin Professional Publishing, 1995b, pp. 333-355.

Macedo, Rosemary. "Tactical Style Allocation Using Small Cap Strategies," in *Small Cap Stocks,* Robert A. Klein and Jess Lederman, eds. Chicago, IL: Probus Publishing, 1993.

Meier, John. "Do Styles Make Sense Globally? Growth versus Value." BARRA International Research Conference in Berkeley, California, May 1992.

Sharpe, William F. "Investor Wealth and Expected Return" in *Quantifying the Market Risk Premium Phenomenon for Investment Decision Making,* William F. Sharpe and Katrina F Sherrerd, eds. New York, NY: Institute of Chartered Financial Analysts, September 26–27, 1989.

Shefrin, Hersh, and Meir Statman. "Behavioral Capital Asset Pricing Theory." *The Journal of Financial and Quantitative Analysis,* September 1994.

Shefrin, Hersh, and Meir Statman. "Making Sense of Beta, Size and Book-to-Market." *Journal of Portfolio Management,* Winter 1995.

Solt, Michael E., and Meir Statman. "Good Companies, Bad Stocks." *Journal of Portfolio Management,* Summer 1989.

Style Indexes: Powerful Tools for Building Global Stock-Selection Models

David A. Umstead
Senior Vice President

Michael P. McElroy
Senior Vice President

H. David Shea
Vice President

Dennis Fogarty
Vice President

Independence International Associates, Inc.,
a subsidiary of Independence Investment Associates, Inc.

Introduction

The Dow Jones Index, arguably the best-known stock market index in the world, celebrated its 100th anniversary on May 26, 1996. For over a century, investors have relied on this benchmark as a barometer of the ups and downs on Wall Street. Over the years, indexes have played an increasingly important role in the investment community. In the early 1970s, indexes moved into the mainstream of investment management with the introduction of the first index funds. At this point, people began to think about indexes as investment portfolios. Index funds proliferated, and the simplest form of quantitative investing was born.

Index funds came into being with very strong theoretical and empirical credentials. The capital asset pricing model led us to the insight that, under certain simplifying assumptions, *all* investors should hold the market portfolio. Efficient market theory, under similar assumptions, told us that security prices reflect all knowable information and that security price *changes* are therefore unpredictable. The efficient market hypothesis was supported by a wide variety of empirical studies.

The first index funds were designed to track the U.S. equity market as measured by indexes such at the Standard & Poor's 500, but it was not too long before researchers such as Stattman;[1] Banz;[2] Reinganum;[3] Basu;[4] and Rosenberg, Reid, and Lanstein[5] noticed that a variety of very simple factor models tended to outperform the market with a consistency that was far greater than could be explained by chance. Price/book, market capitalization, and price/earnings models exhibited statistically significant spreads versus the overall market. This early style research led to a number of investment products designed to exploit these pricing anomalies.

Capaul, Rowley, and Sharpe[6] were among the first to extend style analysis to the international equity markets. They used price/book ratios to split each market index into two subindexes; a low price/book index (called value) and a high price/book index (called growth). They rebalanced their indexes semiannually, and, at each rebalance, the indexes were constructed so each contained half the capitalization of the market index. This allowed comparison of two subindexes with roughly equal liquidity, and which, therefore, represented equally viable strategies for large institutional investors. Allocating the same amount of capitalization to each subindex also controlled the country allocation in regional aggregations. In other words, their global value and growth indexes each had the same country allocation as their global market index.

Capaul, Rowley, and Sharpe analyzed six markets (France, Germany, Switzerland, the United Kingdom, Japan, and the United States) over the 11 and one-half-year period from January 1981 through June 1992. They found a significant value/growth *risk* factor in each country. The returns for their value and growth indexes varied far more from month to month than would be expected if the securities had been selected randomly. When they looked for evidence of value or growth as a *return* factor, they found that value stocks outperformed growth stocks on average in each country, but the spreads were not significant in any single country. The spread for their six-country global index, however, was significant. It averaged 3.44 percentage points per year with a standard deviation of 5.89 resulting in a t-statistic of 1.98.

Umstead[7] extended Capaul, Rowley, and Sharpe's work to 20 markets over the 20-year period from January 1975 to December 1994. He found statistically significant price/book spreads in Japan and France (t-statistics of 2.6 and 2.4, respectively) and a highly significant spread (t-statistic of 3.0) for the Europe/Pacific region. Umstead concluded:

Twenty years of results in 20 markets make it clear that passive investors in the Europe/Pacific region should focus their portfolios on the value end of these markets. The results are profound. The size, consistency and statistical significance of the value/growth spread is extraordinary. We have found that country diversification is the key to controlling the volatility of the spread. We have decomposed the spread and found that value-added comes from both sector selection and stock selection within sector. We have looked at different levels of aggressiveness and found a clear, direct relationship between value and return. We have assessed turnover and transaction costs and found them to be modest. Finally, we have surveyed the literature and found a number of solid theoretical reasons for the value/growth spread. In summary, we have identified a tremendous opportunity for astute investors to capture higher returns in the passive portion of their portfolios.

Where do we go from here? Table 1 provides some guidance. It shows annualized value/growth spread statistics for 22 countries and various regions over the 21-year period from January 1975 through December 1995. Table 1 demonstrates the power of global diversification in capturing the spread. The 3.91 percentage point average annual spread for the global aggregate has the highest t-statistic (3.48) in Table 1.

Table 1 points out, however, that only three individual markets (France, Japan, and Malaysia) have t-statistics at or above 2.0 and that four (Denmark, Italy, Norway, and Switzerland) have *negative* value spreads. So, while we can draw comfort from global diversification, we are left with some nagging doubts about style risk within each country. Even in Japan, where the spread averages 6.66 percentage points per year and the t-statistic is 2.97, we face a standard deviation of 10.29, which means that in one year out of six we can expect the value index to underperform the growth index by at least 3.63 percentage points.

The indexes behind the data in Table 1 have been published by Independence International Associates (IIA)[8] since mid-1993, and the indexes are widely used in the industry. The indexes are a by-product of the quantitative research effort at IIA. IIA is a quantitatively-based global money-management firm, and our interest in these indexes is using them to gain a better understanding of the similarities and differences in the pricing of securities across markets. See Umstead[9] for discussion of some of the detailed research behind the indexes presented in Table 1. Our approach in this chapter will be to treat these indexes as a base-case for comparative analysis. Our software allows us to easily modify our computational methodology, and it can be very instructive to look at alternative construction rules. This kind of comparative analysis is a key part of our continuous search for increasingly better stock-selection models.

TABLE 1. Annualized Spread Statistics, Top Half versus Bottom Half, January 1975–December 1995

Low P/B versus High P/B

	Months	Avg	Std	t-stat	Conf	%Pos
Austria	252	1.99	13.19	0.69	75.5	54.0
Belgium	252	3.54	9.67	1.68	95.5	55.6
Denmark	252	-1.66	16.35	-0.46	67.9	50.0
Finland	96	0.01	19.17	0.00	50.0	52.1
France	252	4.18	9.57	2.00	97.7	56.7
Germany	252	2.50	7.58	1.51	93.5	56.3
Ireland	60	7.98	11.25	1.59	94.3	66.7
Italy	252	-2.17	12.71	-0.78	78.2	48.4
Netherlands	252	1.13	10.26	0.50	69.2	54.0
Norway	252	-1.55	21.69	-0.33	62.8	50.8
Spain	252	2.09	17.05	0.56	71.3	53.2
Sweden	252	2.92	14.33	0.93	82.4	52.4
Switzerland	252	-0.14	9.26	-0.07	52.7	49.6
United Kingdom	252	3.10	8.73	1.63	94.9	54.4
Europe	252	1.96	4.73	1.90	97.1	57.9
Australia	252	3.43	11.04	1.42	92.2	55.2
Hong Kong	252	1.52	12.66	0.55	70.9	47.6
Japan	252	6.66	10.29	2.97	99.8	62.3
Malaysia	252	6.21	13.03	2.18	98.5	52.8
New Zealand	96	2.70	16.91	0.45	67.4	51.0
Singapore	252	2.51	11.43	1.00	84.2	52.0
Pacific	252	6.08	9.07	3.07	99.9	61.5
Canada	252	3.14	10.61	1.36	91.2	57.5
United States	252	2.76	7.66	1.66	95.2	56.7
North America	252	2.78	7.14	1.79	96.3	56.0
Europe-Pacific	252	3.98	5.70	3.20	99.9	61.5
EuroPac x Japan	252	2.17	4.20	2.37	99.1	59.9
Pacific x Japan	252	3.13	6.60	2.17	98.5	53.2
Global x US	252	3.95	5.49	3.29	99.9	61.1
Global	252	3.91	5.15	3.48	100.0	61.5

Source: Independence International Associates, Inc.

Base-Case Methodology

Table 2 is a schematic of the method used to create the IIA Value and Growth Indexes presented in Table 1. The methodology is quite simple. Imagine that Table 2 represents all the stocks in the XYZ stock market. For each stock, we collect two pieces of information: price/book ratio and

TABLE 2. Schematic of the Method IIA Uses to Create Its Value and Growth Indices

	Company	Cap		Price-to-Book
	A	$2 bil		0.6
	B	10		0.8
	C	1		0.9
	D	15		1.0
Value	E	3	50%	1.1
	F	4		1.2
	G	5		1.5
	H	5		1.7
	I	5		2.0
	J	15		2.1
	K	10		2.4
Growth	L	5	50%	3.4
	M	10		4.6
	N	10		5.2
		$100 bil		

capitalization. We sort by price/book (from low to high) and sum the capitalization data, starting from the top, until we have accumulated exactly half of the capitalization of the XYZ market. All stocks above this point in the table are designated value stocks, all stocks below are growth. We then capitalization-weight the stocks on each constituent list in order to create value and growth subindexes for the XYZ market.

Any stock in Table 2 with a price/book ratio of 2.0 or less is a value stock and any stock with a price/book ratio more than 2.0 is a growth stock. The exact break point between value and growth varies from market to market and varies over time within each market. In other words, the definitions of value and growth are relative rather than absolute. The sort procedure is repeated semiannually on January 1 and July 1. At each rebalance we identify a new constituent list for each index. The turnover in the base-case indexes averages about 15 percent at each rebalance.

For each stock, we use its price/book ratio exactly as it was published in the Morgan Stanley Capital International *Perspective* at the time of the rebalance.[10] MSCI has published fundamental data on a monthly basis since January 1975. This database is a unique resource in the industry. It is unmatched in terms of its length (over 21 years), number of companies and countries, consistency of presentation, lack of survivor bias and known publication dates. The database currently covers over 2,500 companies in 22 countries. The decision rules behind our style indexes and models operate with the data as the data were available to investors at each decision point. There is no survivor bias in the application of the decision rules. In other words, the rules are allowed to select companies that have since disappeared. There is no uncertainty about whether the data were available to the market. The decision rules operate only with data that were published within a few days of the month-end on which the rule is assumed to have been applied.[11]

Alternative Value Models

Dividend yield is often used as a discriminator of value and growth securities. One possible advantage of dividend yield over price/book (P/B) is that the yield measure does not depend on accounting information. Dividend yield may be a better discriminator in countries where the accounting is particularly obscure. Price/earnings (P/E) ratio is also routinely used as a style-classification variable. Price/earnings ratios are obviously quite susceptible to accounting vagaries, but they are certainly worth looking at, given their usefulness as discriminators in the U.S. equity market.

Table 3 compares annualized spread statistics for these two new sets of indexes to our base-case index. For the global aggregate, we see very little difference between price/book and dividend yield as sort variables. The P/B-based global value index outperforms the P/B-based global growth index by an average of 3.91 percentage points per year with a standard deviation of 5.15 percent and a t-statistic of 3.48. The yield-based global value index outperforms the yield-based global growth index by an average of 3.82 percentage points per year with a standard deviation of 5.23 percent and a t-statistic of 3.35. Country by country, however, we see some dramatic differences. Dividend yield provides considerably larger spreads in Austria, Italy, Netherlands, and New Zealand. Globally this is offset by a lowering of spreads in most markets especially in Denmark, the United Kingdom, and Australia. Three individual markets (Italy, Japan, and New Zealand) have t-statistics above 2.0, and six (Denmark, Finland, Norway, Switzerland, Hong Kong, and Singapore) have *negative* spreads.

Looking at price/earnings as a sort variable, we see that the P/E-based global value index outperforms the P/E-based global growth index by an average of 3.00 percentage points per year, with a standard deviation of 4.57 percent and a t-statistic of 3.01. Price/earnings works well globally, but it is not as powerful as price/book. We see three countries (Spain, Japan, and Canada) with t-statistics above 2.0, but price/earnings spreads are lower than price/book spreads in all but five countries. We

TABLE 3. Annualized Spread Statistics, Top Half versus Bottom Half, January 1975–December 1995

		Low P/B versus High P/B			High Yield versus Low Yield			Low P/E versus High P/E		
	Months	Avg	Std	t-stat	Avg	Std	t-stat	Avg	Std	t-stat
Austria	252	1.99	13.19	0.69	5.30	13.27	1.83	1.25	13.19	0.44
Belgium	252	3.54	9.67	1.68	4.08	10.60	1.77	3.31	9.95	1.52
Denmark	252	-1.66	16.35	-0.46	-4.54	16.20	-1.29	-1.40	15.29	-0.42
Finland	96	0.01	19.17	0.00	-1.50	15.99	-0.27	-1.43	13.70	-0.30
France	252	4.18	9.57	2.00	4.03	10.41	1.78	2.22	7.20	1.41
Germany	252	2.50	7.58	1.51	1.41	7.85	0.82	0.16	6.81	0.11
Ireland	60	7.98	11.25	1.59	7.20	14.24	1.13	-0.48	12.38	-0.09
Italy	252	-2.17	12.71	-0.78	6.10	12.22	2.29	1.42	9.77	0.67
Netherlands	252	1.13	10.26	0.50	4.71	11.41	1.89	2.73	11.87	1.05
Norway	252	-1.55	21.69	-0.33	-1.42	18.55	-0.35	-5.54	21.00	-1.21
Spain	252	2.09	17.05	0.56	1.40	17.36	0.37	7.17	11.95	2.75
Sweden	252	2.92	14.33	0.93	1.69	12.98	0.60	1.68	12.08	0.64
Switzerland	252	-0.14	9.26	-0.07	-0.29	8.21	-0.16	0.29	7.15	0.19
United Kingdom	252	3.10	8.73	1.63	1.18	8.74	0.62	0.04	7.73	0.02
Europe	252	1.96	4.73	1.90	1.70	4.41	1.77	0.75	3.95	0.87
Australia	252	3.43	11.04	1.42	0.83	12.85	0.30	2.32	12.17	0.88
Hong Kong	252	1.52	12.66	0.55	-0.48	12.89	-0.17	0.68	10.57	0.29
Japan	252	6.66	10.29	2.97	5.59	10.40	2.46	4.62	9.53	2.22
Malaysia	252	6.21	13.03	2.18	4.73	13.83	1.57	4.41	13.55	1.49
New Zealand	96	2.70	16.91	0.45	11.28	12.78	2.50	0.05	12.78	0.01
Singapore	252	2.51	11.43	1.00	-0.85	11.63	-0.34	2.16	10.50	0.94
Pacific	252	6.08	9.07	3.07	5.07	9.01	2.58	4.33	8.24	2.41
Canada	252	3.14	10.61	1.36	2.12	11.25	0.87	5.86	10.67	2.52
United States	252	2.76	7.66	1.66	3.25	8.24	1.81	2.53	7.01	1.65
North America	252	2.78	7.14	1.79	3.16	7.78	1.86	2.76	6.57	1.92
Europe-Pacific	252	3.98	5.70	3.20	3.63	5.44	3.06	2.61	5.01	2.39
EuroPac x Japan	252	2.17	4.20	2.37	1.73	3.97	1.99	1.12	3.46	1.48
Pacific x Japan	252	3.13	6.60	2.17	1.03	7.33	0.64	2.41	6.51	1.70
Global x US	252	3.95	5.49	3.29	3.59	5.26	3.13	2.92	4.81	2.79
Global	252	3.91	5.15	3.48	3.82	5.23	3.35	3.00	4.57	3.01

Source: Independence International Associates, Inc.

see four markets (Denmark, Finland, Ireland, and Norway) with *negative* price/earnings spreads.

In summary, the three most common rules of thumb for valuing securities—P/B, yield, and P/E—require no forecasting ability and lead to very successful global investment strategies for investors that systematically hold low-priced stocks. Globally, the P/E spreads are 80 to 90 basis points lower, which probably reflects their sensitivity to accounting problems, but P/E is the clear best choice of the three valuation models in Spain and Canada.

Cherry Picking the Best Value Index

We use Table 3 to pick the best of the three valuation models, country by country, to arrive at a global value index which uses 10 P/B models, six dividend-yield models, and two P/E models. In four countries (Denmark, Finland, Norway, and Switzerland), none of the valuation models produce convincing results, and we therefore use the market index rather than the subindexes for these markets.

Table 4 shows results for these hybrid value and growth indexes. Globally the hybrid value index outperforms the hybrid growth index by an average of 4.40 percentage points per year with a standard deviation of 5.16 percent and a t-statistic of 3.91. This is a modest improvement over the pure P/B index. The spread averages 49 basis points higher, and the t-statistic improves from 3.48 to 3.91.

Understanding Norway

Purists will argue that picking the best of our three valuation models is nothing more than a data-mining exercise. They have a point. We need to know a lot more about why each model works, or why it does not work, before we can intelligently make such a choice.

Norway is a good example. Table 3 suggests that a value strategy is foolhardy in Norway. All three value/growth spreads are negative. A value strategy based on P/B generates a spread which averages -1.55 percentage points per year, the dividend-yield spread averages -1.42, and P/E averages -5.54. The t-statistic for the P/E spread is not significant, but at -1.21 we might be persuaded that a P/E-based *growth* strategy is the way to go.

Table 5 shows year-by-year spreads for our three value models in Norway. It is immediately obvious that the 21-year averages cited in Table 3 are not representative. The averages are distorted by events in 1979. The P/B spread is -309.41 percentage points in 1979, the yield spread is -191.07 and the P/E spread is -241.83. Figure 1 plots value relative to growth in Norway for each set of indexes. This highlights the fact that 1979 was unusual. The plot for the P/B-based index shows a strong upward trend from 1980 on.

TABLE 4.   Annualized Spread Statistics, Top Half versus Bottom Half, January 1975–December 1995

Best Performing Value Model

	Model	Months	Avg	Std	t-stat	Conf	%Pos
Austria	Yield	252	5.30	13.27	1.83	96.7	57.9
Belgium	Yield	252	4.08	10.60	1.77	96.2	54.0
Denmark	Index	252	0.00	—	—	—	—
Finland	Index	96	0.00	—	—	—	—
France	P/B	252	4.18	9.57	2.00	97.7	56.7
Germany	P/B	252	2.50	7.58	1.51	93.5	56.3
Ireland	P/B	60	7.98	11.25	1.59	94.3	66.7
Italy	Yield	252	6.10	12.22	2.29	98.9	55.2
Netherlands	Yield	252	4.71	11.41	1.89	97.1	52.8
Norway	Index	252	0.00	—	—	—	—
Spain	P/E	252	7.17	11.95	2.75	99.7	58.7
Sweden	P/B	252	2.92	14.33	0.93	82.4	52.4
Switzerland	Index	252	0.00	—	—	—	—
United Kingdom	P/B	252	3.10	8.73	1.63	94.9	54.4
Europe		252	2.77	4.39	2.89	99.8	60.3
Australia	P/B	252	3.43	11.04	1.42	92.2	55.2
Hong Kong	P/B	252	1.52	12.66	0.55	70.9	47.6
Japan	P/B	252	6.66	10.29	2.97	99.8	62.3
Malaysia	P/B	252	6.21	13.03	2.18	98.5	52.8
New Zealand	Yield	96	11.28	12.78	2.50	99.3	62.5
Singapore	P/B	252	2.51	11.43	1.00	84.2	52.0
Pacific		252	6.11	9.07	3.09	99.9	61.9
Canada	P/E	252	5.86	10.67	2.52	99.4	56.3
United States	Yield	252	3.25	8.24	1.81	96.5	55.6
North America		252	3.43	7.71	2.04	97.9	55.2
Europe-Pacific		252	4.48	5.60	3.67	100.0	66.3
EuroPac x Japan		252	2.90	3.94	3.37	100.0	62.7
Pacific x Japan		252	3.26	6.62	2.25	98.8	53.6
Global x US		252	4.66	5.33	4.01	100.0	65.9
Global		252	4.40	5.16	3.91	100.0	61.9

Source: Independence International Associates, Inc.

Table 6 shows position reports for our P/B-based value and growth indexes as of the rebalance dates at the beginning, middle and end of 1979. This table, analogous to the schematic shown in Table 2, shows the 12 stocks in our Norwegian market index sorted by price/book. Table 6 shows stock price, various fundamentals, and each security's weight in our market index, our value index, and our growth index. The last col-

TABLE 5. Calendar Year Return Spreads for Norway, Top Half
versus Bottom Half, 1975–1995

Norway	Low P/B versus High P/B	High Yield versus Low Yield	High P/E versus Low P/E
1975	1.37	3.14	-12.18
1976	8.85	11.49	39.72
1977	-8 47	-6.38	-1.15
1978	21.21	20.14	0.02
1979	-309.41	-191.07	-241.83
1980	11.42	9.14	11.00
1981	23.74	24.35	6.23
1982	7.75	8.02	-5.99
1983	-21.14	-41.84	13.12
1984	14.43	12.75	-2.47
1985	-1.80	1.45	4.09
1986	20.29	5.98	13.15
1987	22.12	6.44	-2.95
1988	-1.00	-30.61	-65.91
1989	18.29	4.88	-10.76
1990	1.72	17.84	-13.28
1991	-31.08	-24.69	-5.24
1992	9.56	15.60	7.74
1993	46.40	12.32	12.79
1994	-7.60	-3.18	5.06
1995	-4.02	6.45	0.24

Source: Independence International Associates, Inc.

umn on the right shows cumulative market weight and is the basis for
determining the break point between value and growth.

The top panel of Table 6 shows that on January 1, 1979, our Norway
value index contained 10 stocks and our growth index contained three.
One stock, Hafslund Nycomed with a price/book of 0.83, fell on the
break point between value and growth and was, therefore, allocated
partly to value and partly to growth. The break point is the point at which
the cumulative market-capitalization percentage, shown in the right-most
column, reaches exactly 50 percent.

We can see that the Norwegian market was dominated by Norsk
Hydro at the beginning of 1979. The stock, which was selling at 178 krone,
had a capitalization of U.S. $405 million and represented 42.5 percent of
the market index. With a P/B ratio of 0.93, Norsk Hydro fell into the
growth group. Since each stock in the value and growth indexes, except
the one on the break point, starts out at the rebalance date with a weight
twice its market weight, Norsk Hydro was 84.9 percent of our growth

FIGURE 1.   Cumulative Spread for Norway,
                      January 1975–December 1995

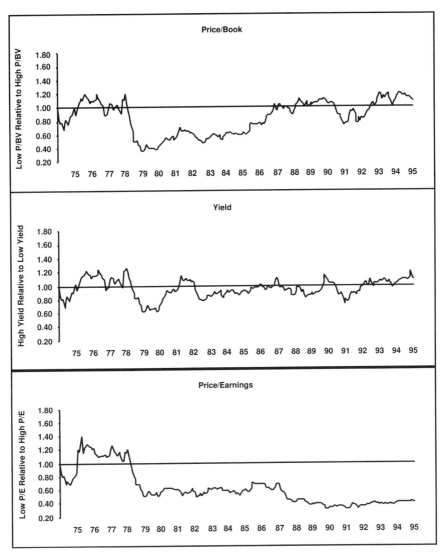

Source: Independence International Associates, Inc.

TABLE 6. Security Position Reports for Norway, January 1979–January 1980

	Industry	Price	P/B	P/E	Yield	Cap	MKT	Weights Low P/B	Weights High P/B	Weights Cum. MKT
January 1, 1979										
Borregaard	Multi-Ind	73.0	0.31	0.0	0.0	38M	4.0	8.0		4.0
Aker A	Buildings	97.0	0.36	2.1	10.3	31M	3.3	6.5		7.2
Elkem A	NonFerrous	76.5	0.37	50.3	4.6	84M	8.8	17.6		16.0
Uni Storebrand A	Insurance	88.5	0.47	11.6	7.9	23M	2.4	4.8		18.4
DNL	Airlines	60.0	0.52	6.5	11.7	16M	1.7	3.4		20.1
Orkla A	NonFerrous	50.0	0.53	0.0	0.0	16M	1.7	3.4		21.8
Bergen Bank	Banking	107.0	0.64	13.3	8.5	85M	8.9	17.8		30.7
Norske Creditbank	Banking	119.0	0.64	6.4	9.2	108M	11.3	22.6		42.0
Christiania Bank A	Banking	118.0	0.74	8.7	9.4	70M	7.3	14.7		49.4
Hafslund Nycomed A	Utilities	210.0	0.83	8.8	5.2	38M	4.0	1.3	6.7	53.4
Norsk Hydro	Chemicals	178.0	0.93	14.4	5.4	405M	42.5		84.9	95.8
Kosmos	Shipping	280.0	1.48	19.0	7.1	40M	4.2		8.4	100.0
July 1, 1979										
Borregaard	Multi-Ind	70.0	0.25	4.8	0.0	37M	2.1	4.2		2.1
Aker A	Buildings	76.0	0.40	3.8	13.2	35M	2.0	4.0		4.1
DNL	Airlines	70.0	0.47	2.2	11.4	18M	1.0	2.0		5.1
Christiania Bank A	Banking	115.0	0.59	7.1	9.6	67M	3.8	7.6		8.9
Bergen Bank	Banking	102.0	0.62	15.8	5.9	80M	4.5	9.0		13.4
Kosmos	Shipping	490.0	0.63	33.4	4.1	69M	3.9	7.8		17.3
Norske Creditbank	Banking	115.0	0.63	5.8	9.6	117M	6.6	13.2		23.9
Uni Storebrand A	Insurance	110.0	0.66	15.9	9.1	41M	2.3	4.6		26.2
Elkem A	NonFerrous	109.0	0.71	33.6	3.7	117M	6.6	13.2		32.8
Orkla A	NonFerrous	81.0	0.89	21.0	0.0	25M	1.4	2.8		34.2
Hafslund Nycomed A	Utilities	270.0	1.18	19.6	4.1	48M	2.7	5.4		36.9
Norsk Hydro	Chemicals	500.0	2.08	45.3	1.9	1B	63.1	26.2	100.0	100.0
January 1, 1980										
Borregaard	Multi-Ind	73.5	0.26	1.8	0.0	40M	1.5	3.0		1.5
Aker A	Buildings	80.0	0.42	1.3	12.5	38M	1.4	2.8		2.9
DNL	Airlines	70.0	0.47	0.6	11.4	18M	0.7	1.3		3.6
Elkem A	NonFerrous	87.0	0.56	3.0	4.6	97M	3.6	7.2		7.2
Christiania Bank A	Banking	121.0	0.62	0.0	9.1	74M	2.8	5.5		9.9
Bergen Bank	Banking	108.0	0.66	0.0	5.6	88M	3.3	6.5		13.2
Norske Creditbank	Banking	122.0	0.67	0.0	9.0	129M	4.8	9.6		18.0
Uni Storebrand A	Insurance	120.0	0.72	0.0	8.3	47M	1.8	3.5		19.7
Kosmos	Shipping	510.0	1.02	4.2	2.0	74M	2.8	5.5		22.5
Hafslund Nycomed A	Utilities	245.0	1.07	6.6	4.5	45M	1.7	3.3		24.1
Orkla A	NonFerrous	100.0	1.09	13.0	0.0	32M	1.2	2.4		25.3
Norsk Hydro	Chemicals	695.0	3.21	6.5	1.4	2B	74.7	49.3	100.0	100.0

Source: Independence International Associates, Inc.

index, and the growth index needed only two stocks and a portion of Hafslund Nycomed in order to encompass half of the capitalization of the Norwegian market.

Six months later, at the July 1, 1979 rebalance, Norsk Hydro's stock price had rocketed to 500 krone. Its P/B was 2.08. It represented 63.1 percent of the Norwegian market and, therefore, 100 percent of the growth index and 26.2 percent of the value index. By the time of the January 1, 1980 rebalance, the stock was selling at 695 krone. Norsk Hydro's P/B at this point was 3.21, and it represented 74.7 percent of the Norwegian market and, thus, 100 percent of our growth index and 49.3 percent of our value index.

Our historic value/growth spread statistics for Norway are not meaningful. Norsk Hydro so dominated the market in the late 1970s and early 1980s that it completely invalidates our statistical test of value versus growth. If Norsk Hydro had been an average performer during this period it would not have mattered. But, Norsk Hydro, benefiting enormously from the second global energy crisis in 1979, produced a U.S. dollar total return of 376 percent that year. The remainder of the Norwegian market returned just 22 percent.

The value/growth spread within the remainder of the Norwegian market is not unlike the spreads in most other markets. We can see this by computing a new set of P/B-based value and growth indexes for Norway. We neutralize the impact of Norsk Hydro by assigning half to the value side of the market and half to the growth side at every rebalance, regardless of where it ranks in the sort. The spread statistics for these new indexes are dramatically different. Whereas the P/B spread including Norsk Hydro averaged -1.55 percentage points per year, without Norsk Hydro it improves to 1.81 percentage points with a standard deviation of 10.86 and a t-statistic of 0.80. Figure 2 plots value relative to growth for this new index. We can see that the spread is still quite inconsistent until the most recent three years, but we should keep in mind that it is measured over a very small number of stocks for most of the period.

Since 1979, the Norwegian market has matured and diversified. Table 7 shows the position report for our P/B-based value and growth indexes in Norway as of our July 1, 1996 rebalance. At this date, there are 29 stocks in our market index for Norway and Norsk Hydro, with a market cap of U.S. $11 billion, represents only 33.2 percent of the market. Norsk Hydro falls on the break point between value and growth and represents 57.0 percent of growth and 9.5 percent of value.

In summary, if we neutralize the effect of Norsk Hydro the value/ growth spreads in Norway are not unlike most markets. Norsk Hydro is such a large percentage of the Norwegian market that it needs to be han-

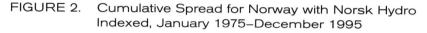

FIGURE 2.   Cumulative Spread for Norway with Norsk Hydro
            Indexed, January 1975–December 1995

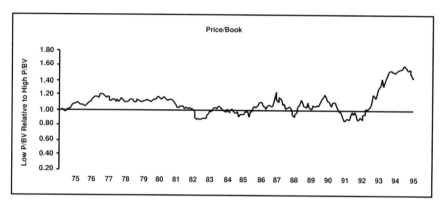

Source: Independence International Associates, Inc.

dled as a special case in the model-building process and in the risk management of the portfolios built to exploit these models.

Beware of the Accounting in Italy

Table 3 shows that the value/growth spread in Italy, if we define it using
P/B, has averaged -2.17 percentage points per year with a standard deviation of 12.71 percent and a t-statistic of -0.78. Using P/E, it has averaged
1.42 percentage points with a standard deviation of 9.77 and a t-statistic
of 0.67. Using yield, it has averaged 6.10 percentage points with a standard deviation of 12.22 percent and a t-statistic of 2.29. Figure 3 plots
value relative to growth for the three sets of value and growth indexes.
The charts confirm that the summary statistics for Italy in Table 3 are representative.

The data suggest that Italy is one of the best value markets in the
world as long as the model being used does not require any accounting
information. Our yield-based value model shows some cyclicality, as
most models do, but overall the record is very convincing. Our P/E-
based model is marginal, and our P/B-based model is perverse. Our suspicion is that there are severe accounting problems in Italy. For example,
we should not expect our P/B and P/E-based models to work well for
companies that do not have consolidated reporting. Historically, many
companies in Italy fall into this category.

TABLE 7.   Security Position Report for Norway, July 1996

| | | | | | | | | Weights | | |
| | | | | | | | | Low | High | Cum. |
	Industry	Price	P/B	P/E	Yield	Cap	MKT	P/B	P/B	MKT
July 1, 1996										
Norske Skogindustrier B	Forest	181	0.90	2.7	3.3	170M	0.5	1.0		0.5
Norske Skogindustrier A	Forest	196	0.98	2.9	3.1	800M	2.4	4.7		2.9
Sas Norge B	Airlines	70.5	0.99	7.7	4.7	510M	1.5	3.0		4.4
Den Norske Bank	Banking	19.7	1.03	4.7	6.3	2B	5.8	11.5		10.1
Christiania Bank	Banking	15.3	1.06	3.2	7.2	1B	3.8	7.7		14.0
Kvaerner B	Machine	251	1.17	6.3	2.6	373M	1.1	2.2		15.1
Aker B	Multi-Ind	116	1.18	9.0	3.9	157M	0.5	0.9		15.5
Aker A	Multi-Ind	124.5	1.27	9.7	3.6	764M	2.3	4.5		17.8
Kvaerner A	Machine	274.5	1.28	6.8	2.4	1B	4.2	8.4		22.0
Elkem	NonFerrous	89.5	1.38	4.9	5.0	679M	2.0	4.0		24.0
Dyno Industrier	Chemicals	144	1.38	24.9	2.8	563M	1.7	3.3		25.7
Nycomed B	Health	90	1.43	8.1	0.0	580M	1.7	3.4		27.4
Helicopter Services Gp	Airlines	75	1.45	10.4	4.0	233M	0.7	1.4		28.1
Bergesen B	Shipping	131	1.48	24.6	0.8	457M	1.4	2.7		29.5
Nycomed A	Health	93.5	1.48	8.4	0.0	872M	2.6	5.2		32.0
Bergesen A	Shipping	135	1.52	25.3	0.7	1B	3.3	6.5		35.3
Leif Hoegh	Shipping	113	1.72	9.0	2.7	522M	1.6	3.1		36.9
Orkla B	Multi-Ind	316	1.83	10.5	1.9	450M	1.3	2.7		38.2
Orkla A	Multi-Ind	342	1.99	11.3	1.8	2B	6.2	12.3		44.3
Unitor	Brd&Pub Sv	105	2.04	19.9	2.9	312M	0.9	1.9		45.3
Norsk Hydro	Energy Src	318	2.24	10.2	1.9	11B	33.2	9.5	57.0	78.5
Petroleum Geo-services	Energy Equ	186	2.41	22.0	0.0	775M	2.3		4.6	80.8
NCL Holding	Leisure	14.8	2.44	-1.8	0.0	247M	0.7		1.5	81.5
Uni Storebrand Ord	Insurance	29.2	2.44	6.0	0.0	1B	3.7		7.4	85.2
Saga Petroleum A	Energy Src	95.5	2.53	17.1	2.6	2B	5.9		11.9	91.1
Hafslund B	Utilities	41	3.19	17.0	0.0	264M	0.8		1.6	91.9
Schibsted	Broad&Pub	84	3.64	17.1	1.5	895M	2.7		5.3	94.6
Hafslund A	Utilities	47	3.65	19.5	0.0	438M	1.3		2.6	95.9
Transocean	Energy Equ	168.5	3.87	86.9	0.0	1B	4.2		8.3	100.0

Source: Independence International Associates, Inc.

Japan: A Great Market for Multivariate Value Models

Table 3 shows that the statistics for all three of our value models in Japan are impressive. The value/growth spread for our P/B-based model averages 6.66 percentage points with a standard deviation of 10.29 and a t-statistic of 2.97. The dividend yield-based model averages 5.59 percentage points with a standard deviation of 10.40 and a t-statistic of 2.46. The P/E-based model averages 4.62 percentage points with a standard deviation of 9.53 percent and a t-statistic of 2.22.

Table 8 shows the year-by-year spreads. We see remarkable consistency for all three sets. P/B works every year but three; yield and P/E

FIGURE 3. Cumulative Spread for Italy,
January 1975–December 1995

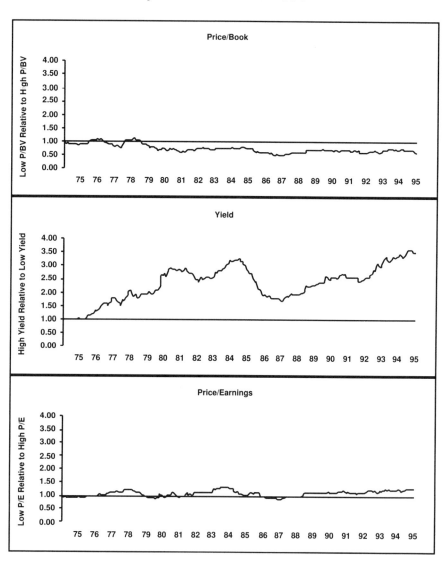

Source: Independence International Associates, Inc.

TABLE 8. Calendar Year Return Spreads for Japan, Top Half
versus Bottom Half, 1975–1995

Japan	Low P/B versus High P/B	High Yield versus Low Yield	High P/E versus Low P/E
1975	19.66	-1.22	23.22
1976	6.81	-12.50	10.34
1977	21.61	23.17	2.44
1978	6.19	2.34	7.45
1979	3.31	-3.62	0.15
1980	6.99	3.58	4.52
1981	26.27	12.87	16.16
1982	7.83	-6.44	7.65
1983	-3.18	-5.25	-3.13
1984	-19.39	21.73	-9.43
1985	6.81	22.90	3.09
1986	-5.64	21.38	21.21
1987	0.01	0.34	-1.10
1988	17.64	26.44	14.93
1989	14.33	8.87	3.47
1990	6.06	2.44	6.88
1991	2.83	0.71	-2.22
1992	12.62	10.03	10.78
1993	5.64	6.76	2.52
1994	15.61	6.68	-0.69
1995	6.43	3.39	1.73

Source: Independence International Associates, Inc.

work every year but five. Remarkably, in every year but two, 1983 and 1984, at least two out of three models work. This is clearly a market where multivariate modeling makes sense.

Figure 4 plots our value index relative to our growth index for the three sets of indexes. P/B offers a cumulative spread of 4.36 to 1, yield 3.2 to 1 and P/E 2.8 to 1. The yield model is particularly successful at avoiding the underperformance of the P/B model in 1984. Table 8 shows that our P/B-based value index *underperformed* its growth counterpart by 19.39 percentage points. Our yield-based value index *outperformed* its growth counterpart by 21.73 percentage points. This period is clearly worth further investigation. Could accounting again be the culprit?

We *can* blame the data, but this time it is not the book value or earnings data that are the problem, it is the price data. So we cannot blame the accountants, but we can blame the regulators. Banks are highly regulated in Japan, as they are in most countries. Prior to 1984, however, the Japanese brand of regulation was quite unique. The *market prices* of bank

FIGURE 4.   Cumulative Spread for Japan,
              January 1975–December 1995

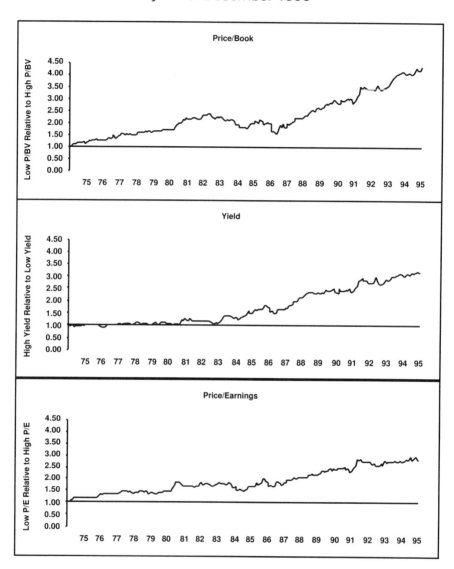

Source: Independence International Associates, Inc.

stocks were controlled in much the same manner that the Federal Reserve Bank in the United States controls the discount rate. At the end of 1984, Sumitomo, Fuji, Mitsubishi, and Sanwa banks all traded at 500 yen and had traded at that price for two years. Industrial Bank of Japan had traded at 400 yen for two years. Daiichi Kangyo had traded at 484 yen for two years. These were obviously not market-determined prices, so we should not expect any of our valuation models—P/B, dividend yield, or P/E—to work during this period.

In January 1984, the Japanese bank stocks were suddenly allowed to trade freely. Their prices doubled within a couple months and the great Japanese speculative bubble was off and running. Our position report for January 1, 1984, shows the P/B break point between value and growth in Japan at 2.19. On this basis, all of the very large city banks fell into the growth half of the market, with P/Bs ranging from 2.19 to 2.78. The yield break point was 1.2 percent, and, fortuitously, every bank had enough yield (some just barely enough) to get into the value half of the market.[12] The Japanese market was up 17 percent in 1984, but the banks were up 125 percent. The value/growth spread for the P/B-based index reflects a bank allocation at the start of the year, which was 8.9 percent for the value index and 16.6 percent for the growth index. The spread for the yield-based index reflects a bank allocation of 24.3 percent for the value index and only 1.1 percent for the growth index. No wonder the value/growth spread was positive for the yield-based indexes and negative for the P/B-based set.

So here again is another situation where results are out of character and we find a rational explanation. Our P/B model in Japan is a disaster in 1984 and our yield model goes through the roof. But neither is telling us anything, because we have (1) a one-time deregulation of stock prices for the largest industry in the market, and (2) we are testing models which going into this period have faulty data.

Are Value Models Better than Small-Cap Models?

Capitalization was one of the first sort variables to receive wide exposure in the academic literature,[13] so it is certainly worth comparing the information content of capitalization spreads to those that are fundamentally based. Table 9 compares annualized spread statistics for a set of small-cap and large-cap indexes to our base-case index. The cap-based indexes are computed identically to the P/B-based indexes, except that we sort by capitalization instead of P/B.

The record for the capitalization spreads looks quite random. At the global level, we see a small spread in favor of the small-cap index, but it is

TABLE 9. Annualized Spread Statistics, Top Half versus Bottom Half, January 1975–December 1995

	Months	Low P/B versus High P/B			Small Cap versus Large Cap		
		Avg	Std	t-stat	Avg	Std	t-stat
Austria	252	1.99	13.19	0.69	5.46	12.10	2.07
Belgium	252	3.54	9.67	1.68	0.51	9.04	0.26
Denmark	252	-1.66	16.35	-0.46	1.97	15.32	0.59
Finland	96	0.01	19.17	0.00	-1.01	18.22	-0.16
France	252	4.18	9.57	2.00	0.00	9.67	0.00
Germany	252	2.50	7.58	1.51	-0.01	7.28	0.00
Ireland	60	7.98	11.25	1.59	-1.35	13.42	-0.22
Italy	252	-2.17	12.71	-0.78	-2.24	11.96	-0.86
Netherlands	252	1.13	10.26	0.50	-3.81	15.86	-1.10
Norway	252	-1.55	21.69	-0.33	-5.90	24.97	-1.08
Spain	252	2.09	17.05	0.56	1.88	12.96	0.66
Sweden	252	2.92	14.33	0.93	1.83	11.33	0.74
Switzerland	252	-0.14	9.26	-0.07	-2.67	7.45	-1.64
United Kingdom	252	3.10	8.73	1.63	0.62	8.86	0.32
Europe	252	1.96	4.73	1.90	-0.15	4.99	-0.14
Australia	252	3.43	11.04	1.42	0.73	11.73	0.28
Hong Kong	252	1.52	12.66	0.55	5.28	13.14	1.84
Japan	252	6.66	10.29	2.97	1.38	10.44	0.61
Malaysia	252	6.21	13.03	2.18	0.65	13.97	0.21
New Zealand	96	2.70	16.91	0.45	-3.85	13.97	-0.78
Singapore	252	2.51	11.43	1.00	0.00	15.17	0.00
Pacific	252	6.08	9.07	3.07	1.69	9.29	0.83
Canada	252	3.14	10.61	1.36	1.28	8.52	0.69
United States	252	2.76	7.66	1.66	1.50	6.95	0.99
North America	252	2.78	7.14	1.79	1.47	6.54	1.03
Europe-Pacific	252	3.98	5.70	3.20	0.96	6.14	0.71
EuroPac x Japan	252	2.17	4.20	2.37	0.12	4.46	0.12
Pacific x Japan	252	3.13	6.60	2.17	1.88	7.36	1.17
Global x US	252	3.95	5.49	3.29	1.03	5.94	0.79
Global	252	3.91	5.15	3.48	1.55	4.98	1.42

Source: Independence International Associates, Inc.

not statistically significant. The spread is negative in eight out of 22 countries. Table 9 makes one wonder why anyone would want to build a global investment strategy solely around small-capitalization stocks.

The theoretical arguments for the existence of a small-cap spread have never been very convincing. The rationale seems to center mostly around the belief that small-cap companies are less widely followed and, therefore, are more likely to contain undiscovered jewels. But aren't there also likely to be undiscovered disasters as well?

Where the spreads do exist there is always the fear that for liquidity reasons they are not achievable in practice or, as Roll[14] has pointed out, nontrading effects may cause risk to be dramatically understated.

Why Do Value Models Work?

Capaul, Rowley, and Sharpe[15] argue there are things that matter to investors beyond just return and risk. Considerations such as taxes and comfort level can lead investors to be quite willing to pay up for growth stocks. The tax argument is analogous to the explanation of the spread in the United States bond market between taxable corporates and tax-free municipals. Taxable investors are willing to pay more for munis, because of the muni's favorable tax status. Munis are therefore overpriced for tax-free investors. Similarly, taxable investors should be willing to pay more for low-yielding growth stocks, thus making them overpriced for tax-free investors. Growth stock investors expect most of their return in the form of capital gains; value investors expect a larger percentage of their return to be from income dividends. For most investors in most countries, capital gains are taxed more favorably than dividends. In many countries, capital gains are not taxed at all.

The comfort-level argument is simply that high-multiple stocks are in the consensus. This creates a comfort level that may be worth something to many investors. Investors that must select their portfolio holdings from an approved list fall into this category. The more hurdles a stock must overcome to make the approved list, the more likely it will be in the consensus.

Shefrin and Statman[16] point out that an ancillary benefit of in-the-consensus stocks is the ability to externalize blame. If a highly touted growth stock goes haywire, the investor can point to all the glowing research reports in his or her files and argue that the poor performance was bad luck. If a value stock goes south, the investor is vulnerable to looking stupid, especially if the client can point to a host of sell recommendations from the brokerage community.

Lakonishok, Shleifer, and Vishny[17] argue that value models outperform because investors are prone to behavioral errors. For example, investors try to forecast the future by extrapolating the past. This leads them to willingly pay up for companies that have recently generated strong revenues and profits (i.e., growth companies). Vice versa, they need a large discount to entice them into companies with recent weak revenues and profits (i.e., value companies). Since trends rarely continue in competitive markets, growth investors are set up for a preponderance of negative surprises, while value investors are more likely to reap positive surprises and the excess return that goes with it.

Lakonishok, Shleifer, and Vishny also point out that investors are prone to cognitive error. Investors often make a leap of faith that a good company is a good investment. Once investors have formed an opinion that a company is a good company, it is difficult for them to separate that conclusion from the really important question which is whether or not the stock is a good stock. They may be right that the company is well-managed with great products, strong market share, and so forth; but, if the market already recognizes this and reflects this in the stock price, the stock is not a great investment.

Behavioral economists assure us that being expert does not provide immunity from behavioral errors. In fact, some research shows that the more expert the person is, the *more* likely it is that he or she will make these types of errors. Experts are much more prone to overconfidence for example.

Fama and French[18] argue that value stocks outperform because they are riskier. They believe the value premium is a risk premium. Many researchers such as Capaul, Rowley, and Sharpe,[19] and Umstead[20] have shown that the realized volatility of the value half of most equity markets has been no higher than the volatility of the growth half. Fama and French argue that the expectation of risk is there; it simply has yet to come home to roost. There is no way to dispute this argument short of looking at more and more markets over longer and longer periods of time. Unfortunately, the Fama and French study of the U.S. market is the longest available, and it goes back only to July 1963. Value models may well have performed poorly in the depression years in the late 1920s and 1930s.

It is our view that value models work for a combination of all of the above reasons. To the extent that taxes are part of the reason, we need to be concerned that tax laws can change. To the extent that behavioral factors are the reason, we should be concerned that investors will learn from their mistakes. One of the great advantages that quantitative managers have over traditional managers is they will not make behavioral errors if they have the discipline to stick to their models. To the extent that there are more and more quantitative firms coming into the industry, there may eventually be enough discipline and structure in place to eliminate the opportunities created by more emotional investors. We should be concerned that value stocks may indeed be riskier and that the risk will some day be realized.

All this said, there is no doubt that there has been tremendous opportunity for adding value from the disciplined application of very simple valuation models applied either regionally or globally. The evidence is pervasive, and we believe it is very unlikely that the opportunity will disappear in the foreseeable future. The tax advantage of capital gains is not likely to disappear any time soon, human behavior typically changes at a glacial pace, and, even if Fama and French are correct, it does not make sense to design an investment strategy around the next global depression.

Other Ways to Measure the Growth Side of the Market

Each of the fundamental variables—P/B, yield and P/E—discussed so far represent a simple valuation model. They compare some measure of value to current price. One criticism we often hear is that these measures do a reasonably good job of identifying the kinds of stocks that price-driven value managers buy, but they do not accurately identify the selections of most growth managers.

We have therefore constructed a set of indexes derived from a direct measure of next-year's earnings growth.[21] These indexes "cheat" in that they require information not available to the market at the rebalance date. Nevertheless, they offer insights into the potential usefulness of forecast earnings for picking stocks. We should expect considerable variation from market to market depending on the quality of the accounting and the degree of disclosure. If these indexes do not perform well, it will certainly tell us something about the viability of growth investing in global markets.

Table 10 compares annualized spread statistics for these indexes to our base-case indexes. Next-year's earnings growth works everywhere! Globally, the high-earnings-growth index outperforms the low-earnings-growth index by 11.05 percentage points per year with a standard deviation of 4.16 percent and a t-statistic of 12.18. Seventeen out of 22 markets have t-statistics above 2.0. These data leave no doubt about the usefulness of accurate forecasts of next-year's earnings.

Next-year's earnings growth offers tremendous potential for value-added. We often hear that U.S. investors are overly focused on short-term earnings. If so, they are clearly not alone. Selecting stocks based on accurate forecasts of next-year's earnings growth can be a tremendously successful strategy in every developed market.

TABLE 10. Annualized Spread Statistics, Top Half versus
Bottom Half, January 1975–December 1995

	Months	Low P/B versus High P/B			High Forward Earnings Growth versus Low Forward Earnings Growth		
		Avg	Std	t-stat	Avg	Std	t-stat
Austria	252	1.99	13.19	0.69	3.94	11.79	1.53
Belgium	252	3.54	9.67	1.68	5.91	9.80	2.76
Denmark	252	-1.66	16.35	-0.46	9.44	14.40	3.00
Finland	96	0.01	19.17	0.00	8.13	9.08	2.53
France	252	4.18	9.57	2.00	11.04	7.27	6.96
Germany	252	2.50	7.58	1.51	2.91	6.15	2.17
Ireland	60	7.98	11.25	1.59	8.79	12.70	1.55
Italy	252	-2.17	12.71	-0.78	8.23	8.86	4.26
Netherlands	252	1.13	10.26	0.50	5.20	13.05	1.82
Norway	252	-1.55	21.69	-0.33	6.08	16.43	1.70
Spain	252	2.09	17.05	0.56	7.38	11.89	2.85
Sweden	252	2.92	14.33	0.93	10.36	10.81	4.39
Switzerland	252	-0.14	9.26	-0.07	6.44	7.15	4.13
United Kingdom	252	3.10	8.73	1.63	11.74	7.28	7.40
Europe	252	1.96	4.73	1.90	8.55	3.85	10.18
Australia	252	3.43	11.04	1.42	14.76	8.73	7.75
Hong Kong	252	1.52	12.66	0.55	13.05	11.30	5.29
Japan	252	6.66	10.29	2.97	7.66	8.91	3.94
Malaysia	252	6.21	13.03	2.18	13.57	11.48	5.42
New Zealand	96	2.70	16.91	0.45	1.90	13.32	0.40
Singapore	252	2.51	11.43	1.00	9.84	11.53	3.91
Pacific	252	6.08	9.07	3.07	8.56	7.86	4.99
Canada	252	3.14	10.61	1.36	12.35	7.64	7.41
United States	252	2.76	7.66	1.66	13.90	6.22	10.25
North America	252	2.78	7.14	1.79	13.76	5.91	10.68
Europe-Pacific	252	3.98	5.70	3.20	8.45	4.74	8.17
EuroPac x Japan	252	2.17	4.20	2.37	9.13	3.49	11.98
Pacific x Japan	252	3.13	6.60	2.17	13.26	5.90	10.30
Global x US	252	3.95	5.49	3.29	8.67	4.49	8.84
Global	252	3.91	5.15	3.48	11.05	4.16	12.18

Source: Independence International Associates, Inc.

How Difficult Is It to Forecast Next-Year's Earnings?

It order to get some feel for the difficulty in coming up with a stock ranking that reflects next-year's earnings, we have computed a second set of indexes based on last-year's earnings growth. If we can rank based on last-year's earnings growth and achieve spreads that are nearly as large and consistent as those based on next-year's earnings growth, we will be encouraged to build more sophisticated time-series models for forecasting earnings. Table 11 compares spreads.[22]

TABLE 11.   Annualized Spread Statistics, Top Half versus Bottom Half, January 1976–December 1995

		High Forward Earnings Growth versus Low Forward Earnings Growth			High Trailing Earnings Growth versus Low Trailing Earnings Growth		
	Months	Avg	Std	t-stat	Avg	Std	t-stat
Austria	240	4.14	12.07	1.54	6.61	11.31	2.61
Belgium	240	6.07	9.93	2.73	0.25	9.32	0.12
Denmark	240	9.60	14.71	2.92	-0.94	11.46	-0.36
Finland	96	8.13	9.08	2.53	2.00	10.17	0.56
France	240	11.71	7.38	7.09	0.50	7.37	0.31
Germany	240	2.98	6.26	2.13	-1.37	5.71	-1.07
Ireland	60	8.79	12.70	1.55	2.23	11.90	0.42
Italy	240	8.70	9.05	4.30	-2.37	7.80	-1.36
Netherlands	240	5.76	13.16	1.96	-3.24	13.19	-1.10
Norway	240	6.48	16.82	1.72	-4.37	15.46	-1.26
Spain	240	7.78	12.11	2.87	1.67	10.74	0.70
Sweden	240	10.63	10.97	4.33	1.21	11.17	0.48
Switzerland	240	6.55	6.99	4.19	2.12	6.55	1.45
United Kingdom	240	11.88	7.42	7.16	-2.08	7.17	-1.30
Europe	240	8.83	3.90	10.12	-0.97	3.63	-1.19
Australia	240	14.53	8.68	7.48	-1.92	8.76	-0.98
Hong Kong	240	13.18	11.39	5.18	4.34	10.83	1.79
Japan	240	7.77	9.03	3.85	0.86	9.07	0.42
Malaysia	240	14.70	11.21	5.86	-1.10	11.58	-0.43
New Zealand	96	1.90	13.32	0.40	3.07	15.21	0.57
Singapore	240	10.17	11.75	3.87	3.46	10.39	1.49
Pacific	240	8.62	7.97	4.84	0.76	8.06	0.42
Canada	240	12.61	7.78	7.25	-0.66	8.60	-0.34
United States	240	14.25	6.25	10.19	0.51	6.44	0.35
North America	240	14.10	5.94	10.62	0.40	5.90	0.31
Europe-Pacific	240	8.65	4.82	8.03	-0.04	4.97	-0.04
EuroPac x Japan	240	9.38	3.53	11.89	-0.65	3.23	-0.90
Pacific x Japan	240	13.21	5.88	10.05	1.24	5.81	0.96
Global x US	240	8.86	4.56	8.68	-0.09	4.76	-0.08
Global	240	11.30	4.19	12.07	0.00	4.20	0.00

Source: Independence International Associates, Inc.

The record for spreads based on last-year's earnings growth is not encouraging. At the global level, we see a spread of exactly 0.00 and the spreads are negative in nine out of 22 countries. Extrapolation of last-year's earnings growth has worked well in just a few markets; Austria, Hong Kong, Singapore, and Switzerland. In Austria, we see the perverse result that last-year's earnings growth has been more useful than next-year's earnings growth. This obviously needs more research. In Hong Kong, Singapore, and perhaps Switzerland, projecting trends may work because of a disproportionate number of outstanding growth companies that are often able to sustain excess earnings growth and excess returns for several years in a row.

The primary message from Table 11 is that naive extrapolation of earnings growth does not work in most markets. Does this mean that it is hopeless to strive for the fantastic spreads in Table 10? Not necessarily. How about the cadre of professional security analysts? Electronic databases of analysts' earnings estimates now make it possible to systematically exploit this information. Coggin and Hunter[23] and Conroy and Harris[24] have found that analysts' consensus-earnings forecasts provide more accurate earnings estimates than a number of time-series methods. Elton and Gruber[25] have shown that consensus forecasts per se are not adequate to earn excess returns, but they also show that knowing the change in the consensus-earnings estimate is more useful than knowing the change in the actual earnings. This observation led researchers such as Wheeler[26] and Arnott[27] to create successful U.S. stock-selection models that rely on simple measures of the recent trend in estimate revisions. These models work because consensus estimates change in a predictable fashion. Analysts tend to change their earnings forecasts gradually. If they think earnings are going up $1.00, they might revise their forecast $0.50 this month and $0.50 next month. The latter revision would come only after seeing some confirmation in the revisions of other analysts. Feedback effects from analyst to analyst introduce trends in the consensus numbers.

Change in Consensus-Earnings Forecasts

In order to see whether earnings-estimate-revision models work outside the United States, we use the Institutional Brokers Estimate System (I/B/E/S) database to compute a new sort variable. I/B/E/S has been compiling security analysts' earnings-per-share forecasts since 1971. For many years I/B/E/S limited its coverage to the United States, but in 1986 they began international coverage which now extends to over 16,000 securities in 47 countries.

We construct a monthly measure of earnings-estimate changes for each security in our MSCI database beginning in January 1987.[28] We sort on this measure to create a set of indexes which distinguish between companies where earnings estimates have recently been revised upwards and those where estimates have been revised downwards. Table 12 shows annualized top-*quintile* versus bottom-*quintile*[29] spread statistics for the nine-year period from January 1987 to December 1995. The table compares the indexes discussed in the prior two sections to this new set of indexes.

It is not surprising that the top- versus bottom-quintile spreads based on next-year's earnings growth are enormous. They range from a

TABLE 12.   Annualized Spread Statistics, Top Quintile versus Bottom Quintile, January 1987–December 1995

		High Forward Earnings Growth versus Low Forward Earnings Growth			High Trailing Earnings Growth versus Low Trailing Earnings Growth			High Change in Consensus versus Low Change in Consensus		
	Months	Avg	Std	t-stat	Avg	Std	t-stat	Avg	Std	t-stat
Austria	108	4.73	17.38	0.82	2.74	15.31	0.54	11.16	16.65	2.01
Belgium	108	15.35	15.16	3.04	-4.50	17.99	-0.75	-5.02	15.24	-0.99
Denmark	108	6.01	12.86	1.40	-8.51	13.56	-1.88	15.17	19.01	2.39
Finland	96	11.64	12.00	2.74	-1.59	17.83	-0.25	11.93	20.73	1.63
France	108	16.84	9.81	5.15	1.46	9.45	0.46	12.04	12.89	2.80
Germany	108	2.32	9.12	0.76	-1.17	8.99	-0.39	4.30	13.18	0.98
Ireland	60	13.79	20.03	1.54	10.96	19.83	1.24	3.68	18.14	0.45
Italy	108	2.71	13.60	0.60	-1.66	12.58	-0.40	11.38	16.63	2.05
Netherlands	108	10.46	12.52	2.51	-8.34	12.86	-1.95	-1.10	10.87	-0.30
Norway	108	7.00	17.59	1.19	-10.35	15.52	-2.00	2.17	24.10	0.27
Spain	108	10.54	11.76	2.69	3.51	14.16	0.74	2.30	19.12	0.36
Sweden	108	3.81	14.93	0.77	-6.33	16.92	-1.12	1.13	25.05	0.13
Switzerland	108	16.62	10.32	4.83	-0.91	10.92	-0.25	11.03	12.32	2.69
United Kingdom	108	16.77	8.81	5.71	0.70	8.62	0.24	5.86	11.13	1.58
Australia	108	23.83	11.96	5.98	-0.26	15.05	-0.05	15.57	14.94	3.13
Hong Kong	108	23.25	12.39	5.63	6.31	13.18	1.44	11.28	14.98	2.26
Japan	108	8.36	15.49	1.62	-5.06	14.46	-1.05	0.07	12.66	0.02
Malaysia	108	25.32	14.51	5.24	4.04	16.07	0.75	15.91	16.57	2.88
New Zealand	96	21.26	25.88	2.32	-12.48	25.68	-1.37	9.23	26.49	0.99
Singapore	108	12.80	15.78	2.43	8.13	12.79	1.91	9.61	14.58	1.98
Canada	108	17.95	8.57	6.28	0.07	9.95	0.02	7.79	11.27	2.07
United States	108	15.82	6.99	6.79	-1.57	5.60	-0.84	3.04	9.47	0.96
Europe-Pacific	108	11.45	9.09	3.78	-2.67	8.36	-0.96	3.79	7.28	1.56
Global	108	13.23	6.52	6.09	-2.34	5.49	-1.28	3.65	6.38	1.71

Source: Independence International Associates, Inc.

low of 2.32 percentage points per year in Germany to a high of 25.32 percentage points in Malaysia. Globally, the spread averages 13.23 percentage points over nine years with a standard deviation of 6.52 and a t-statistic of 6.09. The global top versus bottom half spread in Table 11 averages 11.30 percentage points over 20 years, with a standard deviation of 4.19 and a t-statistic of 12.07. We should expect larger spreads when we exclude the middle three quintiles, and we should expect higher volatility. The higher volatility combined with the shorter measurement period accounts for the lower t-statistic.

The top- versus bottom-quintile spreads based on last-year's earnings growth are generally perverse. The spreads in Table 12 are negative in 13 out of 22 countries. Globally, the trailing-earnings-growth spread averages -2.34 percentage points, with a standard deviation of 5.49 and a t-statistic of -1.28. These results are consistent with Lakonishok, Shleifer, and Vishny[30] who show that U.S. companies with the lowest growth in sales (measured over the prior five years) outperform companies with the highest sales growth.

The top- versus bottom-quintile spreads based on the change in the consensus forecast suggest that estimate-revision models work quite well in most markets outside of the United States. The spreads are positive in 20 out of 22 countries, and statistically significant in nine. Globally, the spread averages 3.65 percentage points per year with a standard deviation of 6.38 and a t-statistic of 1.71.

Our estimate-revision model does not work in Japan, and this accounts for the relatively low t-statistic for the global spread. The large amount of cross-holdings in the Japanese equity market may explain why stock-price movements are not linked to estimate revisions. Chudler[31] reports that as of March 29, 1996, domestic corporations owned 26.3 percent of the First Section of the Japanese equity market and domestic banks owned another 15.6 percent. He also shows that 39.2 percent of the corporate portfolio was invested in Japanese banks. This interlocking ownership creates a privileged class of shareholders with a much longer investment horizon than the typical outside investor. In addition, these special owners are likely to have inside information about their portfolio holdings and are, therefore, probably far less interested in the opinions of professional security analysts who are forced to work exclusively with publicly-reported information. Finally, these insiders are not arms-length owners. They have a whole host of business objectives unrelated to the performance of their stock portfolio. For instance, if a manufacturing company owns shares in a bank, and the bank is providing the debt financing for the manufacturer, the manufacturer may be more concerned with the interest charges on the loan than with the performance of the bank's stock. If the bank in turn owns shares of the manufacturer, the bank will be of two minds as well.

If prices in the Japanese market are being set by insiders with very long-term investment horizons, we should expect to see price movements that are insensitive to shifts in the short-term earnings outlook. This would also explain why simple valuation ratios in Japan tend to be very high, and why they tend to be exceptionally useful guides to stock selection. The farther ahead the market's discounting process operates, the more likely it will be proven wrong and the more likely the simple valuation model will be proven right. In other words, if investors tend to err by extrapolating recent experience, the farther ahead the extrapolation, the larger the error. Table 3 shows that Japan is quite unique as a value market. The t-statistic for the P/B spread in Japan is the highest of any market over the last 21 years. The t-statistic for yield is the second highest, and for P/E it is the third highest. Table 8 shows that these spreads are positive almost every year. Table 10 shows, quite amazingly, that perfect knowledge of next-year's earnings is only moderately more useful than current P/B. P/B in Japan provides a spread which averages 6.66 percentage points with a standard deviation of 10.29 and a t-statistic of 2.97, while next-year's earnings delivers a 7.66 percentage point spread with a standard deviation of 8.91 and a t-statistic of 3.94. By comparison, perfect knowledge of next-year's earnings in the United States produces a spread of 13.76 percentage points with a standard deviation of 5.91 and a t-statistic of 10.68, whereas P/B delivers only 2.76 percentage points with a standard deviation of 7.66 and a t-statistic of 1.66.

Summary and Conclusions

We have used our style-index methodology as a research tool to gain a better understanding of the similarities and differences in the pricing of securities across markets. We have carefully compared the three most common valuation models country by country and documented their power and rostbustness. We saw results that were out of character in some countries for some of the models in some time periods. We probed a few of these and we were able to find a rational explanation in every case. When one or more of the models did not work, it was either because of a single dominant stock that invalidated the statistical comparison or because of data problems of one sort or another. The harder we look the more convinced we become that simple valuation techniques are powerful stock-selection models in virtually all of the developed markets of the world.

We explored the academic explanations for this phenomenon and found three general lines of thought. Value stocks outperform because investors (1) have rational preferences for characteristics in addition to more return and less risk, (2) are prone to various types of decision making errors, or (3) perceive low-priced stocks to be riskier. It would be nice to know which, if any, of these explanations are correct, because that would be very useful in assessing the likelihood that the spread will continue. The best we can do at this point is to assume there is an element of truth in all three.

We addressed the criticism that growth is not necessarily the opposite of value. We tried a straightforward approach to the identification of growth stocks; we measured earnings growth directly; next-year's first, then last-year's. We found that the spreads from knowing next-year's earnings growth are generally two to three times larger than the spreads that can be gleaned from sorting by current P/B, current yield, or trailing P/E. We found that last-year's earnings growth is not a useful stock-selection model in most markets.

Several articles in the research literature lead us to consider revisions in analysts' consensus forecasts as a direct approach to identifying growth stocks. Researchers have shown that (1) stock-price movements are more closely tied to changes in consensus-earnings estimates than they are to changes in actual earnings, and (2) consensus estimates change in predictable patterns. We indeed found that an estimate-revision model works quite well in identifying small numbers of stocks that are likely to produce excess returns.

So, we have identified lots of opportunity for quantitative stock-selection models in the global markets. How do we take advantage of this? How should we use these models in practice? Should we simply cherry pick the highest spreads, regardless of volatility, assuming that future model performance will be similar to past model performance? Should we use expectational data, historical data, or both? Should we use single-factor models in each country or multifactor models?

Grinold and Kahn[32] describe techniques for combining single-factor stock-selection models to produce an optimal multifactor model which has higher spreads and lower volatility than any individual model by itself. We have developed a number of useful rules of thumb for applying these techniques. First, ensure that individual models are robust and statistically significant. Second, to the extent possible, provide enough "different" models (as measured by the correlations between them) to allow multiple sources of information to be included in the solution. The more varied the information sources, the less volatile the final solution. Finally, subject all models to a reality check. In many markets outside of the

United States, there are not many stocks, and often one or two are much, much larger than any of the others. We saw this in the case of Norsk Hydro in Norway in the late 1970s and early 1980s. These kinds of situations need to be handled as special cases in the model-building phase. All models must be reviewed country by country and period by period in order to identify data irregularities, such as the prices of Japanese banks prior to 1984, which can wreak havoc with the model-development process.

The analytic software which we have developed to build and maintain our style indexes is an ideal tool for the research and development of global stock-selection models. This chapter represents a brief summary of work in progress.

Endnotes

1. Dennis Stattman, "Book Values and Stock Returns," *The Chicago MBA: A Journal of Selected Papers* (1980), pp. 25-45.

2. Rolf W. Banz, "The Relationship between Return and Market Value of Common Stocks," *Journal of Financial Economics* (March 1981), pp. 779-794.

3. M. R. Reinganum. "Abnormal Returns in Small Firm Portfolios," *Financial Analysts Journal* (March/April 1981).

4. S. Basu, "Investment Performance of Common Stocks in Relation to Their Price-Earnings Ratios: A Test of the Efficient Market Hypothesis," *The Journal of Finance* (1983).

5. Barr Rosenberg, Ken Reid, and Ron Lanstein, "Persuasive Evidence of Market Inefficiency," *Journal of Portfolio Management* (1985), pp. 9-17.

6. Carlo Capaul, Ian Rowley, and William F. Sharpe, "International Value and Growth Stock Returns," *Financial Analysts Journal* (January-February 1993), pp. 27-36.

7. David A. Umstead, "International Equity Style Management," in *Equity Style Management* edited by Robert A. Klein and Jess Lederman (Irwin 1995), pp. 118-141. Umstead presented earlier versions of his work, entitled "Style Life Cycles in International Equity Investing: What Works Long Term," to The Q Group (Spring 1993) and "Value Investing: A Style for All Seasons" to INQUIRE Europe (September 1993).

8. The indexes were originally published by Boston International Advisors, Inc. Independence Investment Associates, Inc., purchased Boston International Advisors on October 1, 1996. Boston International Advisors now operates as Independence International Associates, Inc., a subsidiary of Independence Investment Associates, Inc.

9. Umstead, "International Equity Style Management."

10. Historically many Malaysia stocks traded jointly on the Kuala Lumpur and Singapore stock exchanges, and MSCI published data for these companies in a "country" called Singapore/Malaysia. MSCI began coverage of Malaysia as a separate country on May 1, 1993. We have supplemented our MSCI data with data from the International Finance Corporation, and we have split "Singapore/Malaysia" into two separate countries all the way back to January 1, 1975.

11. We doubt that the few days lag makes a difference. If we lag our data a full month, we see very little impact on results.

12. Several banks had yields of exactly 1.2 percent and, thus, fell exactly on the break point. All stocks falling on the break point are allocated in proportion to whatever is needed to split the market exactly in half. In this case, all but a small fraction of the market cap of each stock on the break point was allocated to the value half of the market. Using divided yield, we often have lots of ties in the early periods because our data are only calculated to one decimal place for yield.

13. Banz, "Relationship between Return and Market Value"; and Reinganum, "Abnormal Returns in Small Firm Portfolios."

14. Richard Roll, "A Possible Explanation of the Small Firm Effect," *The Journal of Finance* (1981), pp. 879-888.

15. Capaul, "International Value and Growth Stock Returns."

16. Hersh Shefrin and Meir Statman, "A Behavioral Framework for Expected Stock Returns," working paper presented to The Q Group (Fall 1993).

17. Josef Lakonishok, Andrei Shleifer, and Robert W. Vishny, "Contrarian Investment, Extrapolation, and Risk," working paper presented to The Berkeley Program in Finance (Spring 1994)

18. Eugene F. Fama and Kenneth R. French, "The Cross-Section of Expected Stock Returns," *The Journal of Finance* (1992) pp. 427-465.

19. Capaul, "International Value and Growth Stock Returns."

20. Umstead, "International Equity Style Management."

21. Next-year's earnings growth is computed from the earnings as reported in the Morgan Stanley Capital International *Perspective* on the rebalance date versus the earnings reported in the *Perspective* 12 months later.

22. Last-year's earnings growth is computed from the earnings as reported in the Morgan Stanley Capital International *Perspective* on the rebalance date versus the earnings reported in the *Perspective* 12 months prior. The comparisons in Table 11 cover the period from January 1976 to December 1995. The data in this table start one year later than the data in the previous tables. This is necessary because computation of last-year's earnings growth was not possible until January 1976.

23. T. Daniel Coggin and John E. Hunter, "Analysts' EPS Forecasts Nearer Actual than Statistical Models," *Journal of Business Forecasting* (Winter 1982-1983), pp. 20-23.

24. Robert Conroy and Robert S. Harris, "Consensus Forecasts of Corporate Earnings: Analysts' Forecasts and Time-Series Methods," *Management Science* (June 1987), pp. 725-738.

25. Edwin J. Elton and Martin J. Gruber, "Expectations and Share Prices," *Management Science* (September 1981), pp. 975-987.

26. Langdon B. Wheeler, "Changes in Consensus Earnings Estimates and Their Impact on Stock Returns," working paper presented to The Q Group (Spring 1990).

27. Robert Arnott, "The Use and Misuse of Consensus Earnings," *Journal of Portfolio Management* (Spring 1985), pp. 18-27.

28. The exact construction of this measure is proprietary.

29. This table compares top- and bottom-*quintile* spreads rather than top- and bottom-*half* spreads because, in most months, a small percentage of companies experience a change in consensus forecast. Our ranking on consensus-forecast change is therefore useful only in the tails. In other words, the middle quintiles of this sort are often not meaningful, because many companies in this range have a zero value for the ranking variable.

30. Josef Lakonishok, Andrei Shleifer, and Robert W. Vishny, "Contrarian Investment, Extrapolation, and Risk," *The Journal of Finance* (December 1994), pp. 1553.

31. Craig Chudler, "Japan Equity Strategy Review," Salomon Brothers' *Japanese Equity Research Report* (September 1996), pp. 31.

32. Richard C. Grinold and Ronald N. Kahn, *Active Portfolio Management* (Chicago: Probus Publishing, 1995).

The Case for Global Small Stocks

Lawrence S. Speidell
Director of Global/Systematic Portfolio
  Management and Research

Douglas Stone
Director of Research
Nicholas Applegate

Introduction

Investors are now aware of the opportunities available through international investing. Between 1992 and 1997, it is estimated that investors increased international investment exposure from 5 percent of equities to 10 percent. The driving forces in globalizing portfolios have been the prospect of higher returns and the benefit of diversification. These arguments remain powerful, but there is an added opportunity for international investors: the diversification of investment styles, particularly by adding exposure to smaller capitalization stocks. The definition of investment styles has been a significant result of the developing maturity of institutional investing in the United States over the past 25 years. As a result of this maturing, several benefits have emerged, including improved diversification and improved measurement of investment managers' results. Now, after establishing initial positions in international investments over the last decade, U.S. institutional investors are beginning to pay increasing attention to distinctions in international investment styles.

Regarding domestic investments, institutional investors and consultants have developed a style framework which typically includes four major categories or quadrants: large-capitalization value stocks, large-capitalization growth stocks, small-capitalization value stocks and small-capitalization growth stocks. A similar framework is likely to develop internationally as more institutions move a greater portion of their assets outside the United States. As international style distinctions develop, there will be some important shifts in asset allocation toward styles not presently represented in most institutional investors' portfolios. The most significant style diversification opportunity today is in the small-stock sector of global markets.

While growth-versus-value distinctions are important, they are often difficult to quantify, especially in high-growth economies where even basic industrials are often considered to be growth stocks. Small capitalization stocks, however, are underowned by global institutions. Most global investors have bought popular large-cap stocks and neglected a broader cross section of companies in foreign markets.

That international indices typically represent large-capitalization stocks is well known. We analyzed the Morgan Stanley Capital International (MSCI) country indices for the United Kingdom, Germany, France, and Japan. Using Sharpe's (1988) effective mix methodology, these indices can be analyzed in terms of capitalization (from small to large) and in terms of value to growth. Not surprising, the returns for these country indices mirror those of large-cap stocks. Approximately 75 percent of the index returns in each country can be attributed to large-company returns, a reflection of a significant large-stock bias.[1]

The institutional bias toward large cap is natural for several reasons: first, it is easier. Conducting broad research in international markets is difficult because of language barriers and reporting differences. These challenges often deter managers and analysts. Second, many large non-U.S. stocks are also available in the form of American Depository Receipts (ADRs), which often offer more liquid trading, improved information disclosure, and simplified custody. Finally, some studies have indicated that stocks within many foreign markets move together. Thus, owning one or two large stocks in a market gives good exposure to the market as a whole. These conditions, however, may be changing.

Just as growth stock investors in the United States in the early 1970s bid up the large "nifty fifty" growth stocks, global investors today may have created many two-tier markets in which the best opportunities may be found in smaller stocks. We examine this pattern to see where it may be worth digging deeper within markets, to find opportunities which may not be well known but may offer high rewards. If this is so, investors will begin to discriminate among international investment managers in the same way they have in the U.S. market. Our analysis of small-capitalization stocks focuses on returns, valuation, and diversification.

Returns

In the United States, there has been a well-documented small-stock effect in which, as shown in Figure 1, small stocks have exhibited long-term outperformance characterized by strong periods ranging from nine to 14 years. A new period of outperformance may have begun in 1990.

For the United Kingdom and France, the historical small-stock results are shown in Figure 2. In this analysis, we measured returns of large stocks by using the proxy of the Morgan Stanley Capital International (MSCI) Index for each developed country. These indexes have a bias toward large stocks because they are capitalization-weighted. For small-capitalization stocks in each developed market, we used the Salomon Extended Market Index (EMI), which is composed of the smallest 20 percent of market capitalization in each market, although it often includes more than 50 percent of the stocks. In Figure 2, the market performance is shown by the thick line and the small-stock performance by the dotted line. Relative performance of small stocks divided by all stocks is represented by the dashed line. In each developed market, smaller stocks underperformed in the early 1990s, but this reversed in the United Kingdom in the second half of 1992 and in France in 1993.

FIGURE 1.

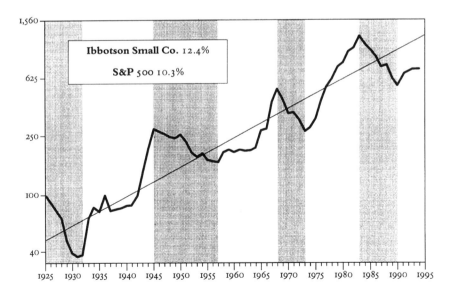

Ibbotson Small Co. 12.4%

S&P 500 10.3%

Source: Ibbotson Associates

FIGURE 2.

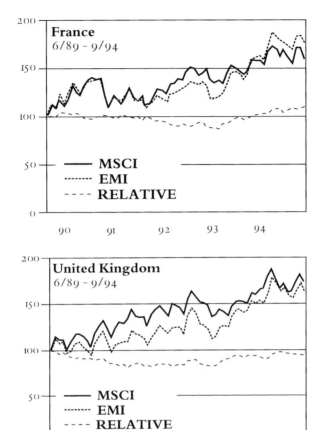

Source: MSCI

A similar analysis of the behavior of small stocks is presented for one of the emerging countries, Malaysia, in Figure 3. In these countries we used the International Finance Corporation (IFC) Investable Index as a proxy for large stocks while for small stocks we used data from Wilshire Associates. Wilshire defines small stocks as those between the 67th and 95th percentiles of size. As shown, small stocks in Malaysia have done especially well since mid-1992.

FIGURE 3.

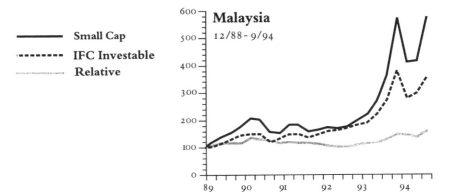

Source: MSCI

There may be a relationship between small-stock relative performance and economic activity, particularly among the trends of industrial production. In the United States, France, and the United Kingdom, the revival of small stocks occurred near the trough in industrial production. This same behavior may be occurring in Germany and Japan, although their economic cycles are at different stages.

An econometric analysis of the small-capitalization returns and changes in industrial production for five countries indicates that monthly changes in industrial production appear to lead small-stock returns. Table 1 shows the results of a Granger causality test indicating that in the United States, industrial production does not lead small-cap returns as it

TABLE 1. Does Industrial Production Lead Small Stock Returns?

Results of a Granger Causality Test with 18 Months Data

Country	F Test	p Value
Japan	1.92	.173**
Germany	2.49	.095*
France	3.22	.048*
United Kingdom	2.91	.063*
United States	1.16	.435

*Denotes significance at the 10% confidence level.
**Denotes significance at the 20% confidence level.

Source: International Monetary Fund

does in other countries. This statistical test measures the ability of one variable to forecast another variable. A significant result indicates that changes in industrial production are useful for forecasting small-company stock returns. In no case did small-stock returns lead industrial production.

Our analysis of returns leads to two conclusions: first, small stocks do behave differently from large stocks in most markets. Second, there has been an improvement in small-stock returns in several markets recently.

Valuation

The valuation of small stocks versus large stocks in developed markets is presented in Figure 4. It shows the market profile of price-to-book values for deciles of market capitalization ranging from decile 1, the smallest 10 percent of stocks, to decile 10, the largest stocks in each market.

Although the pattern is not perfectly regular, the smaller stocks in the United States, United Kingdom, Germany and France are generally cheaper than the larger stocks. In the United States, for example, stocks in

FIGURE 4.

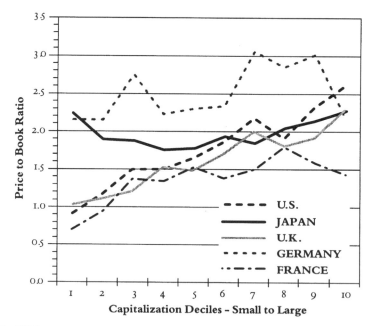

Source: MSCI

the smallest decile sell at a median price-to-book value ratio of less than 1.0x, whereas stocks in the largest decile sell at more than 2.5x. The only exception to this pattern is Japan where small stocks do not presently sell at a discount.

Figure 5 presents the same analysis of valuation for several emerging markets. While there are more irregularities, the overall picture is similar to that of the developed countries. The smaller companies are cheaper, especially in Thailand, where the largest three deciles sell at four times book value while the price of many smaller stocks is only one times book value.

A similar analysis for Peru is presented in Figure 6. Peru is an interesting market because the country has achieved 10 percent GNP growth and inflation is now down to 16 percent compared with 7600 percent in 1990. Our data were obtained from Banco De Credito, the nation's largest bank. As shown in Figure 6, Peru's market is characterized by a steep discount for smaller stocks. For example, Peru's largest beer manufacturer, Backus, with a $796 million market capitalization, sells at 3.1 times book value compared with 1.7x for Compania Nacional Cerreccera (CNC), the second largest brewer with a $196 million market capitalization.

Although our analysis has focused on only one measure of value, price to book, there is evidence that smaller stocks are definitely valued

FIGURE 5.

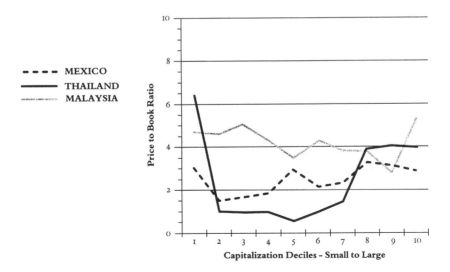

Source: MSCI

FIGURE 6.

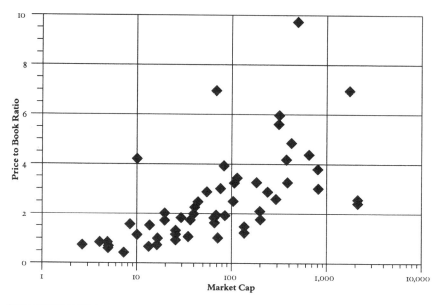

Source: MSCI and Salomon

differently in many markets and may often be cheaper than larger capitalization issues.

Diversification

Another important feature of global small stocks is their diversification benefit relative to the U.S. market. Figure 7 shows the correlation of several developed markets with the U.S. market. These correlations have been calculated over moving 12-quarter windows to show changes in the relative relationships of markets. For each country, the correlation has been calculated for the market as a whole versus the S&P 500 using the MSCI country indices. Then the same calculation has been done using the Salomon EMI, with those results shown by the gray line in each chart. In all cases, the correlations of these developed markets with the United States have declined during the period. This may be the result of the different patterns of monetary policy and industrial production. While this decline may not be permanent, there is some evidence that developed market correlations may rise during periods of high volatility.[2] Nevertheless, in every case, smaller stocks show much lower correlations with the

FIGURE 7.

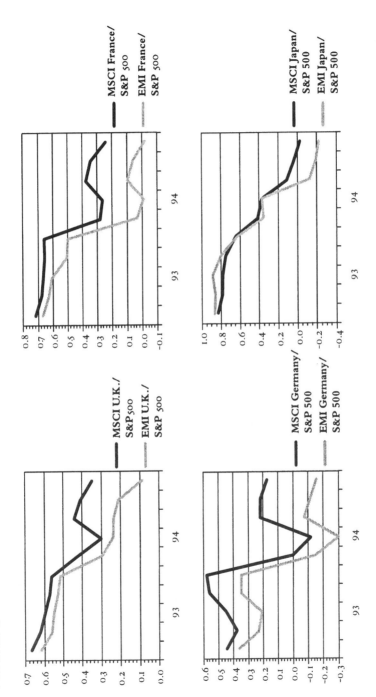

Source: MSCI and Salomon

211

U.S. market than each country's market as a whole. In the case of Japan and Germany, smaller stocks have even exhibited a negative correlation with the U.S. market.

A similar study is presented for several of the emerging markets in Figure 8: Brazil, Thailand, Mexico, and the Philippines. For emerging markets, the correlations with the U.S. market were calculated for large stocks using the International Finance Corporation (IFC) Investable Index and for small stocks using the Wilshire Small Capitalization Index. Generally, the overall emerging market correlations with the United States are lower than those for developed markets. Thus, there is often a further diversification benefit from owning the smaller stocks within emerging markets.

Asset Allocation Inputs and Methods

To analyze the utility of investing in small companies around the world, we developed an asset allocation model that takes into account expected returns, volatilities, and the correlations between assets. We use a probabilistic approach that incorporates uncertainty into the calculations. Our model concentrates on the equity portion of a plan's assets and treats the non-equity asset classes as given.

This model was based on the concept of estimation error as noted in Lummer, *et. al.* (1994) and in Michaud (1989). Estimation error arises whenever statistical estimates of returns, variances and correlations are calculated. This in turn will lead to overinvesting in some asset classes and underinvesting in others. Monte Carlo allows us to include the notion of estimation error directly into the allocation process. The standard deviations were assumed to come from normal distributions based on their historical patterns, while the expected returns were all set equal at an annualized rate of 11 percent. The resulting efficient frontier is sometimes called the "fuzzy efficient frontier." The idea that expected returns might be the same for similar asset classes was first developed by Hensel and Turner (1993) and we have adopted this approach.

Table 2 lists the asset classes used in this study along with various return and volatility assumptions. Because the Salomon indices began in mid-1989, the short history runs from July 1989 to September 1994. The long history encompasses all data for each asset class. Common stock, for example, is represented by the S&P 500 Index and starts in January 1926. The consensus forecasts are the averages of several consulting firms' standard inputs. The firms are Callan Associates, SEI Capital Resources, Frank Russell Co., and Wilshire Associates. The fourth column shows the

FIGURE 8.

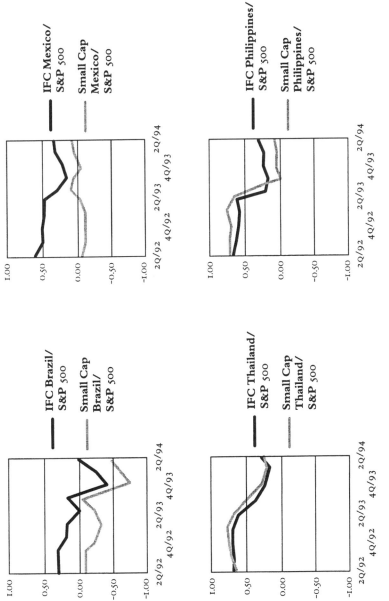

Source: IFC and Wilshire

213

TABLE 2. Expected Annualized Returns and Standard
          Deviations

	Short Historical	Long Historical	Consensus Forecasts	Forward Looking Estimates
Common Stock (S&P 500)				
Return	11.08	11.76	10.44	11.00
Standard Deviation	12.67	19.90	17.90	16.00
International Stock (Morgan Stanley Capital International EAFE)				
Return	7.01	14.14	10.93	11.00
Standard Deviation	20.34	17.42	20.68	20.68
U.S. Small Cap Stocks (Russell 20000				
Return	11.27	16.15	NA	11.00
Standard Deviation	16.50	19.14	NA	17.90
Emerging Markets (International Finance Corporation)				
Return	12.41	21.70	NA	11.00
Standard Deviation	21.32	23.39	NA	28.00
International Small Cap Stock (Salomon Extended Market Index)				
Return	6.98	6.98	NA	11.00
Standard Deviation	21.70	21.70	NA	20.68

Source: Nicholas-Applegate & Heitman/JMB Advisory Corp.

inputs used in this study and represents our estimates for future returns
and volatilities.

In addition to returns, we used a correlation matrix estimated with
monthly data from 1989 to 1994. These correlations are displayed in Table
3. Figures 9 and 10 show the rolling five-year annualized returns and

TABLE 3. Correlations between Asset Classes

Asset Class	S&P 500	MSCI EAFE	Cash	U.S. Small Cap	Emrg. Markets	Int'l Small Cap
S&P 500	1.000					
MSCI EAFE	0.550	1.000				
Cash	0.041	-0.044	1.000			
U.S. Small Cap	0.804	0.330	-0.149	1.000		
Emrg. Markets	0.273	0.359	-0.277	0.335	1.000	
Int'l Small Cap	0.400	0.800	-0.018	0.283	0.383	1.000

Source: Nicholas-Applegate

FIGURE 9.

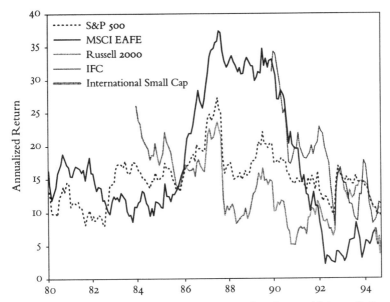

Source: Nicholas Applegate Capital Management, Ibbotson Associates, and Salomon Brothers.

FIGURE 10.

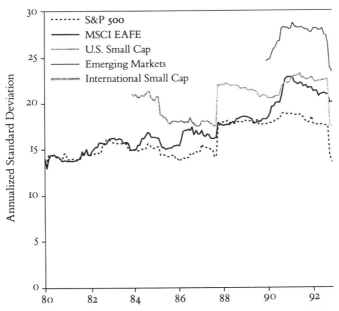

Source: Nicholas Applegate Capital Management, Ibbotson Associates, and Salomon Brothers.

standard deviations for these asset classes. In the last two or three years, the annualized standard deviations across all asset classes have decreased dramatically from relatively high levels in the late 1980s. This is due, in part, to the volatility of October 1987 rolling out of the equations.

The rolling five-year annualized returns for the S&P 500 ranged from a low of 7.9 percent in 1982 to a high of 27.4 percent in July 1987. At the end of the third quarter 1994, the annualized return was 9.5 percent. Which number is the correct one to use? In order to assess the information content present in the forecasts, we used the short-term and long-term returns and standard deviations from Table 2 and analyzed the allocations that resulted from using these numbers in an allocation model.

Asset Allocation Results

Table 4 shows the results of using both sets of historical inputs for a moderate risk investor. The short-term history produced allocations where, at a moderate risk level, approximately 77 percent of the assets were allocated to the S&P 500 with the remaining amounts invested in emerging markets. The long-term returns and standard deviations, however, suggest that an investor willing to take on a moderate amount of risk should not invest any money in large companies in the United States. Forty-six percent of the portfolio would be invested in the IFC emerging markets index—certainly not a moderate risk policy.

Next, we performed asset allocation optimization using the consensus forecasts in a model that excluded international small stocks. Later we reintroduced them to see if it made a difference. Finally, we used our own forward-looking estimates. The standard asset-allocation model was modified to run in a probabilistic fashion.

Adding small international stocks to a well-diversified portfolio adds about 150 basis points, on average, to the expected return at moderate levels of risk tolerance. As Figure 11 graphically demonstrates, not only are U.S. small-cap stocks in the mix, but international small-cap stocks are chosen at every risk level.

TABLE 4. Allocations for Moderate Risk Portfolios Using Historical Data

	U.S. Large Cap Stocks	U.S. Small Cap Stocks	Int'l Stocks	Emrg. Markets
Short-Term History	77%	0%	0%	23%
Long-Term History	0%	28%	26%	46%

Figure 11 indicates that the resulting portfolios, based on our estimates, show a reasonable mix of assets. This figure presents efficient portfolios at different risk levels with global small stocks. A moderate-risk
investor would be 59 percent invested in the United States, 22 percent in
the Morgan Stanley Capital International Europe, Australia, Far East
(EAFE) Index, 14 percent in international small stocks, and 5 percent in
the emerging markets. At virtually all levels of risk, some amount of global small-capitalization stocks are included.

Adding small global stocks to a well-diversified portfolio adds, on
average, over 100 basis points of return at normal levels of risk. Figure 12
shows the results of a Monte Carlo simulation and compares portfolios
with small-capitalization stocks and those without. Figure 11 shows the
average weights of the simulated portfolios while Figure 12 displays
ellipse charts showing where the portfolios plot in a risk-return framework. At each level of risk tolerance, two sets of portfolios are compared:
one without international small-cap stocks, and one with.

The initials NS in the legend of Figure 12 refer to no small-cap
stocks. The chart shows that at the conservative end of the spectrum, the
addition of international small-cap stocks does not make much of a difference. At higher risk-tolerances, the addition of international small-cap
stocks increases both the return and the risk of simulated portfolios. Figure 12, therefore, shows the "fuzzy efficient frontier." One can see that the
shape of the frontier slopes upward and to the right, indicating that
higher risk is associated with higher return.

FIGURE 11.

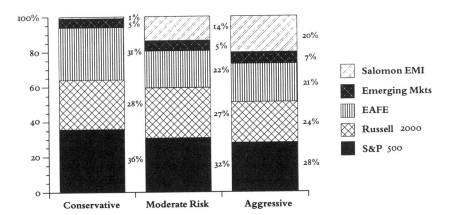

Source: Nicholas Applegate Capital Management

FIGURE 12.

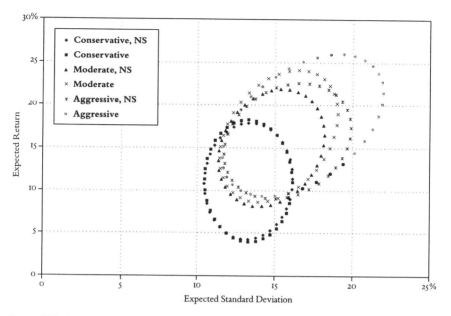

Source: Nicholas Applegate Capital Management

The results show that small stocks can play an effective role in diversifying portfolios across a wide range of risk tolerances.

Conclusion

We have examined the global evidence of small-stock returns, valuations, and correlations. There appear to be several advantages to investing in small stocks around the world:

- small stocks behave differently and are viewed differently than large stocks;
- recent relative returns of small stocks have improved significantly in many non-U.S. markets;
- the valuations of smaller stocks appear low relative to their larger counterparts in many markets;
- smaller stocks appear to offer greater diversification benefits to a U.S. investor than the large-cap sectors of both developed and emerging countries; and,

- the results from extensive asset allocation modeling indicate that global small stocks can play a dramatic role in diversification by increasing expected return at most risk levels.

In addition, there is growing interest in smaller stocks in international and emerging markets, as evidenced by a Wilshire study of small-cap results published in the fall of 1994, and the announcement by MSCI of international small-cap indices to be introduced in 1995 or early 1996. As international investors become more conscious of the opportunity for international style diversification, there are likely to be significant shifts in asset allocation. One segment with significant potential for increased allocations is global small-capitalization stocks. Our conclusions suggest this is an excellent time to invest in smaller stocks around the world.

Endnotes

1. The style indices were developed using the techniques of Capual, Rowley, and Sharpe (1993) and are available from Boston International Advisors.
2. See also "Global Diversification in a Shrinking World" by Lawrence S. Speidell and Ross Sappenfield, *Journal of Portfolio Management,* Fall 1992.

Bibliography

Capaul, Carlo; Ian Rowley; and William F. Sharpe. "International Value and Growth Stock Returns." *Financial Analysts Journa,* January/February 1993.

Hensel, Chris, and Andy Turner. "Were Returns from Stocks and Bonds of Different Countries Different in the 1980s?" *Management Science,* vol. 39, no. 7 (1993).

Lummer, Scott L.; Mark W. Riepe; and Lawrence B. Siegel. "Taming Your Optimizer: A Guide through the Pitfalls of Mean-Variance Optimization." *Global Asset Allocation: Techniques for Optimizing Portfolio Management.* New York: John Wiley & Sons, 1994.

Michaud, Richard O. "The Markowitz Optimization Enigma: Is 'Optimized' Optimal?" *Financial Analysts Journal,* January/February 1989.

Sharpe, William F. "Determining a Fund's Effective Asset Mix," *Investment Management Review,* September/October 1988.

Speidell, Lawrence S., and Ross Sappenfield. "Global Diversification in a Shrinking World." *Journal of Portfolio Management,* Fall 1992.

Wurtzebach, Charles H. "Real Estate Investing: A Disciplined Approach." Institute for Fiduciary Education Winter Seminar for Public Funds Program, January 1995.

The Cross-Sectional Determinants of Emerging Equity Market Returns*

Geert Bekaert
Associate Professor, Stanford University
Faculty Research Fellow, National Bureau of Economic
  Research

Claude B. Erb
Managing Director
First Chicago NBD Investment Management Co.

Campbell R. Harvey
Professor, Duke University
Research Associate, National Bureau of Economic Research

Tadas E. Viskanta
Vice President
First Chicago NBD Investment Management Co.

Introduction

Regulatory changes, currency devaluations, failed economic plans, coups, and other national financial "shocks" are notoriously difficult to predict and may have disastrous consequences for global portfolios. These features often define the difference between investment in the capital markets of developed versus emerging economies.

Research on emerging markets has suggested three market characteristics: high average returns, high volatility, and low correlations both across the emerging markets and with developed markets. Indeed, the lesson of volatility was learned the hard way by many investors in December 1994 when the Mexican stock market began a fall that would reduce equity value in U.S. dollars by 80 percent over the next three months.

*Some of the results in this chapter were presented at the conference on *The Future of Emerging Market Capital Flows* at New York University, May 23–24, 1996.

But, we have learned far more about these fledgling markets. First, we need to be careful in interpreting the average performance of these markets. Errunza and Losq (1985) and Harvey (1995) point out that the International Finance Corporation (IFC) backfilled some of the index data resulting in a survivorship bias in the average returns. In addition, the countries that are currently chosen by the IFC are the ones that have a proven track record. This selection of winners induces another type of selection bias. Finally, Goetzmann and Jorion (1996) detail a re-emerging market bias. Some markets, like Argentina, have a long history beginning in the last half of the 19th century. At one point in the 1920s, Argentina's market capitalization exceeded that of the United Kingdom. However, this market submerged. To sample returns from 1976 (as the IFC does), only measures the "re-emergence" period. A longer-horizon mean, in this case, would be lower than the one calculated from 1976. This insight is consistent with the out-of-sample portfolio simulations carried out by Harvey (1993) indicating that the performance of the dynamic strategy was affected by the initial five years. It must also be realized that exposure as measured by the IFC is not necessarily attainable for world investors because of investment restrictions, high transactions costs, poor liquidity, and so forth [see Bekaert and Urias (1996)].

Second, we have learned that the emerging market returns are more predictable than developed market returns. Harvey (1995) details much higher explanatory power for emerging equity markets than for developed market returns. The sources of this predictability could be time-varying risk exposures and/or time-varying risk premiums, such as in Ferson and Harvey's (1991, 1993) study of U.S. and international markets. The predictability could also be induced by fundamental inefficiencies.

In many countries, the predictability is of a remarkably simple form: autocorrelation. For example, Harvey (1995) details 0.25 autocorrelation coefficient for Mexico in a sample that ends in June 1992. An investor who followed a strategy based on autocorrelation in this country would have lost 35 percent like everyone else in December 1994. However, the investor would have been completely out of the market in the next three months (or short, if possible). Momentum appears to be important for many of these markets.

Third, we have learned that the structure of the returns distribution is potentially unstable. Bekaert, Erb, Harvey, and Viskanta (1996) present evidence that the distribution of emerging equity market returns is different in the 1990s than in the 1980s. Garcia and Ghysels (1994) reject the structural stability of the prediction regressions presented in Harvey (1995). These regressions allow for the influence of both local and world information. Bekaert and Harvey (1995, 1996a) present a model which explains the results of Garcia and Ghysels. The Bekaert and Harvey model allows for the relative influence of local and world information to change through time. They hypothesize that as a market becomes more "integrated" into world capital markets, the world information becomes relatively more important. Bekaert and Harvey (1996a) find that the changing relative importance of world information also influences volatility.

Fourth, the Bekaert and Harvey (1996a) framework suggests that the increasing influence of world factors on emerging expected returns may manifest itself in increased correlation with developed market benchmarks.

The goal of this chapter is to explore cross-sectional determinants of emerging-markets market strategies. We begin by examining some of the issues involved in using emerging-market equity data. These issues include investibility, survivorship, and nonnormality. We then investigate a wide variety of cross-sectional strategies. We attempt to answer the question of what matters in emerging-equity-market investing. We try to link the cross-section of expected returns to political, economic, and financial risk, as well as a number of fundamental attributes, such as price to book value. Some concluding remarks are made in the last section.

The Challenges of Emerging Market Data

Which Emerging Market Benchmarks Should Be Used?

The three main sources of emerging market benchmarks are the International Finance Corporation (IFC), Morgan Stanley Capital International (MSCI) and ING Barings' Emerging Markets Indices (BEMI). All provide country benchmark indices which are based on a value-weighted portfolio of a subset of stocks which account for a substantial amount of the market capitalization within each emerging market.

The IFC produces two types of indices: global (IFCG) and investable (IFCI). For nine countries, data exist back to 1976. Currently, the IFC provides data on 27 countries.[1] MSCI also produces both emerging markets global (EMG) and emerging-markets free indices (EMF) which resembles the IFCI. ING Barings only focuses on investible indices. Our chapter focuses on the global indices. Part of the interest in studying emerging markets is the impact capital market liberalizations have on the returns. Hence, we study markets before and after they are accessible to international investors.[2]

IFC, MSCI, and ING Barings all use different hierarchical processes in the company selection for their indices. MSCI follows the same technique that it uses in its·popular developed-country benchmarks. First, the market is analyzed from the perspective of capitalization and industry categories. Next, a target of 60 percent coverage of the total capitalization of each market, with industry weightings approximating the total market's weightings is established. Finally, companies are selected based on liquidity, float, and cross-ownership to fulfill these goals.

In contrast, the IFC's order of preference is: size, liquidity, and industry. The IFC primarily targets the largest and most actively traded stocks in each market, with a goal of 60 percent of total market capitalization at the end of each year. As a second objective, the index targets 60 percent of the trading volume during the year. Industry is of tertiary priority.

ING Baring's indices focus on foreign institutional investibility for the global emerging markets. Their indices only contain the most accessible securities in the 20 markets they track. As a result, the number of securities tracked by BEMI is far less than MSCI and IFC.[3] Aside from investibility, the primary factor for both company and country selection is liquidity. ING Barings considers other factors, including frequent financial reporting and the availability of high-quality data.

Although there are some hierarchical differences in the structure of construction, there is little difference in the behavior of the IFCG and the EMG. Table 1A details the difference between the IFCG and the EMG returns over identical samples for each index. The data are available through June 1996. Of the 22 countries where there is MSCI and IFC data, the returns indices have greater than 94 percent correlation. The volatility differences are quite small, as is the tracking error of the two indices.[4]

The only country where substantial deviations occur is Argentina. The IFC index produced a 10.3 percent lower average return and a 20.8 percent lower volatility. For this country, the correlation between the IFC index and the MSCI index is only 76 percent. However, much of the tracking error is due to 1988–1989 data. When we redo the comparison for Argentina beginning in January 1990, the tracking error drops from 61.9 percent to 10.6 percent. The correlation increases from 76 percent to 99 percent. There is no difference in the mean returns and little difference in the volatilities. Hence, even for Argentina, there is does not appear to be a substantive difference between the MSCI and IFC indices.

Table 1B examines the differences between the MSCI free and the BEMI investible indices. The average tracking error is 9.6 percent. The countries with the highest tracking errors are Argentina, Brazil, and Tur-

TABLE 1A.   Comparison of IFC and MSCI Emerging Market
             Global Indices

Country	Start Date	Ave. Return Difference IFCG-MSCI	Volatility Difference IFCG-MSCI	Tracking Error IFCG-MSCI	Correlation IFCG vs. MSCI
Argentina	Jan-88	10.3%	-20.8%	61.0%	0.76
Brazil	Jan-88	-1.9%	2.3%	19.1%	0.96
Chile	Jan-88	-1.7%	-0.8%	7.5%	0.96
Colombia	Jan-93	3.2%	-1.6%	7.8%	0.96
Greece	Jan-88	-6.6%	0.8%	11.8%	0.96
India	Jan-93	-4.5%	-1.7%	6.5%	0.98
Indonesia	Jan-90	1.0%	2.2%	8.9%	0.96
Jordan	Jan-88	4.4%	0.0%	11.7%	0.76
Malaysia	Jan-88	-0.6%	0.1%	4.7%	0.98
Mexico	Jan-88	-1.2%	-1.3%	10.8%	0.96
Pakistan	Jan-93	0.1%	2.1%	4.4%	0.99
Peru	Jan-93	0.5%	2.6%	6.8%	0.99
Philippines	Jan-88	-1.4%	-0.1%	9.7%	0.95
Poland	Jan-93	8.7%	3.2%	14.6%	0.99
Portugal	Jan-88	0.2%	0.5%	6.3%	0.96
South Africa	Jan-93	1.2%	-0.2%	3.1%	0.99
South Korea	Jan-88	0.2%	0.3%	6.6%	0.97
Sri Lanka	Jan-93	-1.3%	-0.4%	5.8%	0.98
Taiwan	Jan-88	-1.1%	-1.1%	7.1%	0.99
Thailand	Jan-88	-0.8%	0.5%	5.2%	0.98
Turkey	Jan-88	-2.8%	-2.6%	21.8%	0.94
Venezuela	Jan-93	3.0%	-2.0%	9.1%	0.98
Average		0.4%	-0.8%	11.4%	0.95

Monthly returns in US Dollars.
Data through June 1996.

Source: IFC Global Indices, MSCI EM Global Indices.

key. Nevertheless, the correlation of the indices averages 95 percent and is above 94 percent in 14 of the 17 countries.

Table 1C measures the differences between the Barings and IFC investibles. The tracking error is slightly less than the BEMI–MSCI Free, at 9.4 percent. The average correlation of the indices is 96 percent. There are only three countries of 18 that have correlations less than 94 percent.

The IFC family of indices presents the longest history and, as a result, we choose to focus on the IFC. In addition, we study total market returns measured in U.S. dollars. The local currency returns are not, in general, available to international investors. Furthermore, hedged returns are not available either. Table 2 presents the total sample of emerging

TABLE 1B. Comparison of Barings and MSCI Emerging
Market Indices

Country	Start Date	Ave. Return Difference BEMI-MSCI	Volatility Difference BEMI-MSCI	Tracking Error BEMI-MSCI	Correlation IFCG vs. BEMI-MSCI
Argentina	Jan-92	-2.1%	-4.0%	13.7%	0.93
Brazil	Jan-92	5.7%	-3.2%	19.5%	0.90
Chile	Nov-93	1.4%	0.9%	8.7%	0.94
Colombia	May-95	1.6%	0.3%	6.1%	0.97
Greece	Jan-92	-5.6%	1.7%	6.3%	0.97
Indonesia	Jan-92	5.5%	-3.9%	8.5%	0.96
Malaysia	Jan-92	-3.0%	-1.6%	6.3%	0.97
Mexico*	Jan-92	2.1%	1.1%	11.3%	0.96
Pakistan	Jun-93	-11.7%	2.0%	9.9%	0.94
Peru	Jun-93	3.2%	1.6%	11.5%	0.96
Philippines*	Jan-92	-3.5%	4.1%	8.1%	0.98
Portugal	Jan-92	-0.4%	-0.8%	5.8%	0.96
South Africa	Jun-95	-6.0%	4.4%	9.8%	0.85
South Korea	Jan-92	3.4%	0.6%	7.3%	0.96
Taiwan	Jan-92	-4.4%	4.5%	7.1%	0.99
Thailand	Jan-92	-2.6%	0.7%	7.9%	0.96
Turkey	Jan-92	-6.7%	2.6%	15.4%	0.96
Average		-1.4%	0.6%	9.6%	0.95

Monthly returns in US Dollars.
Data through June 1996.

Source: Barings Emerging Market Indices, MSCI EM (*Free where applicable) Indices.

markets followed by the IFC and some summary measures of capitalization (in U.S. dollars) along with the number of countries in each index and the weight in the IFC Composite as of June 1996.

Summary Analysis of Emerging Market Returns

Some summary statistics for the emerging market returns over the common period of July 1991 to June 1996 are presented in Table 3 for the sample of 27 countries followed by the IFC global indices. We examine the mean returns, volatility, skewness, and kurtosis of the returns.

Consistent with the evidence in Harvey (1995) and Bekaert and Harvey (1996a), there are significant deviations from normality in the distributions of many of the emerging market returns. For the past five years, normality can be rejected by the Bera–Jarque (1982) test in 13 of 20 countries.

TABLE 1C. Comparison of Barings and IFC Emerging Market Investable Indices

Country	Start Date	Ave. Return Difference BEMI-IFCI	Volatility Difference BEMI-IFCI	Tracking Error BEMI-IFCI	Correlation IFC vs. BEMI
Argentina	Jan-92	4.3%	3.0%	13.0%	0.93
Brazil	Jan-92	6.4%	4.8%	20.3%	0.90
Chile	Nov-93	2.8%	0.6%	8.4%	0.95
China	Feb-96	-2.1%	-6.6%	7.1%	0.99
Colombia	May-95	-3.2%	-2.1%	5.0%	0.98
Greece	Jan-92	-5.8%	-0.1%	3.6%	0.99
Indonesia	Jan-92	9.1%	3.7%	7.9%	0.96
Malaysia	Jan-92	-1.3%	2.9%	7.7%	0.96
Mexico	Jan-92	1.4%	-0.3%	8.7%	0.97
Pakistan	Jun-94	-2.5%	0.1%	8.5%	0.96
Peru	Jun-94	-1.1%	-3.3%	12.0%	0.95
Philippines	Jan-92	-3.4%	-1.1%	8.9%	0.97
Portugal	Jan-92	0.7%	0.6%	5.8%	0.96
South Africa	Jun-95	-5.7%	-4.1%	9.2%	0.89
South Korea	Jan-92	-0.6%	-0.7%	7.7%	0.96
Taiwan	Jan-92	-5.2%	-2.6%	5.4%	0.99
Thailand	Jan-92	-3.1%	1.4%	8.1%	0.97
Turkey	Jan-92	-1.6%	3.4%	21.0%	0.94
Average		-0.6%	0.0%	9.4%	0.96

Monthly returns in US Dollars.
Data through June 1996.

Source: Barings Emerging Market Indices, IFCI Emerging Market Indices.

We also investigate how these summary statistics change from the 1980s to the 1990s. Figures 1 and 2 show the means and volatilities in the 1980s and 1990s. Most of the capital market liberalizations took place before 1992. The graph shows that the mean returns in many countries are much lower in the 1990s compared to the 1980s. For example, the four countries who had greater than 65 percent returns in the 1980s all had less than 25 percent returns in the 1990s. Volatility is also lower in many countries. These results support the idea presented in Bekaert and Harvey (1995, 1996a) that time-varying world market integration impacts the distribution of returns.

We also detail the skewness and excess kurtosis over the 1980s and 1990s. Figures 3A and 3B show that the absolute value of the skewness parameter has shrunk for many (12 of 19) countries from the 1980s to the

TABLE 2. Market Weights in the IFC Indices—June 1996

Market	No. of Stocks	Market Capital-ization (US$ Mil)	Weight in IFC Composite	No. of Stocks	Market Capital-ization (US$ Mil)	Weight in IFC Composite
	IFC Global Indices			*IFC Investable Indices*		
Latin America						
Argentina	35	25647	2.1	31	25461	3.8
Brazil	86	113553	9.4	68	76216	11.3
Chile	47	43085	3.6	43	42655	6.3
Colombia	28	6875	0.6	15	5519	0.8
Mexico	81	70922	5.9	65	63547	9.4
Peru	37	8423	0.7	21	7811	1.2
Venezuela	16	3814	0.3	5	2576	0.4
East Asia						
China	172	46186	3.8	24	3534	0.5
Korea	151	110558	9.2	145	20580	3.1
Philippines	46	46420	3.9	35	23430	3.5
Taiwan, China	83	154781	12.9	83	31561	4.7
South Asia						
India	131	79987	6.7	76	16670	2.5
Indonesia	45	55767	4.6	44	28254	4.2
Malaysia	123	165530	13.8	123	138973	20.6
Pakistan	68	7153	0.6	25	5417	0.8
Sri Lanka	44	1071	0.1	5	372	0.1
Thailand	73	91149	7.6	72	29156	4.3
EMEA						
Czech Republic	69	13541	1.1	5	5653	0.8
Greece	53	10416	0.9	47	9899	1.5
Hungary	16	3592	0.3	8	3069	0.5
Jordan	51	3029	0.3	8	1022	0.2
Nigeria	35	2090	0.2	0	0	0.0
Poland	23	4935	0.4	22	4918	0.7
Portugal	30	13045	1.1	26	9634	1.4
South Africa	63	99577	8.3	63	99577	14.7
Turkey	54	19783	1.6	54	19783	2.9
Zimbabwe	23	1831	0.2	5	420	0.1
Regions						
Composite	1683	1202760	100.0	1118	675707	100.0
Latin America	330	272319	22.6	248	223785	33.1
Asia	936	758603	63.1	632	297947	44.1
EMEA	417	171838	14.3	238	153976	22.8

TABLE 3. Summary Statistics: July 1991–June 1996

Country	Start Date	Arithmetic Return	Geometric Return	Standard Deviation	Skewness	Kurtosis	First Order Autocorrelation	Beta MSCI World	Beta MSCI AC World	Beta IFCG Composite
Argentina	Jul-91	38.6%	29.5%	56.6%	3.08	16.94	0.06	1.54	1.71	0.89
Brazil	Jul-91	36.0%	28.3%	48.6%	0.79	1.72	0.11	1.12	1.36	1.31
Chile	Jul-91	22.8%	21.4%	26.1%	0.36	-0.32	0.21	0.28	0.40	0.67
China	Jan-93									
Colombia	Jul-91	39.3%	37.3%	40.3%	1.33	1.95	0.52	0.03	0.09	0.31
Czech Republic	Jan-95									
Greece	Jul-91	3.4%	0.8%	22.6%	-0.40	0.58	0.02	0.45	0.46	0.24
Hungary	Jan-93									
India	Jul-91	15.6%	9.4%	37.2%	0.61	1.24	0.23	-0.70	-0.57	0.74
Indonesia	Jul-91	12.9%	9.3%	28.6%	0.14	0.18	0.16	0.48	0.64	1.02
Jordan	Jul-91	8.3%	7.6%	14.3%	0.36	-0.72	0.07	0.14	0.15	0.10
Malaysia	Jul-91	19.9%	18.5%	23.9%	-0.04	1.03	-0.14	0.57	0.67	0.88
Mexico	Jul-91	11.2%	4.2%	36.3%	-1.10	2.39	0.31	0.83	1.09	1.35
Nigeria	Jul-91	42.1%	17.7%	69.5%	1.13	11.78	-0.03	1.15	1.13	-0.07
Pakistan	Jul-91	20.7%	16.0%	35.3%	1.07	1.94	0.29	0.12	0.21	0.53
Peru	Jan-93									
Philippines	Jul-91	27.0%	25.9%	28.6%	1.34	4.46	0.04	0.45	0.60	1.06
Poland	Jan-93									
Portugal	Jul-91	11.5%	10.1%	19.4%	0.32	1.67	0.00	0.98	1.00	0.22
South Africa	Jan-93									
South Korea	Jul-91	7.2%	3.6%	27.5%	0.85	1.07	0.03	0.50	0.62	0.75
Sri Lanka	Jan-93									
Taiwan	Jul-91	11.6%	5.3%	38.5%	2.08	6.30	0.08	0.86	1.09	1.49
Thailand	Jul-91	22.7%	20.3%	29.6%	1.08	1.98	0.02	0.15	0.31	1.11
Turkey	Jul-91	20.0%	2.6%	61.0%	0.58	0.39	0.04	-0.22	-0.09	0.88
Venezuela	Jul-91	4.1%	-7.7%	47.7%	-0.45	1.53	-0.17	0.46	0.57	0.63
Zimbabwe	Jul-91	5.6%	-0.3%	35.0%	0.36	0.81	0.31	0.89	0.96	0.55
MSCI World	Jul-91	12.4%	12.5%	10.2%	-0.23	-0.37	-0.25	1.00	1.01	0.19
MSCI AC World	Jul-91	12.2%	12.4%	10.1%	-0.14	-0.43	-0.21	0.98	1.00	0.24
IFCG Composite	Jul-91	12.1%	11.3%	16.7%	0.89	3.15	0.38	0.51	0.67	1.00

Source: IFC Global Indices, MSCI EM Indices. Monthly returns in US dollars.

‑

FIGURE 1. Emerging Market Returns, 1980s vs. 1990s
IFC Global Indices—Total Returns US$

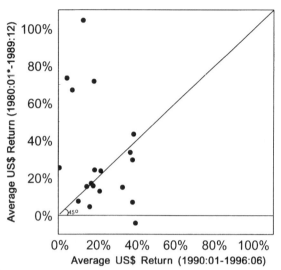

*Or inception, if later.

FIGURE 2. Emerging Market Volatility, 1980s vs. 1990s
IFC Global Indices—Total Returns US$

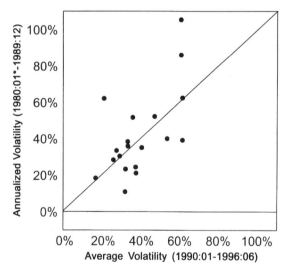

*Or inception, if later.

FIGURE 3A. Emerging Market Skewness, 1980s vs. 1990s
IFC Global Indices—Total Returns US$

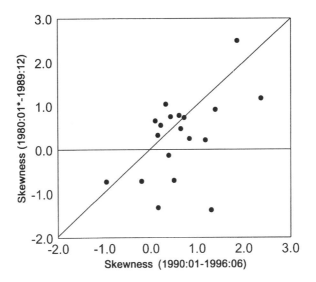

*Or inception, if later.

FIGURE 3B. Emerging Market Absolute Skewness,
1980s vs. 1990s
IFC Global Indices—Total Returns US$

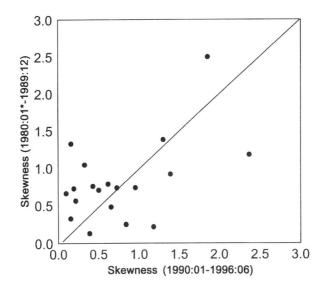

*Or inception, if later.

1990s. For excess kurtosis, there is no particular pattern over the 1980s and 1990s as is clear from Figure 4.

We looked at the patterns in correlations following Bekaert and Harvey (1996a) who present a model of conditional correlation where the means, volatilities, and covariances are influenced by both local and world information. Their model predicts that as a market becomes more integrated with world capital markets, the relative influence of world and local information changes. Figure 5 shows that the correlations generally have increased over the longer horizon. Correlations have increased in 11 of 19 countries, remained the same in six countries and decreased in only two countries. This suggests that the benefits of diversification have decreased for many emerging markets. However, the correlations are still sufficiently low to attract most global portfolio investors.

The betas presented in Figure 6 mimic the correlations. For many countries, the beta with respect to the MSCI–all countries index has increased from the 1980s to the 1990s. This suggests that country returns are more affected by world market returns, and this is consistent with the impact of degree of capital market integration detailed in Bekaert and Harvey (1995, 1996a).

FIGURE 4.   Emerging Market Excess Kurtosis, 1980s vs. 1990s IFC Global Indices–Total Returns US$

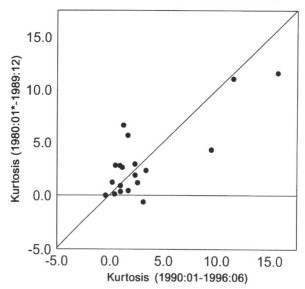

*Or inception, if later.

FIGURE 5.   Emerging Market Correlations, 1980s vs. 1990s
            IFC Global Indices—Total Returns US$

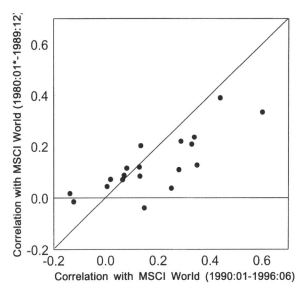

*Or inception, if later.

FIGURE 6.   Emerging Market Betas, 1980s vs. 1990s
            IFC Global Indices—Total Returns US$

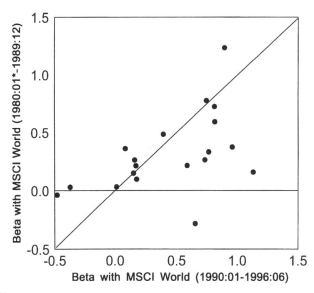

*Or inception, if later.

Cross-Sectional Portfolio Strategies for Emerging Market Returns

Asset Pricing Theory and Emerging Market Returns

Risk is notoriously difficult to measure in emerging market returns. A simple implementation of the capital asset pricing model (CAPM) of Sharpe (1964) and Lintner (1965) is problematic. In these markets, there is little relation between the risk measured by the CAPM and expected returns.

Consider Figure 7 which plots the average returns versus beta against the world–all countries index over the 1980s and the 1990s. The betas over the past five years, July 1991 to June 1996 are presented in Table 3. In the 1980s, there is a positive relation between beta and average returns, the t-statistic on the beta coefficient is 1.5, which is marginally significant at conventional levels.

The beta-average returns relation appears stronger over the 1990s. However, as is obvious from Figure 7, there is one influential observation—Poland—which had a high average return and very high beta. If the average returns are regressed on the betas, the t-statistic is 3.2, and the R-square measure is 27 percent. When Poland is removed from the analysis, the t-statistic drops to 0.4 and the R-square is 0 percent.

FIGURE 7.   Risk and Return
             IFCG Indices

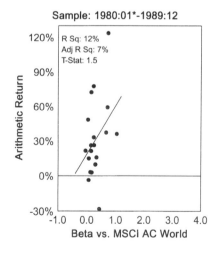
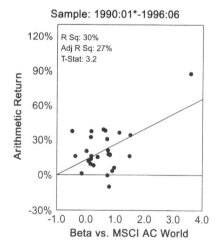

*Or inception, if later.

The failure of the CAPM to explain emerging market returns could be interpreted in a number of ways. First, following Roll and Ross (1994) and Kandel and Stambaugh (1995), the benchmark world portfolio may not be mean-variance efficient. Second, perhaps a multifactor representation, following Merton (1973), Ross (1976), and Chen, Roll, and Ross (1986) is more appropriate for emerging markets. Third, following Ferson and Harvey (1991), an examination of average returns and average risk could be misleading if the risk and expected returns change through time. Finally, the CAPM is not the appropriate framework if these markets are not integrated into world capital markets. In integrated capital markets, the projects of identical risk command identical expected returns, irrespective of domicile [see Stulz (1981a,b); Solnik (1983); Campbell and Hamao (1992); Chan, Karolyi, and Stulz (1992); Heston, Rouwenhorst, and Wessels (1995); Bekaert (1995); Harvey (1991, 1995); and Bekaert and Harvey (1995)].

It is likely that many of these markets are not fully integrated into world capital markets. As a result, the beta suggested by the CAPM may not be that useful in explaining the cross-section of average returns. Indeed, in completely segmented capital markets, the volatility is the correct measure of risk. The relation between average returns and volatility is detailed in Figure 8. Similar to the beta graph, there is a positive relation which is now significant at conventional levels of confidence (R-square is 33 percent in the 1980s, and 36 percent in 1990s). However, it should be noted that even among the segmented markets, the relation between volatility and expected returns may appear weak because the premium accorded to volatility could vary across countries [see Bekaert and Harvey (1995)].

We examine two attributes based on asset pricing theory in our portfolio strategies: the trailing three-year beta against the MSCI–all countries index and the trailing three-year conditional volatility. If markets were perfectly integrated and a world version of the CAPM held, then higher-beta countries should earn higher expected-returns. If markets were perfectly segmented and a local version of the CAPM held, then higher-volatility countries should have higher expected returns, assuming that risk aversion is the same across countries.

Alternative Risk Attributes

Following Ferson and Harvey (1994), Erb, Harvey, and Viskanta (1995a, 1996b) and others, we examine the relation between some country-specific risk attributes and the distribution of returns. We group these attributes into the following categories:

FIGURE 8.   Risk and Return
             IFCG Indices

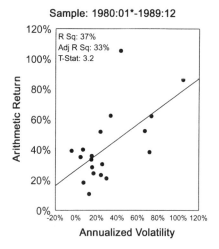
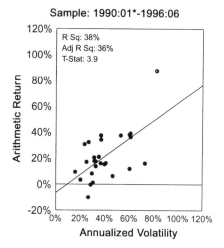

*Or inception, if later.

Survey-Based Measures

The first of these measures is *Institutional Investor's* country credit rating (IICCR). *Institutional Investor's* country credit ratings are based on a survey of leading international banks who are asked to rate each country on a scale from zero to 100 (where 100 represents the maximum creditworthiness). *Institutional Investor* averages these ratings, providing greater weights to respondents with higher worldwide exposure and more sophisticated country analysis systems. These ratings have appeared in the March and September issues of *Institutional Investor* since 1979, and the ratings now cover over 135 countries, for additional details see Erb, Harvey, and Viskanta (1996a).

Whenever a survey or expert panel is used to subjectively rate creditworthiness, it is hard to exactly define the parameters taken into account. At any given point in time, an expert's recommendation will be based on those factors that the expert feels are relevant. In a recent survey of participants, the most important factors for assessing emerging markets' credit rating were (1) debt service, (2) political outlook, (3) economic outlook, (4) financial reserves/current account, and (5) trade balance/foreign direct investment.

The next four measures are from Political Risk Services' *International Country Risk Guide*. They include the political risk index (ICRGP), economic risk index (ICRGE), financial risk index (ICRGF), and the composite risk index (ICRGC). The political index is studied in Harlow (1993) and Diamonte, Liew, and Stevens (1996). Erb, Harvey, and Viskanta (1996b) examine the information in all four of the ICRG risk indices.

On a monthly basis, *ICRG* uses a blend of quantitative and qualitative measures to calculate risk indices for political, financial, and economic risk, as well as a composite index. Five financial factors, 13 political and six economic factors are used. Each factor is assigned a numerical rating within a specified range. A higher score represents lower risk; for additional details see Erb, Harvey, and Viskanta (1996b).

The composite index is simply a linear combination of the three subindices. The political risk is weighted twice that of either financial or economic risk. *ICRG*, as well as many of the other providers, think of country risk as being composed of two primary components: ability to pay and willingness to pay. Political risk is associated with a willingness to pay, while financial and economic risk are associated with an ability to pay.

We also include *Euromoney's* country credit risk (EMCCR). *Euromoney's* rating system is based on both qualitative and quantitative methods. The political component is a qualitative survey of experts. The economic component is quantitative and based on *Euromoney's* global economic projections. The financial component is also quantitative and based on (1) debt indicators, (2) debt in default or rescheduled, (3) credit rating (Moody's or Standard and Poors), (4) access to bank finance, (5) access to short-term financing, and (6) access to international bond and syndicated loan markets.

Macroeconomy

The survey-based measures indirectly gauge the future macroeconomic conditions in each country. One of the primary economic measures that influences these ratings is the inflationary environment. Ferson and Harvey (1993, 1994) argue that asset exposure versus world inflation helps explain both the cross-section and time-series of expected returns in 18 developed markets. Erb, Harvey, and Viskanta (1995b) examine the interaction of inflation and asset returns in emerging markets. We use a trailing 12-month measure of inflation represented by the consumer price index reported in the International Financial Statistics database of the International Monetary Fund. This variable is lagged by six months to allow for reporting delays. In the case of Taiwan, who is not a member of the IMF, we use inflation reported in their national accounts.

Demographics

Bakshi and Chen (1994) propose a life-cycle investment hypothesis. Younger investors have a higher demand for housing than for equities. As age increases, more investment is allocated to the stock market. As a result, a rise in average age should be accompanied by a rise in the stock market. Bakshi and Chen (1994) find support for this hypothesis using U.S. data. Erb, Harvey, and Viskanta (1996c) find that average-age growth explains the risk premiums in a number of developed countries. We examine three variables: population growth, average age, and average-age growth. All of these data are based on annual statistics compiled by the United Nations.

Market Integration

Bekaert and Harvey (1996a) argue that the size of the trade sector to the total economy is a reasonable proxy for the openness of both the economy and the investment sector. They use exports plus imports divided by GDP as an instrument for market integration. This variable, along with other proxies for market integration, is used in a function which assigns time-varying weights to world versus local information. Bekaert and Harvey find that increases in this ratio are associated with the increased importance of world relative to local information for both the mean and the volatility of the country's stock returns.

Bekaert and Harvey (1996a) also suggest that the size of the stock market serves as a proxy for the degree of financial integration. Larger market size suggests that the country is more likely to be integrated into world capital markets. We specify this variable as the ratio of market capitalization to the previous year's gross domestic product (GDP).

Persistence

A number of researchers have pointed to momentum as an important firm-specific attribute [see Jegadeesh and Titman (1993), Asness, Liew and Stevens (1996), Ferson and Harvey (1996)]. We examine two measures of momentum: the lagged monthly return and the lagged quarterly return from four months ago to one month ago (i.e., the quarterly return lagged by an extra month).

Size

We follow a number of papers, beginning with Banz (1981), that document a relation between firm size and expected returns. Recently, Berk (1995, 1996) has argued that size measured by market capitalization should be a proxy for risk. This attribute has recently been studied on a country-level basis by Keppler and Traub (1993) and by Asness, Liew, and Stevens (1996) who find that size helps explain the cross-section of expected returns in a sample of developed markets.

Fundamental Valuation Measures

Following a number of papers that link "fundamental attributes" to asset valuation [see, for example, Chan, Hamao, and Lakonishok (1991); Keppler (1991); Fama and French (1992); and Ferson and Harvey (1994)], we use three valuation ratios: price to book value, price to earnings, and price to dividend. Value-weighted indices of company-level data are produced by the IFC. Ferson and Harvey (1996) show that some of these ratios, most notably price to book, appear to capture information regarding changing risk in a sample of 21 developed countries. In addition, sudden changes in these ratios may also reflect changes in the degree of market integration [see Bekaert and Harvey (1996b)]. A change in the marginal investor from domestic to international could lead to a change in the fundamental valuation ratios and a change in the riskiness.

Summary Statistics

Some summary measures for many of these attributes are included in Table 4. The March 1996 value of the attribute is reported. In the lower panel, the rank/order correlation of all of the attributes is reported. Most of the correlations follow from intuition. Consider the ICRG indices. These indices are highly correlated with the *Euromoney* and *Institutional Investor* country credit risk measures. All of the survey measures are negatively correlated with inflation (high inflation means low rating). The most negative correlation with inflation is found for the ICRG economic risk index. Average age is positively correlated with the survey risk indices, indicating that low average-age is associated with a low rating. Size is positively related to the ICRG ratings (smaller markets appear riskier). There is also a positive relation between the size of the trade sector and the ICRG ratings. The lowest correlations are found for the ICRG indices and the fundamental attributes.

TABLE 4. Country Attributes—March 1996

Country	ICRGC	ICRGP	ICRGF	ICRGE	IICCR	EMCRR	IN-FLATE	TRDGDP	MKCP-GDP	POPGR	AAGEGR	AVEAGE	MKTCAP	BETA	VOL	P/E	P/B	P/D
Argentina	72.5	76.0	35.0	34.0	38.4	57.2	0.7%	0.13	0.08	1.2%	0.3%	30.9	22308	1.9	35%	16.7	1.4	29.2
Brazil	65.5	64.0	34.0	33.0	35.8	55.4	29.2%	0.14	0.23	1.7%	0.8%	27.1	93940	0.6	43%	40.3	0.5	28.9
Chile	80.5	76.0	43.0	41.5	59.2	79.8	7.6%	0.42	0.88	1.6%	0.6%	29.0	39421	1.0	27%	15.9	1.9	26.1
China	72.0	68.0	38.0	38.0	56.4	70.8			0.07	1.0%	0.9%	29.6	29495	0.8	72%	31.8	2.0	37.6
Colombia	66.0	58.0	39.0	35.0	46.7	62.6	19.1%	0.61	0.12	1.6%	0.9%	26.2	6659	0.1	28%	12.0	1.0	36.8
Czech Rep.	82.5	82.0	42.0	40.5	60.1	74.6	8.6%		0.29				12346			13.4	1.0	87.7
Greece	75.0	76.0	38.0	36.0	49.8	73.3	8.5%	0.60	0.11	0.3%	0.6%	38.9	11200	0.9	18%	10.8	2.1	24.6
Hungary	76.0	79.0	40.0	32.5	43.6	67.7	29.6%	0.50	0.02	-0.5%	0.2%	37.3	2957	1.9	43%	21.4	1.1	125.0
India	67.0	62.0	36.0	36.0	45.8	66.7	9.7%	0.17	0.19	1.9%	0.5%	26.0	71141	0.4	29%	14.3	2.3	65.8
Indonesia	70.5	65.0	39.0	37.0	51.8	73.2	10.5%	0.44	0.22	1.5%	0.8%	26.2	54571	1.1	30%	26.6	3.5	112.4
Jordan	74.5	73.0	38.0	38.0	30.5	54.3	7.0%	1.30	0.58	4.6%	0.3%	21.4	3276	0.2	15%	15.6	1.7	50.0
Malaysia	79.5	75.0	43.0	41.0	68.4	84.5	3.3%	1.66	1.97	2.3%	0.6%	24.8	162134	1.1	29%	28.4	3.7	83.3
Mexico	69.5	66.0	40.0	33.0	41.2	58.8	43.8%	0.37	0.25	2.0%	0.9%	24.8	65162	1.6	42%	18.6	1.7	117.6
Nigeria	50.5	54.0	23.0	24.0	14.8	32.3	69.9%	0.41	0.04	3.0%	0.0%	21.5	1712	1.4	81%	12.2	3.3	23.3
Pakistan	60.0	54.0	34.0	31.5	29.5	50.7	9.8%	0.35	0.13	2.8%	0.3%	21.9	6647	0.1	29%	16.4	2.1	45.7
Peru	64.0	59.0	34.0	34.5	27.2	47.5	11.6%	0.20	0.14				7422	1.6	38%	13.8	2.7	90.1
Philippines	68.5	63.0	37.0	36.5	38.1	63.5	12.3%	0.54	0.46	2.1%	0.6%	24.0	39729	1.2	32%	21.2	3.8	153.8
Poland	77.5	77.0	41.0	37.0	40.2	56.5	20.4%	0.38	0.02	0.1%	0.6%	34.3	3893	4.0	88%	8.5	1.8	84.7
Portugal	83.5	83.0	43.0	41.0	68.8	81.9	2.5%	0.56	0.13	-0.1%	0.6%	36.6	11405	1.0	19%	14.8	1.5	35.1
South Africa	76.0	75.0	41.0	35.5	46.3	64.9	6.8%	0.38	1.28	2.2%	0.2%	25.0	105981	0.9	25%	19.2	2.7	49.0
South Korea	82.0	77.0	46.0	41.0	72.0	85.0	4.5%	0.54	0.32	1.0%	1.0%	30.5	125037	0.6	20%	21.0	1.3	54.3
Sri Lanka	66.5	61.0	36.0	35.5	32.5	50.6	11.8%	0.81	0.11	1.3%	0.9%	28.2	1315	0.0	32%	8.9	1.5	39.8
Taiwan	83.0	75.0	48.0	43.0	78.9	91.5	3.0%	0.87	0.48				114475	1.2	38%	21.6	2.8	85.5
Thailand	76.5	69.0	43.0	41.0	63.4	82.1	5.4%	0.65	0.66	1.0%	1.2%	27.9	95036	1.2	33%	20.5	3.1	55.9
Turkey	60.5	55.0	36.0	30.0	40.4	58.4	78.9%	0.32	0.14	1.9%	0.6%	26.5	20641	0.6	64%	12.2	3.7	40.2
Venezuela	64.5	65.0	33.0	31.0	30.1	44.7	78.1%	0.40	0.05	2.2%	0.8%	25.1	2652	0.1	49%	16.3	2.6	63.3
Zimbabwe	63.5	66.0	28.0	32.5	32.2	50.5	25.8%	0.75	0.16	2.4%	0.2%	21.4	1677	0.4	33%	8.2	1.4	21.1

TABLE 4 (continued)

Rank Correlations

Country	ICRGC	ICRGP	ICRGF	ICRGE	IICCR	EMCRR	IN-FLATE	TRDGDP	MKCP-GDP	POPGR	AAGEGR	AVEAGE	MKTCAP	BETA	VOL	P/E	P/B	P/D
ICRGC	1.00	0.89	0.90	0.84	0.82	0.82	-0.70	0.40	0.38	-0.59	0.25	0.57	0.47	0.36	-0.38	0.28	-0.17	0.23
ICRGP		1.00	0.68	0.59	0.61	0.61	-0.55	0.24	0.13	-0.59	0.04	0.61	0.23	0.40	-0.27	0.15	-0.36	0.09
ICRGF			1.00	0.83	0.88	0.88	-0.59	0.43	0.50	-0.50	0.42	0.44	0.58	0.28	-0.38	0.31	-0.03	0.30
ICRGE				1.00	0.79	0.81	-0.76	0.52	0.55	-0.39	0.43	0.33	0.54	0.15	-0.47	0.29	0.03	0.17
IICCR					1.00	0.97	-0.61	0.39	0.41	-0.58	0.54	0.53	0.66	0.16	-0.36	0.36	-0.02	0.13
EMCRR						1.00	-0.65	0.38	0.48	-0.54	0.44	0.48	0.71	0.22	-0.40	0.45	0.06	0.21
INFLATE							1.00	-0.31	-0.49	0.24	-0.10	-0.27	-0.50	-0.14	0.66	-0.28	0.02	0.06
TRDGDP								1.00	0.30	0.02	0.18	-0.11	-0.06	-0.19	-0.43	-0.02	0.06	-0.01
MKCPGDP									1.00	0.35	0.11	-0.38	0.69	-0.05	-0.50	0.38	0.24	0.21
POPGR										1.00	-0.47	-0.95	-0.09	-0.37	-0.04	-0.05	0.35	-0.07
AAGEGR											1.00	0.39	0.36	-0.14	-0.04	0.26	-0.12	0.11
AVEAGE												1.00	0.07	0.30	0.02	0.02	-0.36	-0.09
MKTCAP													1.00	0.23	-0.21	0.68	0.26	0.27
BETA														1.00	0.35	0.22	0.20	0.38
VOL															1.00	0.05	0.13	0.18
P/E																1.00	0.15	0.37
P/B																	1.00	0.27
P/D																		1.00

Legend

ICRGC	International Country Risk Guide Composite Index
ICRGP	International Country Risk Guide Political Index
ICRGF	International Country Risk Guide Financial Index
ICRGE	International Country Risk Guide Economic Index
II CCR	Institutional Investor Country Credit Ratings
EMCRR	Euromoney Country Risk Ratings
INFLATE	Annual Consumer Inflation: IFS Database
TRDGDP	(Exports+Imports)/GDP: IFS Database
MKCPGDP	IFC Global Market Capitalization/GDP
POPGR	Annual Growth in Population - UN Data
AAGEGR	Annual Growth in Average Age of Population - UN Data
AVEAGE	Average Age of Population - UN Data
MKTCAP	IFC Global Market Capitalization
BETA	IFC Global Beta with MSCI AC World - 36 months trailing
VOL	IFC Global Volatility - 36 months trailing
MOM-1	Trailing USD Total Return - Prior Month
MOM-2-4	Trailing USD Total Return - Months -4 to -2
P/E*	IFC Global Price/Earnings Ratio
P/B*	IFC Global Price/Book Ratio
P/D	IFC Global Price/Dividend Ratio

What Matters in Choosing an Emerging Market for Portfolio Investment?

Portfolio Approach

A commonly used technique in examining the cross-sectional importance of a fundamental variable is to form unique portfolios based on their ranking. We will examine the country risk variables by forming portfolios based on the risk level itself. These portfolios are investible with respect to the attribute. That is, lagged attribute information is used to determine which countries are in the portfolios, and the analysis is conducted out of sample. Given the small number of emerging markets, we examine only three portfolios: high, middle, and low attribute. In each case, we track the returns to portfolios that are equally weighted by country, those that are weighted by each country's equity market capitalization, and those that are weighted by value of trading volume. To reduce potential transactions costs, the minimum holding period that we consider is quarterly. We also examine strategies that have semiannual rebalancing.

Table 5A presents the results of the quarterly portfolio strategies over the January 1985–June 1996 period. This portfolio includes all the countries in the IFC–Global database. However, for much of this period, many of the returns were not attainable due to investment restrictions [see Bekaert and Urias (1996)]. To address this problem, Table 5B examines the same strategies evaluated over the past five years. In the late 1980s and early 1990s, most of these market experienced substantial liberalizations. Tables 5C and 5D display the same strategies with semiannual rebalancing. Tables 5E and 5F examine quarterly and semiannual strategies over the past five years using only the investible indices. The very last column in each of the tables reports the abnormal excess return with respect to the MSCI–all-country portfolio. The annualized abnormal returns are large in absolute magnitude for many of the attributes.

ICRG

Consider the results for the ICRG composite index (ICRGC). With equal weighting, the low-rating portfolio averaged 30.8 percent annual return with 30.3 percent volatility. The high-rating portfolio had both higher returns, 34.1 percent, and lower volatility of 27.6 percent. The alpha measure is 6.5 percent on an annual basis. The results are even more impressive with the capitalization weights. The alpha increases to 14.2 percent. The most impressive results occur over the past 5 years (Table 5B) where the capitalization-weighted alpha is 24.3 percent for the ICRGC.[5] Similar results are documented for the semiannual holding periods in Tables 5C

TABLE 5A. Emerging Market Risk Level Portfolio Strategy
IFCG Indices–Quarterly Rebalancing: January 1985–June 1996

	High Tritile						Low Tritile							Low-High Attribute			
Risk Attribute	Average Annual Return	Standard Dev.	MSCI AC World Beta	MSCI AC World Alpha	Skew-ness	Kurto-sis	Average Annual Turnover	Average Annual Return	Standard Dev.	MSCI AC World Beta	MSCI AC World Alpha	Skew-ness	Kurto-sis	Average Annual Turnover	Average Annual Return	Standard Dev.	MSCI AC World Alpha
Equal Weighted																	
ICRGC	30.8%	30.3%	0.82	16.3%*	1.59	6.53	56%	34.1%	27.6%	0.03	28.4%***	1.46	4.28	64%	3.3%	36.5%	6.5%
ICRGP	31.6%	31.9%	0.94	15.8%*	0.72	4.32	69%	28.0%	20.4%	0.07	21.7%***	0.03	-0.12	51%	-3.6%	33.7%	0.3%
ICRGF	26.5%	29.0%	0.76	12.6%	1.76	8.38	52%	36.7%	34.0%	0.05	30.8%***	2.16	8.54	74%	10.2%	43.2%	12.6%
ICRGE	28.0%	28.7%	0.80	13.6%*	1.26	5.30	64%	40.5%	32.3%	0.44	30.3%***	0.20	-0.28	93%	12.6%	32.3%	11.1%
II CCR	28.3%	28.0%	0.84	13.7%**	1.37	5.71	32%	38.7%	28.3%	0.46	28.2%***	0.37	0.52	45%	10.5%	30.7%	9.0%
EMCRR	27.6%	27.9%	0.82	13.2%*	1.41	5.89	40%	45.2%	31.6%	0.62	32.9%***	0.44	0.16	57%	17.6%*	34.7%	14.1%
INFLATE	52.4%	35.9%	0.54	41.2%***	0.31	0.35	68%	21.3%	20.2%	0.48	10.5%*	0.71	1.93	64%	-31.1%***	32.5%	-36.3%***
TRDGDP	28.6%	28.4%	0.85	13.7%*	1.40	5.67	37%	37.4%	30.7%	0.25	29.2%***	0.47	-0.08	40%	8.8%	33.0%	9.8%
MKCPGDP	23.8%	32.1%	0.84	9.0%	1.83	9.74	62%	46.6%	28.4%	-0.01	41.2%***	0.26	0.63	76%	22.8%**	38.2%	26.6%**
POPGR	23.9%	19.1%	-0.02	18.6%***	0.03	0.55	27%	36.9%	33.7%	0.87	22.0%**	1.07	2.29	41%	13.0%	36.1%	-2.2%
AAGEGR	37.8%	30.9%	1.03	21.0%**	0.47	1.96	38%	22.0%	25.2%	0.07	15.8%**	1.13	1.94	32%	-15.7%	35.8%	-10.9%
AVEAGE	43.2%	35.9%	0.95	27.7%***	1.14	2.14	43%	27.5%	20.2%	0.49	16.6%***	-0.23	0.72	25%	-15.7%	33.1%	-16.6%
MKTCAP	24.9%	26.4%	0.79	10.7%	-0.36	2.96	49%	44.2%	27.1%	0.11	37.5%***	-0.25	-0.32	69%	19.3%*	34.9%	21.2%**
BETA	37.8%	32.8%	0.40	28.0%***	1.40	3.74	103%	29.1%	25.3%	0.44	18.9%**	0.20	-0.16	104%	-8.7%	37.0%	-14.7%
VOL	27.8%	39.8%	0.50	17.0%	1.40	5.32	69%	28.2%	21.0%	0.46	17.6%***	0.98	2.21	67%	0.5%	42.4%	-5.0%
MOM-1	38.3%	30.1%	0.84	23.9%***	0.20	0.15	272%	24.3%	27.2%	0.48	13.3%	1.12	2.69	277%	-13.9%	31.5%	-16.1%
MOM-2-4	37.8%	38.0%	0.79	23.8%**	1.21	5.92	269%	29.7%	27.1%	0.25	21.5%**	0.71	1.13	267%	-8.0%	44.2%	-7.9%
P/E*	19.6%	28.6%	0.87	8.0%	0.17	2.84	102%	38.9%	25.3%	0.19	32.1%***	-0.32	0.13	107%	19.3%*	31.7%	18.7%*
P/B*	19.8%	28.0%	0.87	8.0%	0.75	1.98	96%	47.4%	27.5%	0.38	39.4%***	0.34	0.16	112%	27.6%***	30.4%	25.9%***
P/D	29.6%	36.9%	0.58	17.9%	1.26	3.09	110%	28.4%	22.5%	0.54	16.9%**	0.22	-0.51	83%	-1.2%	39.5%	-6.5%

TABLE 5A (continued)

	High Tritile						Low Tritile							Low-High Attribute			
Risk Attribute	Average Annual Return	Standard Dev.	MSCI AC World Beta	MSCI AC World Alpha	Skewness	Kurtosis	Average Annual Turnover	Average Annual Return	Standard Dev.	MSCI AC World Beta	MSCI AC World Alpha	Skewness	Kurtosis	Average Annual Turnover	Average Annual Return	Standard Dev.	MSCI AC World Alpha
Capitalization Weighted																	
ICRGC	22.5%	34.8%	0.67	9.5%	0.32	1.50	22%	31.4%	34.0%	-0.31	29.3%***	1.40	3.02	46%	8.9%	43.6%	14.2%
ICRGP	20.1%	39.4%	0.73	6.5%	0.17	1.17	41%	26.5%	28.9%	-0.29	23.8%***	1.17	3.05	36%	6.4%	44.4%	11.8%
ICRGF	20.5%	37.9%	0.70	7.3%	1.01	4.00	21%	29.1%	40.2%	0.05	23.2%*	1.50	5.88	61%	8.6%	55.4%	10.3%
ICRGE	20.9%	34.5%	0.69	7.7%	0.21	1.51	24%	30.6%	44.4%	0.76	16.7%	0.06	0.41	55%	9.7%	45.1%	3.4%
IICCR	19.9%	32.4%	0.66	7.1%	0.32	1.37	17%	31.8%	41.2%	0.89	16.4%	-0.33	1.08	39%	12.0%	37.1%	3.7%
EMCRR	19.7%	32.7%	0.64	7.1%	0.33	1.30	20%	39.2%	43.0%	1.18	20.7%	-0.11	-0.35	69%	19.5%	42.7%	8.0%
INFLATE	31.9%	42.8%	0.82	17.4%	-0.17	0.47	32%	19.9%	34.5%	0.62	7.5%	0.08	0.65	25%	-12.0%	45.3%	-15.5%
TRDGDP	24.2%	39.3%	0.77	10.1%	0.23	1.27	15%	23.3%	34.3%	0.45	12.9%	-0.50	0.38	20%	-0.9%	42.4%	-2.7%
MKCPGDP	20.2%	39.8%	0.88	4.9%	0.33	2.31	31%	34.0%	31.6%	-0.09	29.7%***	1.01	2.83	59%	13.9%	46.2%	19.2%
POPGR	18.8%	21.4%	0.35	9.3%	-0.11	1.90	14%	22.0%	28.5%	1.01	5.5%	0.91	2.33	16%	3.2%	27.9%	-9.5%
AAGEGR	23.8%	34.4%	1.08	6.5%	-0.05	0.95	17%	12.0%	20.0%	0.31	3.0%	0.04	1.20	16%	-11.8%	31.8%	-9.1%
AVEAGE	25.2%	32.5%	1.08	8.1%	0.93	1.74	21%	30.7%	35.8%	1.03	14.0%	-0.86	3.10	13%	5.5%	34.4%	0.3%
MKTCAP	18.0%	32.9%	0.66	5.2%	-0.23	1.23	23%	43.5%	29.9%	0.05	37.5%***	0.41	0.39	54%	25.5%**	41.0%	26.8%***
BETA	34.1%	47.9%	0.15	27.0%*	1.88	7.65	69%	29.2%	35.4%	0.23	21.3%*	0.48	-0.26	88%	-4.9%	52.5%	-11.4%
VOL	13.5%	49.7%	0.57	1.9%	-0.15	0.09	32%	30.2%	28.6%	0.40	20.3%**	0.27	0.18	47%	16.7%	52.5%	12.8%
MOM-1	27.2%	31.8%	0.69	14.4%	-0.46	0.98	283%	24.1%	43.4%	0.70	10.7%	1.37	4.60	272%	-3.1%	44.4%	-9.2%
MOM-2-4	16.9%	48.6%	0.79	2.8%	1.42	7.18	177%	24.6%	32.6%	0.29	16.0%	0.70	0.41	194%	7.7%	54.3%	7.7%
P/E*	14.4%	34.7%	0.97	1.9%	-0.50	0.87	53%	28.9%	36.4%	0.64	18.8%	0.25	1.04	78%	14.5%	43.4%	11.4%
P/B*	12.5%	40.7%	0.79	1.2%	0.10	0.84	55%	29.7%	31.2%	0.79	18.6%**	0.66	1.32	54%	17.2%	39.1%	11.9%
P/D	20.6%	41.1%	0.71	7.3%	0.00	1.08	64%	22.5%	24.6%	0.59	10.5%	0.38	0.04	73%	1.8%	40.9%	-2.4%

	Average Annual Return	Standard Dev.	MSCI AC World Beta	MSCI AC World Alpha	Skewness	Kurtosis
IFC Composite	19.3%	29.6%	0.60	7.1%*	0.04	1.17
MSCI AC World	16.4%	15.4%	1.00		-0.56	2.43

TABLE 5A (continued)

Notes:

Significance level: * 10%, ** 5%, *** 1%.

IFC Global and MSCI World Indices in US dollars: Unhedged.

From January 1985-December 1987 the MSCI World Index was substituted for the MSCI All Country (AC) World Index.

Price/Earnings and Price/Book ratios are unavailable until January 1986.

Portfolios were formed by sorting the countries into three tritiles based on the level of the attribute.

Portfolios were reformed quarterly.

Legend

ICRGC	International Country Risk Guide Composite Index
ICRGP	International Country Risk Guide Political Index
ICRGF	International Country Risk Guide Financial Index
ICRGE	International Country Risk Guide Economic Index
II CCR	Institutional Investor Country Credit Ratings
EMCRR	Euromoney Country Risk Ratings
INFLATE	Annual Consumer Inflation: IFS Database
TRDGDP	(Exports+Imports)/GDP: IFS Database
MKCPGDP	IFC Global Market Capitalization/GDP
POPGR	Annual Growth in Population - UN Data
AAGEGR	Annual Growth in Average Age of Population - UN Data
AVEAGE	Average Age of Population - UN Data
MKTCAP	IFC Global Market Capitalization
BETA	IFC Global Beta with MSCI AC World - 36 months trailing
VOL	IFC Global Volatility - 36 months trailing
MOM-1	Trailing USD Total Return - Prior Month
MOM-2-4	Trailing USD Total Return - Months -4 to -2
P/E*	IFC Global Price/Earnings Ratio
P/B*	IFC Global Price/Book Ratio
P/D	IFC Global Price/Dividend Ratio

245

Risk Attribute	High Tritile							Low Tritile						Low-High Attribute			
	Average Annual Return	Standard Dev.	MSCI AC World Beta	MSCI AC World Alpha	Skew-ness	Kurto-sis	Average Annual Turnover	Average Annual Return	Standard Dev.	MSCI AC World Beta	MSCI AC World Alpha	Skew-ness	Kurto-sis	Average Annual Turnover	Average Annual Return	Standard Dev.	MSCI AC World Alpha
Equal Weighted																	
ICRGC	22.0%	22.6%	0.83	10.5%	1.51	3.75	41%	25.3%	26.2%	0.56	16.1%	0.25	-0.89	74%	3.3%	22.1%	1.5%
ICRGP	17.2%	24.0%	1.13	3.3%	0.78	1.11	74%	23.3%	25.2%	0.06	18.2%	0.13	-0.53	67%	6.1%	21.1%	10.8%
ICRGF	14.2%	20.1%	0.18	7.9%	1.25	3.32	45%	27.6%	27.7%	0.74	17.3%	-0.03	-0.18	60%	13.4%	25.9%	5.3%
ICRGE	17.7%	20.0%	0.66	7.5%	1.86	4.75	61%	32.5%	30.4%	0.16	26.7%	-0.14	-1.15	77%	14.9%	27.4%	15.1%
II CCR	12.1%	19.3%	0.51	3.3%	1.34	2.05	25%	30.7%	30.2%	1.51	13.8%	-0.02	-0.60	37%	18.7%	27.0%	6.3%
EMCRR	22.0%	19.2%	1.09	8.5%	0.80	0.21	7%	36.6%	49.8%	2.37	9.4%	0.00	-0.92	12%	14.6%	43.0%	-4.8%
INFLATE	39.7%	36.3%	1.23	25.3%	0.07	-1.07	53%	14.6%	20.9%	0.66	4.3%	1.90	5.97	51%	-25.0%	35.0%	-25.2%
TRDGDP	14.2%	23.7%	0.80	2.6%	2.05	5.74	31%	39.2%	34.1%	1.14	25.6%	0.32	-0.47	40%	25.0%	30.2%	18.9%
MKCPGDP	11.2%	22.1%	0.60	1.6%	2.31	7.45	45%	37.3%	30.6%	0.66	27.9%*	-0.07	-0.49	74%	26.1%	33.5%	22.3%
POPGR	19.4%	24.6%	1.35	4.0%	0.13	-0.06	28%	21.4%	23.1%	1.23	7.1%	0.08	-0.91	35%	2.0%	20.5%	-1.1%
AAGEGR	23.4%	25.8%	0.28	16.4%	0.46	0.03	34%	20.7%	24.7%	1.44	5.0%	-0.15	-1.00	32%	-2.7%	24.1%	-15.6%
AVEAGE	23.6%	23.4%	1.18	9.9%	0.06	-0.93	30%	18.4%	25.4%	1.08	5.1%	0.11	0.18	29%	-5.2%	22.0%	-8.9%
MKTCAP	17.5%	23.9%	0.08	12.0%	1.07	1.84	43%	32.8%	33.9%	1.85	13.4%	-0.06	-1.07	69%	15.4%	35.8%	-2.6%
BETA	24.7%	20.6%	0.14	19.0%*	-0.35	0.21	84%	17.0%	24.9%	1.54	0.4%	0.71	-0.12	69%	-7.6%	25.9%	-22.7%*
VOL	25.4%	25.2%	1.23	11.4%	-0.52	-0.83	62%	22.3%	26.3%	0.99	9.6%	1.63	2.37	70%	-3.1%	26.9%	-5.9%
MOM-1	13.5%	22.8%	0.90	1.7%	0.79	0.80	265%	27.0%	24.9%	0.68	16.8%	0.13	-0.42	282%	13.5%	18.4%	11.0%
MOM-2-4	20.1%	27.9%	1.02	8.1%	0.67	-0.45	271%	23.3%	21.9%	0.71	12.9%	0.22	-0.06	266%	3.2%	22.0%	0.6%
P/E*	12.6%	22.0%	0.45	5.0%	0.74	-0.09	94%	31.8%	32.5%	1.67	13.3%	-0.06	-0.82	108%	19.2%*	29.9%	4.2%
P/B*	16.1%	24.2%	0.17	10.0%	1.61	3.97	76%	32.2%	27.4%	1.49	15.3%	0.06	-0.56	94%	16.2%	29.6%	1.2%
P/D	16.6%	25.5%	0.54	7.8%	0.73	1.34	99%	20.3%	24.4%	1.63	2.8%	0.00	-0.71	68%	3.8%	25.8%	-9.1%

TABLE 5B (continued)

Risk Attribute	High Tritile						Low Tritile							Low-High Attribute			
	Average Annual Return	Standard Dev.	MSCI AC World Beta	MSCI AC World Alpha	Skew-ness	Kurto-sis	Average Annual Turnover	Average Annual Return	Standard Dev.	MSCI AC World Beta	MSCI AC World Alpha	Skew-ness	Kurto-sis	Average Annual Turnover	Average Annual Return	Standard Dev.	MSCI AC World Alpha
Capitalization Weighted																	
ICRGC	13.5%	25.2%	0.43	5.2%	1.94	5.78	23%	30.1%	37.3%	-0.97	33.6%*	1.38	2.54	51%	16.6%	36.3%	24.3%
ICRGP	11.0%	24.6%	0.47	2.4%	1.58	4.15	49%	32.3%	38.9%	-2.01	43.8%**	1.14	0.87	53%	21.4%	34.7%	37.3%**
ICRGF	9.9%	25.0%	0.55	0.5%	1.74	4.70	15%	19.3%	33.1%	-1.35	26.0%	0.18	-0.49	26%	9.4%	39.8%	21.4%
ICRGE	13.5%	23.8%	0.62	3.5%	1.84	5.10	26%	34.3%	40.0%	-0.92	37.0%*	0.72	0.99	54%	20.8%	38.0%	29.3%
IICCR	11.1%	24.2%	0.66	0.9%	1.84	5.07	12%	30.6%	36.8%	0.73	20.0%	0.30	0.72	18%	19.5%	35.9%	14.9%
EMCRR	10.7%	24.1%	0.65	0.5%	1.88	5.20	15%	28.9%	37.8%	0.81	17.7%	0.29	0.64	84%	18.3%	37.4%	13.0%
INFLATE	28.7%	39.0%	0.90	16.8%	0.62	0.91	36%	10.8%	26.1%	0.85	-1.1%	1.90	5.51	18%	-17.9%	39.9%	-22.0%
TRDGDP	14.7%	32.0%	0.70	3.8%	2.08	6.83	10%	22.1%	29.4%	-0.24	19.5%	0.02	-0.48	15%	7.4%	30.8%	11.6%
MKCPGDP	10.0%	24.5%	0.44	1.7%	2.05	6.20	26%	23.5%	30.7%	-0.39	22.8%	0.75	0.25	40%	13.5%	29.2%	17.0%
POPGR	20.8%	22.1%	0.72	10.3%	0.96	3.51	21%	10.1%	21.5%	0.76	-0.5%	1.25	1.44	18%	-10.7%**	19.6%	-15.0%
AAGEGR	14.7%	26.7%	0.31	7.4%	0.31	0.05	15%	12.0%	20.7%	0.65	2.5%	0.33	1.64	23%	-2.7%	22.9%	-9.1%
AVEAGE	10.6%	18.5%	0.48	2.4%	0.78	-0.36	14%	18.6%	31.7%	0.34	11.2%	0.33	0.36	17%	8.0%	23.4%	4.7%
MKTCAP	13.0%	24.0%	0.34	5.4%	1.29	2.60	21%	28.9%	31.0%	1.54	12.3%	0.09	-0.69	52%	15.9%	34.0%	2.8%
BETA	22.1%	26.7%	0.33	14.6%	1.53	2.31	69%	22.5%	31.7%	0.10	17.7%	0.55	-0.57	77%	0.4%	28.4%	-1.1%
VOL	11.0%	27.2%	1.00	-1.8%	0.95	1.25	42%	17.5%	30.0%	-0.30	14.7%	1.09	1.82	57%	6.6%	29.4%	12.4%
MOM-1	7.8%	21.1%	0.14	2.3%	0.53	1.04	295%	24.1%	31.5%	0.20	17.1%	0.76	2.82	267%	16.3%	23.5%	10.6%
MOM-2-4	2.7%	25.2%	-0.43	2.1%	0.56	0.41	200%	19.5%	28.7%	1.00	7.0%	1.29	2.13	225%	16.8%*	21.7%	0.8%
P/E*	4.7%	23.4%	0.13	-0.7%	1.33	3.12	62%	23.6%	32.4%	0.69	13.1%	-0.37	0.47	76%	18.9%	28.9%	9.7%
P/B*	8.2%	25.0%	0.20	1.8%	1.04	2.42	44%	18.7%	25.0%	1.03	5.7%	0.43	0.82	49%	10.5%	26.6%	-0.3%
P/D	6.4%	26.6%	-0.05	1.9%	1.14	1.42	71%	14.4%	22.7%	1.20	0.4%	-0.16	-1.16	76%	8.0%	27.1%	-5.7%

	Average Annual Return	Standard Dev.	MSCI AC World Beta	MSCI AC World Alpha	Skew-ness	Kurto-sis
IFC Composite	13.3%	23.6%	0.37	5.5%**	1.23	2.66
MSCI AC World	12.1%	6.8%	1.00		-1.28	3.17

247

248

TABLE 5B *(continued)*

Notes:

Significance level: * 10%, ** 5%, *** 1%.

IFC Global and MSCI World Indices in US dollars: Unhedged.

From January 1985-December 1987 the MSCI World Index was substituted for the MSCI All Country (AC) World Index.

Price/Earnings and Price/Book ratios are unavailable until January 1986.

Portfolios were formed by sorting the countries into three tritiles based on the level of the attribute.

Portfolios were reformed quarterly.

Legend

ICRGC	International Country Risk Guide Composite Index
ICRGP	International Country Risk Guide Political Index
ICRGF	International Country Risk Guide Financial Index
ICRGE	International Country Risk Guide Economic Index
II CCR	Institutional Investor Country Credit Ratings
EMCRR	Euromoney Country Risk Ratings
INFLATE	Annual Consumer Inflation: IFS Database
TRDGDP	(Exports+Imports)/GDP: IFS Database
MKCPGDP	IFC Global Market Capitalization/GDP
POPGR	Annual Growth in Population - UN Data
AAGEGR	Annual Growth in Average Age of Population - UN Data
AVEAGE	Average Age of Population - UN Data
MKTCAP	IFC Global Market Capitalization
BETA	IFC Global Beta with MSCI AC World - 36 months trailing
VOL	IFC Global Volatility - 36 months trailing
MOM-1	Trailing USD Total Return - Prior Month
MOM-2-4	Trailing USD Total Return - Months -4 to -2
P/E*	IFC Global Price/Earnings Ratio
P/B*	IFC Global Price/Book Ratio
P/D	IFC Global Price/Dividend Ratio

TABLE 5C. Emerging Market Risk Level Portfolio Strategy
IFCG Indices–Semi-Annual Rebalancing: January 1985–June 1996

Risk Attribute	High Tritile							Low Tritile							Low-High Attribute		
	Average Annual Return	Standard Dev.	MSCI AC World Beta	MSCI AC World Alpha	Skew-ness	Kurto-sis	Average Annual Turnover	Average Annual Return	Standard Dev.	MSCI AC World Beta	MSCI AC World Alpha	Skew-ness	Kurto-sis	Average Annual Turnover	Average Annual Return	Standard Dev.	MSCI AC World Alpha
Equal Weighted																	
ICRGC	26.4%	25.9%	1.20	11.8%	1.29	1.33	42%	34.6%	27.4%	0.77	22.2%***	0.74	0.78	49%	8.3%	24.1%	4.8%
ICRGP	32.9%	30.5%	1.05	16.6%*	0.80	0.26	53%	29.2%	22.6%	0.74	17.3%**	0.33	-0.43	44%	-3.7%	31.3%	-5.0%
ICRGF	28.1%	22.7%	0.77	17.2%**	0.46	-0.23	45%	37.2%	29.8%	0.84	22.3%**	0.43	-0.30	59%	9.1%	25.0%	-0.6%
ICRGE	27.6%	26.7%	0.93	14.5%	1.06	1.08	48%	38.7%	34.2%	1.00	23.1%**	0.00	-0.74	70%	11.1%	28.5%	2.9%
II CCR	25.9%	24.6%	0.95	12.5%*	0.54	-0.19	28%	39.9%	30.2%	1.08	24.3%***	0.35	-0.66	43%	14.1%	29.4%	6.2%
EMCRR	27.0%	25.1%	0.94	13.4%*	0.48	-0.40	34%	43.0%	33.2%	1.55	22.3%**	0.03	-1.42	52%	16.0%*	30.6%	3.2%
INFLATE	57.3%	35.1%	1.09	40.8%***	-0.08	-0.97	64%	21.4%	22.2%	0.77	9.3%	1.47	2.27	52%	-35.9%***	29.2%	-37.2%***
TRDGDP	26.9%	28.2%	1.19	11.7%	1.36	1.99	34%	37.3%	34.9%	0.82	23.8%**	0.83	-0.36	37%	10.4%	33.0%	6.5%
MKCPGDP	22.7%	23.0%	0.95	8.2%	1.15	0.60	43%	52.2%	30.9%	0.61	40.8%***	-0.04	-0.21	70%	29.6%***	29.9%	26.9%***
POPGR	25.7%	24.0%	-0.40	21.6%***	0.80	-0.11	27%	36.8%	27.8%	0.91	23.2%***	0.01	-0.85	37%	11.0%	33.7%	-4.1%
AAGEGR	36.5%	28.0%	1.11	21.0%**	0.09	-0.99	34%	22.5%	24.8%	0.30	13.4%	0.84	-0.01	28%	-14.0%	29.6%	-13.3%
AVEAGE	41.6%	31.8%	1.21	24.3%***	0.55	0.01	39%	30.0%	24.1%	0.86	15.3%**	0.55	-0.36	24%	-11.5%	27.3%	-14.6%
MKTCAP	23.5%	24.1%	1.02	7.7%	0.64	-0.16	35%	47.6%	30.9%	0.38	36.5%***	0.10	-0.87	59%	24.2%**	34.4%	23.2%**
BETA	32.4%	27.7%	0.33	26.9%***	0.06	-1.20	74%	40.9%	37.4%	0.45	25.7%**	0.32	-0.95	79%	8.4%	49.5%	-6.8%
VOL	30.9%	38.8%	0.88	17.9%	0.52	-0.38	57%	30.1%	22.1%	0.55	17.8%***	0.85	0.18	54%	-0.8%	43.4%	-5.8%
MOM-1	37.9%	33.9%	1.75	13.9%*	0.52	-1.25	148%	23.7%	27.1%	0.64	15.4%*	0.84	0.05	142%	-14.2%	36.3%	-4.2%
MOM-2-4	43.9%	38.7%	1.09	26.6%**	1.12	0.97	144%	28.0%	31.8%	0.51	18.1%*	1.24	1.79	141%	-15.8%	51.1%	-14.2%
P/E*	18.8%	25.9%	0.73	7.3%	0.50	0.06	71%	50.4%	33.5%	0.22	44.0%***	0.56	0.53	90%	31.6%***	31.1%	31.2%***
P/B*	15.5%	28.2%	1.08	3.5%	0.93	1.67	61%	50.4%	32.4%	0.52	43.4%***	0.06	-0.93	85%	34.9%***	39.6%	34.4%***
P/D	25.1%	29.6%	0.81	8.9%	0.79	0.70	76%	39.1%	30.1%	1.19	25.0%***	0.13	-0.56	72%	14.0%	37.8%	10.4%

TABLE 5C (continued)

	High Tritile							Low Tritile							Low-High Attribute		
Risk Attribute	Average Annual Return	Standard Dev.	MSCI AC World Beta	MSCI AC World Alpha	Skew-ness	Kurto-sis	Average Annual Turnover	Average Annual Return	Standard Dev.	MSCI AC World Beta	MSCI AC World Alpha	Skew-ness	Kurto-sis	Average Annual Turnover	Average Annual Return	Standard Dev.	MSCI AC World Alpha
Capitalization Weighted																	
ICRGC	19.5%	16.9%	1.18	5.4%	0.92	0.51	10%	27.0%	27.3%	0.47	17.9%**	1.08	1.58	35%	7.5%	25.9%	6.8%
ICRGP	18.2%	14.5%	1.23	2.4%	0.45	-0.22	26%	23.7%	23.1%	0.35	14.9%*	0.93	2.10	19%	5.5%	29.4%	6.9%
ICRGF	19.0%	16.8%	0.98	8.1%	0.95	0.76	13%	27.1%	34.1%	1.08	9.7%	0.62	-0.28	29%	8.1%	28.5%	-4.1%
ICRGE	19.3%	16.6%	1.08	6.1%	0.86	0.45	15%	25.1%	39.2%	1.15	6.8%	0.08	-0.74	37%	5.9%	35.1%	-5.0%
II CCR	17.8%	15.3%	1.07	6.1%	0.87	0.55	8%	29.7%	37.0%	1.44	12.5%	0.27	0.66	10%	11.9%	32.3%	0.9%
EMCRR	18.9%	16.3%	1.05	5.8%	0.83	0.38	7%	35.4%	49.4%	2.35	8.1%	0.03	-0.96	12%	16.5%	41.4%	-3.33%
INFLATE	28.4%	23.3%	1.20	10.5%	0.05	-1.40	16%	21.8%	34.7%	1.15	8.4%	1.29	1.55	16%	-6.6%	38.2%	-7.7%
TRDGDP	21.5%	17.6%	1.26	7.0%	0.95	0.82	8%	22.0%	33.1%	0.68	7.9%	0.18	-0.67	10%	0.5%	34.1%	-4.7%
MKCPGDP	19.0%	15.3%	1.33	1.1%	0.75	-0.10	16%	34.7%	24.0%	0.77	21.8%***	-0.69	-0.19	32%	15.7%**	27.1%	15.0%*
POPGR	19.3%	17.7%	0.37	10.0%	0.83	1.79	9%	21.4%	22.4%	1.02	5.8%	0.58	-0.89	9%	2.0%	28.8%	-9.8%
AAGEGR	20.0%	17.2%	0.95	2.8%	0.76	-0.10	9%	14.2%	20.3%	0.51	3.8%	0.45	1.08	11%	-5.9%	26.6%	-4.7%
AVEGAE	23.2%	20.8%	1.10	5.5%	0.83	1.49	14%	30.5%	38.2%	1.16	12.3%	0.57	1.05	9%	7.4%	44.5%	1.2%
MKTCAP	17.4%	14.5%	1.00	2.7%	0.69	0.37	13%	43.4%	32.0%	0.15	34.0%***	0.43	-0.23	31%	26.1%**	44.9%	25.7%*
BETA	25.1%	19.1%	0.70	15.3%	0.63	-0.23	37%	36.4%	36.8%	0.88	17.8%*	1.23	1.42	32%	11.3%	55.4%	-3.2%
VOL	19.5%	8.0%	0.87	5.8%	0.44	-0.38	21%	30.5%	27.5%	0.84	16.9%**	0.51	-0.40	28%	11.0%	52.9%	5.4%
MOM-1	22.8%	19.2%	1.74	-0.1%	0.28	-0.31	155%	17.4%	38.1%	0.83	9.7%	0.95	1.52	142%	-5.4%	43.0%	4.2%
MOM-2-4	25.3%	20.8%	1.24	7.7%	1.09	1.83	78%	25.2%	39.6%	0.70	13.8%	1.20	2.01	100%	-0.1%	52.8%	0.4%
P/E*	13.0%	7.9%	1.26	-1.0%	0.50	-0.18	31%	36.3%	41.0%	0.95	27.4%**	1.03	0.63	37%	23.3%**	33.7%	22.9%**
P/B*	11.7%	5.3%	1.09	1.0%	0.93	0.74	28%	33.9%	35.7%	1.02	25.3%**	1.35	1.58	27%	22.2%*	39.3%	18.7%
P/D	19.1%	14.7%	1.41	0.5%	0.41	-0.11	32%	27.2%	28.4%	1.15	13.7%	0.30	-0.68	42%	8.1%	33.6%	7.5%

	Average Annual Return	Standard Dev.	MSCI AC World Beta	MSCI AC World Alpha	Skew-ness	Kurto-sis
IFC Composite	18.3%	26.7%	0.77	4.2%*	0.74	0.29
MSCI AC World	16.6%	15.4%	1.00		0.13	0.02

250

TABLE 5C (*continued*)

Notes:

Significance level: * 10%, ** 5%, *** 1%.

IFC Global and MSCI World Indices in US dollars: Unhedged.

From January 1985-December 1987 the MSCI World Index was substituted for the MSCI All Country (AC) World Index.

Price/Earnings and Price/Book ratios are unavailable until January 1986.

Portfolios were formed by sorting the countries into three tritiles based on the level of the attribute.

Portfolios were reformed semi-annually.

Legend

ICRGC	International Country Risk Guide Composite Index
ICRGP	International Country Risk Guide Political Index
ICRGF	International Country Risk Guide Financial Index
ICRGE	International Country Risk Guide Economic Index
II CCR	Institutional Investor Country Credit Ratings
EMCRR	Euromoney Country Risk Ratings
INFLATE	Annual Consumer Inflation: IFS Database
TRDGDP	(Exports+Imports)/GDP: IFS Database
MKCPGDP	IFC Global Market Capitalization/GDP
POPGR	Annual Growth in Population - UN Data
AAGEGR	Annual Growth in Average Age of Population - UN Data
AVEAGE	Average Age of Population - UN Data
MKTCAP	IFC Global Market Capitalization
BETA	IFC Global Beta with MSCI AC World - 36 months trailing
VOL	IFC Global Volatility - 36 months trailing
MOM-1	Trailing USD Total Return - Prior Month
MOM-2-4	Trailing USD Total Return - Months -4 to -2
P/E*	IFC Global Price/Earnings Ratio
P/B*	IFC Global Price/Book Ratio
P/D	IFC Global Price/Dividend Ratio

Risk Attribute	High Tritile							Low Tritile							Low-High Attribute		
	Average Annual Return	Standard Dev.	MSCI AC World Beta	MSCI AC World Alpha	Skewness	Kurtosis	Average Annual Turnover	Average Annual Return	Standard Dev.	MSCI AC World Beta	MSCI AC World Alpha	Skewness	Kurtosis	Average Annual Turnover	Average Annual Return	Standard Dev.	MSCI AC World Alpha
Equal Weighted																	
ICRGC	16.7%	26.2%	0.64	6.5%	2.40	6.49	34%	24.9%	26.6%	0.94	12.1%	0.53	0.39	57%	8.2%	19.2%	1.5%
ICRGP	18.5%	29.2%	1.49	1.1%	1.28	1.19	52%	20.9%	23.2%	0.28	13.8%	1.01	1.00	53%	2.4%	19.6%	8.6%
ICRGF	14.5%	21.8%	0.07	8.8%	1.95	4.49	42%	30.3%	30.5%	1.80	10.5%	0.17	-1.21	51%	15.7%	25.7%	-2.4%
ICRGE	18.4%	27.6%	0.54	8.6%	2.68	7.79	52%	29.6%	31.7%	1.71	10.9%	-0.18	-0.66	56%	11.3%	24.3%	-1.9%
II CCR	11.8%	21.3%	0.27	4.7%	1.33	1.93	22%	33.3%	34.6%	2.25	9.5%	0.72	-0.36	37%	21.5%	27.5%	0.6%
EMCRR	11.4%	25.0%	0.59	1.3%	1.93	4.33	6%	29.2%	33.0%	1.34	12.9%	-0.09	-1.70	16%	17.8%	26.9%	7.5%
INFLATE	43.1%	39.8%	2.68	16.0%	0.28	-1.56	49%	16.5%	25.9%	0.63	5.8%	2.44	6.39	47%	-26.6%	33.7%	-14.3%
TRDGDP	15.4%	32.6%	0.69	4.2%	2.65	7.56	31%	39.6%	43.9%	2.88	10.9%	0.88	-0.73	40%	24.1%	37.1%	2.6%
MKCPGDP	12.8%	24.1%	0.60	2.6%	2.35	6.18	34%	35.4%	36.5%	2.15	13.7%	0.85	0.62	63%	22.6%	37.5%	6.9%
POPGR	20.0%	25.4%	1.51	2.9%	0.87	0.80	27%	24.2%	30.0%	1.66	5.7%	0.79	0.04	36%	4.2%	18.0%	-1.3%
AAGEGR	20.7%	24.0%	0.71	9.9%	1.08	0.77	29%	23.7%	31.2%	1.66	5.7%	0.74	-0.70	30%	3.0%	20.5%	-8.4%
AVEAGE	26.0%	27.7%	1.61	8.2%	0.50	-1.24	30%	19.6%	25.7%	1.15	5.4%	1.25	1.46	24%	-6.3%	15.5%	-6.9%
MKTCAP	16.5%	22.7%	0.40	8.1%	1.94	4.67	29%	38.4%	38.6%	2.68	11.4%	0.60	-1.00	58%	21.9%	31.7%	-0.8%
BETA	24.3%	23.7%	0.52	15.3%	0.68	-0.27	55%	23.9%	39.7%	2.83	-3.7%	0.71	-0.39	64%	-0.4%	34.5%	-23.0%
VOL	26.7%	31.4%	2.00	5.8%	-0.47	-1.22	52%	23.5%	28.7%	1.51	6.3%	1.34	0.68	57%	-3.2%	30.3%	-3.6%
MOM-1	19.8%	27.6%	1.34	4.4%	0.96	-0.14	131%	24.2%	31.1%	1.63	6.0%	1.20	0.68	141%	4.5%	14.0%	-2.5%
MOM-2-4	21.2%	32.8%	1.56	4.4%	1.00	0.35	132%	20.6%	25.0%	1.31	4.6%	0.52	0.03	133%	-0.6%	26.1%	-3.9%
P/E*	15.1%	25.0%	0.87	3.5%	0.90	0.68	69%	36.0%	35.5%	1.76	16.4%	0.65	0.16	89%	21.0%**	18.2%	8.8%
P/B*	16.6%	30.1%	0.23	10.0%	1.70	3.82	51%	31.7%	30.9%	2.11	9.1%	0.10	-2.01	76%	15.0%	34.1%	-5.0%
P/D	18.0%	25.5%	0.96	5.6%	0.77	0.23	62%	23.2%	29.1%	2.23	0.3%	0.06	-1.27	58%	5.3%	15.7%	-9.4%

TABLE 5D (continued)

Risk Attribute	High Tritile							Low Tritile							Low-High Attribute		
	Average Annual Return	Standard Dev.	MSCI AC World Beta	MSCI AC World Alpha	Skew-ness	Kurto-sis	Average Annual Turnover	Average Annual Return	Standard Dev.	MSCI AC World Beta	MSCI AC World Alpha	Skew-ness	Kurto-sis	Average Annual Turnover	Average Annual Return	Standard Dev.	MSCI AC World Alpha
Capitalization Weighted																	
ICRGC	11.1%	23.2%	0.53	1.7%	2.67	7.87	9%	26.2%	27.4%	-0.47	25.9%	0.41	-0.42	43%	15.0%	24.5%	20.1%
ICRGP	11.7%	23.6%	0.51	2.6%	2.02	4.63	32%	28.4%	31.6%	-1.06	32.3%*	0.92	0.23	32%	16.6%*	18.3%	25.6%***
ICRGF	9.8%	24.6%	0.41	1.2%	2.50	7.07	11%	17.5%	27.1%	0.03	13.1%	0.40	-0.91	14%	7.6%	25.8%	7.7%
ICRGE	13.6%	25.8%	0.59	3.4%	2.03	4.69	22%	24.1%	29.3%	0.47	15.8%	0.31	-0.81	43%	10.5%	21.7%	8.2%
II CCR	10.9%	24.8%	0.51	1.5%	2.01	4.72	7%	28.2%	30.3%	1.27	12.8%	-0.22	-1.73	9%	17.2%*	26.3%	7.2%
EMCRR	14.5%	22.8%	0.69	3.6%	1.03	0.30	30%	36.2%	32.0%	1.80	16.2%	0.48	-0.98	49%	21.7%*	25.9%	8.4%
INFLATE	27.4%	33.0%	1.57	9.6%	0.15	-1.58	21%	11.1%	27.4%	0.70	-0.1%	2.41	6.44	12%	-16.3%	33.3%	-13.8%
TRDGDP	14.6%	35.2%	0.63	3.8%	2.18	5.56	5%	19.1%	26.5%	0.79	8.0%	0.90	0.34	9%	4.5%	23.8%	0.0%
MKCPGDP	10.8%	25.0%	0.57	0.9%	2.39	6.35	11%	21.9%	26.7%	1.36	6.7%	-0.62	-0.97	25%	11.1%	26.3%	1.7%
POPGR	19.8%	24.5%	0.61	9.8%	2.32	6.70	17%	9.5%	18.8%	0.56	0.0%	2.05	5.32	12%	-10.4%**	10.3%	-13.9%**
AAGEGR	13.2%	20.6%	0.51	3.9%	1.36	2.70	10%	16.9%	22.9%	0.73	6.1%	0.88	2.89	18%	3.6%	18.8%	-2.0%
AVEAGE	9.8%	11.1%	0.27	3.0%	1.28	2.11	10%	18.4%	33.2%	0.97	5.4%	1.47	2.72	15%	8.5%	25.9%	-1.7%
MKTCAP	12.9%	23.1%	0.53	3.3%	2.13	5.28	15%	35.1%	37.3%	2.32	11.4%	1.03	1.17	29%	22.2%	37.8%	4.0%
BETA	18.9%	27.0%	0.32	11.2%	0.66	-0.38	37%	23.2%	34.2%	1.44	7.5%	0.74	-0.69	41%	4.3%	30.4%	-7.8%
VOL	14.9%	32.7%	1.12	0.5%	0.30	-1.44	24%	15.8%	27.0%	0.15	9.3%	2.23	5.94	29%	0.9%	33.1%	4.6%
MOM-1	12.7%	23.8%	0.42	4.2%	1.79	3.83	161%	11.7%	28.1%	1.17	-3.3%	0.92	0.95	144%	-1.0%	18.4%	-11.7%
MOM-2-4	13.3%	26.4%	0.71	3.3%	0.54	-0.53	85%	23.3%	31.6%	1.54	5.2%	0.97	-0.11	119%	9.9%**	23.8%	-2.3%
P/E*	8.2%	27.4%	0.69	-2.6%	1.55	3.38	35%	26.1%	30.8%	0.15	19.7%	1.17	3.11	45%	18.0%**	16.4%	18.1%*
P/B*	11.2%	33.9%	0.39	2.6%	2.14	5.45	24%	17.0%	18.9%	0.93	4.1%	-0.33	-1.03	29%	5.7%	31.2%	-2.6%
P/D	8.3%	23.7%	0.24	1.2%	0.91	0.86	44%	11.9%	26.0%	1.33	-3.5%	0.35	-0.81	56%	3.7%	14.6%	-8.8%

	Average Annual Return	Standard Dev.	MSCI AC World Beta	MSCI AC World Alpha	Skew-ness	Kurto-sis
IFC Composite	13.2%	24.4%	0.61	3.1%*	2.10	5.26
MSCI AC World	12.4%	8.5%	1.00		-0.56	0.52

253

TABLE 5D (continued)

Notes:

Significance level: * 10‰, ** 5‰, *** 1%.

IFC Global and MSCI World Indices in US dollars: Unhedged.

From January 1985-December 1987 the MSCI World Index was substituted for the MSCI All Country (AC) World Index.

Price/Earnings and Price/Book ratios are unavailable until January 1986.

Portfolios were formed by sorting the countries into three tritiles based on the level of the attribute.

Portfolios were reformed semi-annually.

Legend

ICRGC	International Country Risk Guide Composite Index
ICRGP	International Country Risk Guide Political Index
ICRGF	International Country Risk Guide Financial Index
ICRGE	International Country Risk Guide Economic Index
II CCR	Institutional Investor Country Credit Ratings
EMCRR	Euromoney Country Risk Ratings
INFLATE	Annual Consumer Inflation: IFS Database
TRDGDP	(Exports+Imports)/GDP: IFS Database
MKCPGDP	IFC Global Market Capitalization/GDP
POPGR	Annual Growth in Population - UN Data
AAGEGR	Annual Growth in Average Age of Population - UN Data
AVEAGE	Average Age of Population - UN Data
MKTCAP	IFC Global Market Capitalization
BETA	IFC Global Beta with MSCI AC World - 36 months trailing
VOL	IFC Global Volatility - 36 months trailing
MOM-1	Trailing USD Total Return - Prior Month
MOM-2-4	Trailing USD Total Return - Months -4 to -2
P/E*	IFC Global Price/Earnings Ratio
P/B*	IFC Global Price/Book Ratio
P/D	IFC Global Price/Dividend Ratio

254

TABLE 5E. Emerging Market Risk Level Portfolio Strategy
IFCG Indices–Quarterly Rebalancing: July 1991–June 1996

Risk Attribute	High Tritile						Low Tritile							Low-High Attribute			
	Average Annual Return	Standard Dev.	MSCI AC World Beta	MSCI AC World Alpha	Skew-ness	Kurto-sis	Average Annual Turnover	Average Annual Return	Standard Dev.	MSCI AC World Beta	MSCI AC World Alpha	Skew-ness	Kurto-sis	Average Annual Turnover	Average Annual Return	Standard Dev.	MSCI AC World Alpha
Equal Weighted																	
ICRGC	21.3%	24.5%	1.11	7.8%	1.41	2.65	55%	36.9%	29.7%	1.58	19.6%	0.29	-0.92	83%	15.6%	20.0%	7.7%
ICRGP	21.0%	26.6%	1.53	3.8%	0.77	0.36	77%	28.6%	29.8%	0.54	19.4%	0.96	0.19	79%	7.6%	20.1%	11.5%
ICRGF	16.1%	22.4%	0.29	8.7%	1.63	4.91	49%	32.2%	28.4%	1.51	15.8%	0.43	-0.64	88%	16.1%	26.4%	2.9%
ICRGE	17.8%	21.9%	0.43	9.6%	1.57	3.63	72%	36.5%	30.4%	1.11	23.0%	-0.23	-1.48	76%	18.7%	26.7%	9.3%
II CCR	13.2%	23.6%	0.54	3.8%	1.55	4.21	31%	41.1%	32.6%	1.54	24.0%	0.21	-0.74	44%	27.9%*	29.2%	16.1%
EMCRR	12.2%	21.5%	0.64	2.1%	1.51	3.81	46%	41.3%	33.7%	1.47	25.0%	0.67	0.22	57%	29.2%*	29.6%	18.8%
INFLATE	43.6%	42.4%	1.89	24.1%	0.66	0.14	57%	14.2%	23.5%	0.55	4.6%	1.33	3.89	51%	-29.4%	40.5%	-23.6%
TRDGDP	20.1%	24.3%	0.26	12.6%	1.57	3.68	38%	37.2%	34.4%	1.81	18.2%	0.70	0.51	45%	17.1%	27.4%	1.4%
MKCPGDP	15.0%	23.5%	0.48	6.3%	2.28	8.00	59%	38.7%	38.5%	1.75	20.5%	1.23	2.89	89%	23.7%	38.3%	10.0%
POPGR	26.9%	28.2%	1.55	9.9%	1.14	1.23	29%	23.7%	25.5%	1.47	7.1%	0.43	-0.29	44%	-3.2%	16.5%	-6.9%
AAGEGR	24.1%	30.2%	0.60	14.4%	1.21	1.91	41%	26.6%	26.6%	1.70	8.6%	0.59	-0.49	40%	2.5%	19.8%	-9.9%
AVEAGE	25.0%	26.2%	1.55	8.1%	0.27	-0.57	38%	27.5%	25.6%	0.93	15.3%	0.91	0.87	28%	2.5%	20.8%	3.1%
MKTCAP	22.5%	25.0%	0.55	13.8%	-0.01	-1.08	46%	31.3%	30.6%	1.33	15.4%	0.97	0.25	86%	8.7%	24.6%	-2.6%
BETA	25.2%	26.4%	-0.33	23.2%	0.19	-0.65	87%	33.4%	36.9%	1.94	13.6%	1.21	1.39	97%	8.2%	43.5%	-13.8%
VOL	30.4%	32.8%	1.54	14.0%	0.13	-1.50	81%	17.4%	17.2%	0.49	8.6%	1.77	3.86	53%	-12.9%	30.7%	-9.5%
MOM-1	16.5%	24.0%	1.21	2.2%	0.92	0.33	271%	35.8%	28.1%	1.24	21.2%	0.32	0.19	293%	19.3%**	16.5%	14.9%*
MOM-2-4	30.8%	34.9%	1.99	10.9%	1.57	2.89	298%	28.5%	25.5%	0.52	19.4%	0.29	0.00	302%	-2.2%	30.6%	4.4%
P/E	17.3%	26.7%	1.55	1.0%	1.27	1.67	126%	33.9%	29.9%	1.07	20.0%	0.40	-0.41	130%	16.5%*	26.1%	14.9%
P/B	11.6%	27.3%	1.03	-1.7%	1.33	3.09	91%	44.2%	32.1%	1.21	30.0%*	0.52	-0.69	120%	32.6%	37.0%	27.5%
P/D	29.2%	33.7%	1.13	15.9%	0.78	0.26	104%	16.1%	22.4%	1.07	2.6%	0.23	-0.63	92%	-13.1%	32.9%	-17.3%

TABLE 5E (continued)

	High Tritile						Low Tritile							Low-High Attribute			
Risk Attribute	Average Annual Return	Standard Dev.	MSCI AC World Beta	MSCI AC World Alpha	Skew-ness	Kurto-sis	Average Annual Turnover	Average Annual Return	Standard Dev.	MSCI AC World Beta	MSCI AC World Alpha	Skew-ness	Kurto-sis	Average Annual Turnover	Average Annual Return	Standard Dev.	MSCI AC World Alpha
Capitalization Weighted																	
ICRGC	23.5%	26.2%	0.22	16.9%	0.90	1.98	42%	37.6%	37.2%	1.17	23.5%	0.81	1.70	77%	14.1%	35.5%	2.4%
ICRGP	17.3%	26.9%	0.44	9.1%	0.74	1.33	68%	31.9%	35.4%	0.30	24.5%	1.00	0.80	52%	14.6%	31.3%	11.3%
ICRGF	14.5%	27.7%	0.29	7.1%	0.81	2.17	20%	24.1%	27.9%	0.80	13.8%	0.16	-0.52	69%	9.6%	35.4%	2.5%
ICRGE	23.0%	23.2%	0.38	15.0%	0.48	1.77	27%	29.9%	36.0%	0.38	22.2%	0.21	0.82	53%	6.9%	31.7%	3.1%
II CCR	19.3%	26.1%	0.47	10.5%	0.70	2.76	10%	36.0%	40.1%	0.73	25.6%	0.27	0.40	25%	16.7%	39.5%	11.0%
EMCRR	18.1%	25.2%	0.55	8.7%	0.74	2.67	21%	37.0%	39.3%	0.75	26.6%	0.43	0.35	45%	18.9%	38.3%	13.8%
INFLATE	27.7%	38.2%	1.31	12.8%	0.60	0.40	42%	15.6%	29.6%	0.64	5.2%	0.50	1.74	24%	-12.1%	35.1%	-11.7%
TRDGDP	21.3%	29.4%	0.52	12.0%	0.85	3.48	10%	21.6%	28.1%	0.49	13.2%	-0.04	-0.55	14%	0.4%	23.9%	-2.9%
MKCPGDP	16.2%	24.6%	0.09	10.7%	1.16	3.16	32%	26.5%	28.3%	0.79	16.1%	0.42	-0.47	39%	10.3%	23.2%	1.3%
POPGR	20.7%	25.9%	0.52	11.8%	0.52	0.96	17%	16.0%	24.7%	1.07	3.1%	0.78	1.63	33%	-4.7%	13.4%	-12.8%*
AAGEGR	17.9%	34.0%	0.19	11.6%	-0.02	-0.38	22%	19.6%	21.8%	0.98	7.0%	0.68	1.84	20%	1.7%	26.9%	-8.7%
AVEAGE	15.5%	22.6%	0.97	3.7%	0.08	0.69	24%	20.9%	25.7%	0.38	13.0%	0.55	1.00	16%	5.4%	19.3%	5.2%
MKTCAP	18.7%	29.1%	0.48	10.2%	0.02	-0.48	14%	22.9%	23.9%	1.15	8.9%	0.84	0.86	37%	4.2%	25.9%	-5.4%
BETA	25.5%	31.6%	-0.11	21.8%	0.92	2.07	67%	35.7%	45.8%	2.78	9.6%	1.44	3.57	63%	10.2%	54.9%	-16.3%
VOL	26.6%	35.1%	1.03	14.1%	0.28	-0.36	23%	19.2%	26.3%	0.48	10.1%	1.10	2.67	43%	-7.4%	32.5%	-8.1%
MOM-1	10.3%	23.6%	0.13	5.0%	0.20	-0.84	300%	33.9%	30.3%	0.67	23.6%	-0.10	1.03	328%	23.6%*	24.0%	14.5%
MOM-2-4	7.7%	25.7%	0.80	-2.3%	-0.28	-0.29	186%	34.9%	27.2%	0.02	29.9%**	0.48	0.12	199%	27.3%***	27.2%	28.0%*
P/E	15.0%	25.9%	1.47	-1.1%	0.02	1.29	72%	25.7%	31.9%	0.20	19.3%	-0.30	0.44	85%	10.7%	26.6%	16.2%
P/B	12.3%	27.5%	1.35	-3.5%	0.35	1.56	46%	31.1%	31.4%	0.70	21.1%	-0.23	-0.58	63%	18.8%	35.8%	20.5%
P/D	30.8%	36.7%	0.19	24.6%	0.19	-0.41	89%	10.7%	25.0%	1.13	-3.2%	0.01	-0.54	66%	-20.1%	40.2%	-31.9%

| | High Tritile | | | | | | | Low Tritile | | | | | | | Low-High Attribute | | | |
Risk Attribute	Average Annual Return	Standard Dev.	MSCI AC World Beta	MSCI AC World Alpha	Skew-ness	Kurto-sis	Average Annual Turnover	Average Annual Return	Standard Dev.	MSCI AC World Beta	MSCI AC World Alpha	Skew-ness	Kurto-sis	Average Annual Turnover	Average Annual Return	Standard Dev.	MSCI AC World Alpha
Liquidity Weighted																	
ICRGC	16.8%	28.3%	0.25	9.7%	1.32	2.94	35%	42.4%	38.4%	1.18	28.1%	0.70	1.07	71%	25.6%	40.2%	14.3%
ICRGP	11.4%	27.7%	0.64	1.4%	0.74	1.66	48%	38.8%	39.2%	0.23	32.0%	1.28	2.62	68%	27.4%**	34.9%	26.5%
ICRGF	9.8%	29.3%	0.23	2.7%	1.06	2.38	10%	30.3%	28.6%	1.27	16.1%	-0.07	-0.39	69%	20.4%	39.2%	9.2%
ICRGE	16.8%	26.2%	0.33	9.1%	1.34	4.28	15%	34.4%	37.9%	0.58	24.9%	0.07	0.60	45%	17.6%	34.8%	11.7%
IICCR	14.9%	26.4%	0.30	7.4%	1.35	4.38	9%	42.5%	46.7%	0.82	31.7%	0.26	0.04	14%	27.5%	49.6%	20.2%
EMCRR	15.2%	26.2%	0.45	6.4%	1.33	4.21	29%	45.8%	45.8%	1.12	32.6%	0.31	-0.13	42%	30.6%	48.6%	22.0%
INFLATE	29.8%	39.0%	1.56	12.9%	0.65	0.79	31%	11.0%	29.5%	0.49	1.7%	0.94	2.76	26%	-18.8%	38.1%	-15.3%
TRDGDP	20.1%	24.3%	0.26	12.6%	1.57	3.68	38%	37.2%	34.4%	1.81	18.2%	0.70	0.51	45%	17.1%	27.4%	1.4%
MKCPGDP	9.8%	29.0%	0.09	4.1%	1.63	4.72	38%	32.7%	30.8%	0.74	22.8%	0.04	-0.61	31%	22.9%	28.2%	14.6%
POPGR	17.2%	33.2%	0.79	6.2%	0.13	0.17	5%	15.8%	25.4%	0.60	6.4%	1.29	3.08	33%	-1.4%	14.8%	-4.0%
AAGEGR	19.7%	34.8%	0.19	13.4%	-0.16	-0.21	21%	14.8%	27.3%	1.53	-1.9%	0.45	1.28	14%	-4.9%	28.0%	-19.4%
AVEAGE	12.8%	22.3%	0.76	2.3%	0.02	0.59	23%	17.6%	33.5%	0.43	9.4%	0.15	0.09	5%	4.9%	20.1%	3.0%
MKTCAP	22.1%	31.9%	0.71	11.8%	-0.30	-0.49	8%	25.3%	32.1%	1.34	9.6%	1.12	0.55	51%	3.3%	25.5%	-6.4%
BETA	29.1%	32.7%	-0.38	27.4%	0.60	0.99	54%	49.0%	61.8%	4.15	12.5%	2.01	5.98	65%	19.9%	71.0%	-19.1%
VOL	31.9%	37.0%	0.92	20.3%	0.48	0.41	14%	20.0%	28.3%	0.61	9.8%	1.44	3.99	39%	-12.0%	36.7%	-14.6%
MOM-1	7.5%	25.6%	-0.12	4.2%	0.25	-1.30	319%	32.1%	32.5%	0.88	19.9%	0.15	1.87	323%	24.6%*	27.3%	11.6%
MOM-2-4	-1.3%	28.1%	0.69	-11.0%	-0.23	-0.58	184%	35.0%	28.3%	0.27	27.9%*	0.35	-0.17	215%	36.4%***	31.4%	34.8%**
P/E	10.8%	25.4%	1.35	-4.3%	0.07	1.83	62%	34.2%	42.8%	0.55	24.9%	0.43	0.62	67%	23.5%	35.1%	25.0%
P/B	10.5%	28.1%	1.23	-4.3%	0.28	1.36	47%	40.7%	38.3%	0.58	31.7%	0.17	-0.55	52%	30.2%	46.5%	31.9%
P/D	36.1%	39.1%	0.49	27.6%	0.46	-0.45	82%	11.0%	34.5%	2.50	-13.9%	0.49	-0.14	60%	-25.1%	47.3%	-45.6%*

TABLE 5E (continued)

IFC Composite	17.3%	26.5%	0.66	7.3%**	0.41	0.12
MSCI AC World	12.1%	6.8%	1.00	-1.28		3.17

Notes:

Significance level: * 10%, ** 5%, *** 1%.

IFC Investables and MSCI World Indices in US dollars: Unhedged.

Portfolios were formed by sorting the countries into three tritiles based on the level of the attribute.

Portfolios were reformed semi-annually.

Liquidity weighted portfolios based on IFC USD value traded - 12 month average.

Legend

ICRGC	International Country Risk Guide Composite Index
ICRGP	International Country Risk Guide Political Index
ICRGF	International Country Risk Guide Financial Index
ICRGE	International Country Risk Guide Economic Index
II CCR	Institutional Investor Country Credit Ratings
EMCRR	Euromoney Country Risk Ratings
INFLATE	Annual Consumer Inflation: IFS Database
TRDGDP	(Exports+Imports)/GDP: IFS Database
MKCPGDP	IFC Global Market Capitalization/GDP
POPGR	Annual Growth in Population - UN Data
AAGEGR	Annual Growth in Average Age of Population - UN Data
AVEAGE	Average Age of Population - UN Data
MKTCAP	IFC Global Market Capitalization
BETA	IFC Global Beta with MSCI AC World - 36 months trailing
VOL	IFC Global Volatility - 36 months trailing
MOM-1	Trailing USD Total Return - Prior Month
MOM-2-4	Trailing USD Total Return - Months -4 to -2
P/E*	IFC Global Price/Earnings Ratio
P/B*	IFC Global Price/Book Ratio
P/D	IFC Global Price/Dividend Ratio

TABLE 5F. Emerging Market Risk Level Portfolio Strategy
IFCG Indices—Semi-Annual Rebalancing: July 1991–June 1996

	High Tritile						Low Tritile							Low-High Attribute			
Risk Attribute	Average Annual Return	Standard Dev.	MSCI AC World Beta	MSCI AC World Alpha	Skew-ness	Kurto-sis	Average Annual Turnover	Average Annual Return	Standard Dev.	MSCI AC World Beta	MSCI AC World Alpha	Skew-ness	Kurto-sis	Average Annual Turnover	Average Annual Return	Standard Dev.	MSCI AC World Alpha
Equal Weighted																	
ICRGC	18.4%	31.8%	1.37	2.1%	2.15	5.16	50%	36.3%	40.2%	2.11	14.4%	0.95	0.00	73%	18.0%	24.7%	8.1%
ICRGP	25.2%	36.7%	2.09	2.5%	1.34	1.66	57%	24.5%	30.2%	0.76	13.4%	1.33	2.05	55%	-0.7%	17.5%	6.7%
ICRGF	17.0%	25.9%	0.25	9.5%	2.13	5.30	45%	38.2%	40.7%	2.72	11.1%	0.84	-0.39	76%	21.2%	35.5%	-2.5%
ICRGE	18.7%	24.0%	0.48	9.7%	2.16	5.79	48%	34.8%	36.7%	1.91	14.6%	0.66	-0.71	55%	16.1%	25.1%	0.7%
II CCR	12.9%	26.0%	0.39	4.4%	2.03	5.00	28%	44.7%	45.8%	2.59	18.3%	0.96	-0.51	43%	31.8%**	37.3%	9.8%
EMCRR	13.7%	24.5%	0.84	1.3%	1.58	2.12	38%	44.5%	45.0%	2.54	18.8%	1.06	-0.15	57%	30.8%***	38.4%	13.3%
INFLATE	49.5%	53.0%	3.48	16.3%	0.95	-0.18	55%	17.1%	28.6%	0.63	6.3%	2.21	5.50	46%	-32.4%	49.8%	-14.2%
TRDGDP	21.2%	34.2%	0.24	13.4%	2.56	7.27	38%	38.7%	47.5%	3.28	6.7%	1.08	-0.27	46%	17.5%	41.8%	-10.8%
MKCPGDP	16.2%	21.6%	0.46	7.3%	2.01	4.99	44%	40.4%	53.6%	3.16	10.4%	1.34	1.67	65%	24.2%	49.9%	-1.0%
POPGR	28.3%	36.5%	2.31	4.6%	1.25	0.16	30%	27.1%	36.4%	2.20	3.7%	1.15	0.76	45%	-1.2%	15.3%	-5.0%
AAGEGR	22.6%	31.6%	0.87	10.5%	1.46	1.04	38%	29.4%	39.9%	2.37	5.6%	1.32	0.33	36%	6.8%	18.0%	-9.1%
AVEAGE	28.1%	34.9%	2.11	5.8%	0.76	-0.62	39%	28.1%	30.4%	1.35	12.1%	1.28	1.01	28%	0.1%	10.2%	2.2%
MKTCAP	22.6%	28.5%	1.33	7.1%	1.32	0.47	31%	28.6%	37.3%	1.76	8.8%	1.11	1.45	67%	6.0%	20.8%	-2.4%
BETA	23.5%	22.1%	0.75	12.6%	0.47	-1.57	63%	32.5%	38.1%	2.27	9.4%	0.76	-0.04	93%	9.0%	33.5%	-7.4%
VOL	33.6%	43.9%	3.04	4.4%	0.46	-1.13	60%	15.2%	17.4%	0.49	6.2%	1.04	0.92	36%	-18.3%	40.1%	-2.3%
MOM-1	24.4%	38.3%	2.33	1.0%	1.34	1.23	144%	31.5%	39.8%	1.96	10.7%	1.03	-0.11	152%	7.2%*	16.2%	5.6%
MOM-2-4	25.9%	38.9%	1.98	4.9%	1.56	1.90	154%	29.3%	38.5%	2.37	4.8%	0.96	-0.45	158%	3.4%	14.2%	-4.2%
P/E	20.4%	31.0%	1.66	2.4%	1.41	0.57	93%	41.9%	34.4%	1.48	24.5%	0.77	-0.01	101%	21.4%***	15.7%	18.0%*
P/B	11.6%	32.3%	0.47	2.6%	1.98	4.81	66%	52.1%	57.1%	2.90	24.4%	2.31	6.06	93%	40.6%	62.1%	17.7%
P/D	33.3%	43.8%	2.24	10.3%	1.43	1.46	74%	17.7%	30.4%	1.48	0.6%	0.27	-0.89	67%	-15.6%	42.3%	-13.8%

TABLE 5F (continued)

Risk Attribute	High Tritile							Low Tritile							Low-High Attribute		
	Average Annual Return	Standard Dev.	MSCI AC World Beta	MSCI AC World Alpha	Skewness	Kurtosis	Average Annual Turnover	Average Annual Return	Standard Dev.	MSCI AC World Beta	MSCI AC World Alpha	Skewness	Kurtosis	Average Annual Turnover	Average Annual Return	Standard Dev.	MSCI AC World Alpha
Capitalization Weighted																	
ICRGC	16.6%	29.6%	1.04	2.7%	2.02	5.52	23%	31.8%	34.1%	1.64	13.8%	0.00	-1.86	45%	15.3%	37.6%	6.9%
ICRGP	21.8%	30.5%	0.71	11.0%	1.67	4.50	42%	25.3%	32.3%	0.22	18.6%	1.79	3.28	36%	3.6%	17.0%	3.5%
ICRGF	14.9%	30.1%	0.17	8.1%	2.15	5.74	16%	22.1%	30.6%	1.43	6.6%	0.37	0.20	61%	7.1%	35.7%	-5.7%
ICRGE	24.9%	29.7%	0.55	14.9%	1.89	4.69	21%	26.0%	29.4%	0.97	13.3%	0.53	-0.71	44%	1.1%	24.4%	-5.7%
II CCR	19.8%	31.2%	0.50	10.3%	1.81	4.76	5%	34.6%	35.7%	1.60	16.9%	0.19	-1.24	16%	14.8%	38.1%	2.5%
EMCRR	19.5%	30.3%	0.67	8.6%	1.71	4.12	7%	37.3%	36.3%	1.74	18.4%	0.34	-1.24	17%	17.8%	36.0%	5.7%
INFLATE	30.1%	32.0%	1.74	11.1%	0.13	-2.06	24%	18.1%	34.6%	0.62	7.2%	1.97	4.80	14%	-12.0%	37.4%	-8.1%
TRDGDP	22.6%	37.1%	0.54	12.5%	2.03	5.60	6%	19.4%	28.4%	1.46	2.7%	1.17	1.01	8%	-3.2%	26.5%	-13.9%
MKCPGDP	18.8%	25.4%	0.38	10.4%	1.82	4.59	27%	29.3%	35.4%	2.53	4.4%	0.66	-0.22	26%	10.5%	34.6%	-10.2%
POPGR	20.8%	25.8%	1.08	6.8%	1.70	4.12	13%	17.4%	30.7%	1.40	1.3%	1.41	1.99	28%	-3.3%	15.5%	-9.6%
AAGEGR	15.8%	27.9%	0.54	6.4%	1.25	1.84	18%	20.7%	25.2%	1.35	4.6%	1.61	3.34	15%	4.9%	20.8%	-5.9%
AVEAGE	16.3%	26.4%	1.18	2.4%	0.73	0.35	19%	20.9%	25.4%	0.89	8.4%	1.78	4.67	13%	4.6%	20.1%	1.8%
MKTCAP	18.1%	27.8%	1.07	4.4%	1.57	3.08	8%	21.5%	26.0%	1.40	4.9%	0.96	0.50	22%	3.4%	21.0%	-3.6%
BETA	28.4%	25.9%	0.60	18.1%	1.00	0.22	49%	36.7%	52.9%	3.19	6.6%	1.10	1.46	34%	8.3%	50.4%	-15.7%
VOL	26.9%	34.0%	2.13	4.9%	-0.02	-1.95	15%	17.3%	32.3%	0.54	7.2%	1.81	4.45	42%	-9.6%	35.2%	-1.8%
MOM-1	14.2%	21.0%	0.90	2.6%	0.33	-1.04	152%	22.0%	38.0%	2.02	0.2%	1.03	0.28	179%	7.7%	28.2%	-6.5%
MOM-2-4	15.6%	31.4%	1.45	-0.5%	0.79	0.64	92%	18.2%	32.4%	1.71	-1.3%	1.57	2.93	78%	2.6%	25.1%	-4.9%
P/E	16.2%	32.4%	1.73	-3.0%	1.42	3.15	30%	29.4%	29.1%	-0.06	25.2%	0.30	0.48	46%	13.3%	24.5%	24.0%**
P/B	14.5%	34.3%	0.73	3.1%	1.96	5.54	33%	38.1%	36.9%	1.93	17.7%	1.30	2.04	39%	23.5%	44.0%	10.5%
P/D	31.0%	35.5%	1.25	16.2%	0.91	0.15	47%	13.6%	32.3%	1.42	-2.7%	0.13	-0.76	47%	-17.4%	37.4%	-23.0%

260

TABLE 5F (continued)

Risk Attribute	High Tritile							Low Tritile							Low-High Attribute		
	Average Annual Return	Standard Dev.	MSCI AC World Beta	MSCI AC World Alpha	Skew-ness	Kurto-sis	Average Annual Turnover	Average Annual Return	Standard Dev.	MSCI AC World Beta	MSCI AC World Alpha	Skew-ness	Kurto-sis	Average Annual Turnover	Average Annual Return	Standard Dev.	MSCI AC World Alpha
Liquidity Weighted																	
ICRGC	12.4%	27.1%	0.84	0.2%	1.91	4.70	21%	33.6%	33.7%	1.97	12.8%	-0.02	-2.12	40%	21.2%	37.0%	8.5%
ICRGP	15.6%	27.9%	0.75	4.5%	1.88	4.73	24%	31.9%	29.9%	0.56	22.4%	0.85	-0.39	52%	16.4%**	21.1%	13.8%
ICRGF	10.9%	31.1%	0.14	4.1%	2.04	5.02	5%	26.3%	29.0%	2.05	5.9%	-0.47	0.36	68%	15.4%	39.4%	-2.4%
ICRGE	18.0%	29.4%	0.42	9.1%	2.11	5.77	9%	29.2%	30.9%	1.33	13.4%	0.16	-1.34	42%	11.3%	25.0%	0.1%
II CCR	16.0%	30.6%	0.33	7.8%	1.95	5.00	4%	39.6%	42.9%	2.07	18.5%	0.94	0.96	12%	23.6%	49.2%	6.6%
EMCRR	17.9%	30.9%	0.69	6.5%	1.65	3.40	13%	47.7%	45.0%	2.81	19.9%	0.69	-0.53	17%	29.7%	46.7%	9.3%
INFLATE	31.2%	36.4%	2.29	7.9%	0.22	-1.99	19%	13.1%	32.6%	0.44	3.7%	2.01	4.84	12%	-18.1%	41.9%	-8.3%
TRDGDP	17.1%	30.7%	0.40	8.7%	1.50	5.39	13%	20.3%	36.9%	1.19	6.1%	-0.60	-0.02	8%	3.1%	32.5%	-6.7%
MKCPGDP	12.5%	31.0%	0.24	5.2%	1.96	5.05	28%	34.3%	39.3%	2.74	7.6%	0.78	-0.24	19%	21.8%	39.2%	-1.6%
POPGR	16.2%	34.3%	1.31	0.6%	1.39	2.15	2%	17.6%	29.5%	0.96	4.8%	2.05	4.48	29%	1.3%	14.4%	0.1%
AAGEGR	16.3%	27.2%	0.48	7.3%	1.05	1.72	18%	16.8%	34.8%	1.92	-3.6%	1.61	3.94	9%	0.5%	24.8%	-15.0%
AVEAGE	14.6%	24.9%	1.06	1.4%	1.44	1.36	19%	16.1%	33.1%	0.90	3.6%	1.48	3.03	2%	1.5%	20.6%	-1.9%
MKTCAP	19.7%	29.0%	1.41	3.1%	1.16	1.33	4%	27.3%	39.3%	2.13	4.4%	1.32	1.91	13%	7.6%	18.6%	-2.9%
BETA	26.4%	27.8%	0.62	15.7%	0.43	-0.84	41%	61.6%	82.7%	5.98	8.4%	1.50	2.12	39%	35.2%	79.8%	-11.4%
VOL	31.4%	36.0%	2.07	9.7%	0.02	-2.15	11%	17.8%	33.2%	0.66	6.7%	1.94	4.94	39%	-13.6%	37.8%	-7.1%
MOM-1	5.7%	23.3%	0.59	-4.0%	0.56	-1.53	165%	18.0%	35.7%	2.00	-3.3%	0.85	-0.39	173%	12.3%	32.5%	-3.4%
MOM-2-4	5.3%	31.5%	1.19	-9.2%	1.16	2.52	98%	25.3%	41.4%	2.01	2.9%	1.70	3.57	91%	19.9%**	21.5%	8.0%
P/E	13.2%	29.2%	1.63	-5.2%	1.02	1.21	24%	34.7%	34.4%	0.23	28.0%	0.17	-0.55	40%	21.5%*	23.4%	29.1%**
P/B	11.6%	38.8%	1.18	-3.4%	1.70	3.70	27%	42.9%	45.3%	2.39	19.0%	1.80	4.09	17%	31.3%	56.2%	18.3%
P/D	37.8%	45.4%	1.99	17.2%	1.41	2.44	43%	12.5%	43.8%	2.85	-16.2%	0.45	-1.10	30%	-25.4%	53.8%	-37.5%

TABLE 5F (continued)

IFC Composite	17.2%	27.8%	1.15	2.7%*	1.71	3.94
MSCI AC World	12.4%	8.5%	1.00	-0.56		0.52

Notes:

Significance level: * 10%, ** 5%, *** 1%.

IFC Investables and MSCI World Indices in US dollars: Unhedged.

Portfolios were formed by sorting the countries into three tritiles based on the level of the attribute.

Portfolios were reformed semi-annually.

Liquidity weighted portfolios based on IFC USD value traded - 12 month average.

Legend

ICRGC	International Country Risk Guide Composite Index	AAGEGR	Annual Growth in Average Age of Population - UN Data
ICRGP	International Country Risk Guide Political Index	AVEAGE	Average Age of Population - UN Data
ICRGF	International Country Risk Guide Financial Index	MKTCAP	IFC Global Market Capitalization
ICRGE	International Country Risk Guide Economic Index	BETA	IFC Global Beta with MSCI AC World - 36 months trailing
II CCR	Institutional Investor Country Credit Ratings	VOL	IFC Global Volatility - 36 months trailing
EMCRR	Euromoney Country Risk Ratings	MOM-1	Trailing USD Total Return - Prior Month
INFLATE	Annual Consumer Inflation: IFS Database	MOM-2-4	Trailing USD Total Return - Months -4 to -2
TRDGDP	(Exports+Imports)/GDP: IFS Database	P/E*	IFC Global Price/Earnings Ratio
MKCPGDP	IFC Global Market Capitalization/GDP	P/B*	IFC Global Price/Book Ratio
POPGR	Annual Growth in Population - UN Data	P/D	IFC Global Price/Dividend Ratio

and 5D. The investible strategies detailed in Tables 5E and 5F also indicate that there is information in the risk ratings. In all three portfolio-
weighting schemes and over both rebalancing rules, the ICRG earns positive abnormal returns. Interestingly, the ICRGC composite is not even the
most successful attribute. The ICRG economic-risk and political-risk
attributes consistently produce higher abnormal returns. These results are
consistent with those presented in Erb, Harvey, and Viskanta (1996b).

Institutional Investor and *Euromoney*

Both the *Institutional Investor* and the *Euromoney* credit ratings provide
less impressive discrimination between high and low expected-return
securities. None of the abnormal returns are significantly different from
zero and the performance deteriorates in the past five years. For example,
the EMCCR provided impressive abnormal performance in the overall
period (14.4 percent alpha with equal weighting). In the past five years,
the abnormal returns were negative. However, the negative returns are
largely due to noninvestible countries. Tables 5E and 5F show that the
EMCCR generates 18.8 percent, 13.8 percent, and 22.0 percent alpha over
the equal capitalization-weighted and liquidity-weighted strategies with
quarterly rebalancing.

Inflation

Inflation appears to be an important instrument in portfolio selection. In
this case, the high-attribute portfolio has much higher expected returns
than the low-attribute portfolio. However, in contrast to some of the
ICRG results, the high-attribute portfolio has much higher volatility than
the low-attribute portfolio. The high minus low equally weighted portfolio results in an alpha of 36.3 percent over the full sample and 25.2 percent
over the past five years. The alphas are smaller for the capitalization-
weighted portfolios but still large compared to other attributes. In addition, the results are robust to less frequent rebalancing. Finally, inflation is
an important attribute in all of the investible strategies.

Trade Sector

Trade to GDP has some ability to distinguish between high and low
expected returns. Countries with small trade sectors have higher
expected returns than countries with large trade sectors. This is consistent
with the Bekaert and Harvey (1996b) idea that the size of the trade sector
serves as a proxy for market integration. In addition, the beta of the low-

attribute portfolio may be low because the market is not intregrated. The size of the trade-sector attribute produces a 12.6 percent alpha in the full sample with the equally weighted portfolio and 18.9 percent over the last five years. The alphas are lower for the capitalization-weighted portfolio strategies. The alphas are also low for the investible strategies in Tables 5E and 5F.

Market Size

Market size to GDP provides significant information regarding portfolio performance. This is consistent with the arguments of Bekaert and Harvey (1996b) that the size of the equity market relative to economic activity is an important indicator of financial market integration. For the equally weighted portfolios, the alpha is 26.6 percent in the overall period and 22.3 percent in the last five years. The value-weighted portfolios produce equally impressive results. In the overall period, the alpha is 18.7 percent, and in the last five years, 21.6 percent. With quarterly rebalancing, the investible alphas are 10.0 percent, 1.3 percent, and 14.6 percent for the three weighting schemes.

Market size itself provides less information regarding portfolio performance. This contrasts with the results of Asness, Liew, and Stevens (1996) for developed countries. For equally weighted portfolios, the low-minus high-size portfolio produced 21.2 percent alpha in the overall period but -2.6 percent in the last five years. Similarly, the capitalization-weighted portfolios produced a 22.1 percent alpha over the full sample and only a 3.3 percent abnormal return in the last five years. Market capitalization has no information when the investible strategies are examined. For each of the three weighting schemes and over the two rebalancing strategies, capitalization always produces negative abnormal returns.

Demographics

The three demographic variables: population growth, average-age growth, and average age offer only limited ability to discriminate between high and low expected-return countries. The demographic asset pricing theory presented in Bakshi and Chen (1994) is most appropriate for time-series analysis of developed countries. That is, holding other factors constant, an increasing average age will be associated with higher demand for equities. It is difficult, if not impossible, to hold other factors constant in emerging markets. For example, a changing degree of market integration could confound the relation between demographics and returns. In addition, given that the age dynamics are predictable, the demographic analysis is best directed at explaining long-horizon expected returns [see Erb, Harvey, and Viskanta (1996c)].

For the equally-weighted-portfolio strategy, low minus high average-age growth produces an alpha of 10.9 percent in the overall period and 15.6 percent in the last five years. With capitalization weighting, the alpha is 9.3 percent in the overall period and 6.9 percent over the last five years. Examining the investible strategies, average-age growth delivers 9.9 percent, 8.7 percent, and 19.4 percent over the three quarterly-weighting schemes. The other variables, average age and population growth, produce inconsistent results over the different portfolio formation techniques and time periods.

Momentum

The evidence for the momentum variables is inconsistent. For example, the capitalization-weighted strategy which examines the previous month's return produces an alpha of -9.8 percent in the overall period and 10.3 percent in the last five years. The momentum strategies do better when the investible indices are examined. In the quarterly strategies, the relative lagged return produces 14.9 percent, 14.5 percent, and 11.6 percent over the three weighting schemes. It is important to note that this strategy induces dramatically more turnover than any of the other attributes.

Valuation

The final set of attributes involves the traditional accounting ratios. While dividend yields (DP) are available on all the indices one year after the market enters the IFC data, the price to book (PB) and price to earnings (PE) ratios are only available from January 1986. Hence, the evaluation of the PB and PE ratios is over a different sample than all of the other portfolio simulations.

Of the three accounting attributes, PE produces the most consistent results. For equally weighted strategies, the alpha for the overall period is 18.7 percent and 4.2 percent in the last five years. For the capitalization-weighted strategies, the alpha for the overall period is 10.9 percent and 8.9 percent in the last five years. With the investibles, the quarterly strategies produced 14.9 percent, 16.2 percent, and 25.0 percent over the three weighting methods. The portfolio results for PB and PD are inconsistent across portfolio weighting schemes using the global data. However, with the investible strategies, low minus high PB produces more impressive results than low minus high PE. As is expected, the portfolio's strategy needs to be reversed for dividend yield. The high minus low PD produces consistently high abnormal performance over each of the investible strategies.

Asset Pricing Theory

Tables 5A to 5F also present results based on two risk attributes implied by asset pricing theory: the trailing three-year beta and the trailing three-year volatility. The beta is measured against the MSCI–all countries world index, and beta is only a valid risk measure if these markets are integrated into world capital markets. The results are intriguing. In the global strategies, the low- minus high-beta portfolio always earns a negative return, which is what one would expect from asset pricing theory. However, it is important to note that the "beta" of the investment strategies (buy low-beta portfolio or buy high-beta portfolios) are not that different. At first, this appears puzzling. Remember, a trailing beta was used to form the portfolio. The beta of the portfolio is not the weighted sum of the individual country betas because the portfolio is based on an out-of-sample use of the trailing betas. Similar results are observed in the investible strategies.

Volatility also has some ability to distinguish between high and low expected returns. In the global strategies, the high- minus low-volatility strategies produce positive excess returns for the equally weighted portfolios and negative excess returns for the capitalization-weighted portfolios. In the investible strategies, the excess returns are positive for equal capitalization-weighted and liquidity-weighted strategies.

Summary

These results suggest that there are a number of useful attributes in discriminating among those countries which will experience high and low expected returns. It is likely, as argued in Ferson and Harvey (1994, 1996), that these attributes are related to risk. Unfortunately, determining the appropriate measure of risk is difficult in emerging markets.

Trading Emerging Market Portfolios

The cost of trading is high in emerging markets. Table 6 presents estimates of transactions costs from Barings Securities. The percent spread calculation is the difference between the offer and bid price divided by the average of the offer and bid price. Barings uses the midpoint in the divisor in order to avoid the problems caused by large fluctuations in the current price.

The percent spreads in Table 6 are based on snapshots of individual stocks during the weeks of July 17 and July 24, 1995. The country spreads are calculated by capitalization weighting the percentage spreads of the individual firms within each country.

TABLE 6.   Estimated Transaction Costs in the Emerging Markets

Baring Securities Emerging Market Index Spread Analysis

Country	Basis Points	BEMI	+Standalones
Argentina	155	5.9%	5.5%
Brazil	85	15.7%	14.4%
Chile	393	6.5%	5.9%
China	134	0.0%	1.7%
Colombia*	100	0.0%	1.1%
Greece	48	1.8%	1.7%
India*	150	0.0%	4.4%
Indonesia	112	3.1%	2.9%
Jordan	58	0.0%	0.3%
Malaysia	69	14.3%	13.1%
Mexico	93	11.7%	10.7%
Pakistan	38	0.6%	0.5%
Peru	111	2.3%	2.1%
Philippines	94	4.5%	4.1%
Poland*	150	0.0%	0.7%
Portugal	93	1.9%	1.8%
South Africa	112	12.2%	11.2%
South Korea	41	4.6%	4.2%
Taiwan	47	5.2%	4.8%
Thailand	70	8.2%	7.5%
Turkey	160	1.6%	1.5%

*Spread numbers are approximate.

Global Spread (Basis Points)

Index	Cap Weight	Cap Weight +Standalones	Equal Weight	Equal Weight +Standalones
Global	108	110	108	110
Asia	69	80	67	84
Europe+Africa	108	109	103	104
Latin America	146	145	167	156

Please note that these figures represent spreads only, and do not include either commissions or taxes. Countries and weights differ from both IFC and MSCI.

Source: Baring Securities (July 1995)

The percentage spreads are, in many countries, much larger than one would expect in developed markets. The spread in Chile is close to 400 basis points. In both Argentina and Turkey, the percentage spread is more than 150 basis points. These high transactions costs reinforce the need to minimize trading. Indeed, many investment managers do not practice active stock-selection strategies in emerging markets because of the massive transactions costs. "Active" management in emerging markets is often interpreted in the context of country selection rather than stock selection.

While the portfolio analysis in Tables 5A to 5F does not explicitly account for transactions costs, we do include a measure of average turnover. Approximate transactions costs can be estimated with the turnover data. Assume that one-way transactions costs are 200 basis points for each country. If a portfolio experienced 100 percent turnover, this would imply that the average return should be adjusted down by 400 basis points. The highest turnover is found with the momentum strategies. The turnover is so high that it is unlikely that these strategies could be successfully implemented in the form specified here. The lowest turnover is found with the demographic variables. This is not unexpected given that the data are only available annually and there is little variation over the years.

The most impressive ratios of low/high portfolio returns to turnover are found for the survey risk attributes and for the market integration measures, trade to GDP and market capitalization to GDP.

Conclusions

The idea of this chapter is to explore what matters for emerging market investment. The traditional beta-risk paradigm is problematic in emerging markets because a number of the markets are unlikely to be fully integrated into world capital markets. Indeed, in a completely segmented market, country variance (which is usually considered idiosyncratic) is the appropriate measure of risk. We explore a group of risk attributes that have been successfully applied in developed markets. These attributes include traditional risk attributes like beta and volatility as well as a wide range of country characteristics including political risk, inflation, demographics, market integration, and fundamental values. We find that a number of these attributes such as market capitalization to GDP, inflation, price earnings ratios, and survey-based risk measures identify high and low expected-return environments.

Endnotes

1.   The IFC announced on June 20, 1996, that 17 new emerging markets will be added September 30, 1996.

2.   Over the July 1989–June 1996 period, the correlation between the IFCI and the MSCI EMF indices is 92 percent. Over the July 1991–March 1996 period, the correlation between the IFCI and the MSCI EMF is 98 percent. The correlation between the EMG (EMF) and the MSCI world–all countries is 45 percent (45 percent).

3.   The IFCI index contains 1,116 securities, MSCI 868 and BEMI 417 as of May 1996.

4.   Tracking error, in this case, is the standard deviation of the difference between the index returns.

5.   Some caution needs to be exercised in interpreting the "alpha" as an abnormal return. The abnormal return depends on the benchmark. We also report the average returns and volatility of the IFC index, 13.3 percent and 23.6 percent. An alternative comparison would be to compare the Sharpe ratios of the investment strategies to that of the IFC composite.

References

Asness, Cliff S.; John M. Liew; and Ross L. Stevens. "Parallels between the Cross-Sectional Predictability of Stock and Country Returns." Working paper, Goldman Sachs Asset Management, New York, 1996.

Bakshi, Gurdip S., and Zhiwu Chen. "Baby Boom, Population Aging, and Capital Markets." *Journal of Business* 67, 1994, pp. 165-202.

Banz, Rolf W. "The Relationship between Return and Market Value of Common Stocks." *Journal of Financial Economics* 9, 1981, pp. 3-18.

Bekaert, Geert. "Market Integration and Investment Barriers in Emerging Equity Markets." *World Bank Economic Review* 9, 1995, pp. 75-107.

Bekaert, Geert; Claude Erb; Campbell R. Harvey; and Tadas Viskanta. "The Behavior of Emerging Market Returns," in *The Future of Emerging Market Capital Flows*, Edward Altman, Richard Levich, and Jianping Mei, eds., forthcoming, 1996.

Bekaert, Geert, and Campbell R. Harvey. "Time-Varying World Market Integration," *Journal of Finance* 50, 1995, pp. 403-444.

Bekaert, Geert, and Campbell R. Harvey. "Emerging Equity Market Volatility." *Journal of Financial Economics*, forthcoming, 1996a.

Bekaert, Geert, and Campbell R. Harvey. "Speculators and Emerging Equity Markets," Working paper, Duke University and Stanford University, 1996b.

Bekaert, Geert, and Michael Urias. "Diversification, Integration and Emerging Market Closed End Funds." *Journal of Finance* 51, 1996, pp. 835-868.

Bera, Anil, and Carlos Jarque. "Model Specification Tests: A Simultaneous Approach." *Journal of Econometrics* 20, 1982, pp. 59-82.

Berk, Jonathan. "A Critique of Size Related Anomalies." *Review of Financial Studies* 8, 1995, pp. 275-286.

Berk, Jonathan. "An Empirical Re-Examination of the Relation between Firm Size and Return." Unpublished manuscript, University of British Columbia, 1996.

Black, Fischer. "Capital Market Equilibrium with Restricted Borrowing." *Journal of Business* 45, 1972, pp. 444-455.

Brennan, M. J. "Agency and Asset Pricing." Unpublished manuscript, UCLA and London Business School, 1993.

Campbell, John Y., and Yasushi Hamao. "Predictable Bond and Stock Returns in the United States and Japan: A Study of Long-Term Capital Market Integration." *Journal of Finance* 47, 1992, pp. 43-70.

Chan, K. C.; G. Andrew Karolyi; and Rene Stulz. "Global Financial Markets and the Risk Premium on U.S. Equity." *Journal of Financial Economics* 32, 1992, pp. 137-168.

Chan, K. C.; Yasushi Hamao; and Josef Lakonishok. "Fundamentals and Stock Returns in Japan." *Journal of Finance* 46, 1991, pp. 1739-1744.

Chen, Nai-fu; Richard R. Roll; and Stephen A. Ross. "Economic Forces and the Stock Market." *Journal of Business* 59, 1986, pp. 383-403.

Christie, A. A. "The Stochastic Behavior of Common Stock Variances: Value, Leverage, and Interest Rate Effects." *Journal of Financial Economics* 23, 1982, pp. 407-432.

Diamonte, Robin; John M. Liew; and Ross L. Stevens. "Political Risk in Emerging and Developed Markets." *Financial Analysts Journal*, forthcoming, 1996.

Erb, Claude B.; Campbell R. Harvey; and Tadas E. Viskanta. "Forecasting International Equity Correlations. *Financial Analysts Journal,* November-December, 1994, pp. 32-45.

Erb, Claude B.; Campbell R. Harvey; and Tadas E. Viskanta. "Country Risk and Global Equity Selection. *Journal of Portfolio Management* 21, Winter 1995a, pp. 74-83.

Erb, Claude B.; Campbell R. Harvey; and Tadas E. Viskanta. "Inflation and World Equity Selection." *Financial Analysts Journal,* November-December, 1995b, pp. 28-42.

Erb, Claude B.; Campbell R. Harvey; and Tadas E. Viskanta. "Expected Returns and Volatility in 135 Countries." *Journal of Portfolio Management*, 1996a, pp. 32-48. Also in http://www.duke.edu/ ~charvey/Country_risk/couindex.htm.

Erb, Claude B.; Campbell R. Harvey; and Tadas E. Viskanta. "Political Risk, Economic Risk and Financial Risk." *Financial Analysts Journal,* forthcoming, 1996b. Also in http://www.duke.edu/~charvey/Country_risk/couindex.htm.

Erb, Claude B.; Campbell R. Harvey; and Tadas E. Viskanta. "Demographics and International Investment." Working paper, Duke University, 1996c. Also in http://www.duke.edu/ ~charvey/Country_risk/couindex.htm.

Errunza, Vihang R. "Emerging Markets: Some New Concepts." *Journal of Portfolio Management*, Spring 1994, pp. 82-87.

Errunza, Vihang R., and Etienne Losq. The Behavior of Stock Prices on LDC Markets." *Journal of Banking and Finance* 9, 1985, pp. 561-575.

Fama, Eugene F., and Kenneth French. "The Cross-Section of Expected Stock Returns." *Journal of Finance* 59, 1992, pp. 427-465.

Ferson, Wayne E., and Campbell R. Harvey. "The Variation of Economic Risk Premiums." *Journal of Political Economy* 99, 1991, pp. 285-315.

Ferson, Wayne E., and Campbell R. Harvey. "The Risk and Predictability of International Equity Returns." *Review of Financial Studies* 6, 1993, pp. 527-566.

Ferson, Wayne E., and Campbell R. Harvey. "An Exploratory Investigation of the Fundamental Determinants of National Equity Market Returns," in *The Internationalization of Equity Markets*, Jeffrey Frankel, ed. Chicago, IL: University of Chicago Press, 1994, pp. 59-138.

Ferson, Wayne E., and Campbell R. Harvey. "Modeling the Fundamental Determinants of National Equity Market Returns." Working paper, Duke University, 1996.

Garcia, Rene, and Eric Ghysels. "Structural Change and Asset Pricing in Emerging Markets." Unpublished working paper, Université de Montreal, 1994.

Goetzmann, William N., and Philippe Jorion. "Re-Emerging Markets." Working paper, Yale University, 1996.

Hansen, Lars P. "Large Sample Properties of Generalized Method of Moments Estimators." *Econometrica* 50, 1982, pp. 1029-1054.

Harlow, W. Van. *Political Risk and Asset Markets*. Boston, MA: Fidelity Investments Monograph, 1993.

Harvey, Campbell R. "The World Price of Covariance Risk." *Journal of Finance* 46, 1991, pp. 111-157.

Harvey, Campbell R. "Portfolio Enhancement Using Emerging Markets and Conditioning Information," in *Portfolio Investment in Developing Countries*, Stijn Claessens and Shan Gooptu, eds. Washington, D.C.: The World Bank Discussion Series, 1993, pp. 110-144.

Harvey, Campbell R. "Predictable Risk and Returns in Emerging Markets." *Review of Financial Studies* 8, 1995, pp. 773-816.

Harvey, C. R., and A. Siddique. "Conditional Skewness in Asset Pricing Tests." Working paper, Fuqua School of Business, Duke University, 1995.

Heston, Steven L.; K. Geert Rouwenhorst; and Roberto E. Wessels. "Capital Market Integration and the International Cost of Funds." *Journal of Empirical Finance* 2, 1995, pp. 173-198.

Jegadeesh, Narasimhanand, and Sheridan Titman. "Returns to Buying Winners and Selling Losers: Implications for Stock Market Efficiency." *Journal of Finance* 48, 1993, pp. 65-92.

Jorion, Philippe. "The Pricing of Exchange Rate Risk in the Stock Market." *Journal of Financial and Quantitative Analysis* 26, 1991, pp. 363-376.

Keppler, A. Michael. "The Importance of Dividend Yields in Country Selection." *Journal of Portfolio Management,* Winter 1991, pp. 24-29.

Keppler, A. Michael, and Heydon D. Traub. "The Small Country Effect: Small Markets Beat Large Markets." *Journal of Investing,* Fall 1993, pp. 17-24.

Lintner, John. "The Valuation of Risk Assets and the Selection of Risky Investments in Stock Portfolios and Capital Budgets." *Review of Economics and Statistics* 47, 1965, pp. 13-37.

Longin, Francois, and Bruno Solnik. "Is the Correlation in International Equity Returns Constant: 1960-1990?" *Journal of International Money and Finance* 14, 1995, pp. 3-26.

Merton, Robert C. "An Intertemporal Capital Asset Pricing Model." *Econometrica* 41, 1973, pp. 867-887.

Nelson, Daniel B. "Conditional Heteroskedasticity in Asset Returns." *Econometrica* 59, 1991, pp. 347-370.

Roll, Richard, and Stephen A. Ross. "On the Cross-Sectional Relation between Expected Returns and Betas." *Journal of Finance* 49, 1994, pp. 101-121.

Ross, Stephen A. "The Arbitrage Theory of Capital Asset Pricing." *Journal of Economic Theory* 13, 1976, pp. 341-360.

Schwert, G. William. "Why Does Stock Market Volatility Change over Time?" *Journal of Finance* 44, 1989, pp. 1115-1154.

Sharpe, William. "Capital Asset Prices: A Theory of Market Equilibrium under Conditions of Risk." *Journal of Finance* 19, 1964, pp. 425-442.

Solnik, Bruno. "International Arbitrage Pricing Theory." *Journal of Finance* 38, 1983, pp. 449-457.

Stulz, Rene. "On the Effects of Barriers to International Investment." *Journal of Finance* 36, 1981a, pp. 923-934.

Stulz, Rene. "A Model of International Asset Pricing." *Journal of Financial Economics* 9, 1981b, pp. 383-406.

Prediction of Currency Movements

Michael F. Wilcox
President
Alford Associates, Inc.

The Challenge

"Almost all [international managers having EAFE (Europe, Australia, and Far East) index mandates from U.S. pension funds] have negative value-added in the currency-management function," according to a 1996 report by Intersec Research Corp.[1] Over the eight-year period ending December 31, 1995, this group of managers, on average, added more than 2 percent per annum to the returns of the EAFE index through active management *despite* having squandered more than 1 percent per year in currency losses. They could have outperformed EAFE by more than 3 percent per year, in other words, if they had focused exclusively on stock selection and market allocation.

The evidence, thus, suggests that most money managers are either poor currency forecasters or have not been successful in integrating their forecasts into their portfolios. This chapter will address both of these issues, focusing first on a practical, easy-to-implement method for forecasting currency-exchange rates, and then providing some suggestions for using these forecasts in conjunction with the management of portfolios containing foreign securities.

The Response

In the context of institutional money management, currency management most often involves making a decision whether or not to hedge exposure to foreign currencies. These exposures have been acquired in the normal course of business, by investing in foreign securities.

Most economists agree that the concept of purchasing-power parity (PPP) describes an important component of how foreign-exchange (FX) rates ought, in theory, to be determined. There is much less agreement as to how well the theory describes real-world conditions. We will describe a PPP-based methodology that has proven its efficacy over time.

The procedures we describe in this chapter, by selectively hedging portions of foreign-currency exposure, added 3 percent per year to the returns of an EAFE-like portfolio in a simulation that we performed. The simulation covered the same time-period described by the Intersec study mentioned above.

For the most part, this chapter addresses currency hedging as if that were the only application of interest to our readers. We realize that there will be those, particularly in the fixed-income area, who have the latitude to undertake more aggressive strategies and to invest in currencies that appear undervalued in the hope of adding value through the appreciation of those currencies. For such readers, we offer assurances that the success of the system described here is symmetrical—that is to say, it is just as good at predicting currency appreciation as it is at warning of potential depreciation.

Results of Our Simulation

Figure 1 shows the pattern of growth experienced by two portfolios containing the same underlying equity investments. The dark line, which gained about 62 percent over the period from January 1, 1988, to June 30, 1996, represents a capitalization-weighted portfolio of the largest non-US equity markets: namely, Japan, the United Kingdom, Germany, France, Switzerland, Holland, and Italy. Because this group represents about 90 percent of the capitalization of EAFE, the performance of this portfolio will be, for our purpose of comparing with the Intersec results, very nearly the same as the performance of the EAFE. We chose to use only markets where currency hedging is cost-effective for most money managers. Very large portfolios might benefit by hedging currencies in the smaller markets, but our goal was to demonstrate that the exercise will be beneficial even if done selectively.

The lighter line represents a portfolio that gained about 87 percent over this time period. The superior growth of this partly hedged portfolio (which translates to a better than 3 percent per year advantage) is attributable to selective hedging of foreign-currency (i.e. nondollar) exposures. When a currency appeared overvalued according to the algorithm

FIGURE 1.   Unhedged versus Part-Hedged

Non-U.S. Equities

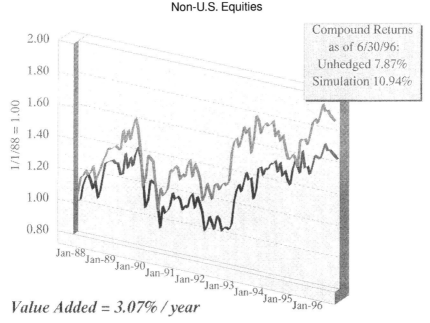

Value Added = 3.07% / year

Source: Alford Associates, Inc.

described in this chapter, we hedged a portion of its exposure (again, in accordance with the methodology laid out below).

No transaction charges were assessed against the partly-hedged portfolio, but turnover is low under our guidelines, and spreads in the FX markets are tight, so trading costs would, in reality, penalize performance by only a few basis points per year.

Our message here is that, in practice, a currency-forecasting technique based on PPP works very well, although, to be consistently successful, care must be taken to evaluate results only over long periods of time. By "long", we mean five years or more. The approach we describe is a valuation-based approach that is suitable only for those who have the temperament to make money, on average, only half the time. In the short run, there are many forces (such as international portfolio flows, central-bank interventions, and governmental fiscal policy actions) that move the FX markets in what may seem, in retrospect, like perfectly understandable ways, but we have yet to discover a way to improve our PPP-based forecasts by taking into account these other economic forces.

Organization of the Chapter

This chapter starts with a quick overview of relevant terminology, basic concepts, and some empirical observations, then reviews alternate theories for explaining currency movements, based on so-called structural models of exchange-rate determination. Most of the methods proposed by economists have proven to be impractical to implement in the context of money management, so the focus of this chapter is on the frame of reference that has proven its power in practice and in extensive backtesting—that of purchasing-power parity. The chapter concludes with some advice about applying forecasts to real-world portfolios to achieve the kind of results our simulation suggests are attainable. Practitioners with experience in the foreign-exchange markets may well want to skip the review in the first part of the chapter and, after reading the next section relating to our terminology, turn to the section entitled Implementing a PPP-Based Forecasting System.

Forecasting Horizon and Other Conventions Used in This Chapter

For ease of exposition, all examples given in this chapter use a one-year forecasting horizon. This is a convenience that makes it easier to think about interest rates and inflation statistics, which are typically quoted as annual rates, but the reader should keep in mind that, in practice, the actual forecasting horizon of interest may be different (typically, shorter than a year).

It is our expectation that forecasts made in the framework outlined here will come to pass in a matter of months rather than days, though there will of course be periods when the forecasts are directionally correct over time periods of only a few days or weeks. The principles enunciated in this chapter are best applied to time horizons of several months to several years, and it is our intention to provide a framework that is useful for money managers, whose investment horizon is fairly long, not necessarily for traders or speculators, who may have a more short-term orientation.

Also, in presenting examples of various investment strategies, we have in most cases rounded results to the nearest percentage point or currency unit (cent or dollar, as appropriate, in illustrations involving the United States), unless more precision is needed for clarity.

We have used formulas and statistics sparingly, on the presumption that our readers are capable of grasping the essence of our methodology from the figures and descriptions. The process we describe is a highly quantitative one, but no one step is terribly complicated. In the few formulas we do provide (though not in all of the illustrations and examples we provide), we have used the convention of quoting currency-exchange rates in units of home currency per unit of foreign currency (usually called the *American convention).*

$$FX = \frac{\text{Home Currency (\$)}}{\text{Foreign Currency}}$$

For dollar-based investors, this formula produces the dollar price of the foreign currency, but the reader should be cautious, because among the major currencies, only the pound sterling is typically quoted this way in the press, with most other currencies (except the Australian dollar) being quoted according to the *European convention* of units of currency per dollar. In the sometimes confusing terminology of the FX markets (akin to fixed-income investors who sometimes talk about a bond going "up" by a certain amount of yield when they mean the price of the bond went up while the yield went down), a rise in the quoted rate of a currency usually means that the value of that currency (in dollar terms) went down.

The Task at Hand

Before we set out to forecast the future course of foreign-exchange fluctuations, let us be clear about what it is that we are attempting to accomplish. If our job is to hedge foreign-currency exposure, it is important to remember that predicting currency movements is of no value unless the actions we take in response to our forecasts result in returns that are superior to those attained by investors who undertake no hedging. Thus, our success should be measured in portfolio performance, not in statistics that tell us how closely our forecasts were correlated with actual rates at the close of our time horizon (although, of course, such measures can be useful in determining if we have produced usable information).

To be successful forecasters, we need not have perfect predictive ability—we need only to be able to do a better job than a naive forecaster would do. At first blush, the benchmark for our task appears quite simple: like the weather, the best naive forecast would be for no change. This turns our not to be the case, however, because we are dealing with money, and, in the world of investments, money is not left idle for a year, but is invested in instruments that will produce income.

Components of Expected (and Actual) Return for Currencies

There are two sources of return from owning a foreign currency. The first, and rather obvious, cause for a change in the value of one's holding is a change in the exchange rate over the holding period. The second involves the alternative investment results that obtain over the investment period in the countries in question.

It is easy to think about these two sources of return if we are talking about cash investments, because one can imagine exchanging dollars for another currency on the spot market (i.e. at today's exchange-rate), investing that (foreign) cash in interest-bearing bank deposits or short-term government securities denominated in that currency, and then exchanging the foreign cash for dollars when the holding period is over. In this scenario, the number of dollars obtained at the end of the holding period will be a function of both the then-prevailing exchange rate and the amount of (foreign) interest accrued during the investment period. When we translate our foreign holding back into dollars, however, we should not compare how much money we have with how much we started with, but rather with how much we would have had if we had kept our dollars invested in short-term dollar investments of similar risk. Thus, it is conceivable that we could make money, in an absolute sense, from both appreciation in the foreign currency and from the interest on our foreign investments, and still lose money relative to what we might have earned in dollar deposits if domestic interest rates were high enough. In that case, we could not claim to have added value through our cleverness in investing abroad, but instead would have to admit that we had a negative return from our currency management.

Similarly, if we are dealing with other forms of investment, (such as bonds, stocks, or even direct investment), it is also important to take into account the interest rate environment prevailing in the two countries over the relevant investment horizon. Any hedging to be considered (assuming it is opportunistic and therefore of a limited time horizon) will of necessity be done with short-term instruments (otherwise, it is not hedging, which requires isolation of the currency risk so that risk can be neutralized).

In the case we address directly in this chapter (hedging the currency exposure in a global equity portfolio), interest rate considerations are very much in evidence. Toward the end of the chapter, we will explain exactly how to take into account interest rate differentials when deciding how much to hedge, but for now it is important for the reader to understand that hedging is usually done in the forward market, and that forward contracts are explicitly priced to account for interest rate differences, as explained in the next section. For most institutional investors, the most cost-effective way to hedge foreign-currency exposure is to sell that currency forward, on the presumption that it will decline in value (relative to the dollar), so that when the forward contract is settled, settlement can be made with units of the foreign currency that can then be bought at a lower price than is now available. Thus, if interest rates are properly taken into account, the investor will end up with more dollars than would have been the case if the hedging had not been done.

Covered-Interest Arbitrage

The principle of covered-interest arbitrage is that currencies will be exchanged for each other in a forward contract at a ratio that reflects the difference in interest rates between the two countries.[2] Specifically, the premium (or discount) that must be paid to buy a foreign currency in a forward contract is

$$f = \frac{F}{S} - 1$$

where f designates the forward premium (or, if negative, discount), which is simply a function of the current spot rate for the foreign currency (S) and the forward rate for that currency (F). The forward rate itself is determined, under arbitrage arguments, by the difference in (default-free) interest rates between the foreign country (i_f) and the domestic market (i_d):

$$F = S\frac{(1 + i_d t)}{(1 + i_f t)}$$

where t is the length of time in the forward contract (as a fraction of a year, assuming interest rates are quoted as simple rates).

According to this description, it can be seen that the currency of the country with the higher interest rate can by purchased forward at a discount. The amount of the discount will exactly reflect the difference between interest rates in the two countries for the time period of the contract. If the discount is less than the interest rate differential, it would be possible to make riskless arbitrage profits by selling forward the higher rate currency and, with money borrowed at the lower interest rate, buying an appropriate amount (as determined by the discount) of that high-rate currency in the spot market, investing the proceeds in interest-bearing securities denominated in that currency. When the time comes to settle the forward contract, regardless of the then-prevailing exchange rate, there would have accumulated more than enough of the high-rate currency to settle the forward contract and (after exchanging back into the low-rate currency) repay the loan, and a riskless arbitrage profit would have been earned.

The arbitrage can be done in reverse if the discount is too great. In that case, the high-rate currency is bought forward, and interest-bearing instruments of the same maturity are sold short in that market (i.e. denominated in the high-rate currency) and the proceeds are invested in an interest-bearing note in the low-rate currency. When the position is unwound, there will be a residual profit that was earned at no risk to the arbitrageur.

In practice, the FX markets for the major currencies are so liquid that this principle of covered-interest arbitrage does, in fact, describe the pricing of forward contracts very well. For developing or smaller markets, the expenses associated with even this simple arbitrage can be significant enough so that the forward premium may seem to violate the arbitrage argument until those costs are taken into account.

Doing Better than a Naive Forecast

Let us reduce some of these abstractions to a numerical example. Our task is to predict the level of a given currency-exchange rate at some point in the future (one year ahead, to use our standard time frame). As we know from the principle of covered-interest arbitrage, a naive forecast would depend on the one-year interest rates prevailing in the two countries.

If, for example, a dollar can be exchanged for 110 yen at the present moment, how many yen will it take to buy back that dollar in a year's time? Suppose that at the beginning of the year, we had been able to purchase (default-free) one-year government securities that offered a yield of 1 percent in Japan while similar securities offered 5 percent in the United States Under those conditions, we would have to anticipate a 4 percent appreciation in the value of the yen (to 106 ¥/$) in order to remain indifferent between the two currencies. With a rise of 4 percent in the yen plus 1 percent interest on our yen holding, we would end up with $1.05 for each dollar invested in yen. If, however, we anticipated less of a rise in the yen, we could have simply bought U.S. government securities and ended up with $1.05. Or, if we knew that the yen would rise more than 4 percent, we would buy yen with our dollar and earn the 1 percent available from Japanese government bonds plus that appreciation in the yen, to end up with more than $1.05.

To put it another way, the principle of covered-interest arbitrage tells us that we should be able to enter into a one-year forward contract to buy yen for about 106 per dollar (reflecting the 4 percent interest-rate differential between the two countries). In other words, a naive forecast of the ¥/$ rate a year hence would be 106. Our task, as forecasters, is to do better than that, not better than predicting no change. Our goal, as money managers, is to use our currency forecast to make more than the 5 percent that is available in U.S. Treasury bills. If we correctly forecast a rise of more than 4 percent for the yen, we can add value by investing in yen- rather than dollar-denominated bonds. If we own yen-denominated equities (or other securities) and correctly forecast that the yen will gain less than 4 percent, we can benefit by hedging some or all of our yen exposure back into dollars by selling yen forward. Note carefully that we might want to hedge a currency position even if we expect that currency to appreciate relative to the dollar, provided that interest rates in that country are sufficiently below those available in the United States.

In practice, the opportunity-set for capitalizing on prowess in the FX markets is usually limited to hedging currency exposure created by owning foreign securities. Most money managers are not permitted to establish short positions in currencies or to cross-hedge (use proxy currencies that provide more liquidity—for example, selling forward the deutsche mark to hedge a guilder position when no underlying mark-denominated assets are held). Thus, the only decision is to hedge or not to hedge (or to be a little more sophisticated about it: how much to hedge). Obviously, being limited by this one-sided approach lessens the value-added that could be achieved if one had the ability to fully capture good forecasts. Most of our comments focus on hedging, but keep in mind that there are many other ways to profit from making currency forecasts.

One natural question that arises is: how good is the naive forecasting guideline that we have just mentioned? Is it truly a bogey that is hard to beat? As it turns out, forward rates have, at least in recent years, not been good (i.e., unbiased) predictors of future spot rates.

Forward-Rate Bias

The principle of covered-interest arbitrage (also called covered-interest parity) ensures that forward currency contracts to exchange one currency for another are priced solely to reflect interest rate differentials between the two countries. While it may be possible for currency arbitrageurs to make profits when this relationship is momentarily violated, for all practical purposes it is impossible for money managers to achieve incremental returns by simply transferring funds from one country to another to take advantage of higher interest rates, provided that the currency risk is hedged away with a forward contract.

As outlined in the previous section, a naive forecast of FX movement is that currency-exchange rates will change by exactly enough so that the net return will be the same in all countries. If this were true, then there would be no need to hedge currency risk, but history tells us that this is a far cry from describing the real world. If, however, as many have argued, this proposition (called the theory of uncovered-interest parity) holds, on average, over longer periods of time, this might persuade some investors that there is no need to forecast or hedge currencies in the context of managing an international portfolio of assets. In fact, the theory has fared very poorly in the real world over the past 20 years. Clarke and Kritzman present empirical evidence that for seven major currencies (relative to the dollar) the forward rate failed, in a consistently biased manner, to predict the future spot rate. They call this the *forward-rate bias*, and observe that "when the forward rate was priced at a discount to the spot rate (foreign interest rates exceeded domestic interest rates), the spot rate did not depreciate to the level predicted by the forward rate... In contrast, during the months when the forward rate was priced at a premium to the spot rate, the spot rate failed to rise to the level predicted by the forward rate..." They conclude that "a hedger's best strategy is to hedge more of a low-interest-rate currency and less of a high-interest-rate currency exposure." [3]

Why might this be so (that the forward rate underpredicts the appreciation that accrues to a high-interest-rate currency)? While we are not aware of any studies that have found a convincing explanation for this bias, it would be reasonable to assume that there is some underlying macroeconomic connection between high interest rates and the stimulation of forces that ultimately (even if indirectly) lead to a strengthening of a currency. Otherwise, how could this phenomenon have persisted for the past 20 years? Its remarkable consistency gives us some comfort that it will continue, perhaps not each and every year, but at least more often than not.

If this is true, adjustments such as Clarke and Kritzman suggest (by either lowering one's estimate of the return expected from a low-interest-rate currency, or simply increasing the amount of hedging done against such a currency) will improve portfolio results.

Nonrandom Behavior of the Foreign-Exchange Markets

Several studies[4] have shown that FX markets violate the cherished assumption of many academics that prices change in random fashion. It is now part of the folklore of the markets that currency values change in discernable trends. If this is true, then profits can be made by implementing trading rules that require no forecasting ability.

Can These Trends Be Used in Forecasting?

Because of the regular appearance of trends in the FX markets, many traders have been successful at implementing trading rules that depend on the existence of these trends. We believe it is dangerous to use such systems in isolation, but when combined with the insights from a PPP-based valuation, the combination can be a powerful trading tool.

Is There an Economic Rationale for This Seemingly Inefficient Behavior?

Many observers advance the explanation that there are players in the FX markets who are not profit-motivated, and so the markets do not work as traditional finance theory calls for them to. This, to many, is particularly surprising in light of the fact that the FX market is the largest market in the world when measured by the value of trades conducted during a given day, and spreads are razor-thin in comparison with other markets—symptoms of presumed efficiency. It is thought that there is enough opportunity for low-cost arbitrage that currencies should not stray too far from their "true" value, but this presumption is clearly violated in the real world.

In our view, the existence of central-bank intervention is more of a psychological influence on the markets than an economic one; though, granted, its effect can be quite real in moving the markets. Many other participants in the FX market may be simply price-takers, such as corporations who hedge their contractual currency exposures or routinely translate their foreign sales into their home currency, and investors (in either physical or financial assets) who, without consideration of currency valuation per se, trade in one currency for another because they see better profit opportunities in the assets of another country. Nonetheless, these participants, over time, will slowly move the market price to a new equilibrium as they become part of the structural forces responding to unequal purchasing power in different countries. The trouble, from the viewpoint of those who desire instantaneous adjustment, is that these very forces are slow-acting, because they require such things as building factories to take advantage of low wages, and other long-range activities. But, once set in motion, these same instruments of change will exert inexorable forces on the currency markets, as goods and services change hands in new patterns that respond to the slow, macroeconomic adjustments being made.

Thus, we have, in our view, a case of turning around the proverbial ocean-liner; it takes time for the system to respond, but, once it does, powers are set in motion that generate real trends in the way currencies are traded. So, a currency will move toward its fair value—but these self-same forces will cause the currency to move beyond its fair value, since they are not turned off any more easily than they were initiated in the first place. As a result, the currency will move far beyond its fair value before countervailing forces begin to reverse the process. All of this describes our view of the markets, and it is meant only as an anecdotal explanation for why currencies seem to trade in two- to four-year cycles. Whether this or any other explanation is wholly adequate may be irrelevant as long as the markets continue to behave in the fashion we have observed. Our system of forecasting does not depend so much on understanding what causes currencies to fluctuate around their fair value as it does on being able to measure that fair value and hence market deviations from that value.

Structural Models to Explain Foreign-Exchange Movements

There are three[5] broad classes of economic theories that address exchange-rate determination. While there is much overlap among the various theories, and it is often a matter of emphasis rather than an exclusive reliance on a single mechanism, it is still fair to say that theories can be divided into (1) those that view currency-exchange rates as the relative price of money, which is known as the monetary approach; (2) those that view exchange rates as the relative price of goods, or the purchasing-power parity approach; and (3) those that rely on a combination of trade, monetary, and financial flows to explain exchange-rate behavior, which is termed the portfolio-balance approach.

While in many ways, the latter (portfolio-balance) approach might seem preferable, since it takes into account the broadest spectrum of economic activity, for our purposes it is not the easiest to use. Among other problems, this theory relies on risk preferences, which are highly conditional, potentially volatile, and subjective. It is equally hard to observe supply and demand schedules, but one must try to predict how exchange rates would respond to movements along those schedules, or to changes in these functions. While this may be all very well and good when the concern is understanding the way economies operate, and in devising government policies designed to optimize the economic well-being of a nation, these theories are of limited practical value in forecasting exchange-rates in the context of portfolio management. Much of the data needed to evaluate these theories are either not available (risk preferences and the like can only be inferred from behavior) or are collected with too much of a time lag to be of much value. This is not to dismiss these theories as being of no value to the international portfolio manager; quite the contrary, we suggest that being aware of their general outlines is quite beneficial to being able to evaluate whether the PPP-derived forecasts make sense, and what international events might trigger or encourage movement in the FX markets.

Similar comments can be made about monetary theories. The monetary approach attempts to explain currency-exchange rates as a function of money stocks and flows. In a sense, PPP is not too much different, since presumably monetary policies have a strong bearing on inflation rates, but we believe it best to use something (like prices) that can be measured directly, rather than something (like money supply) that more indirectly affects the FX markets. Also, it is not particularly comforting to observe the lack of universal agreement among economists as to what response FX rates should have to various combinations of monetary and fiscal policy.

Availability, Reliability, and Timeliness of Structural Data

Beyond the fact that there is no agreement in academia as to what impact fiscal and monetary policies are likely to have on FX rates, many academic empirical studies that address this issue use data that would not have been available in advance. The goal of these studies is generally quite different from that of the investment manager, in that the economists are often in search of policy prescriptions that could guide governmental actions. Unfortunately, though, this means that even if we became convinced of the validity of one of these models, we might not be able to use it in a forecasting role. Also, a common flaw of most academic studies is that they do not control for valuation. Instead, they generally (if only implicitly) assume that currencies are "efficiently" priced (i.e. fairly valued), whereas our experience warns us that results of many such studies would be critically dependent on a currency's placement in the valuation cycle when the study begins. A certain amount of exchange-rate movement would have come about with no intervention or change in fiscal or monetary policy, so this should be factored out when looking at the result of such actions. No wonder nearly identical studies often come to opposite conclusions!

Our task is to identify the course of these valuation cycles, with the faith that structural changes and governmental policy actions will, in fact, not operate so quickly as to remove the profit opportunities that we identify. It is to that job that we now turn our attention.

Implementing a PPP-Based Forecasting System

For purposes of the simulation and illustrations presented in this chapter, we have employed the simplest and most straightforward versions of the many possible data series that are available or can be constructed. We always use the CPI, for example, to calculate inflation, and we use a 60-month historical window (where appropriate). We chose to take this simplified approach to demonstrate that, even with these parameters, our PPP-based system is robust enough to provide good results in forecasting currency movements.

Readers are invited to experiment with alternative measures (such as using export prices instead of consumer prices), or by varying the time window used as a historical reference base, but the methodology we describe will work very well, in our experience, in all markets, by employing only the most basic data. Naturally, improvements are possible by studying the unique characteristics of each country and market, but these incremental benefits are, in our perception, marginal in nature compared with the overall benefit of using the basic approach we advocate. Using export prices or fiddling with the time window will improve results in some countries. We have found, for example, that there is generally a correspondence between the length of the window and the volatility of the currency—more volatile markets need more observations to collect a representative statistical sample.

We do not mean to suggest that these refinements are a waste of time; quite the contrary, we are constantly searching for ways to improve our calculations. The incremental value added will come in basis points, however, not in percentage points. so these subtle modifications are just that—improvements at the margin; or, in other words, the kind of tinkering that quants love to do with their models, but that add only a few basis points per year to returns.

Our methodology is based on our belief that purchasing-power parity (PPP) theory describes market behavior over long periods of time; currency-exchange rates will ultimately reflect relative changes in price levels between countries. Having said that, however, we admit to begging the questions: How long? and Which prices?

As to the first of these issues, we are convinced, after several years of real-time experience with this methodology, and having done additional back-testing covering more than 15 years, that currencies do tend to gravitate toward their true PPP value (as we define it in this chapter). We must admit, however, that this observation is true only on average. Whether we look at monthly, quarterly, or annual periods, only about half the time does a currency move in the direction predicted by our PPP calculation. Fortunately, the moves toward fair value are, on average, larger than the moves away from it, so using the fair PPP value as a predictive measure is profitable from an investment standpoint. Be warned, however, that this is not an approach that will produce positive value added each and every quarter—we will describe, at the end of the chapter, some suggestions for reducing the inherent volatility of these results in a practical investment context, but the underlying process is a choppy one. The reasons for this seeming inefficiency in a market reputed to be the world's most liquid is a function of the mismatch of the speed of adjustment in the financial and physical markets. Real-world macroeconomic forces are slow and lumbering from the point of view of the fast-paced electronic investment world in which prices and information are broadcast about the globe instantaneously. These macroeconomic forces, nonetheless, create an effective negative feedback system that works to correct the excesses of both real and financial markets. The reader might ask, in response to this admission of erratic predictive ability, "Why not use a more stable approach, then?" We wish we knew a better alternative, but the PPP framework is the only system we have found that will, over time, consistently perform well in a real-time, investment-oriented environment.

Anecdotally, currency cycles (that is, the complete trip from fair value to maximum undervaluation, back to maximum overvaluation, returning to fair value) typically take anywhere from two to four years. Since for about half of this time, a currency is moving in the "wrong" direction, one should not expect to consistently achieve profitable results over any period shorter than four years. Naturally, there will be many subperiods during that time when results will be favorable (but only slightly more than half of them, in our experience, as we mentioned above), and specific results will depend both on the length of a particular cycle and at what point in the cycle an investment program begins. Given all of this, it should be clear that it would be dangerous to set a client's expectations too high. Nonetheless, for those willing to wait out the gyrations of the macroeconomic forces that work their magic (albeit slowly), the prospect of adding 3 percent per year to portfolio returns should provide ample incentive to stick with the process.

As to the second question (which prices?), our experience has been that any reasonable proxy of price levels within a country will serve well. In most cases, we use the consumer price index (CPI) (in the United Kingdom, consumer prices are measured by what is known as the Retail Price Index, or RPI), partly because it is, in most countries, the most readily available, the most carefully constructed, and, usually, the most frequently updated. Then, too, the CPI is followed closely by many market participants, including central banks, and so may very well influence market prices directly, not just through its macroeconomic links. Also, the CPI closely tracks any other indicator of inflation over the time periods that are relevant to our analysis.

Presumably, though, currencies are exchanged for each other to buy things that can be physically transferred from country to country, such as automobiles, computers, and foodstuffs. Yet the CPI measures the price level of many things which cannot be transported, such as housing costs. Might it not be better to use a measure of the relative cost in each country of manufacturing export goods (e.g., automobiles), or perhaps use some other more-specialized index of export prices? It is changes in the prices of *tradeable* goods that should influence changes in foreign-exchange rates. After all, if a non-exportable commodity (a residence, for example) or service (such as a restaurant dinner) rises (or falls) in price, this would hardly induce someone in a foreign country to make a transaction in the FX market. However, if computer parts or agricultural goods or some other highly fungible product can be made more cheaply because of manufacturing efficiencies (e.g., keeping a tight cap on wages) or by technological innovation, then a country might expect to see its currency appreciate in response to demand for its products.

Ultimately, which measure of inflation is the proper one to use is an empirical issue, but in most countries, we have yet to find an index that works better than the CPI. Also, keep in mind that it is relative prices between two countries that is of interest in valuing their currencies relative to each other. Although export prices may not always track closely with consumer prices when viewed from the context of one country, when looked at on an international scale, since export goods compete with other export goods (for budgets, if not directly) then it is unlikely that one country will be able to raise prices for its export goods faster than do other countries for extended periods of time. Then too, our experience is that currencies often get misvalued by as much as 20 percent from their PPP value (as calculated by us), and it is unlikely that such large discrepancies would be significantly different even if we used an alternate measure of inflation.

In certain countries, using an index of export prices will improve results.[6] Japan, for example, has, unlike many other industrialized countries, over the past few decades, been a country dedicated to production rather than consumption. Much of the engineering and manufacturing talent of the nation has been devoted to improving sales abroad, and that emphasis has seen the price of exported goods decline in yen terms. But this is not the whole story. In almost every country, export prices have risen more slowly than consumer prices over the past few decades. The reason for this is intuitive: in a competitive world economy, only countries that succeed in keeping their production costs from rising will be able to find markets for their exports—technological innovation can create new markets or can give a country a temporary edge, but in the long run, imitation and substitution will reward low-cost producers. Nonetheless, Japan has done a better job than most other industrialized countries in lowering the prices of its exports. Over the past 15 years, Japan's CPI has risen more slowly than in the U.S. CPI: the gap is more than 2 percent per year (2.1 percent in Japan versus 4.5 percent in the United States). Over the same time period, Japan's export prices have actually fallen by more than 2 percent per year, while those of the United States have risen by a like amount. This means that Japan has enjoyed nearly a 5 percent per year advantage over the United States in terms of its export prices, which is remarkably close to the annualized appreciation of the yen relative to the dollar over that time span.

Trade flows, portfolio flows, political, fiscal, and monetary actions, and other considerations may move market values away from their PPP levels for periods of time (often for many months), and our challenge is to distinguish between temporary dislocations in the exchange rate (which present profit opportunities) and permanent changes brought about by structural changes in the global economy. A country running a trade surplus with another country, for example, may be perfectly content to invest its accumulated foreign currency in the capital markets of that other country, in which case the trade imbalance will have little or no effect on the currency-exchange rate. Should, however, investors in the surplus country decide to repatriate their money or invest it in a different country, the FX transactions resulting from this shift in the demand schedule could have a large impact on the market value of the currencies involved.

Identifying and predicting the macroeconomic forces that determine the timing of exchange-rate movements is difficult at best. Our technique of projecting PPP value and basing our forecasts on the idea that the market value will eventually be driven toward that level works well, and our research has failed to uncover any other method that is as successful at predicting returns in foreign-exchange markets, or that can even be used to supplement this process.

Measuring Inflation

Figure 2 shows the pattern of consumer price inflation in France and the United States over a 15.5-year period beginning in 1981. Notice that in the first half of this period, inflation in France was typically higher than in the United States. After 1987, however, this pattern reversed itself and France experienced a rate of inflation that averaged about 1 percent less than that in the United States.

A technical note: consumer-price inflation is normally reported by governments and therefore the press as the simple year-over-year percentage change in the consumer-price index constructed by the government. We show here a slight variation: we have computed the natural log of the ratio of the index to itself a year earlier. This computation produces a continuous rate of change, which in the lower end of the scale is nearly indistinguishable from the simple rate of change (e.g., a 3 percent simple

FIGURE 2.   Consumer Price Inflation

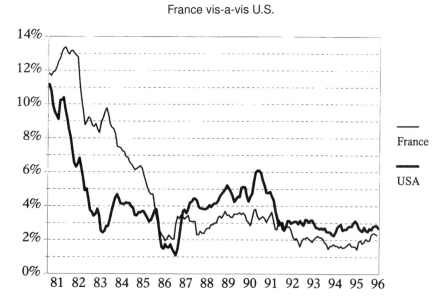

France vis-a-vis U.S.

Source: Alford Associates, Inc.

rate is almost identical to its continuous version of 2.96 percent), but has the effect of compressing the scale in the early 1980s, (e.g., a 13-percent simple rate equals a 12.22 percent continuous rate). There are computational and statistical reasons, as well as visual ones, for preferring continuous rates, but either may be used provided that one is careful about how they are used in calculations and in forecasting algorithms.

Figure 3 shows the pattern of changes in export prices for the same period for the same two countries. Notice that, in both France and the United States, the series is more volatile, and inflation was at times negative. The net compound result over this time period was that export prices in both countries rose less than consumer prices (about 70 percent in France and 45 percent in the United States, compared with 120 percent and 100 percent, respectively). It might seem that there is a lot of information contained in these price series that is relevant to the franc/dollar exchange rate and that is not captured in the CPI. To steal a look ahead, however, Figure 4 depicts alternate valuations for the FX rate that we would forecast with each of these price series. As might be expected, the export-price series produces the more volatile forecast, but that does not make it better. In fact, our finding in France is that it provides a worse

FIGURE 3.   Export Price Inflation

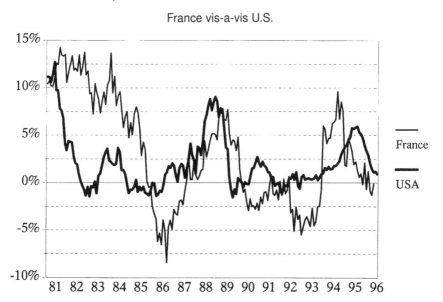

France vis-a-vis U.S.

Source: Alford Associates, Inc.

FIGURE 4.   French Franc

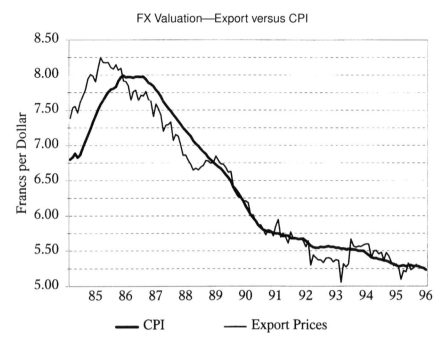

FX Valuation—Export versus CPI

Source: Alford Associates, Inc.

prediction of actual FX movement. Perhaps what is most notable is that the results are quite close to each other.

We will now look at how we derive these forecasts.

Purchasing-Power Index

Our first step is to compute an index of relative inflation, based on the growth in the consumer-price index (CPI) in each of the two countries of interest. We can use any currency as the base (or numeraire) currency, but the examples given on these pages take the point of view of a dollar-based investor. For the sake of consistency, we will follow through and give all examples using the French franc, though the patterns seen here are very similar for most major currencies, especially the European ones.

Figure 5 relates the inflation experience in France to that of the United States in what we have labeled a *relative purchasing-power index* (RPPI). This index is simply the ratio of the CPIs in the two countries of

FIGURE 5.   Relative Purchasing Power Index

RPPI (France versus U.S. Consumer Prices)

Source: Alford Associates, Inc.

interest. Note that, for France, this relative purchasing-power index was rising in the early 1980s, reflecting the phenomenon shown in Figure 2: that prices in France were rising faster than in the United States. Once France began to have lower inflation than the United States, this RPPI began to fall. The scale on the left (Y) axis, by the way, has no particular meaning. As will become clear as we step through the analysis, it is only of interest whether this series is rising or falling, and by how much, in percentage terms. The level of each index as published by the governments of the two countries, and therefore the ratio of the two price indexes, is completely arbitrary. Regardless of the scale that results from this calculation, the RPPI represents the pattern of relative price movements in the two countries, and that is the crucial piece of information we need.

Forecasting Inflation

Our second step is to forecast inflation in the United States and in the country of comparison. As a reminder: we have chosen, for illustration

here, to forecast one year ahead. Figure 6 shows the result of our methodology as applied to France.

In forecasting inflation, we are, in part, seeking a proxy for investor's inflation expectations. It is important to forecast what inflation will
actually be, since that reality will ultimately influence the value of the
currency-exchange rate. It is also important, however, to understand
what people's inflation expectations are, since these expectations will
become embedded in exchange rates (along with a host of other relevant
factors), thus helping to determine their near-term path.

For these reasons, we combine a mixture of an econometric forecast
of inflation in each country along with a measure of trailing inflation. We
believe that this provides the best blend of expectations—anecdotally,
people are heavily influenced in their inflation outlook by recent experience, but markets are also smart enough to take into account changes that
will modify the future course of inflation. We use the average inflation
experience of the past two years as a proxy for average inflation expectations.

FIGURE 6.   CPI–France

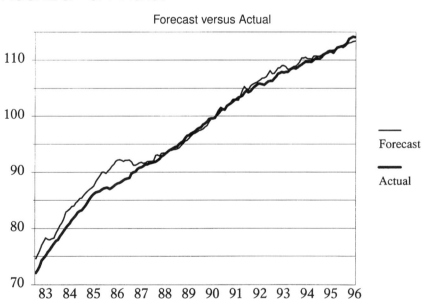

Source: Alford Associates, Inc.

We are aware that other techniques could be employed here that might provide a better inflation forecast. We believe, nonetheless, that errors introduced by any reasonable approach will be minor compared with deviations in market exchange-rates from true economic value. In other words, even having a perfect inflation forecast would not go very far in explaining why exchange rates vary so much from their PPP values, as we calculate them. As mentioned earlier, our experience is that currency-exchange rates often get as much as 20 percent or more away from the value our model ascribes to them. Errors in estimating inflation expectations *differentials* are a small fraction of that. Figure 7 expresses our forecast for the CPI as an inflation rate. Except for the mid-1980s, when the inflation was rapidly deteriorating, the error in our forecast has been about one-half percent per year in France.

Completing the circuit, we substitute our inflation forecast for actual experience in computing a forecast for relative inflation (the RPPI). Figure 8 gives the picture for France. Note that the errors in the forecast are a combination of errors in forecasting inflation in the United States as well

FIGURE 7.   CPI Inflation in France

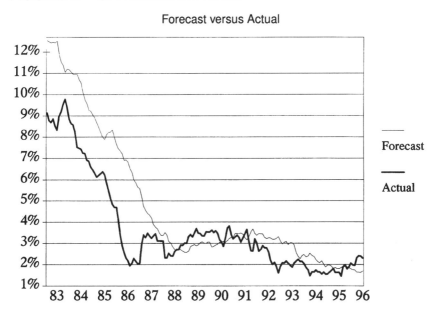

Forecast versus Actual

Source: Alford Associates, Inc.

FIGURE 8. France–RPPI

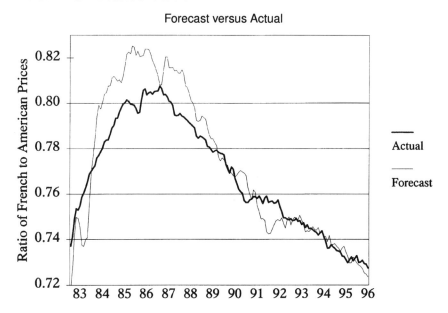

Forecast versus Actual

Source: Alford Associates, Inc.

as in France, since this figure is a comparison of the two. Of course, in some periods, these errors will offset each other, but at other times the errors will be compounded. On balance, the forecast is not too much different from the actual outcome, at least in the context of actual exchange-rate fluctuations, as mentioned in the previous paragraph.

Given all our caveats about how difficult it is to fathom inflation expectations and to forecast inflation accurately, combined with our disclaimer that the errors are relatively insignificant, the reader may very well wonder why we bother at all to go through the exercise of forecasting inflation. Keep in mind that in projecting exchange rates in the context of the PPP paradigm (the goal of this chapter), one must (if only implicitly) forecast inflation. If no conscious projection is made, the unstated assumption is that inflation differentials between the two countries involved will remain unchanged. In our experience, making a stab at an inflation forecast improves results, if only at the margin, so we do it; but we would not find serious fault with an approach that skipped this step.

Pricing the Index: Purchasing-Power Price

The third step in our process is to compute and then forecast the price of the relative purchasing-power index (RPPI) in units of the foreign currency.

This number represents the contemporaneous market price of the relative-price index (RPPI) computed in the first step. If this price were always a "fair" economic value, we would expect it to remain constant. If that held true, changes in the PP Index (that is, relative inflation) would flow through directly to the FX rate. In reality, however, this price ratio will fluctuate, and we can never be sure of when it is in equilibrium. In truth, we don't attach much significance to the concept of equilibrium as defined in its classical economic sense (determined by the interaction of supply and demand schedules). Although it may be true that, at any point in time, an FX rate is in fact the balancing of supply with demand, that observation only begs the important question of what causes these schedules to shift. Clearly, preferences change over time in response to developments in the macroeconomic environment. It is a hopelessly complex task, for our purposes here, to try to determine what influences come to bear on these supply and demand schedules, and to try to predict their precise shape and drift. We will be content to observe that, whatever their cause, changes in supply and demand seem to have the effect of a negative-feedback system. When the price of a currency gets too high, forces come into play that drive that price back down. These agents of change take time to work, and once they are at work, are not easily turned off, so the price tends to drift beyond what would be its long-run equilibrium level. As the price becomes too low, countervailing forces come into play and reverse the decline, sending the currency on its final leg of a cycle. All of this may sound like magic, and in a sense it is wondrous how the world does work, but we are talking about the forces that are commonly recognized to come to bear on FX rates: portfolio adjustments (both in the financial markets and in direct investments), governmental monetary and fiscal policy, central-bank intervention, speculation and arbitrage in the currency markets, and hedging activities by owners of real and financial assets and contracts. Because of the complexity of this system, the FX market is an imperfect negative-feedback mechanism, and therefore tends to overshoot the mark. Because the adjustments required are slow-acting and interrelated, the exact path and timing of the adjustment cannot be predicted, but the general pattern can by used to advantage if one thinks of the price of a currency as a mean-reverting mechanism.

See Figure 9 for an illustration of this relationship in France. Note that in the early 1980s, the franc clearly suffered a precipitous fall relative

FIGURE 9.   France

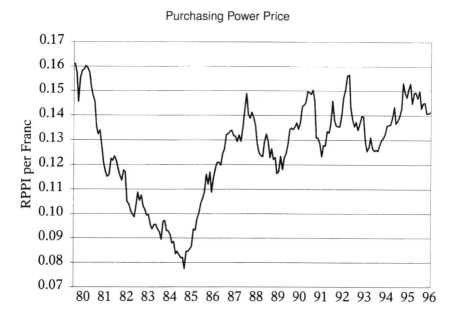

Source: Alford Associates, Inc.

to the dollar in terms of its purchasing power. In fact, this was not unique to the franc; most other currencies showed a similar pattern compared with the dollar. The dollar enjoyed a very long run, pushed up (it is generally agreed) by a combination of a restrictive monetary and expansive fiscal policy in the United States. High real-interest-rates and an expansive domestic economy created an environment in which PPP did not hold very well for a few years. For the past 10 years, however, the franc has traded in a fairly narrow channel—for the last 120 months shown on this figure, the mean of .135 was only slightly higher than for the entire time period shown (.128). In that most recent 10-year period, more than 53 percent of all observations fall within plus or minus 10 percent of the mean (if one assumes that the observations shown are representative of an underlying process that produces normally distributed values). For the entire period shown on the figure, fewer than 25 percent of observations fall within that same band, and for the first 10-year period, only 22 percent of observations are that close to the mean. Clearly the market has become more orderly in recent years, but this only highlights the need to be cautious about using too short a period to define "equilibrium": if only the mid-1980s had been used, the mean value used as a standard would be about 10 percent below what seems in retrospect to have been a fair price.

Forecasting the Price of the RPPI

Figure 10 shows two different attempts to forecast the RPPI price, representing two philosophically different views of the FX market. One forecast (the light line labeled "Regression") is based on a typical time-series econometric approach, which implicitly assumes that past patterns will repeat themselves and that trends, once in place, will persist. The other approach (the darker line identified as "Reversion") is based on a mean-reversion assumption, and will work best if the series does have a tendency to fluctuate around a constant level. As a reminder, we illustrate here the use of a moving 60-month window. In other words, the forecast is based on the premise that the actual price will revert to its mean of the last 60 monthly observations. A shorter window would produce a more volatile forecast series, but the pattern wouldn't be too much different.

FIGURE 10. France

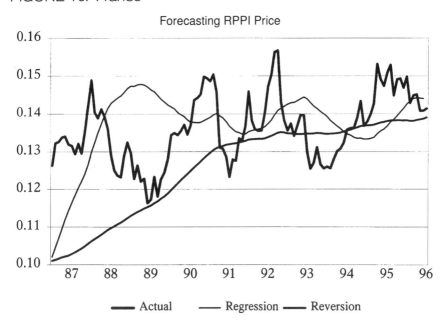

Source: Alford Associates, Inc.

Most currencies complete a full valuation cycle in less time than that, and it is important to include at least one such full cycle. Over time, however, structural changes in the world's economies and markets make older information less and less relevant to today's conditions, so including data that is too old can impair the predictive ability of the analysis. In the end, it is a judgement call as to how long a window of history is relevant.

As it turns out, of the two lines, the reversion method does a better job of forecasting, in the sense defined earlier. Namely, a portfolio strategy based on that assumption has better returns than one using the econometric approach, although in many countries, the regression line has a better "fit" with actual outcomes.

Projecting Exchange Rates

The fourth step in our process is to project a future (in this case, one-year-out) FX rate by assuming that the PP Price will return to some average level as observed in or projected from the time series computed in our second step.

Our forecast of inflation in the two countries over the desired horizon is used to forecast a future PP Index. A future PP price can then be estimated, as described in the previous section. As mentioned, we have often obtained better statistical results with projections based on econometric regressions, but almost always obtained better financial results by using a reversion assumption. Figure 11 shows what happens when an exchange-rate forecast is made with the alternative forecasting methodologies described in the previous section.

As can be seen, the forecasting methods don't produce dramatically different results. Both forecast time series exhibit more stability than the actual FX rate, and both forecasting methods visually seem to be about equally right (or wrong). The discerning eye can perhaps detect that the reversion method is a bit better over this five-year period (ending June 30, 1996), and in fact it does have the better R^2—.2615 versus .1037 for the regression approach. Beyond its better statistical fit, we find the reversion line more appealing because it changes more slowly, which is in accordance with our view of how the world works, and because it more closely tracks the pattern of the RPPI (see Figure 5). In other words, the reversion forecast conforms more closely to what we would expect to see if we believe in the workings of the PPP paradigm.

Figure 12 focuses exclusively on the use of the reversion methodology, and here we show a longer (10.5-year) period. To a statistician, this

FIGURE 11. France

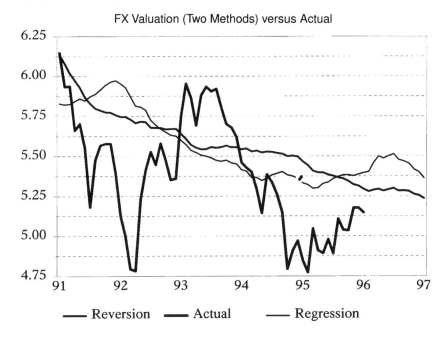

FX Valuation (Two Methods) versus Actual

——— Reversion ——— Actual ——— Regression

Source: Alford Associates, Inc.

figure may not look like a very good forecasting model (and, in fact the R^2 of the entire period shown is only .3153—actually a little better than over the past five years alone of .2615), but remember that our goal is not to forecast FX rates per se. Our job is to make a decision as to whether to hedge a currency or not, and if so how much, and our prize is whether those decisions prove to be profitable.

In this case, the financial success of this model is actually better over the most recent 5-year period than it was in the early years of the figure shown, so looking exclusively at R^2s or other measures of modeling veracity may give us misleading information. We can, of course, draw some comfort from knowing that we have discovered useful information, but it is only if we can translate that information into concrete results (i.e. superior performance) that we should be congratulated. Let us complete, therefore, the description of our framework for using these forecasts in the context of hedging a global equity portfolio.

FIGURE 12. France

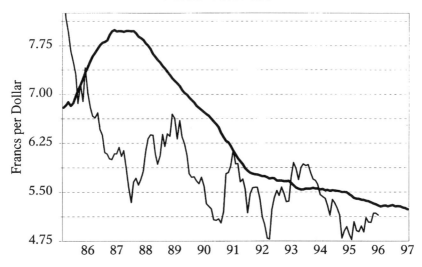

FX Forecast versus Actual

—— Reversion Methodology Forecast —— Actual

Source: Alford Associates, Inc.

Taking a Valuation Perspective

In making portfolio decisions, we find it easier to convert everything to the present tense. Somehow, we'd rather deal with spot rates and current-interest-rate differentials than to keep track of forward rates, although because of the principle of covered-interest parity, we realize that these are equivalent. We also find it helpful to think of our forecast value as a valuation measure rather than as a prediction of a future market level. Again, the two concepts are equivalent, but by translating everything to the present, we find it simpler to think about what action we should take now. By simply shifting the time axis back one year for the forecast series from the previous figure, we can compare our valuation (where we think the FX "ought" to be) directly with the spot rate (where it is). Figure 13 shows this transformation.

FIGURE 13. French Franc

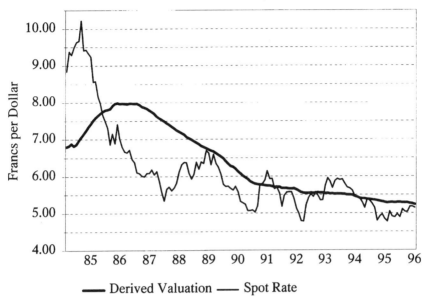

FX Valuation versus Spot

— Derived Valuation —— Spot Rate

Source: Alford Associates, Inc.

Computing an Expected Return

The final element in our forecasting process is to take into account interest rate differentials as well as the valuation just described. It could be that even if a currency is overvalued in accordance with our method of calculating its PPP level, it may not be a candidate for hedging. Remember that the cost of putting on a hedge is reflected in the forward rate that we will obtain when we hedge by selling some of our currency exposure off in the forward market. The price of the forward contract will, under the principle of covered-interest parity, be determined by the difference in interest rates between the United States and the country whose currency we want to hedge. It may be that if interest rates are low in the United States (at least by comparison with the other country), we may have to sell that currency forward at a discount that is more than we anticipate that it will depreciate over our investment-hedging horizon. In that case, we should forego hedging. We therefore have to keep track of both these elements of expected return.

Figure 14 shows the components of expected return. Clearly, misvaluation (the difference in our valuation and the spot, expressed in percentage terms) represents the bulk of the potential for FX gains or losses. Nonetheless, there have been times, such as the period around the middle of 1992 when the French central bank was forced to aggressively raise interest rates to defend the franc, when interest rate differentials have been wide enough to change the sign of the expected return for the franc.

In calculating our expected returns, we combine the percentage misvaluation identified in the previous steps with the interest rate differential over the relevant time horizon. Figure 15 shows the net result of combining these two sources of expected return.

Mapping Expected Returns into Hedging Ratios

The payoff from all of our previous work comes from interpreting our expected returns in a way that can aid portfolio construction. Managers

FIGURE 14. French Franc

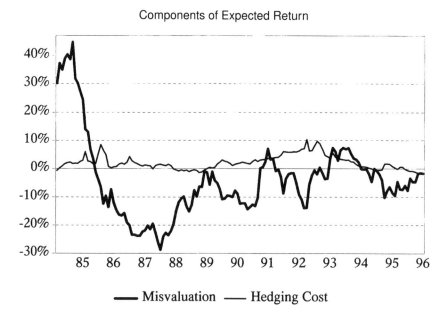

Components of Expected Return

—— Misvaluation —— Hedging Cost

Source: Alford Associates, Inc.

FIGURE 15. French Franc

Net Expected Return

Source: Alford Associates, Inc.

who are using and are comfortable with an optimization framework can take the expected returns derived so far and integrate them directly into a country-allocation analysis that has a full covariance matrix of both local asset-returns and currency-returns.

An alternative that, for us, produces superior results is presented here. Our experience is that this approach, which we term adaptive affine mapping, creates lower turnover and less volatility than does a traditional optimization methodology, while at the same time preserving (and in some cases even enhancing) the incremental returns. This is the process we used in simulating the portfolio presented at the beginning of the chapter.

Note that, for hedging purposes, we are only interested in the negative half of the distribution. When the expected return for a currency is below its historical mean (and here again, we used a 60-month moving window to define "history"), we want to hedge part of our exposure. The question is, "How much?" and the answer is determined by looking at a statistical interpretation of how significant is the current deviation from the mean.

The essence of the approach is a simple one—we transform the expected return directly into a hedge ratio. For each currency, we translate the current expected return into a number between -1 and +1, based on the statistical history of the expected-return time series in that country. We recommend using a sigmoidal function (a process that will be familiar to users of neural networks), although a linear transformation could be used to good advantage as well. In our simulation, we used a normal probability distribution to assess the likelihood of any given expected return being significant.

Figure 16 shows the results of the transformation we made in running the simulation depicted in Figure 1. Again, France is used as an illustration, but we did the same thing in each of the other countries as well. When the "desired exposure" line was negative in any country, we hedged the portion of that currency exposure indicated by the level of the transformed series.

FIGURE 16. French Franc

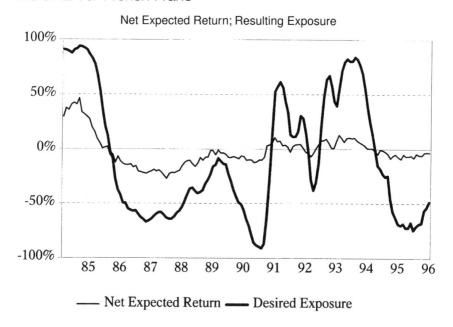

Source: Alford Associates, Inc.

Additional Methods to Reduce Volatility or Further Enhance Returns

Two areas that have already been touched on are the forward-rate bias and the nonrandom behavior of FX markets. While there are conflicting views as to whether these phenomena are transient or permanent features of the FX landscape, our own reasoning and the weight of historical evidence convinces us that these tendencies should be taken seriously—to the point that we think it makes sense to modify expected returns to reflect their existence.

Note that the simulated portfolio results reported in this chapter do not take advantage of these two observations, nor of our view that currency valuations tend to move in cycles. Instead of beginning to hedge the franc in early 1995, for example, when the expected return started to become negative, we could have waited, knowing that the normal tendency of the currency would be to become much more overvalued before turning around. By implementing decision rules such as these, the results of our simulation can be made less volatile and even more productive.

Another feature of real-life investing is that many portfolios will not be able to do as much hedging as would be required to replicate our results. Managers (or clients) may be uncomfortable hedging the majority of a currency exposure. In the case where there are limits, our strategy can simply be stopped when the limit is reached, or the numbers can be rescaled to fit within the constraints. If, for example, there was a restriction against hedging more than 50 percent of exposure to any one currency, the scale of the "desired exposure" series in Figure 16 could simply be changed to be half of what we show at every point on the curve.

Since there are an infinite number of such overlays of decision rules and constraints that could be used, we decided to present only the plain-vanilla version. Volatility could be reduced with constraints, but at the expense of giving up a portion of the excess returns. Decision rules, such as delaying implementation, can improve returns while reducing volatility, but as such rules become less mechanistic and more judgmental, they are hard to simulate.

There are many other potential applications besides the one we illustrated here. If one can do cross-hedging, for example, or take long positions in currencies, the framework presented here could be used to compare the potential returns of two nondollar currencies, or to establish a portfolio of bonds or short-term instruments that has a higher expected return than a domestic-only portfolio of similar duration. For now, we will be content to have conveyed the message that it is possible to add value through the use of disciplined currency management in a global portfolio.

Suggested Areas for Future Research

Our experience in using the expected returns derived in our methodology suggests that they have a shelf life of several months. This is the result of already observed tendencies of the FX markets to exhibit nonrandom behavior; to wit, that monthly changes in FX rates are positively serially correlated, and that currency valuations move in cycles. There are also many alternative ways of computing a reversion target besides simple averaging. For example, an exponential-weighting scheme could be used to give more importance to recent experience. When these phenomena are analyzed with the many other parameters that have been mentioned in this chapter (such as the length of the historical window to be used), it can readily be seen that the search space of all possible prediction methods becomes quite vast. It is not feasible to conduct research by trial and error, nor is it possible to find the best combination of parameters by optimizing one and then testing another. Because of the complex interaction of the assumptions, there is a high degree of danger of locating only a local maximum in the search space. For this reason, we are experimenting with two other approaches that have shown some promise in similar applications: genetic algorithms and simulated annealing. While we can't claim to have made any profound breakthroughs by using these techniques, we do believe they show promise, and they have helped sharpen our thinking on a number of issues.

Because of the complex dynamics involved, some research tools inspired by the study of chaos and nonlinear dynamics may be useful to our efforts. Also, if, as we believe, the FX market is a nonlinear dynamical system that evolves through feedback mechanisms, the path of the FX rate itself or, more likely, of one or more of the intermediate forecasting calculations we make, may profitably be dealt with as a response to a strange attractor. We are currently investigating some recently developed time-series forecasting techniques, such as time-delay embedding, and we are pursuing the use of neural networks.

To date, our work suggests that all of these techniques are overkill. One problem may be that many of the underlying mathematical models were developed after observing natural systems at work. Unfortunately, in the world of human finance, the rules are always changing, and the past may not be prologue. The good news is that the very basic approach we have outlined in this chapter is hard to improve on, but we are hopeful of gaining insights that will prove useful in future versions of our analysis.

Endnotes

1.   Memo from Christopher A. Nowakowski, President, Intersec Research Corp., 66 Gatehouse Road, Stamford CT 06902, telephone (203) 348-7101, fax (203) 348-1906, http://www.intsec.com.

2.   *Currency Management: Concepts and Practices* by Roger G. Clarke and Mark P. Kritzman, The Research Foundation of the Institute of Chartered Financial Analysts, 1996. See pages 14-17 for a more detailed explanation of covered-interest arbirage and the forward premium, including numerical examples.

3.   Roger G. Clarke and Mark P. Kritzman.

4.   For examples of empiracal studies into the nonrandom behavior of foreign-exchange markets and how to exploit these tendencies with technical trading-rules, see Clarke and Kritzman (1996) pages 39-52; William L. Silber "Technical Trading: When It Works and When It Doesn't," *Journal of Derivatives,* Spring 1994, pages 39-44; and Richard Levich who has written several papers on the topic, including "Exchange Rate Behavior: Trends or Random Walks?" Stern School of Business working paper, New York University, 1993, and with Lee Thomas, "The Significance of Technical Trading-Rule Profits in the Foreign Exchange Market: A Bootstrap Approach," National Bureau of Economic Research working paper, no. 3818, 1991.

5.   We follow here the classification scheme proposed by Rudiger Dornbusch in "Exchange Rate Economics: Where Do We Stand?" *Brookings Papers on Economic Activity 1,* 1980, pp. 143-94.

6.   See page 45 in *Currency Forecasting* by Michael R. Rosenberg, Irwin Professional Publishing, 1996.

CHAPTER 11

Portfolio Construction and Risk Management

Ross Paul Bruner
Managing Director
Istituto Mobiliare Italiano

Overview

An Active Approach Enhanced by Quantitative Tools

We take an active approach to portfolio construction and risk management, which is enhanced by a quantitative discipline. In our process, we use quantitative models as the first step in developing a view on sectors, markets, styles, and, ultimately, on shares. We exercise judgment in terms of deciding the appropriate inputs for our models and, finally, in terms of the critical quality leadership decision. The last step is to form a view on the impact of medium-term reference-currency movements on equity performance. Here too, we take an active approach about the decision to hedge reference-currency strength, and we use quantitative-valuation tools to make the process easier and more disciplined.

Equal-Weighted and Capitalization-Weighted Exposure

Our model portfolio (see Table 1) is a 67-stock global fund which is both equal-weighted and capitalization-weighted. Company exposure is equal-weighted (i.e., $1/67 = 1.5$ percent), while sector, market, and style exposure is capitalization-weighted relative to our 3,500-stock global benchmark. Equal-weighting company exposure reduces company-specific risk and introduces a small-capitalization bias into the portfolio. In our experience, equal-weighted strategies outperform capitalization-weighted strategies across sectors, markets, and styles largely as a result of the small-capitalization bias which equal-weighting produces. The

TABLE 1. Global Model Portfolio (local currency)

31-Jul-96 BENCHMARK	Share Price	1-Week % Chg	1-Month % Chg	Q-T-D % Chg	Y-T-D % Chg	P/E FY+1	P/CF FY+1	P/B FY+1	Yield FY+1	ROE FY+1	EPS Y-Y
GLOBAL 3,500-STOCK INDEX		1.3	-5.2	-5.1	3.0	22.1	12.5	3.1	2.8	18.0	17.6
CYCLICAL INDEX (47% vs. 37%)		2.1	-6.1	-5.7	4.7	22.4	12.0	2.9	2.5	16.8	21.1
BASIC MATERIAL (12% vs. 8%)		1.9	-5.2	-4.7	3.4	20.6	10.3	2.6	2.8	17.7	18.0
AIR LIQUIDE(L')	880.0	1.6	-3.0	-4.6	8.5	18.2	9.7	2.4	3.5	13.2	10.0
BAYER AG	49.5	0.7	-7.4	11.2	30.8	11.8	6.6	2.0	3.0	15.1	10.5
BOC GROUP	9.1	-0.4	-1.4	-0.8	1.0	14.2	7.7	2.6	3.0	17.0	11.1
JAMES RIVER CORP	25.3	1.5	-4.7	-3.8	4.7	14.5	3.4	1.0	2.4	6.4	64.2
NISSAN CHEM INDS	702.0	-2.0	-10.7	-3.4	2.5	37.7	26.3	2.9	1.7	7.6	14.1
NKK CORP	305.0	4.5	-7.6	0.0	9.7	27.5	5.3	2.6	0.0	9.2	27.6
PRAXAIR	38.4	5.1	-7.8	12.9	14.1	15.2	8.5	3.8	2.1	24.7	22.9
AVERAGE		1.6	-6.1	1.6	10.2	19.9	9.7	2.4	2.2	13.3	22.9
CONSUMER DURABLE (12% vs. 6%)		2.1	-6.7	-6.8	8.3	22.6	9.9	2.1	2.6	13.0	22.9
BAYER MOTOREN WERK	825.0	-1.4	-6.4	-2.5	12.2	14.8	4.1	1.9	4.0	12.5	18.8
BOSS (HUGO) AG	1,750.0	0.6	1.2	37.3	46.9	15.3	13.0	4.0	4.9	25.8	10.9
CANON INC	2,020.0	0.0	-11.0	0.0	8.0	20.7	8.6	1.9	1.9	9.2	12.3
GENERAL MOTORS CORP	48.8	4.6	-10.3	-7.4	-7.8	6.8	2.1	1.3	6.4	18.6	17.1
HONDA MOTOR CO	2,580.0	3.6	-9.2	10.3	21.1	16.6	9.1	2.1	2.2	12.8	15.2
MINOLTA CAMERA CO	645.0	-1.2	-11.6	5.7	7.0	27.0	7.6	2.8	1.8	10.3	23.8
NIKE -CL B	102.9	4.0	-1.3	47.5	47.8	17.6	16.0	4.7	1.4	26.9	20.8
PIRELLI SPA	2,470.0	2.5	-2.8	14.1	20.5	10.6	4.2	1.1	4.7	10.3	17.1
SONY CORP	6,750.0	0.7	-6.6	3.1	9.0	21.4	7.5	2.4	0.7	10.7	20.5
AVERAGE		1.5	-6.5	12.0	18.3	16.7	8.0	2.5	3.1	15.2	17.4
CONSUMER MERCHANDISE (9% vs. 5%)		1.2	-5.7	-5.6	9.7	20.9	14.4	3.4	2.3	16.2	16.8
BENETTON GROUP SPA	17,855.0	-3.6	-8.7	-4.4	-5.5	12.0	8.6	1.9	2.2	14.4	9.2

TABLE 1 (continued)

31-Jul-96	Share Price	1-Week % Chg	1-Month % Chg	Q-T-D % Chg	Y-T-D % Chg	P/E FY+1	P/CF FY+1	P/B FY+1	Yield FY+1	ROE FY+1	EPS Y-Y
BENCHMARK											
CIRCUIT CITY STORES INC	31.5	-6.0	-13.7	22.3	14.0	13.9	10.2	2.4	0.8	17.5	17.6
COMPTOIRS MODERNES	2,314.0	6.1	-0.3	31.9	45.5	22.4	10.8	3.6	2.0	16.2	12.9
GAP INC	29.8	0.8	-7.4	26.3	41.7	17.0	12.2	4.1	2.1	24.0	16.7
FAMILYMART CO	4,930.0	-1.2	0.8	6.3	16.4	33.5	26.8	4.3	0.9	12.9	7.6
TOYS R US INC	26.4	1.4	-8.3	19.9	21.3	12.9	9.6	1.8	0.0	14.1	14.5
AVERAGE		-0.4	-6.2	17.0	22.2	18.6	13.0	3.0	1.3	16.5	13.1
CONSUMER NON-DURABLE (6% vs.8%)											
COCA-COLA CO	46.9	1.6	-3.5	-3.2	7.7	20.1	14.3	4.9	3.1	26.7	12.9
COLGATE-PALMOLIVE	78.5	2.2	-5.1	24.4	26.3	28.6	25.7	13.0	2.3	45.4	18.0
GILLETTE CO	63.8	-4.6	-7.2	6.1	11.7	16.3	11.4	6.4	2.2	35.2	14.5
KIKKOMAN CORP	811.0	0.8	3.0	18.9	22.3	25.4	20.8	8.2	2.3	32.1	16.2
		-0.5	-9.4	-4.6	6.7	29.8	21.0	1.7	1.6	5.6	-1.1
AVERAGE		-0.5	-4.7	11.2	16.8	25.0	19.7	7.3	2.1	29.6	11.9
CONSUMER SERVICE (6% vs. 5%)											
CANAL PLUS	1,195.0	1.7	-6.9	-6.9	3.9	22.3	14.2	3.9	2.1	16.2	14.3
POLYGRAM NV	93.0	3.0	-5.5	15.7	30.2	29.6	9.8	3.4	1.7	10.9	25.5
TOKYO BROADCASTING	1,750.0	5.9	-7.5	-2.8	9.2	17.7	15.3	4.8	2.3	27.2	13.7
WENDY'S INTERNATIONAL	17.0	0.0	-8.9	-0.6	2.9	50.1	28.5	1.6	1.3	3.2	12.2
		-2.2	-10.5	-17.6	-20.0	11.7	8.1	2.2	1.4	17.0	17.9
AVERAGE		1.7	-8.1	-1.3	5.6	27.3	15.4	3.0	1.7	14.6	17.3
ENERGY (3% vs. 5%)											
COSMO OIL	673.0	-0.8	-4.6	-4.4	6.4	16.9	8.2	2.4	3.4	15.5	9.8
SCHLUMBERGER LTD	80.0	1.5	-1.9	23.0	19.3	31.0	8.5	2.2	2.4	7.1	39.1
		-2.4	-5.6	14.1	15.5	20.6	11.0	3.8	1.8	16.8	18.2
AVERAGE		-0.5	-3.7	18.6	17.4	25.8	9.8	3.0	2.1	12.0	28.7
FINANCIAL (12% vs. 21%)											
ALLSTATE CORP	44.8	1.0	-4.6	-4.2	-0.4	27.2	14.9	2.2	2.9	12.8	22.0
		4.7	-3.8	2.9	8.8	9.9	7.4	1.6	5.0	16.3	16.2

TABLE 1 (continued)

31-Jul-96 BENCHMARK	Share Price	1-Week % Chg	1-Month % Chg	Q-T-D % Chg	Y-T-D % Chg	P/E FY+1	P/CF FY+1	P/B FY+1	Yield FY+1	ROE FY+1	EPS Y-Y
BANKERS TRUST	71.9	1.8	-3.5	10.8	8.1	9.8	7.9	1.1	5.6	11.2	12.7
BANK OF YOKOHAMA	924.0	0.3	-6.5	12.8	9.3	43.4	27.3	2.4	0.5	5.5	82.1
CITICORP	81.9	1.6	-1.5	10.8	21.7	9.8	8.4	2.0	1.5	19.7	12.6
DEAN WITTER DISCOVER	50.9	3.3	-11.7	-6.0	8.2	7.9	7.5	1.4	2.6	17.4	17.0
NATIONSBANK	86.0	3.5	2.1	23.1	23.5	9.6	8.7	1.8	2.4	17.0	11.7
PROVIDENT FINL	4.5	9.5	-3.4	12.1	8.8	14.3	13.2	5.2	3.1	30.7	10.0
SUNTRUST BANKS INC	36.8	2.1	-2.0	6.3	7.3	12.3	10.2	1.7	4.5	13.8	9.9
AVERAGE		3.3	-3.8	9.1	12.0	14.6	11.3	2.2	3.2	16.5	21.5
HEALTH CARE (7%)											
ASTRA AB	271.0	0.4	-5.3	-5.0	2.4	18.7	14.4	5.0	2.1	34.5	15.7
JOHNSON & JOHNSON	47.8	5.0	-5.4	-2.7	3.0	14.8	12.6	4.2	2.4	28.3	15.1
PHARMACIA & UPJOHN	41.1	0.5	-3.8	-0.5	11.7	19.4	15.4	5.1	3.2	26.2	14.4
SMITHKLINE BEECHAM	6.8	2.8	-7.3	-1.2	6.1	16.1	11.8	2.9	1.8	18.0	23.2
		-1.2	-1.7	-6.4	-3.9	16.0	12.9	12.6	2.1	75.9	12.8
TAISO PHARM CO	2,300.0	0.0	-1.7	10.0	12.7	24.7	18.7	2.4	1.9	9.5	6.6
AVERAGE		1.4	-4.0	-0.2	5.9	18.2	14.2	5.4	2.3	31.6	14.4
INDUSTRIAL (9% vs. 12%)											
HITACHI CONST MACH	1,340.0	0.6	-6.0	-5.8	3.5	25.5	14.2	2.6	2.5	13.9	19.2
ILLINOIS TOOLWORKS	64.4	2.3	-2.2	8.1	7.2	44.2	22.7	2.3	0.4	na	35.3
KOMATSU	979.0	3.2	-4.6	4.9	9.1	14.9	11.6	3.0	2.5	20.5	12.2
MITSUBISHI HVY IND	905.0	2.4	-6.8	8.5	15.2	38.2	15.1	1.7	0.8	na	19.6
SYSCO CORP	29.0	2.4	-5.0	6.6	10.0	22.2	15.2	2.3	2.4	10.2	12.1
		1.3	-15.3	-9.4	-10.8	16.5	11.9	3.0	3.0	18.2	na
TELEDYNE INC	36.0	2.9	-1.7	44.0	40.5	12.4	8.6	4.4	1.1	30.1	9.8
AVERAGE		2.4	-5.9	10.5	11.9	24.7	14.2	2.8	1.7	19.7	17.8
TECHNOLOGY (15% vs. 12%)		3.7	-6.5	-5.6	4.8	20.5	11.9	3.8	2.1	20.8	23.8
BRITISH AEROSPACE	9.3	0.4	-4.8	4.1	16.6	11.6	7.9	4.5	4.2	39.0	24.6

TABLE 1 *(continued)*

31-Jul-96 BENCHMARK	Share Price	1-Week % Chg	1-Month % Chg	Q-T-D % Chg	Y-T-D % Chg	P/E FY+1	P/CF FY+1	P/B FY+1	Yield FY+1	ROE FY+1	EPS Y-Y
COMPAQ COMPUTER	54.6	13.2	9.2	15.9	13.8	10.8	9.3	2.3	0.0	21.7	20.5
ERICSSON(LM)TEL	132.5	8.2	-10.2	-5.0	1.9	16.0	11.0	3.7	1.3	20.9	20.3
FUJI PHOTO FILM CO	3,190.0	3.2	-9.1	5.6	7.0	20.2	9.4	1.2	1.3	6.2	6.4
KYOCERA CORP	7,310.0	1.2	-4.7	-3.7	-4.7	19.3	13.8	1.9	2.0	10.1	6.7
MICROSOFT CORP	117.9	2.7	-3.6	27.4	34.3	29.0	26.1	7.8	0.0	27.0	na
MOTOROLA INC	54.0	2.9	-16.3	0.0	-5.3	17.3	8.5	2.5	1.7	14.4	29.3
REUTERS HOLDINGS	6.7	-4.1	-14.2	8.7	14.2	20.0	13.7	8.5	3.1	42.5	14.2
SUN MICROSYSTEMS	54.6	9.0	-9.9	18.8	19.7	16.6	11.9	3.6	0.0	21.9	na
TDK CORP	6,190.0	5.3	-4.6	16.1	17.5	22.7	10.5	2.1	0.8	8.7	-8.3
AVERAGE		4.2	-6.8	8.8	11.5	18.3	12.2	3.8	1.4	21.2	14.2
UTILITY (9% vs. 11%)		0.4	-5.8	-6.0	-4.0	17.1	7.4	2.9	4.0	16.0	8.5
AT&T CORP	52.3	2.7	-15.7	-21.9	-19.3	12.6	7.8	4.4	2.5	na	12.7
CABLE & WIRELESS	4.1	1.8	-3.8	-8.4	-11.5	12.7	7.0	2.8	2.5	19.4	12.8
KOKUSAI DEN (KDD)	11,000.0	-3.5	-0.9	33.5	22.2	42.0	11.3	2.0	1.0	4.7	3.5
KPN	58.3	0.3	-9.6	-8.9	0.0	10.0	4.5	1.8	4.5	16.7	9.4
MCI COMMUNICATIONS	24.6	5.9	-2.5	-14.0	-5.7	12.4	6.2	1.5	0.6	12.2	14.5
VEBA AG	75.0	-0.1	-7.5	13.2	23.1	14.1	5.2	2.1	2.3	13.7	10.4
AVERAGE		1.2	-6.7	-1.1	1.5	17.3	7.0	2.4	2.2	13.3	10.5
MODEL PORTFOLIO (100%)*		1.8	-5.8	7.7	12.2	19.5	11.8	3.3	2.2	18.4	16.9
RELATIVE TO THE MARKET		0.5	-0.6	-0.6	3.7	88.4	94.6	105.4	78.3	102.3	95.6

*Equal-weighted (1/67 = 1.5%) relative to our benchmarks.

TABLE 1 (continued)

Country Rotation Strategy

	Y-T-D % Chg	P/E FY +1	P/CF FY +1	P/B FY +1	Yield FY +1	Index %	Portfolio %
Belgium	6.7	12.3	7.2	1.7	4.8	1.0	0.0
France	9.4	16.4	8.4	2.0	3.8	3.0	4.5
Germany	6.8	20.3	8.9	2.8	2.8	4.0	5.5
Italy	2.0	16.3	8.1	1.6	4.2	2.0	2.5
Japan	0.2	44.6	20.1	2.6	1.2	29.0	28.5
Netherlands	11.6	14.3	9.1	2.9	4.7	2.0	3.0
Spain	8.5	12.1	7.4	1.9	4.7	1.0	0.0
Sweden	8.4	12.6	9.0	2.6	4.1	1.0	3.0
Switzerland	5.2	14.9	10.4	2.6	3.1	3.0	0.0
United Kingdom	1.2	13.2	9.5	3.1	4.3	10.0	9.5
United States	3.3	15.1	10.1	3.8	3.0	44.0	43.5

Source: Compustat, WorldScope, I/B/E/S & IMI estimates.

Portfolio-Weighting Strategy figures in the appendix to this chapter support our view.

Equal-weighting company exposure implies, however, that we can only be overweight a sector, market, or style to the extent that there are enough quality names to own. It is more difficult to implement such an approach in very small, developing, or narrow markets, but it can be done as illustrated by our Italian model portfolio (see Table 2). Our Italian model portfolio is a 33-stock equal-weighted portfolio (i.e., 1/33 = 3 percent) which reflects our thinking on Italian sectors. Notice that our views on Italian sectors are broadly similar to our views on global sectors (see Table 1). In order to implement such an approach in small, developing, or narrow markets, the portfolio will have structural under- and over-weights, which tend to be concentrated in low-growth and high-growth sectors, respectively. This means that large privatized shares, which often represent an extreme weight in a market index will be underrepresented; it also means that smaller growth-oriented shares in newly emerging sectors will be overrepresented. We are long-term investors, and we are comfortable with the implications of such an approach.

Capitalization-weighting sector, country, and style exposure provides a way of incorporating risk-management techniques into the process of portfolio construction. We market-weight sectors, countries, and styles by owning a number names, which on balance fits our fundamental views in terms of sectors, markets, and styles of investing. In other words, adding up the number of names in a particular group (sector, market, or style) and multiplying by the appropriate equal-weight results in our recommended exposure to the group. In general, our sector bets tend to be larger than our country bets, and we generally favor growth-at-a-reasonable-price (GARP) as opposed to pure value. This fits with our notion of owning companies which we perceive to be the quality leaders in a particular sector, country, or style. More important, by capitalization-weighting sectors and then finding quality leaders which also fit our fundamental views on markets and styles, we are able to focus on a smaller group of variables, which makes the process significantly more manageable and does not materially impact our ability to add value (see Chapter 5).

Integrate Risk Management and Construction

We integrate risk management into the construction process by controlling company-specific risk through an equal-weighting discipline and by controlling sector, market, and style risk by capitalization-weighting exposure to these dimensions. As illustrated in Tables 3 and 4, by looking

TABLE 2. Italian Model Portfolio (local currency)*

31-Jul-96 Benchmark	Share Price	1-Week % Chg	1-Month % Chg	Q-T-D % Chg	Y-T-D % Chg	P/E FY+1	P/CF FY+1	P/B FY+1	Yield FY+1	ROE FY+1	EPS Y-Y
ITALY 100-STOCK INDEX		-0.3	-7.5	-8.1	1.6	15.4	7.4	1.5	4.0	10.3	18.8
BASIC MATERIAL (6% vs. 3%)											
BURGO(CARTIERE)	7,300	-0.4	-7.2	-9.1	-16.4	9.5	2.8	0.8	4.2	8.8	37.7
CAFFARO SPA	1,580	-2.7	-12.7	-7.6	-7.9	6.6	2.6	0.6	8.2	8.9	2.9
		-1.9	-6.5	11.1	19.1	7.5	3.4	0.7	6.1	na	15.8
AVERAGE		-2.3	-9.6	1.8	5.6	7.0	3.0	0.7	7.1	8.9	9.4
CONSUMER DURABLE (15% vs. 10%)											
MARZOTTO & FIGLI	8,950	0.6	-5.2	-6.6	-4.4	9.9	3.6	1.0	5.5	10.4	19.8
MERLONI ELETTRODOM	3,200	-0.6	-2.2	-9.6	-5.7	10.9	4.4	1.3	2.6	11.6	16.9
PININFARINA SPA	16,250	-3.9	-4.8	-13.7	-12.9	9.0	3.2	1.2	2.5	12.1	21.1
PIRELLI SPA	2,470	-2.6	-3.3	27.0	17.8	11.8	6.4	1.4	1.8	11.3	33.6
SOGEFI	3,000	2.5	-2.8	14.1	20.5	10.3	4.2	1.1	4.8	10.6	14.3
		1.4	-5.1	-16.7	-10.8	7.7	4.0	1.0	4.0	12.3	9.5
AVERAGE		-0.7	-3.6	0.2	1.8	9.9	4.4	1.2	3.1	11.6	19.1
CONSUMER MERCHANDISE (6% vs. 2%)											
BENETTON GROUP SPA	17,855	-2.1	-8.1	-9.4	-5.2	15.3	8.0	2.2	4.7	9.6	-13.0
RINASCENTE(LA)	9,900	-3.6	-8.7	-4.4	-5.5	12.0	8.6	1.9	2.2	14.4	8.7
		-0.7	-7.9	-2.8	3.0	20.0	8.1	2.7	1.0	12.6	11.3
AVERAGE		-2.1	-8.3	-3.6	-1.2	16.0	8.4	2.3	1.6	13.5	10.0
CONSUMER NON-DURABLE (3% vs. 1%)											
PARMALAT FINANZ	1,920	-1.3	-9.0	-10.2	2.1	8.9	3.1	1.0	3.1	11.8	19.2
		3.4	-3.3	29.1	44.3	11.5	6.0	1.3	2.3	11.5	16.8
AVERAGE		3.4	-3.3	29.1	44.3	11.5	6.0	1.3	2.3	11.5	16.8
CONSUMER SERVICE (6% vs. 1%)											
ARN MONDADORI EDIT	10,650	-0.8	-9.1	-9.9	-10.5	15.0	5.5	1.1	2.7	-2.3	38.0
MEDIASET	6,865	2.2	-8.2	-18.7	-22.6	13.0	6.6	1.3	6.0	9.7	14.2
		-1.2	na	na	na	14.1	14.1	na	na	na	12.2

318

TABLE 2 (continued)

31-Jul-96 Benchmark	Share Price	1-Week % Chg	1-Month % Chg	Q-T-D % Chg	Y-T-D % Chg	P/E FY +1	P/CF FY +1	P/B FY +1	Yield FY +1	ROE FY +1	EPS Y-Y
AVERAGE		0.5	-8.2	-18.7	-22.6	13.5	10.4	1.3	6.0	9.7	13.2
ENERGY (6% vs. 14%)		1.8	-11.7	-10.3	24.7	10.9	4.9	2.0	5.2	18.8	8.3
ENI	6,840	1.9	-12.0	15.8	23.2	10.8	4.9	2.0	5.3	18.8	8.0
SAIPEM	6,210	-1.0	-3.6	56.0	69.7	11.8	7.3	2.3	3.4	19.4	15.3
AVERAGE		0.5	-7.8	35.9	46.5	11.3	6.1	2.2	4.3	19.1	11.7
FINANCIAL (27% vs. 38%)		-0.3	-4.4	-5.7	-8.0	20.5	10.4	1.6	3.5	7.3	12.5
BCA COMM ITALIANA	2,885	0.2	-4.8	-20.5	-14.9	9.5	6.3	0.6	5.2	6.1	18.7
BCA FIDEURAM SPA	3,000	-3.2	-10.7	50.1	63.5	17.2	16.3	2.9	1.5	15.6	16.0
BCA POP DI MILANO	7,200	-1.4	-2.8	3.2	13.4	7.6	5.7	0.7	6.9	9.1	11.3
BCO AMBROS VENETO	3,750	-1.3	-9.0	-20.2	-13.3	10.6	7.7	1.1	4.3	9.9	15.3
CREDITO BERGAMASCO	19,600	0.5	-0.5	2.6	9.8	12.4	10.5	1.3	3.6	9.9	18.3
CREDITO ITALIANO	1,720	2.1	-1.5	-12.7	-7.0	10.4	6.3	0.6	2.0	6.0	22.2
IMI SPA	11,425	-1.9	-9.4	4.9	14.3	10.5	9.3	0.9	7.5	8.6	7.9
INA(IST NAZ ASS)	2,180	1.4	-4.4	-4.8	3.6	17.3	9.3	0.8	2.5	4.3	8.6
ISTIT BCOSAN PAOL	9,145	-0.3	-6.7	-9.5	-2.7	11.3	8.1	0.8	2.6	6.6	15.9
AVERAGE		-0.4	-5.5	-0.8	7.4	11.9	8.8	1.1	4.0	8.5	14.9
HEALTH CARE (3% vs. 1%)		-1.9	-11.7	-13.3	27.1	13.9	6.4	1.9	2.8	12.7	17.9
ESAOTE	5,700	0.0	5.9	na	na	na	na	na	na	na	na
AVERAGE		0.0	5.9	na	na	na	na	na	na	na	na
INDUSTRIAL (9% vs. 6%)		-1.0	-9.2	-10.3	0.2	11.3	4.2	1.0	4.8	8.7	30.5
COMAU FINANZIARIA	1,850	-5.5	1.6	-0.5	5.7	6.4	3.7	0.6	12.5	9.6	9.0
DANIELI & C	9,130	-4.4	-9.6	-13.5	-8.7	12.2	7.8	1.0	4.4	8.0	7.6
SASIB	5,450	-6.3	-11.2	-18.7	-22.1	11.6	7.3	1.2	3.7	10.1	18.1
AVERAGE		-5.4	-6.4	-10.9	-8.4	10.0	6.3	0.9	6.8	9.2	11.6

TABLE 2 (continued)

31-Jul-96 Benchmark	Share Price	1-Week % Chg	1-Month % Chg	Q-T-D % Chg	Y-T-D % Chg	P/E FY+1	P/CF FY+1	P/B FY+1	Yield FY+1	ROE FY+1	EPS Y-Y
TECHNOLOGY (6% vs. 2%)											
ERICSSON	15,000	-2.2	-8.8	-9.0	-22.7	13.0	5.4	1.3	3.3	9.2	117.3
GEWISS	23,300	-4.5	-16.2	-21.9	-25.0	7.8	4.1	0.4	3.6	5.5	9.7
		0.6	-0.4	12.6	16.5	22.7	16.1	6.0	2.1	26.5	17.7
AVERAGE		-1.9	-8.3	-4.7	-4.3	15.3	10.1	3.2	2.9	16.0	13.7
UTILITY (13% vs. 22%)											
EDISON	8,890	-1.2	-9.8	-9.9	11.6	14.8	7.7	1.4	3.3	10.8	18.6
STET	4,620	1.3	-2.4	12.2	30.0	15.2	10.0	2.3	2.1	14.7	23.3
TIM SPA	3,180	-2.0	-9.9	-7.4	2.9	11.9	2.0	1.4	2.8	11.2	15.1
TELECOM ITALIA SPA	2,875	2.3	-8.4	11.2	13.8	21.3	21.3	na	na	na	25.2
		-3.8	-12.5	6.5	16.4	10.7	2.1	1.1	4.2	9.8	15.0
AVERAGE		-0.6	-8.3	5.6	15.8	14.8	8.8	1.6	3.0	11.9	19.7
MODEL PORTFOLIO (100%)*		-1.0	-6.1	1.7	7.4	12.0	7.4	1.4	4.1	11.2	14.9
RELATIVE TO THE MARKET		-0.7	1.4	9.8	5.8	77.8	99.9	95.6	100.6	108.3	79.0

Equal-weighted (1/33 = 3%) relative to our benchmark.

Source: WorldScope, I/B/E/S & IMI estimates.

TABLE 3   Style Weights: By Market

31-Dec-95 Benchmark	Market %	Growth %	Value %	Small %	Large %	Mid-Cap Growth	Mid-Cap Value
GLOBAL 3,500-STOCK INDEX	100.0	100.0	100.0	100.0	100.0	100.0	100.0
AUSTRALIA	1.4	0.3	1.2	4.3	1.0	4.1	3.1
AUSTRIA	0.2	0.0	0.5	1.5	0.1	0.4	0.6
BELGIUM	0.7	0.5	1.7	0.2	0.5	0.6	1.4
CANADA	1.8	1.2	8.9	1.4	1.4	3.1	8.8
DENMARK	0.4	0.7	0.9	2.0	0.1	0.8	2.2
FINLAND	0.2	0.1	1.0	1.1	0.1	0.5	4.5
FRANCE	3.2	2.4	12.8	4.1	2.8	2.5	8.1
GERMANY	3.8	2.5	7.4	4.7	4.0	4.7	1.3
HONG KONG	1.6	4.9	3.4	2.1	1.7	4.9	5.4
IRELAND	0.1	0.2	0.2	0.3	0.0	0.3	0.1
ITALY	1.5	0.7	6.7	3.5	1.3	1.6	9.8
JAPAN	25.5	6.1	16.3	39.6	24.7	14.8	15.5
MALAYSIA	0.9	2.3	0.1	5.0	0.6	10.8	0.2
MEXICO	0.3	0.8	0.3	0.3	0.2	0.0	2.1
NETHERLANDS	2.2	2.7	4.1	1.4	2.6	3.5	2.9
NEW ZEALAND	0.1	0.0	0.6	0.5	0.1	0.9	0.1
NORWAY	0.2	0.0	0.5	0.6	0.1	0.5	1.3
SINGAPORE	1.0	1.9	1.2	2.8	1.0	3.2	3.2
SPAIN	1.0	1.8	3.5	1.7	0.8	1.9	2.3
SWEDEN	1.0	1.0	3.1	0.9	0.8	1.2	2.4
SWITZERLAND	2.7	6.1	2.7	2.4	3.2	4.0	5.7
THAILAND	0.5	1.0	0.0	0.9	0.5	1.0	0.0
UNITED KINGDOM	8.7	8.5	8.1	10.6	8.9	13.2	8.3
UNITED STATES	40.9	54.5	15.2	8.4	43.6	21.5	10.7

Source: Compustat, WorldScope, I/B/E/S & IMI estimates.

TABLE 4.   Style Weights: By Sector

31-Dec-95 Benchmark	Market %	Growth %	Value %	Small %	Large %	Mid-Cap Growth	Value
GLOBAL 3,500-STOCK INDEX	100.0	100.0	100.0	100.0	100.0	100.0	100.0
BASIC MATERIAL	7.5	2.1	11.0	12.1	5.9	9.8	9.3
CONSUMER DURABLE	6.1	1.8	8.7	11.4	5.7	5.4	8.8
CONSUMER MERCHANDISE	4.8	7.6	2.2	7.1	3.9	7.6	6.1
CONSUMER NON-DURABLE	7.8	11.9	4.6	7.7	8.6	5.8	7.0
CONSUMER SERVICE	5.2	5.8	2.4	6.6	4.3	8.6	6.5
ENERGY	5.4	0.5	3.5	1.8	6.2	2.4	1.6
FINANCIAL	21.5	22.6	36.2	8.9	23.4	19.4	20.2
HEALTH CARE	6.9	15.0	0.5	3.1	8.1	3.9	1.3
INDUSTRIAL	11.5	7.5	15.4	32.3	7.6	24.0	31.5
TECHNOLOGY	12.2	17.6	6.1	8.5	13.2	9.0	5.1
UTILITY	11.2	7.6	9.4	0.6	13.0	4.1	2.5

Source: Compustat, WorldScope, I/B/E/S & IMI estimates.

at styles across markets and sectors, we know that a pure growth strategy will have a natural American overweight and a natural Japanese underweight. Similarly, such a portfolio will also have a structural overweight in health care, technology, and consumer nondurable, and a natural underweight in energy, consumer durable, and industrial. This kind of analysis helps to focus our selection process and to control risk by ensuring that there are no unintended sector, market, or style bets in our portfolios.

Equal-weighting company exposure ensures that one position does not determine the performance of the entire portfolio. It also reduces the upside benefit from a single decision. We try to generate performance as much by sector, country, and style bets as by stock selection. The final step in terms of integrating risk management into the construction process is to form a view on the reference currency and to hedge potential strength when it significantly exceeds the cost of execution. Here, too, we use quantitative tools to provide an indication as to how much the reference currency is likely to strengthen. Our currency-valuation model is developed from historical real relative-interest-rate premiums, which we then evaluate in the context of today's term-structure and inflation backdrop.

Methodology

Three-Dimensional Selection Process

Our global equity portfolio is constructed from a series of quantitative management tools organized around three dimensions: sector, country, and style. For each dimension, we evaluate historical and forecast valuation premiums, earnings-per-share (EPS) momentum, estimate error and quality, as well as performance or valuation anomaly (see Chapter 5). Once our sector, market, and style views are in place, we find shares which reflect these views and which are themselves attractive relative to bonds versus a historical average with added characteristic of quality leadership.

Market-Weight Sector, Country, and Style Exposure

We take a market-capitalization-weighted view on sectors, markets, and styles in order to add outperformance to our results, while simultaneously reducing risk. We begin with a view on sectors and with a natural orientation toward growth-at-a-reasonable-price (GARP). Next, we analyze countries in order to see where we feel comfortable with an overweight or underweight position. The last step is to evaluate the relative attractiveness of growth, value, or size. For styles, instead of measuring over- or undervaluation through P/E to bond yield, we evaluate a style P/E multiple relative to its complement (e.g., growth P/E divided by value P/E, or small P/E divided by large P/E) over the last 10 years, and then we compare that figure to the trailing and forecast ratios (see Global Style-Rotation figures in the appendix to this chapter.)

Equal-Weight Company Exposure

We equal-weight company exposure in order to introduce a small-capitalization bias as well as to control risk in our portfolios. Equal-weighted strategies outperform capitalization-weighted strategies, as the Portfolio-Weighting Strategy figures in the appendix to this chapter illustrate. These figures demonstrate the long-term impact of an equal-weighted approach. Across all styles of investing, equal-weighted strategies performed 38 percent better than the cap-weighted styles during the period 1985-1995. Equal-weighted growth (+42 percent), value (+90 percent), small (+44 percent), large (+15 percent), mid-cap growth (+16 percent), and mid-cap value (+23 percent) all significantly outperformed their cap-weighted counterparts in our 11-year analysis. For the three largest markets (United States +78 percent, Japan +50 percent, and United Kingdom +75 percent), the equal-weighted results were 67 percent better, on average, than the cap-weighted market performance.

Separate the Currency Decision

Separating the currency decision from the equity decision is crucial to our understanding equity performance. In our model portfolios, long-term performance-tracking systems, and correlation models, we always use local currency returns. In our view, long-term performance in a given market is driven more by local investors than by international investors. As a consequence, we compare valuation levels with local returns in order to understand the market dynamics and to look at relationships between markets in terms of local price correlation. As we discussed in Chapter 5, it is by looking at local currency (hedged) returns that the importance of the sector dimension is revealed. Introducing a reference currency into the valuation exercise, in a sense, creates a synthetic security which is more difficult to understand, because it is not one security but two.

We evaluate currencies by comparing the reference currency's 10-year real bond yield relative to each of the other currencies over the last five years, and then we compare that figure to trailing and forecast ratios.

These real relative-interest-rates represent the first step in our process of deciding whether there is the potential for significant reference-currency strength. In our model, we use the cumulative consumer-price-index (CPI) rather than the month-to-month rate of change, because we believe that the market has a collective memory with respect to price-level stability and that it is not the marginal change which is important, but, rather, the cumulative effect of monthly changes.

As Tables 5 and 6 indicate, this approach suggests that the dollar remains significantly undervalued against both Europe (+16 percent) and Japan (+23 percent), but that the lira is overvalued relative to Europe (-8 percent) and America (-20 percent) but not to Japan (+2 percent). With respect to sustained lira strength, there may be a rerating of the historical risk premium in process, reflecting enhanced growth with lower inflation, more fiscal restraint, and the possibility of a European-Monetary-Union (EMU). We believe that the EMU will make many historical relationships less meaningful going forward. The valuation premium, whether in terms of sectors, countries, styles, shares, or currency, is the single most important decision, which almost inevitably involves the exercise of judgment. Our model is simply quantifying the extent to which American yields have increased so far this year and the extent to which they have fallen across Europe and Japan, relative to historical real yield-spreads. A double-digit fair-value return target is about the point where we start wondering about hedging reference-currency strength. Ultimately, this decision is based not simply on the trailing ratio but, also, on how the currency looks, given our view of bond yields and price levels six- to nine-months forward.

Construction

Selected by P/E to Inverse Bond Yield

We evaluate stocks relative to bonds by dividing the price-to-earnings ratio by the inverse 10-year government-bond yield, which for us represents a kind of equity risk premium. This method of transformation captures the rate at which equity investors capitalize the EPS relative to the pace of economic activity. In our company selection model (see Table 7), we compute this ratio over the preceding five years on a monthly basis, and we compare that figure to our 1997 estimate of the same. In general, we use consensus 1997 EPS estimates, and we assume that interest rates rise (+75 basis points to be conservative); although, it is important to know where you are in the profit cycle in order to choose the correct inputs for the models (see Chapter 5).

TABLE 5. Currency Strategy: American Dollar

30-Sep-96	Real GBY	CPI Level	10-Year GBY	CPI FY +1	GBY FY +1	Disc /Prem	5-Year Mean	FVRT %
EUROPE / $	6.1	1.15	7.1	1.16	7.5	1.00	˙.16	16.0
YEN / $ *	3.1	1.07	3.3	1.07	3.6	0.51	0.63	22.9
DM / YEN	5.5	1.16	6.4	1.17	6.9	1.76	1.51	-13.9
GLOBAL / $	5.2	1.12	5.8	1.13	6.3	0.86	0.95	10.9
BELGIUM	6.0	1.12	6.7	1.12	7.0	0.96	1.16	20.5
FRANCE	5.8	1.10	6.4	1.11	6.9	0.96	1.16	20.8
GERMANY	5.5	1.16	6.4	1.17	6.9	0.90	1.01	12.2
ITALY	7.6	1.22	9.3	1.23	10.2	1.28	1.63	27.1
NETHERLANDS	5.6	1.13	6.4	1.13	6.7	0.91	1.04	14.1
SPAIN	7.1	1.25	8.9	1.26	9.7	1.19	1.55	30.3
SWEDEN	6.9	1.21	8.3	1.21	9.1	1.16	1.38	18.9
SWITZERLAND	3.8	1.15	4.4	1.15	4.8	0.64	0.74	15.9
UNITED KINGDOM	6.9	1.14	7.9	1.16	8.4	1.11	1.24	11.3

(*) Ten-year average valuation.

Source: OECD & IMI estimates.

TABLE 6. Currency Strategy: Italian Lira

30-Sep-96	Real GBY	CPI Level	10-Year GBY	CPI FY +1	GBY FY +1	Disc /Prem	5-Year Mean	FVRT %
EUROPE / LIRA	6.1	1.15	7.1	1.16	7.5	0.78	0.72	-8.0
YEN / LIRA*	3.1	1.07	3.3	1.07	3.6	0.40	0.41	2.2
$ / LIRA	5.5	1.16	6.4	1.17	6.9	0.78	0.63	-19.8
GLOBAL / LIRA	5.2	1.12	5.8	1.13	6.4	0.68	0.59	-12.9
BELGIUM	6.0	1.12	6.7	1.12	7.0	0.75	0.72	-4.3
FRANCE	5.8	1.10	6.4	1.11	6.9	0.75	0.71	-4.3
GERMANY	5.5	1.16	6.4	1.17	6.9	0.71	0.63	-11.0
ITALY	7.6	1.22	9.3	1.23	10.2	1.00	1.00	0.0
NETHERLANDS	5.6	1.13	6.4	1.13	6.7	0.71	0.65	-9.6
SPAIN	7.1	1.25	8.9	1.26	9.7	0.93	0.96	3.0
SWEDEN	6.9	1.21	8.3	1.21	9.1	0.91	0.86	-5.6
SWITZERLAND	3.8	1.15	4.4	1.15	4.8	0.50	0.46	-8.2
UNITED KINGDOM	6.9	1.14	7.9	1.16	8.4	0.87	0.77	-11.5

(*) Ten-year average valuation.

Source: OECD & IMI estimates.

TABLE 7. Company Selection Model (local currency)

31-Jul-96 Benchmark	Share Price	5-Year P/E	10-Year Yield	P/E FY +1	10-Year FY +1	Inverse Yield	Disc / Prem	5-Year Mean	FVRT %
BRITISH AEROSPACE	9.3	63.6	6.9	13.5	7.7	13.1	1.0	4.5	336.3
SMITHKLINE BEECHAM	6.8	47.4	6.9	18.5	7.7	13.1	1.4	3.8	165.4
PIRELLI SPA	2,470.0	27.7	6.9	11.7	7.7	13.1	0.9	2.0	120.7
ERICSSON(LM)TEL	132.5	33.9	6.9	21.0	7.7	13.1	1.6	2.8	73.8
BOC GROUP	9.1	21.6	6.9	14.4	7.7	13.1	1.1	1.8	59.6
CABLE & WIRELESS	4.1	19.6	6.9	13.4	7.7	13.1	1.0	1.6	55.2
ASTRA AB	271.0	20.7	6.9	16.0	7.7	13.1	1.2	1.7	40.6
BENETTON GROUP SPA	17,855.0	14.9	6.9	12.0	7.7	13.1	0.9	1.2	30.8
BAYER MOTOREN WERK	825.0	19.6	6.9	15.9	7.7	13.1	1.2	1.6	27.0
POLYGRAM NV	93.0	20.1	6.9	17.2	7.7	13.1	1.3	1.6	23.1
AIR LIQUIDE(L')	800.0	19.9	6.9	17.4	7.7	13.1	1.3	1.6	21.6
VEBA AG	75.0	18.0	6.9	15.5	7.7	13.1	1.2	1.4	19.3
REUTERS HOLDINGS	6.7	22.8	6.9	22.6	7.7	13.1	1.7	1.8	6.6
BAYER AG	49.5	13.4	6.9	13.7	7.7	13.1	1.0	1.1	2.2
PROVIDENT FINL	4.5	13.7	6.9	14.5	7.7	13.1	1.1	1.1	-0.7
COMPTOIRS MODERNES	2,314.0	18.9	6.9	24.7	7.7	13.1	1.9	1.5	-19.3
BOSS (HUGO) AG	1,750.0	10.7	6.9	16.1	7.7	13.1	1.2	0.9	-30.0
CANAL PLUS	1,195.0	25.1	6.9	38.0	7.7	13.1	2.9	2.0	-30.3

Source: Compustat, WorldScope, I/B/E/S & IMI estimates.

Exercise Judgment

Making judgments about the inputs (e.g., EPS, valuation premium, and interest rates) separates portfolios which outperform from those that underperform. In Table 7, we highlight European shares from our global model portfolio ranked by the fair-value return target, which is simply the upside potential from our 1997 estimate to the five-year average. Only three out of the 18 have sharply negative return-targets. We think the historical risk premium does not properly reflect the forward growth potential for these shares and that these companies will command a higher valuation-premium going forward. This is a judgment, and it represents the principal reason why our stock-selection decisions are not made by algorithm.

Find Quality Leadership

We think finding quality leadership is largely an exercise in locating consistent long-term profitability. The concept of quality leadership is best understood by finding stocks which exemplify this characterization and, then, by studying the financial characteristics of these companies in order to see what range of values is typically associated with that judgment. In our experience, profitability is best measured by return on equity (ROE), which can also be normalized by dividing by the price-to-book ratio or by adding back goodwill which had been written off in order to account for the cumulative impact of purchase transactions on a company's capital account. Notice that in both of our model portfolios, the ROE is higher than the relevant benchmark.

Conclusion

In short, our active approach incorporates cap-weighting and equal-weighting in order to control risk and to add performance. The Portfolio-Weighting Strategy figures in the appendix to this chapter support our view on the impact of equal-weighted strategies on performance. Quantitative tools enhance the construction process and form the basis for the critical input and selection decisions which follow. We begin by evaluating sectors, followed by markets, and, finally, by styles, before we begin the stock-selection process. Stocks are selected on the same basis as sectors, markets, or styles. Finally, we take a view on reference-currency strength, and we hedge, when necessary.

APPENDIX

Portfolio-Weighting Strategy

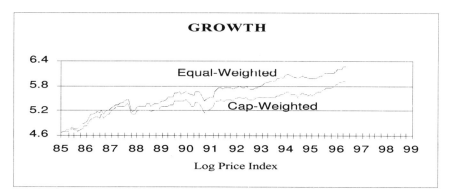

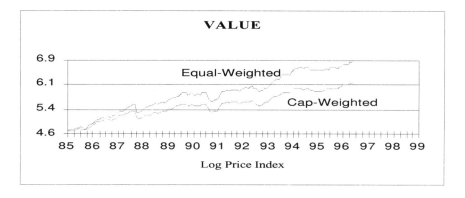

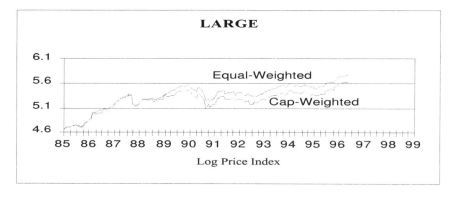

Portfolio-Weighting Strategy

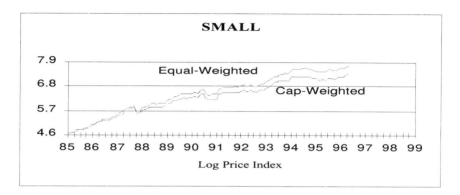

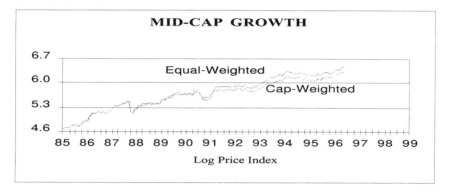

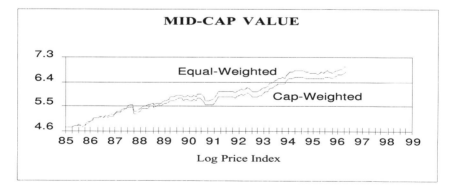

Portfolio-Weighting Strategy

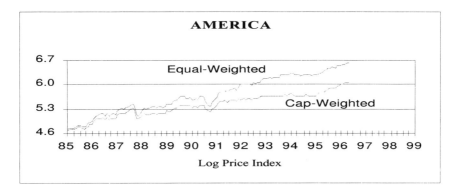

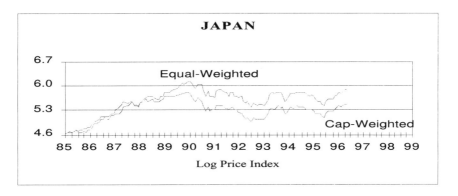

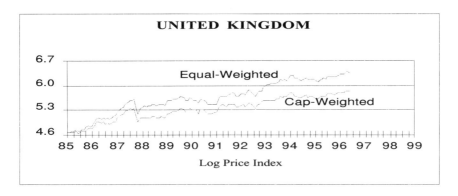

Global Style-Rotation

GROWTH

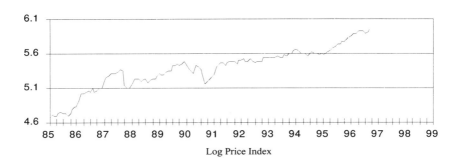

Log Price Index

EQUITY RISK PREMIUM

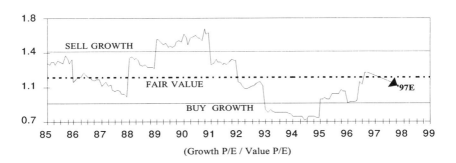

(Growth P/E / Value P/E)

VALUE

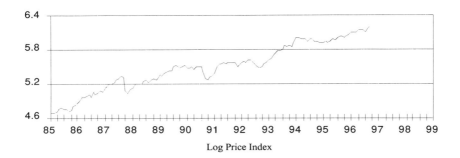

Log Price Index

Global Style-Rotation

SMALL

Log Price Index

EQUITY RISK PREMIUM

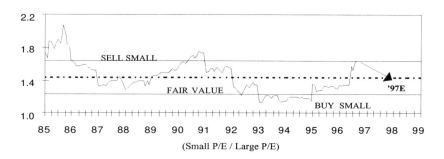

(Small P/E / Large P/E)

LARGE

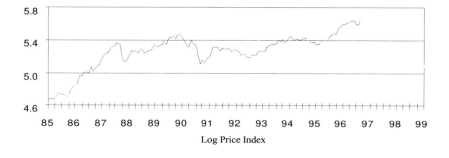

Log Price Index

Global Style-Rotation

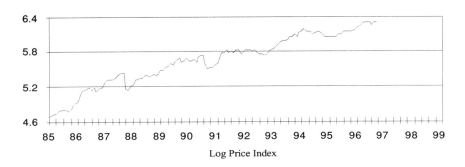

MID-CAP GROWTH

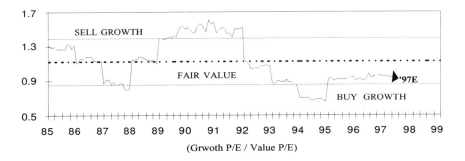

EQUITY RISK PREMIUM

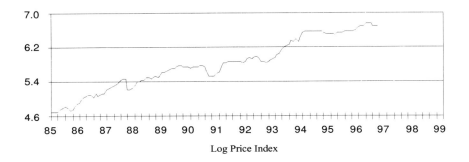

MID-CAP VALUE

CHAPTER 12

Implementing Global Investment Strategies

Wayne H. Wagner
President
Plexus Group

Carole A. Ryavec
Director
Plexus Group

The Investing Process

Why It Is Important to Understand the Transaction Process

Investment management can be viewed as a two-part process: an information process and an implementation process. The information process view is discussed at length throughout this book. The focus in this chapter is the implementation process and its potential for enhancing performance.

Implementation-process analysis seems to be the stepchild of the traditional investing process. An observer studying how professional investment managers spend their time would conclude that a manager's energy is spent reviewing the strength of his or her holdings and, especially, assessing potential buy-candidates. The operative assumption appears to be that this "buying and holding the right stocks" is sufficient to win the investment game (see Figure 1).

FIGURE 1.   The Traditional Management Process

Managers *are* highly successful at identifying attractive buys. In a 1995 study[1] of U.S. managers, Plexus Group found the value of the buy-decisions to be market return plus 1.67 percent over the first six weeks post-decision. Clearly, this part of the process works.

As we shall see, however, the bottom line indicates that other important pieces are missing from the equation of investment performance. Worldwide, professional managers as a group have difficulty keeping pace with the index funds that represent low-cost, zero-insight alternatives to active portfolio management. Something is adrift in the active investment process. Determining where the slippage occurs in the process requires looking at the problem from a complementary, nontraditional view.

An alternative view of investing is not in a buy-plus-hold framework, but as a buy-plus-sell process. This viewpoint focuses on the day-to-day activity of the manager. It views the investment process as one of replacing held stocks with stocks thought to have greater future potential. Under this view, a manager invests *long* with the positive decision on the buy and *short* with the decision to sell the stock, whose future appreciation he or she will not participate in. Thus, the investment value (on paper) is in the *differential* in performance between the stock bought and the stock sold (see Figure 2).

In the 1995 U.S. study, the average stock sold appreciated 5 basis points more than the market. Thus, the paper return between the average sell and the average buy is +162 basis points. Clearly, there is still value on paper, even though the value comes totally from the buy decision.

Of course, these position swaps are not costless. In the U.S. study, we measured the slippage between costless returns and realized returns at 100 basis points on the buys and 103 basis points on the sells, over 2 percent round-trip. Once these costs are incurred, the return net of costs and net of market falls to -41 basis points. Thus, finding the right stocks to buy and to sell is a necessary part of investment management, but is often insufficient to guarantee superior performance.

In contrast to a "picking winners" perspective, the focus here is on the *process* of investing: As Figure 3 shows, selling one stock to buy

FIGURE 2.   The Potential Value of Manager Activity

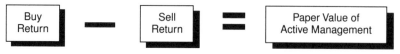

FIGURE 3.   The Investing Process

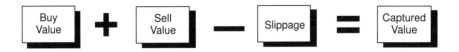

another captures the difference between the buy's return and the sell's return, less the cost of getting from one to the other. Greater success comes when managers combine stock-picking abilities with similar attention to the sell discipline and to the implementation process.

From this perspective, investing is more than mysterious fortune-telling acumen. It is a delicate balancing of all the factors that combine to result in superior performance:

- The breadth of candidates in the potential buying universe.
- The assets under management.
- The number of positions held, and therefore the size of trade required.
- Cash flows and constraints.
- The decision trigger: the process which causes potential actions to become realized decisions. Value-oriented processes will trigger on different events than price-confirming processes.
- The nature of the triggering event, which dictates the trading strategy, the speed of trading, the implementation cost , and the completion rate.
- The quality of the manager's market-intelligence systems and the availability of first-rate trading facilities.

As we shall see, the problems compound in global markets due to market liquidity and transparency problems. Compared to managing global portfolios, the U.S. managers' environment seems benign. Global managers are seldom blessed with the quality of information about individual companies that is available in the United States. Furthermore, global markets, despite their facade of electronic sophistication, seldom have the depth, transparency, and liquidity to easily accommodate institutional sized trading.

Thus, managers need a clear understanding of their own processes, and the processes' strengths, weaknesses, and anticipated costs, when devising a solution that works in global markets.

Taking the Process Global

The framework we will use to describe global-investing processes is that of a successful country-manager deciding to extend his or her range to international investing. The biggest danger a manager faces in going global is making inadvertent analogies that extend beyond the range of tangible experience. Because it works well *here* does not mean it will work well *there*.

We have become acquainted with investing activities of managers based in different countries, we are impressed with the similarity of the core attitudes and thinking processes. Yet there are profound differences in the details that they deal with on a daily basis. Indeed, while U.S. managers find foreign markets confusing in their opacity, foreign managers often find U.S. markets confusing for their clarity!

Some of these market differences are simply a matter of scale. In many countries, the largest companies would be classified as medium or even small companies in the United States. All the problems of implementing small-cap U.S. decisions are amplified in foreign markets.

Other differences are more fundamental:

- Information on companies is more difficult to gather and more difficult to interpret.
- Many companies are closely held, and the floating supply of stock is much less than the outstanding shares. This amplifies market volatility.
- Market structure, despite the prevalence of electronic markets, may be much more primitive. *Caveat emptor,* despite the assurance of the local market authorities.
- Market-information dissemination is often far less revealing than in U.S. markets.
- The local market, often the best source of liquidity, may be open during what for global investors is the middle of the night. Agency problems, especially with limit orders, can become acute.
- Government supervision of the markets may be lax, leaving the local brokers to decide how to organize commission structure, trading, and information dissemination.
- The government may take a protective attitude toward the local market, in effect creating an advantage for local investors over foreign investors.
- Standards of fiduciary behavior are different. In some cases, the standards may be quite strict (e.g., Investment Management Reg-

ulatory Organisation (IMRO) oversight in Great Britain); but more often, they will be perfunctory.

Over time, of course, all this will be known by direct experience. On a more personal level, however, the key to operating effectively in global markets is to know your own strengths and weaknesses. If your firm does not possess a clear understanding of its own capabilities, and of its information sources and usage, extending to global markets will be a series of unpleasant surprises.

A manager extending to global markets must change and extend the capabilities of the firm. Before changing yourself, you need to know yourself. Far too many proud institutions have found that any unexamined weakness can turn into a profound embarrassment. Going global requires that you understand your own firm, how it implicitly depends on the home market, and how you need to grow to accommodate the global-transaction process. Establishing strong discipline for corporate—and personal—conduct, *whatever the prevailing local standards,* is imperative.

The Basics of Implementing Investment Ideas

The appeal of global markets to plan sponsors is enhanced diversification. To investment managers, the added appeal is greater growth and appreciation. Accompanying the growth potential, however, is a more daunting cost structure.

Market structure is an issue that seldom affects the thinking of U.S. managers. U.S. markets can be taken for granted to a far greater degree than global markets. This is a blind spot for U.S. managers that accounts for the difficulty that managers have in beating the benchmark indexes. In global markets, this can be a far more serious problem. Table 1 contrasts typical implementation costs across markets.

TABLE 1. Comparative Costs of Trading

	Large-Cap Stocks ($1 billion U.S. or greater)	Mid-Cap Stocks ($250 million-$1 billion U.S.)	Small-Cap Stocks (less than $250 million U.S.)
U.S. Exchanges	-52 basis points	-97 basis points	-147 basis points
U.K./SEAQ Markets	-66	-83	-1778
Japan	-65	-90	-168
EEC Markets	-64	-148	-163
AsianTigers	-103	-189	-212
Emerging Markets	-176	-249	-377

The higher the cost structure, the more important it is to identify superior prospects. Conversely, high transaction costs leave many good investment ideas unactionable.

What Is Different about Trading International Stocks?

Global market structures sprang up from different roots to service different clientele. Germany, for example, differs from the United States in the role played by the commercial banks, the paucity of private-pension investing, and the lack of cultural support for entrepreneurial start-ups. Each country will have historical cultural compromises that spawned the market structures and business practices in use today.

Over time, all markets may head toward a similar solution as investors and market functionaries realize the advantages of liquidity and transparency. For now, however, new global managers may be amazed at some of the unusual facilities to accommodate modern trading needs:

Hidden trades. Under certain—but frequent—conditions, trades on Stock Exchange Automated Quotations (SEAQ) in London do not have to be revealed for periods extending to days. The purpose of this practice is to protect the brokers who may have taken positions in the stock. This protection does not extend to investors. The net effect is that trades in volume may be executed without you being aware of them.

Warehousing. Warehousing of trades, particularly in Europe, as a broker will accumulate a large position over many days and does not deliver the final shares for five days, or sometimes until the activity is complete. Again, without a public record of activity, trades in volume may be unobservable.

Government restrictions. Government restrictions on foreign investment, as is found in South Korea and Thailand. Foreigners may be locked out of certain buy situations as the stock held by foreigners is capped out. Only if another foreigner wants to sell can shares be bought.

Cabal of local brokers. In underdeveloped markets—India and Turkey, for example—foreign investors are considered fair game for the local brokers. Only in time will they discover that fair markets mean low transaction costs, which attract capital and enrich the brokers as well as the investors.

Cross-holdings. In countries such as Japan and Switzerland, many of the outstanding shares of companies can be held by other industrial or investment companies, thus reducing the apparently large capitalization to a small potential trading volume. Goldman Sachs estimates that half the shares in Japan are locked up in cross-holdings.[2]

What Can Be Done to Alleviate These Trading Problems?

When faced with these problems, a manager has three basic tools to keep the investment strategy successful:

- Apply inventive and experimental trading strategies.
- Alter the investment strategy to make greater use of what is available, rather than what is desirable.
- Respond in the negative to the question: Can I grow this business?

Of course, a manager will adapt the third strategy only when the potential of the first two is exhausted.

Some specific methods we have seen for improving trading effectiveness are

- *Pay up for liquidity.* Recognize that markets with fewer dealers and fewer players require "cutting in" other parties to the information advantage. Get to know the locals. Half a loaf is better than none.
- *Use program trades* to acquire positions in a breadth of companies. Despite the cautions in this chapter, international brokerage is highly competitive. Brokers have been known to buy market share with aggressive bidding on program trades.
- *Use the rapidly developing electronic markets* to their fullest capacity. This usually works only on smaller trades and often does not help in search for liquidity.
- *Create a local presence* by opening a trading desk in the country of interest. Court the local sources of liquidity. This is expensive in the short run, but can be highly effective over the longer term.
- *Trade when you can*, not when you want. Be more anticipatory.
- *Trade what you can*, not what you want. Every global manager sooner or later encounters a need to sell Japan rather than Italy simply because you can reliably get control of the proceeds. Clearing in countries like Italy may be a mess, and cannot be counted on for predictable cash-flow to fund the buys.

None of this works unless the manager is fully aware of the circumstances in which trading is effective in capturing investment value, and the circumstances when it is not. Thus, dramatic gains are available from studying your own trading. A continuing periodic review provides the necessary grist to redesign the investing strategy in order to square decision-value with the implementation opportunities. For example:

- Modify an intensively active strategy to incorporate quantitative techniques.
- Move from price confirmation to strategies to a value orientation. Buy while the market is still dominated by sellers.
- Abandon a *laissez-faire* brokerage attitude in favor of one with strong supervision and control.
- Forego central trading in favor of a local trading capability.

Finally, there is the ultimate accommodation: Close off the business when the asset size and investment strategy prevent the capture of liquidity and the realization of positive value-added.

What Makes Trading Expensive?

There are no standard solutions in investment management. Different investing approaches require unique solutions matched to specific management styles, strengths and needs. A manager needs to know what works in terms of generating information *and* capturing the value. The easiest way for a manager to assess his own process is to trace the decision value from point of decision and compare it to captured value. This approach is called *implementation shortfall*.[3] It provides a direct, side-by-side comparison of the decision strength to the captured value.

The case studies below are derived from using an expanded implementation-shortfall-analysis approach to evaluate decision/implementation effectiveness. They illustrate how global managers can apply this self-knowledge to improve their effectiveness and enhance performance.

Liquidity Constraints

The typical global manager with $500 million invested in U.K./ Europe markets in the late 70's would easily have $5 billion under management by the early 1990s. The firm's research staff and top portfolio managers know the top companies in their market universes, whether Europe, Australia, and Far East (EAFE), global, or regional. They know which brokers give good forecasts and sector coverage. They establish a pattern of rotating within the known investment-universe, which could range from 100 names to 300 names. They often take full percent positions in the favored names.

At $500 million, a manager represents a small percentage of the available liquidity in the universe of stocks. At $5 billion, the trading situation has changed. The manager now must position carefully to accumulate larger shares of liquidity. Obtaining a percentage position means that the manager may need to trade 15 percent to 30 percent or more of daily volume for several days. The following tables look at the cost difference between trading small and trading large. Clearly, increases in trade size add to the average cost of execution (see Table 2).

Momentum Constraints

Managers who routinely wait for confirming price movements frequently encounter an excess of competitors who also want to buy when they want to buy. We call these situations *liquidity demanding,* and they result in expensive trading conditions. Large trades into liquidity demanding situations may double or triple the costs of execution. Momentum is the single most important determinant of transaction costs. Note, in contrast, that buy-trades into markets filled with sellers offer potential gains for *liquidity-supplying* traders (see Table 3).

Value managers, in contrast to momentum managers, avoid adverse momentum. As a result, their transaction costs are usually far less than momentum managers. Occasionally, however, they meet competition in the market to complete the desired trade. The competition may arise from other value managers keying into the same idea, or from other managers responding to different signals.

The choice is to pass up the opportunity to trade or to shift to a more aggressive trading posture. When they step up, they meet the momentum managers head on, and pay more to trade in adverse momentum than in neutral or favorable momentum. As Table 3 shows, there appears to be a larger momentum impact in the United Kingdom than in the United States.

TABLE 2. The Cost of Liquidity

	United States	United Kingdom
Small Trades	-19	-82
Large Trades	-28	-110

TABLE 3. Momentum Effects on Costs

	United States	United Kingdom
Liquidity Demanding	-146	-172
Liquidity Supplying	+75	+18

Cash Constraints

Another problem faced by all managers is cash constraints. Unless excess cash is readily available, the manager is forced to sell existing positions in order to buy new positions. Frequently, the early-in-the-day focus is on buying the attractive stock; selling often waits until later in the day. Then, panic sets in since the manager does not want to inadvertently leverage the account. The result is often faster trading in larger-size trades, and the quality of sell-trading naturally deteriorates.

The trend is for plan sponsors to limit cash positions through "remain fully invested" policies. This directive forces managers to sell in a way that tends to increase costs. Managers are increasingly forced to deal in larger trade-sizes in order to get cash in quickly for investment shifts. Therefore, even if the sell discipline is value in orientation, the trade desk faces greater impact, as shown above. Our database shows a 30-basis-point differential between small trades (less than 15 percent of daily trading volume) and large trades (greater than 30 percent of volume), all other factors being the same.

How do global equity managers deal with the costs of trading? The six cases presented below offer very different solutions. Each case represents a real manager evolving toward a more effective strategy through a better understanding of his or her own investment process.

Case Studies: Adjusting Trading Strategies and/or Investment Style

Case Study 1: Adjustments by a U.S.-Based Global Manager

Manager 1 manages about $1.5 billion in global equities. Roughly one-third of this portfolio's trading is done in U.K. shares.

Table 4 shows the decision strength and execution costs. The decisions had value, yet the realized returns from the activity drained assets from the fund.

The costs of execution in the United Kingdom were very high. For the first quarter, the cost of execution was almost -300 basis points, against a benchmark cost of -150 basis points. In the following quarters, the execution loss drops dramatically, resulting in an increase in the realized return.

These changes result from an explicit four-point program on the part of the manager to reduce costs and to increase the capture of investment value.

TABLE 4. Global Equity Turnover: Potential and Captured
Returns

Qtr	Decision Return	Implementation Cost	Realized Return
1	91 bp	-286 bp	-195 bp
2	80	-196	-116
3	80	-155	-75
4	72	-124	-52
5	101	-102	-1
6	84	-82	+2

1. The manager reconsidered the criteria which turned his buy candidates into buy decisions. The *price trigger* was changed, with respect to the direction and degree of pretrade momentum. The manager enforced a discipline away from reacting to bad news by releasing trades into strong negative momentum. The manager built a more anticipatory selling discipline and combined it with a refusal to sell in panic conditions. Over the time span, trades were released into positive (favorable) momentum, which strongly reduced the cost of selling. Pretrade momentum—price movement in the two days prior to decision—dropped from 3.2 percent adverse price movement to 30 basis points of positive price movement.

2. The manager built up the research function in the firm, expanding the potential decision universe by increasing the number of names on the research list. This expansion changed the *size of trades*, downsizing from almost 50 percent of daily volume to 16 percent of daily volume. Again, reduced cost of selling was the result.

3. The *decision universe* was expanded by widening the capitalization band to admit larger, more-liquid companies. Rather than limiting selections to companies less than $U.S. 1 billion, the manager began to research companies with capitalizations as high as $U.S. 8 billion.

4. In addition to the changing the nature of the decision process, the manager also changed the *procedures governing trading*. The equity team began to measure and monitor brokerage. They hired a trader to arrive early to trade the market in real time. They demanded that every broker report on quality of execution.

The four factors combined to result in a dramatic change in trading characteristics. Expected (benchmark) costs dropped by a factor of three, and execution costs dropped by a factor of ten! An ineffective investing process became capable of benefiting from profitable capture of new ideas.

With the experience of dramatic improvement in U.K. implementation, the manager gained confidence to examine trading in other countries. They applied all of the above disciplines to trading Japan, addressing what for them was another black hole of execution costs.

Perhaps few managers would be willing to apply this fanatical an approach to solving high-execution-cost problems. This extreme but real case exemplifies the adjustments to trading and investment strategies that a manager might use to deal with the higher costs of trading the global market.

Case Study 2: Adjustments by a Large U.S.-Based Global Manager

The equity team for Manager 2 had a different problem. We measured costs at about 30 basis points more than the benchmark costs, yet it was not clear where or why the leakage occurred.

Table 5 shows that U.K. trades cost an average of -110 basis points. The equity team, highly quantitative in orientation, was not willing to change the decision universe. But they were sensitive to the potential return of (1) releasing slightly smaller trade size, (2) experimenting with the timing of the trade releases, and (3) carefully monitoring brokerage, not particularly "policing," but measuring and monitoring each trade.

Table 5 shows the gradual improvement resulting from these adjustments in release strategy and broker communication. Brokerage cost declined from -116 basis points to -61 basis points. The benchmark cost actually increased, reflecting a shift to more difficult trading environment over the year. Despite the increased difficulty, and directly as a result of timing improvements and broker monitoring, recent quarterly results show an ability to trade below benchmark costs.

TABLE 5. U.K. Execution Costs

Quarter	Execution Costs	Benchmark Costs
1	-116	-70
2	-108	-63
3	-67	-74
4	-61	-76

Case Study 3: Adjustments by a Large U.K.-Based Global Manager

The manager in Case 1 was able to adjust strategy without forsaking the basic nature of the decision process. Manager 3 was not able to find easy solutions. With over $50 billion in U.K. equities, Manager 3 found many of his positions in the "Liquidity Penalty Box," with positions representing more than 30 days' volume. Many of the best investment ideas were not implementable: Elephants simply cannot hide in the strawberry patch! The solution is to use the weight to advantage by becoming a value trader, reducing transaction friction by taking contrarian stances. They expect to take trading gains as they (1) accumulate positions at better prices, or (2) wait passively for large block discounts from the brokers. They became the buyer of last resort, and, by necessity, a long-term investor.

Manager 3 was able to increase portfolio return by stepping up its own contrarian view by applying a rigid discipline to the sell side. Instead of reducing positions quickly, Manager 3 lengthened the trading horizon. A sharp increase in performance resulted from changes in decision timing, which gave the desk opportunities to trade at a gain (liquidity supplying.) The net positive trading-return offset a slight short-term decision negative, resulting in value-added from current activity.

Case Study 4: Execution in Japan—Being There

Another solution for the single-market investment manager as it begins to invest abroad is to create a physical presence in its major new markets.

The flow of domestic investment in non-U.S. markets moves in mysterious manners which are not always obvious to offshore investors. A large part of the success in nondomestic markets will be listening to the pulse behind stock flow. Fiscal year-end, cross-holdings, domestic insurance holdings, restrictions on nondomestic investments, and many other constraints make trading both expensive and volatile. No market has been a greater problem for global investors than Japan.

For EAFE managers, the weight of Japan's market capitalization pushed managers into heavy positions of fairly illiquid stocks. Since the end of the roaring 80s, the dearth of Japanese liquidity has intensified. Managers have turned to emerging small-cap stocks in the search for liquidity and diversification. But the hunt has a high cost. Physical presence in the marketplace appears to give the traders a definite advantage over long-distance trading—whether agency or principal.

On the basis of the very expensive trading done for Japan, the Manager decided that it was worth the cost of moving a trade desk to Tokyo.

The following tables show the actual quarter-to-quarter improvement in both execution and captured alpha over the recent period with a full Tokyo presence of portfolio managers and traders. In Table 6, Japanese executions were handled out of New York.

Costs are running about 2.5 percent one way, and roughly twice the expected costs. Over the next two quarters, the trader from London moved to Tokyo and began to get a feel for the market. The immediate improvements were small (see Table 7).

Then, improvement came sharply as the trader began to understand and effectively apply his direct knowledge of the nuances of the market (see Table 8).

Not only have costs come down, but expected costs have fallen as a result of seeking to fill smaller trades and reacting less to price movement in the stock. (The pretrade momentum figures indicate how much the price has moved in the day prior to the trade.)

TABLE 6. Trading Japan from New York

Quarter	Execution Cost	Benchmark Cost	% Daily Volume	Pretrade Momentum
2Q94	-248	-101	55	-84
3Q94	-239	-154	49	-22
4Q94	-188	-131	52	-101
1Q95	-267	-136	57	-91

TABLE 7. Transition-Period Trading

Quarter	Execution Cost	Benchmark Cost	% Daily Volume	Pretrade Momentum
2Q95	-213	-131	51	-62
3Q95	-237	-104	31	-12

TABLE 8. Trading Japan from Tokyo

Quarter	Execution Cost	Benchmark Cost	% Daily Volume	Pretrade Momentum
4Q95	-120	-98	30	-12
1Q96	-108	-101	28	2
2Q96	-65	-99	30	-3

Both the portfolio manager and trader were able to shift styles due to their improved proximity and sensitivity to information. The importance of these critical ingredients was not only missing but *undetectable* when they traded from the United States. Hence, the investment style shifted from reactive to proactive, and trade size reduced from 55 percent of daily volume to around 30 percent of daily volume. Better understanding of the market led both trader and portfolio manager to improvements that they would not have known how to make if the trader had not moved to Tokyo.

Case Study 5: Fine-Tuning the Global-Allocation Strategy

When a manager moves from a market he or she knows well to one that is understood only superficially, the tendency is to rely on "easy" insights and data-intensive approaches such as quantitative modeling for stock selection, sector switches for small-scale alpha capture, and top-down allocation strategies. These are all perfectly valid investment strategies, but may yet fail due to a lack of in-depth fundamental information on markets or specific stocks. Similar to the previous case study, it is difficult for managers to understand that trading insights can improve the decision process. In this case, a global asset-allocator considered trading costs as totally unrelated to the weaknesses in his investment process: "We make market-allocation decisions. They have nothing to do with execution."

The first step toward a low-cost execution was to recognize that a market-allocation decision dependent on buying and selling stocks is not solely a neutral market-allocation decision. It also involves a trading decision, and a need to adjust to market conditions. If the decision to increase an allocation to a market or sector is coincident with other buying pressure from other market participants, there will be competition to complete the position. Whenever there is competition, getting the position earlier rather than later has an advantage. On the other hand, when there is no competition, the allocation decision results in more contrarian situations, and there is no rush to capture the position in a quick series of trades.

The process can be improved by marrying the fundamental allocation strategy to some technical trading indicators, which assess the probable market conditions and dictate the trading strategy. The solution is to create simple mechanical "filters" to watch price trends and liquidity levels for any stock in the allocation universe.

Table 9 shows the cost structure of the asset allocator with and without a stock-specific filter for price trend and volume.

TABLE 9. Refinement of the Allocation Process

	Without Filter		With Filter	
Market	Trading Cost	PAEG/L	Trading Cost	PAEG/L
Japan	-16	-91	-97	-77
U.K.	-18	-49	-50	-45
U.S.	33	-31	-33	-35

Case Study 6: The Emerging Markets

Every global manager's dream is to be the first to discover the fastest-growing emerging market. Unfortunately, the more recent the emergence, the more difficult will be the trading. It may be difficult to accumulate reasonable positions . . . and it may be impossible to lay off these positions when things look grim. Costs will be high, pricing will be fanciful, valuation will be questionable, and clearing may be uncertain.

However emergent the market, sooner or later trading structures will arise to meet the demand to invest in the country. The first rungs on the ladder move from illiquid, long-term investments to slow accumulations and program trades. At later stages, we may see American Depository Receipts (ADRs) trade at attractive costs in U.S. markets. In the process, the price volatility dampens and more ideas become actionable as trading costs lessen.

Conclusion

The central message of these case studies is that transaction costs are real, but not inevitable. There are many actions managers that can take to improve the cost structure and capture more of the investment idea.

Over the past few years, we have seen an industry need for a better definition of best execution. The definition we use[4] is a simple extension of the standard for prudent portfolio management. Best execution is a procedure most likely to flow the maximum investment decision value into portfolios.

Put another way, best execution is the set of trades which best captures the decision value of the portfolio managers' ideas. We believe that the timing of releases from managers, as well as from the trade desk, is an art form, a balancing act requiring experience to estimate the cost of waiting to trade versus the cost of immediate completion. The art form is measurably improved with attention to detail.

Our desire is to forewarn you, not to discourage you. Face it: you have to go global, because the investors and the markets are increasingly global. Some learning curve pain is inevitable. Walking in blindly assuming that what you know from your local experience will carry forward into global markets will be painful. The antidote is self-knowledge. You have to understand your *own* process to pinpoint its weaknesses and improve on it.

Bibliography

Birinyi, Laszlo. "Minimizing Trading Costs." In *Global Equity Markets*, eds. Lederman and Park. Association for Investment Management and Research (AMIR) 1994.

Burnett, Thomas. "International Trading." In *The Complete Guide To Securities Transactions: Enhancing Investment Performance and Controlling Costs*, ed. Wayne H. Wagner. New York: John Wiley & Sons, 1989.

Collins, Bruce M., and Frank J. Fabozzi. "A Methodology for Measuring Transaction Costs." *Financial Analysts Journal*, March-April 1991.

Goldman Sachs. *The Goldman Sachs Cross-Holdings-Adjusted Japan Index*. Goldman Sachs, September 1996.

Loeb, Thomas F. "Trading Cost: The Critical Link between Investment Information and Results." *Financial Analysts Journal*, May-June 1983.

Perold, Andre. "The Implementation Shortfall: Paper versus Reality." *Journal of Portfolio Management*, April 1988.

Plexus Group. "Picking Good Stocks: Necessary, but Sufficient? *Plexus Group Commentary #43*, January 1995.

Wagner, Wayne H., and Michael Banks. "Increasing Portfolio Effectiveness via Transaction-Cost Management." *Journal of Portfolio Management*, Fall 1992.

Wagner, Wayne H., and Mark Edwards. "Best Execution." *Financial Analysts Journal*, January/February 1993.

Wagner, Wayne H., and Mark Edwards. "The Five W's and an H, the What, Why, Where, When, Who, and How of Trading." *Journal of Portfolio Management*, Fall 1991.

Endnotes

1. See *Plexus Group Commentary #43* on "Picking Good Stocks: Necessary, but Sufficient? January 1995.

2. See *The Goldman Sachs Cross-Holdings-Adjusted Japan Index*, Goldman Sachs, September 1996.

3. See Andre Perold, "The Implementation Shortfall: Paper versus Reality," *Journal of Portfolio Management*, April 1988.

4. See Wayne H. Wagner and Mark Edwards, "Best Execution." *Financial Analysts Journal*, January/February 1993.

INDEX

conclusions concerning, 109
custom consensus and, 106-109
defining good data in, 95-99
and fundamental inputs in foreign
  markets, 102-106
overview of critical role of, 93
and why inputs add value, 99-102

G
Global investment strategies
  case studies illustrating, 346-352
  conclusions concerning, 352-353
  investing process for, 337-344
  liquidity constraints and, 344-346
  why trading is expensive, 344
Global sector allocation
  conclusions concerning, 143
  construction of, 123, 129
  methodology of, 112, 119-123
  overview of, 111-112
  results of, 129-130
Global stock and bond
  capitalizations, *see* Bond market
  capitalization; Stock market
  capitalization

H
Harvey, Campbell R., 221
Hedging, currency, 48-49
Hedging ratios, mapping expected
  returns into, 304-306
Human capital, 3-4

I
Indexes, *see* Style indexes
Indicators, 147-150
Inflation
  forecasting, 293-296
  measuring, 290-292
  and portfolio selection, 263

K
Kennedy, William J., Jr., 93

M
Macedo, Rosemary, 145

McElroy, Michael P., 169
Mean reversion, 119
Mean-variance analysis, portfolio
  construction, 81-85

P
Portfolio construction
  mean-variance analysis for 81-85
  and risk management, 311, 317,
    323, 323-325, 329
Portfolio construction tests, 151-159
Purchasing-power index, 292-293
Purchasing-power price, 297-299

Q
Quantitative investing; *see also* Global
  sector allocation; Style-based
  country-selection strategies
  concepts of, 59-67
  dealing with constraints, 85-87
  econometric return models and, 72-81
  introduction to, 57-59
  mean-variance analysis and, 81-85
  multiple-period optimization and,
    87-88
  screening and scoring and, 67-72
  summary of, 88-90

R
Real estate, 4
Returns
  bond market, 21-25
  expected, for currencies, 278-279,
    303-306
  global small stock, 205-208
  greater, from foreign markets, 34-42
  other methods to enhance, 307-308
  stock market, 8-16
Returns, emerging equity market
  choosing benchmarks and, 223-226
  conclusions concerning, 268
  cross-sectional portfolio strategies
    for, 234-239
  introduction to determinants of,
    221-223